"What with the conclusions Whitaker draws from his assembled literature and the accusations he levels at those who consciously deceive consumers eager for magical cures, his book will either blow the lid off a multibillion-dollar industry or cause him to be labeled a crackpot and, perhaps, medicated into obscurity. At the very least, it should prod those who take the drugs to question those who prescribe them."

—*Booklist* (starred review)

"[Whitaker's] arguments are worryingly sane and consistently based on evidence . . . a provocative yet reasonable thesis, one whose astonishing intellectual punch is delivered with the gripping vitality of a novel. Whitaker manages to be damning while remaining stubbornly optimistic in this enthralling and frighteningly persuasive book."

—*New Scientist*

"Strips away psychiatry's carefully constructed and brightly painted architecture, then turns a halogen lamp on the pile of dust that remains. . . . Take everything you know about psychiatry. Turn it upside down. You'll have a pretty good idea of what Whitaker discovered. . . . challenge intrigues you, put this book on your reading list."

—Examiner.com (Portland)

"This is the most alarming book I've read in years. The approach is neither polemical nor ideologically slanted. Relying on medical evidence and historical documentation, Whitaker builds his case like a prosecuting attorney."

—Carl Elliott, MD, PhD; professor, Center for Bioethics, University of Minnesota; and author of *Better Than Well*

"Every so often a book comes along that exposes a vast deceit. Robert Whitaker has written that sort of book. Scrupulously reported and written in compelling but unemotional style, this book shreds the myth woven around today's psychiatric drugs."

—Nils Bruzelius, former science editor for the *Boston Globe* and the *Washington Post*

Also by Robert Whitaker

Mad in America

The Mapmaker's Wife

On the Laps of Gods

ANATOMY OF AN EPIDEMIC

Magic Bullets,

Psychiatric Drugs,

and the

Astonishing Rise of

Mental Illness

in America

Robert Whitaker

B\D\W\Y

BROADWAY BOOKS

New York

To Lindsay

May you sing "Seasons of Love" again

and be filled with joy

All rights reserved.
Published in the United States by Broadway Books, an imprint of the Crown Publishing Group, a division of Random House LLC, a Penguin Random House Company, New York.
www.crownpublishing.com

BROADWAY BOOKS and its logo, B \ D \ W \ Y, are trademarks of Random House LLC.

Originally published in different form in hardcover in the United States by Crown Publishers, an imprint of the Crown Publishing Group, a division of Random House LLC, New York, in 2010.

Library of Congress Cataloging-in-Publication Data
Whitaker, Robert.
    Anatomy of an epidemic : magic bullets, psychiatric drugs, and the astonishing rise of mental illness in America / Robert Whitaker.
       p. ; cm.
    Includes bibliographical references and index.
    1. Mental illness—United States. 2. Psychotropic drugs—Prescribing—United States.
3. Psychiatry—United States. I. Title.
    [DNLM: 1. Psychiatry—ethics—United States. 2. Psychiatry—history—United States.
3. Mental Disorders—drug therapy—United States. 4. Mental Disorders—
epidemiology—United States. WM 11 AA1 W578a 2010]
    RC443.W437 2010
    616.89—dc22   2009049467

ISBN 978-0-307-45242-9
eBook ISBN 978-0-307-45243-6

Printed in the United States of America

Illustrations by Hadel Studio, Westbury NY
Cover design by Laura Duffy
Cover illustration © Dietrich Madsen/Getty Images

30 29 28 27 26 25 24 23 22

2015 Paperback Edition

CONTENTS

Foreword • *vii*

Part One: The Epidemic

1. A Modern Plague • *3*
2. Anecdotal Thoughts • *12*

Part Two: The Science of Psychiatric Drugs

3. The Roots of an Epidemic • *39*
4. Psychiatry's Magic Bullets • *47*
5. The Hunt for Chemical Imbalances • *67*

Part Three: Outcomes

6. A Paradox Revealed • *89*
7. The Benzo Trap • *126*
8. An Episodic Illness Turns Chronic • *148*
9. The Bipolar Boom • *172*
10. An Epidemic Explained • *205*

11. The Epidemic Spreads to Children • 216

12. Suffer the Children • 247

Part Four: Explication of a Delusion

13. The Rise of an Ideology • 263

14. The Story That Was . . . and Wasn't Told • 283

15. Tallying Up the Profits • 313

Part Five: Solutions

16. Blueprints for Reform • 331

Epilogue • 361

Afterword: Research Update • 363

Notes • 379

Acknowledgments • 411

Index • 413

Anatomy of an Epidemic was first published in 2010, and it is fair to say that it quickly became known as a "controversial" book. At its core, this book investigates the long-term effects of psychiatric drugs, and it ultimately presents a history of science that challenges psychiatry to rethink our current drug-based paradigm of care.

It is now four years later, and the publication of this updated edition provides two opportunities. The first is to recount the response to *Anatomy*, which is a revealing story of its own. The second is to provide an update of relevant studies published since 2010. The new studies add to the body of evidence presented in *Anatomy* in a powerful way. Indeed, I think that the new studies can be seen as *corroborating* the conclusions drawn in *Anatomy*.

In the foreword to the first edition, I told of how I came to write this book. More than ever, I think it is important for readers to know this story. When a book challenges conventional wisdom, those who feel stung by the book may respond by attacking the person who wrote it. The author is biased. The author has an agenda. And so forth. The reviewer switches the focus from the book to the author, and by doing so, seeks to discredit the book.

I came to write about this subject in a very roundabout manner. In 1994, after having worked a number of years as a newspaper reporter, I left daily journalism to cofound a publishing company, CenterWatch, that reported on the business aspects of the clinical testing of drugs. Our readers came from pharmaceutical companies, medical schools, private medical practices, and Wall Street, and for the most part, we wrote about this enterprise in an industry-friendly way. We viewed clinical trials as part of a process that brought improved medical treatments to market, and we reported on the financial aspects of that growing industry. Then, in early 1998, I stumbled upon a story that told of the abuse of psychiatric patients in research settings. Even while I co-owned CenterWatch, I occasionally wrote freelance articles for magazines and newspapers, and that fall I cowrote a series on this problem for the *Boston Globe*.

There were several types of "abuses" that Dolores Kong and I focused on. We looked at studies funded by the National Institute of Mental Health (NIMH) that involved giving schizophrenia patients a drug designed to exacerbate their symptoms (the studies were probing the biology of psychosis). We investigated the deaths that had occurred during the testing of the new atypical antipsychotics. Finally, we reported on studies that involved withdrawing schizophrenia patients from their antipsychotic medications, which we figured was an unethical thing to do. In fact, we thought it was outrageous.

Our reasoning was easy to understand. These drugs were said to be like "insulin for diabetes." I had known that to be "true" for some time, ever since I had covered the medical beat at the *Albany Times Union*. Clearly, then, it was abusive for psychiatric researchers to have run drug-withdrawal studies in which they carefully tallied up the percentage of schizophrenia patients who became sick again and had to be rehospitalized. Would anyone ever conduct a study that involved withdrawing insulin from diabetics to see how fast they became sick again?

That's how we framed the withdrawal studies in our series, and that would have been the end of my writing on psychiatry except for the fact that I was left with an unresolved question, one that nagged at me. While reporting that series, I had come upon two research findings that just didn't make sense. The first was by Harvard Medical School investigators, who in 1994 announced that outcomes for schizophrenia patients in the United States had *worsened* during the past two decades and were now no better than they had been a century earlier. The second was by the World Health Organization, which had twice found that schizophrenia outcomes were much better in poor countries, like India and Nigeria, than in the United States and other rich countries. I interviewed various experts about the WHO findings, and they suggested that the poor outcomes in the United States were due to social policies and cultural values. In the poor countries, families were more supportive of those with schizophrenia, they said. Although this seemed plausible, it wasn't an altogether satisfactory explanation, and after the series ran in the *Boston Globe,* I went back and read all of the scientific articles related to the WHO study on schizophrenia outcomes. It was then that I learned of this startling fact: In the poor countries, only 16 percent of patients were regularly maintained on antipsychotic medications.

I can still remember my feelings of confusion upon seeing that statistic. I had just cowritten a series that had focused, in one of its parts, on how unethical it was to withdraw schizophrenia patients from their medications, and yet here was a study by the World Health Organization that seemingly had found an association between good outcomes and *not* staying continuously on the drugs. I wrote my first book, *Mad in America,* which turned into a history of our country's treatment of the severely mentally ill, to try to understand how that could be.

In short, I began this long intellectual journey as a believer in the conventional wisdom. I believed that psychiatric researchers were discovering the biological causes of mental illnesses and that this knowledge had led to the development of a new generation of psychiatric drugs that helped "balance" brain chemistry. These medications were like "insulin for diabetes." I believed that to be true because that is what I had been told by psychiatrists while writing for newspapers. But then I stumbled upon the Harvard study and the WHO findings, and that set me off on an intellectual quest that ultimately grew into this book, *Anatomy of an Epidemic.*

Although *Anatomy* challenges conventional wisdom, it does so in a conventional manner. Today, medical practices are supposed to be "evidence-based," meaning that they are supported by research findings, and thus, as I investigated the long-term effects of psychiatric medications, I simply tried to flesh out the relevant evidence. What does it show? In essence, this put me into the position of a messenger, holding up psychiatry's own research findings for all to see.

I think that is why *Anatomy* has, at times, provoked rather hostile reactions. I recounted a history of science that arises from research funded by the National Institute of Mental Health and the research institutes of other countries, and if that research ultimately tells of a need to rethink our current paradigm of care, then the book is doubly threatening. The challenge to psychiatry's current practices is coming from its own research on the long-term effects of psychiatric medications. *Anatomy* is not a critique of psychiatry's "medical model"; it's a review of psychiatry's own findings, which simply hadn't been put together before into a larger coherent picture.

Given that is so, those wishing to defend mainstream beliefs may be tempted to kill the messenger. The first review of *Anatomy*, which was published in the *Boston Globe* the day that *Anatomy* was released, fit that bill. The reviewer, Dennis Rosen, an assistant professor of pediatrics at Harvard Medical School, likened me to an AIDS denier. In particular, he compared me to former South African president Thabo Mbeki who by virtue of denying that AIDS was real had caused hundreds of thousands of South Africans to die.

That review served two purposes: First, it presented me to the public as a heretic, someone who should not be listened to. I denied obvious scientific truths. Second, it sent a message to other potential reviewers of *Anatomy* that mine was an *irresponsible* book. It had the potential to do great harm. Rosen's review was meant to silence, and, at first, it worked. No other major newspaper reviewed *Anatomy,* and I had virtually no radio interviews. *Anatomy* seemed destined to quickly disappear from public view.

However, *Time* magazine eventually provided a brief positive review, as did *New Scientist* and *Salon,* and thus a few readers found their way to the book. Then, in the summer of 2010, I was invited to be the keynote speaker at the Alternatives Conference, an annual meeting organized by "peers" and funded by the Substance Abuse and Mental Health Services Administration (SAMHSA). That invitation provoked some concern at SAMHSA, and the invitation was reissued with a caveat: I would only be allowed to speak if a second speaker, a psychiatrist, then gave a rebuttal.

While this was a bit odd, it did serve a purpose: Here was psychiatry's chance to respond to the challenge the book posed and present study findings—if such findings existed—that told of psychiatric medications that improved long-term outcomes. This was a chance for psychiatry to deconstruct the book. I admit I held my breath—was there any compelling evidence I had missed? But at the Alternatives meeting, no rebuttal of that sort was presented. There was no "counter evidence" cited, and thus that forum provided the book with a new public foil. Where was the counter-argument to *Anatomy*? Why wasn't it being made?

At that point, I began hearing from a small number of psychiatrists and providers who wanted to discuss the implications of the research presented in the book. I put them in touch with one another, via the Internet, and eventually that seed of discussion turned into a conference, held in Portland, Oregon, in February of 2011. There, a mix of people—psychiatrists, providers, family members, and peers—discussed the issues raised by *Anatomy* and broke into workshops, led by psychiatrists, that reviewed the long-term-outcomes literature for schizophrenia and depression. Both of those small workshops came to the conclusion that there was, in fact, good reason for psychiatry to rethink prescribing practices, once long-term outcomes were considered.

That conference in turn gave rise to a nonprofit organization, the Foundation for Excellence in Mental Health Care. The Foundation is raising funds to support further research into long-term outcomes and the "optimal" use of psychiatric medications. It is also supporting efforts to develop alternatives to drug-centered approaches to care.

Since that time, I have spoken widely about the outcomes literature presented in this book, and at those forums, which have included grand rounds at medical schools, I sense that there is a growing *societal* interest in rethinking psychiatric care. I have found this same interest when giving talks in Canada and European countries. Many people sense that something is not quite right with our drug-based paradigm of care. The more we use these drugs, the more the burden of mental illness seems to rise in our societies. Why would that be?

The research findings that have been published since 2010 add to this discussion. In this new edition of *Anatomy,* I have added a section—after the epilogue—that updates the research. Four years is not that much time, and yet here is the surprise: Thoughts that were considered heretical in 2010, when *Anatomy* was first published, are now being discussed in mainstream research circles.

part one

----------------------------------- •

The Epidemic

• -----------------------------------

I

A Modern Plague

"That is the essence of science: ask an impertinent
question, and you are on the way to
a pertinent answer."
—JACOB BRONOWSKI (1973)[1]

This is the story of a medical puzzle. The puzzle is of a most curious sort, and yet one that we as a society desperately need to solve, for it tells of a hidden epidemic that is diminishing the lives of millions of Americans, including a rapidly increasing number of children. The epidemic has grown in size and scope over the past five decades, and now disables 850 adults and 250 children *every day*. And those startling numbers only hint at the true scope of this modern plague, for they are only a count of those who have become so ill that their families or caregivers are newly eligible to receive a disability check from the federal government.

Now, here is the puzzle.

As a society, we have come to understand that psychiatry has made great progress in treating mental illness over the past fifty years. Scientists are uncovering the biological causes of mental disorders, and pharmaceutical companies have developed a number of effective medications for these conditions. This story has been told in newspapers, magazines, and books, and evidence of our societal belief in it can be found in our spending habits. In 2007, we spent $25 billion on antidepressants and antipsychotics, and to put that figure in perspective, that was more than the gross domestic product of Cameroon, a nation of 18 million people.[2]

In 1999, U.S. surgeon general David Satcher neatly summed up this story of scientific progress in a 458-page report titled *Mental Health*. The modern era of psychiatry, he explained, could be said to have begun in 1954. Prior to that time, psychiatry lacked treatments that could "prevent patients from becoming chronically ill." But then Thorazine was introduced. This was the first drug that was a specific antidote to a mental disorder—it was an *antipsychotic* medication—and it kicked off a psychopharmacological revolution. Soon *antidepressants* and *antianxiety* agents were discovered, and as a result, today we enjoy "a variety of treatments of well-documented efficacy for the array of clearly defined mental and behavioral disorders that occur across the life span," Satcher wrote. The introduction of Prozac and other "second-generation" psychiatric drugs, the surgeon general added, was "stoked by advances in both neurosciences and molecular biology" and represented yet another leap forward in the treatment of mental disorders.[3]

Medical students training to be psychiatrists read about this history in their textbooks, and the public reads about it in popular accounts of the field. Thorazine, wrote University of Toronto professor Edward Shorter, in his 1997 book, *A History of Psychiatry*, "initiated a revolution in psychiatry, comparable to the introduction of penicillin in general medicine."[4] That was the start of the "psychopharmacology era," and today we can rest assured that science has proved that the drugs in psychiatry's medicine cabinet are beneficial. "We have very effective and safe treatments for a broad array of psychiatric disorders," Richard Friedman, director of the psychopharmacology clinic at Weill Cornell Medical College, informed readers of the *New York Times* on June 19, 2007.[5] Three days later, the *Boston Globe*, in an editorial titled "When Kids Need Meds," echoed this sentiment: "The development of powerful drugs has revolutionized the treatment of mental illness."[6]

Psychiatrists working in countries around the world also understand this to be true. At the 161st annual meeting of the American Psychiatric Association, which was held in May 2008 in Washington, D.C., nearly half of the twenty thousand psychiatrists who attended were foreigners. The hallways were filled with chatter about schizophrenia, bipolar illness, depression, panic disorder, attention deficit/

hyperactivity disorder, and a host of other conditions described in the APA's *Diagnostic and Statistical Manual of Mental Disorders,* and over the course of five days, most of the lectures, workshops, and symposiums told of advances in the field. "We have come a long way in understanding psychiatric disorders, and our knowledge continues to expand," APA president Carolyn Robinowitz told the audience in her opening-day address. "Our work saves and improves so many lives."[7]

But here is the conundrum. Given this great advance in care, we should expect that the number of disabled mentally ill in the United States, on a per-capita basis, would have declined over the past fifty years. We should also expect that the number of disabled mentally ill, on a per-capita basis, would have declined since the arrival in 1988 of Prozac and the other second-generation psychiatric drugs. We should see a two-step drop in disability rates. Instead, as the psychopharmacology revolution has unfolded, the number of disabled mentally ill in the United States has *skyrocketed*. Moreover, this increase in the number of disabled mentally ill has accelerated further since the introduction of Prozac and the other second-generation psychiatric drugs. Most disturbing of all, this modern-day plague has now spread to the nation's children.

The disability numbers, in turn, lead to a much larger question. Why are so many Americans today, while they may not be disabled by mental illness, nevertheless plagued by chronic mental problems—by recurrent depression, by bipolar symptoms, and by crippling anxiety? If we have treatments that effectively address these disorders, why has mental illness become an ever-greater health problem in the United States?

The Epidemic

Now, I promise that this will not just be a book of statistics. We are trying to solve a mystery in this book, and this will lead to an exploration of science and history, and ultimately to a story with many surprising twists. But this mystery arises from an in-depth analysis of government statistics, and so, as a first step, we need to track the disability numbers over the past fifty years to make certain that the epidemic is real.

In 1955, the disabled mentally ill were primarily cared for in state and county mental hospitals. Today, they typically receive either a monthly Supplemental Security Income (SSI) or Social Security Disability Insurance (SSDI) payment, and many live in residential shelters or other subsidized living arrangements. Both statistics provide a rough count of the number of people under governmental care because they have been disabled by mental illness.

In 1955, there were 566,000 people in state and county mental hospitals. However, only 355,000 had a psychiatric diagnosis, as the rest suffered from alcoholism, syphilis-related dementia, Alz-

The Hospitalized Mentally Ill in 1955

	First Admissions	Resident Patients
Psychotic Disorders		
Schizophrenia	28,482	267,603
Manic-depressive	9,679	50,937
Other	1,387	14,734
Psychoneurosis (Anxiety)	6,549	5,415
Personality Disorders	8,730	9,739
All Others	6,497	6,966

Although there were 558,922 resident patients in state and county mental hospitals in 1955, only 355,000 suffered from mental illness. The other 200,000 were elderly patients suffering from dementia, end-stage syphilis, alcoholism, mental retardation, and various neurological syndromes. Source: Silverman, C. *The Epidemiology of Depression* (1968): 139.

heimer's, and mental retardation, a population that would not show up in a count of the disabled mentally ill today.[8] Thus, in 1955, 1 in every 468 Americans was hospitalized due to a mental illness. In 1987, there were 1.25 million people receiving an SSI or SSDI payment because they were disabled by mental illness, or 1 in every 184 Americans.

Now it may be argued that this is an apples-to-oranges comparison. In 1955, societal taboos about mental illness may have led to a reluctance to seek treatment, and thus to low hospitalization rates. It's also possible that a person had to be sicker to get hospitalized in 1955 than to receive SSI or SSDI in 1987, and that's why the 1987 disability rate is so much higher. However, arguments can be made in the other direction, too. The SSI and SSDI numbers only provide a count of the disabled mentally ill less than sixty-five years old, whereas the mental hospitals in 1955 were home to many elderly schizophrenics. There were also many more mentally ill people who were homeless and in jail in 1987 than in 1955, and that population doesn't show up in the disability numbers. The comparison is an imperfect one, but it's the best one we can make to track disability rates between 1955 and 1987.

Fortunately, from 1987 forward it's an apples-to-apples comparison, involving only the SSI and SSDI numbers. The Food and Drug Administration approved Prozac in 1987, and over the next two decades the number of disabled mentally ill on the SSI and SSDI rolls soared to 3.97 million.[9] In 2007, the disability rate was 1 in every 76 Americans. That's more than double the rate in 1987, and six times the rate in 1955. The apples-to-apples comparison proves that something is amiss.

If we drill down into the disability data a bit more, we find a second puzzle. In 1955, major depression and bipolar illness didn't disable many people. There were only 50,937 people in state and county mental hospitals with a diagnosis for one of those affective disorders.[10] But during the 1990s, people struggling with depression and bipolar illness began showing up on the SSI and SSDI rolls in ever-increasing numbers, and today there are an estimated 1.4 million people eighteen to sixty-four years old receiving a federal payment because they are disabled by an affective disorder.[11] Moreover, this trend is accelerating: According to a 2008 report by the U.S. General Accountability Office, 46 percent of the young adults (ages eighteen to twenty-six) who received an SSI or SSDI payment because of a psychiatric disability in 2006 were diagnosed with an affective illness (and another 8 percent were disabled by "anxiety disorder").[12]

The Disabled Mentally Ill in the Prozac Era
SSI and SSDI Recipients Under Age 65 Disabled by Mental Illness, 1987–2007

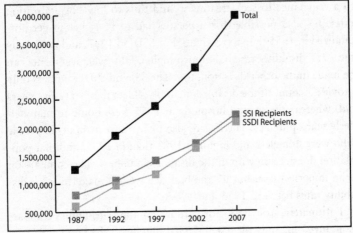

One in every six SSDI recipients also receives an SSI payment; thus the total number of recipients is less than the sum of the SSI and SSDI numbers. Source: Social Security Administration reports, 1987–2007.

This plague of disabling mental illness has now spread to our children, too. In 1987, there were 16,200 children under eighteen years of age who received an SSI payment because they were disabled by a serious mental illness. Such children comprised only 5.5 percent of the 293,000 children on the disability rolls—mental illness was not, at that time, a leading cause of disability among the country's children. But starting in 1990, the number of mentally ill children began to rise dramatically, and by the end of 2007, there were 561,569 such children on the SSI disability rolls. In the short span of twenty years, the number of disabled mentally ill children rose *thirty-five fold*. Mental illness is now the leading cause of disability in children, with the mentally ill group comprising 50 percent of the total number of children on the SSI rolls in 2007.[13]

The baffling nature of this childhood epidemic shows up with particular clarity in the SSI data from 1996 to 2007. Whereas the number of children disabled by mental illness more than doubled during this period, the number of children on the SSI rolls for all other reasons—cancers, retardation, etc.—*declined*, from 728,110 to 559,448. The nation's doctors were apparently making progress in treating all of those other conditions, but when it came to mental disorders, just the opposite was true.

A Scientific Inquiry

The puzzle can now be precisely summed up. On the one hand, we know that many people are helped by psychiatric medications. We know that many people stabilize well on them and will personally attest to how the drugs have helped them lead normal lives. Furthermore, as Satcher noted in his 1999 report, the scientific literature does document that psychiatric medications, at least over the short term, are "effective." Psychiatrists and other physicians who prescribe the drugs will attest to that fact, and many parents of children taking psychiatric drugs will swear by the drugs as well. All of that makes for a powerful consensus: Psychiatric drugs work and help people lead relatively normal lives. And yet, at the same time, we are stuck with these disturbing facts: The number of disabled mentally ill has risen dramatically since 1955, and during the past two decades, a period when the prescribing of psychiatric medications has exploded, the number of adults and children disabled by mental illness has risen at a mind-boggling rate. Thus we arrive at an obvious question, even though it is heretical in kind: Could our drug-based paradigm of care, in some unforeseen way, be fueling this modern-day plague?

My hope is that *Anatomy of an Epidemic* will serve as an exploration of that question. It's also easy to see what we must find if we are to solve this puzzle. We will need to discover a history of science that unfolds over the course of fifty-five years, arises from the very best research, and explains all aspects of our puzzle. The history must reveal why there has been a dramatic increase in the number of disabled mentally ill, it must explain why disabling affective disorders are so much more common now than they were fifty years ago, and it must explain why so many children are being laid low by serious mental illness today. And if we find such a history, we should then be able to explain why it has remained hidden and unknown.

It's also easy to see what is at stake here. The disability numbers only hint at the extraordinary toll that mental illness is exacting on our society. The GAO, in its June 2008 report, concluded that one in every sixteen young adults in the United States is now "seriously mentally ill." There has never been a society that has seen such a plague of mental illness in its newly minted adults, and those who go on the SSI and SSDI rolls at this young age are likely to spend the rest of their lives receiving disability payments. The twenty-year-old who goes on SSI or SSDI will receive more than $1 million in benefits over the next forty or so years, and that is a cost—should this epidemic continue to grow—that our society will not be able to afford.

There is one other, subtler aspect to this epidemic. Over the past twenty-five years, psychiatry has profoundly reshaped our society. Through its *Diagnostic and Statistical Manual,* psychiatry draws a line between what is "normal" and what is not. Our societal understanding of the human mind, which in the past arose from a medley of sources (great works of fiction, scientific investigations, and philosophical and religious writings), is now filtered through the DSM. Indeed, the stories told by psychiatry about "chemical imbalances" in the brain have reshaped our understanding of how the mind works and challenged our conceptions of free will. Are we really the prisoners of our neurotransmitters? Most important, our children are the first in human history to grow up under the constant shadow of "mental illness." Not too long ago, goof-offs, cut-ups, bullies, nerds, shy kids, teachers' pets, and any number of other recognizable types filled the schoolyard, and all were considered more or less normal. Nobody really knew what to expect from such children as adults. That was part of the glorious uncertainty of life—the goof-off in the fifth grade might show up at his high school's twenty-year reunion as a wealthy entrepreneur, the shy girl as an accomplished actress. But today, children diagnosed with mental disorders—most notably, ADHD, depression, and bipolar illness—help populate the schoolyard. These children have been told that they have something wrong with their brains and that they may have to take psychiatric medications the rest of their lives, just like a "diabetic takes insulin." That medical dictum teaches all of the children on the playground a lesson about the nature of humankind, and that lesson differs in a radical way from what children used to be taught.

So here is what is at stake in this investigation: If the conventional history is true, and psychiatry has in fact made great progress in identifying the biological causes of mental disorders and in developing effective treatments for those illnesses, then we can conclude that psychiatry's reshaping of our society has been for the good. As bad as the epidemic of disabling mental illness may be, it is reasonable to assume that without such advances in psychiatry, it would be much worse. The scientific literature will show that millions of children and adults are being helped by psychiatric medications, their lives made richer and fuller, just as APA president Carolyn Robinowitz said in her speech at the APA's 2008 convention. But if we uncover a history of a different sort—a history that shows that the biological causes of mental disorders remain to be discovered and that psychiatric drugs are in fact *fueling* the epidemic of disabling mental illness—what then? We will have documented a history that tells of a society led horribly astray and, one might say, betrayed.

And if that is so, we will spend the final part of this book looking at what we, as a society, might do to forge a different future.

2

Anecdotal Thoughts

*"If we value the pursuit of knowledge, we must be
free to follow wherever that search may lead us."*
—ADLAI STEVENSON (1952)[1]

McLean Hospital in Belmont, Massachusetts, is one of the oldest
mental hospitals in the United States, as it was founded in 1817,
when a type of care known as moral therapy was being popularized
by Quakers. Their belief was that a retreat for the mentally ill
should be built in a pastoral setting, and even today the McLean
campus, with its handsome brick buildings and shaded lawns, feels
like an oasis. On the evening in August 2008 that I came there, in
order to attend a meeting of the Depression and Bipolar Support Alliance, that sense of tranquility was heightened by the weather. It
was one of the most gorgeous nights of the summer, and as I approached the cafeteria where the meeting was to be held, I figured
that attendance that night would be sparse. It was just too nice of a
night to be inside. This was a meeting for people living in the community, which meant they would have to leave their homes and
apartments to come here, and given that the McLean group met five
times a week—there was an afternoon session every Monday, Thurs-
day, Friday, and Saturday, and an evening meeting every Wednes-
day—I reasoned that most people attached to the group would skip
this one.

I was wrong.

There were a hundred or so people filling the cafeteria, a scene that, in a small way, bore witness to the epidemic of disabling mental illness that has erupted in our country over the past twenty years. The Depression and Bipolar Support Alliance (DBSA) was founded in 1985 (known initially as the Depressive and Manic-Depressive Association), with this group at McLean starting up shortly after that, and today the organization counts nearly one thousand of its support groups nationwide. There are seven such groups in the Greater Boston area alone, and most—like the group that meets at McLean—offer people a chance to get together and talk several times a week. The DBSA has grown in lockstep with the epidemic.

The first hour of the meeting was given over to a talk about "flotation therapy," and at first glance, the audience was really not identifiable—at least not by an outsider such as myself—as a patient group. The people here ranged widely in age, the youngest in their late teens and the oldest in their sixties, and although the women outnumbered the men, this gender disparity might have been expected, given that depression affects more women than men. Most in the audience were white, which perhaps reflected the fact that Belmont is an affluent town. Perhaps the one telltale sign that the meeting was for people diagnosed with a mental illness was that a fair number were overweight. People diagnosed with bipolar disorder are often prescribed an atypical antipsychotic, such as Zyprexa, and those drugs regularly cause people to put on the pounds.

After the talk ended, Steve Lappen, one of the DBSA leaders in Boston, listed the various groups that would now meet. There was one for "newcomers," another for "family and friends," a third for "young adults," a fourth for "maintaining stability," and so on, with the last of the eight choices an "observer's group," which Steve had organized for me.

There were nine in our group (excluding myself), and by way of introduction, everyone briefly spoke about how he or she had been doing lately—"I've been having a hard time" was a common refrain—and told of his or her specific diagnosis. The man to my right was a former executive who had lost his job because of his recurring depression, and as we went around the room, such life stories spilled out. A younger woman told of a troubled marriage to a Chinese man who, because of his culture, didn't like to talk about mental illness. Next to her, a former prosecuting attorney spoke of how he'd lost his wife two years ago, and since then "I don't feel like I know who I am." A woman who was an adjunct professor at an area college told of how difficult her work was at the moment, and finally, a nurse who had been recently hospitalized at McLean for depression explained what drove her to that dark place: She had the stress of caring for an ailing father, the stress of her job, and years of living with "an abusive husband."

The one lighter moment in this round of introductions came from the oldest member of the group. He had been doing pretty well lately, and his explanation for his relative happiness was one that Seinfield's George Costanza would have appreciated. "Usually the summer is a hard time for me because everybody seems so happy. But with all the rain we have been having, that hasn't been so much the case this summer," he said.

Over the course of the next hour, the talk jumped from topic to topic. There was a discussion of the stigma that the mentally ill face in our society, particularly in the workplace, and talk too of how family and friends, after a time, lose their empathy. This was clearly why many in the group had come—they found the shared understanding to be helpful. The issue of medication came up, and on this topic, opinions and experiences varied widely. The former executive, while still regularly suffering from depression, said that his medication did "wonders" for him and that his greatest fear was that it would "stop working." Others told of having tried one medication after another before finding a drug regimen that provided some relief. Steve Lappen said that medications had never worked for him, while Dennis Hagler, the other DBSA leader in the meeting (who also agreed to be identified), said that a high dose of an antidepressant has made all the difference in the world in his life. The nurse told of having responded very badly to antidepressants during her recent hospitalization.

"I had an allergic reaction to five different drugs," she said. "I am now trying one of the new atypicals [antipsychotics]. I'm hoping that will work."

After the group sessions ended, people gathered in the cafeteria in clutches of two and three, sharing small talk. That made for a pleasant moment; there was a feeling of social warmth in that room, and you could see that the evening had lifted the spirits of many. It was all so ordinary that this easily could have been the wrap-up moment to a PTA meeting or a church social, and as I walked to the car, it was that ordinariness that struck me most. In the observer's group, there had been a businessman, an engineer, a historian, an attorney, a college professor, a social worker, and a nurse (the other two in the group hadn't spoken of their work histories). Yet, as far as I could tell, only the college professor was currently employed. And that was the puzzle: The people in the observer's group were well educated and they were all taking psychotropic medications, and yet many were so plagued by persistent depression and bipolar symptoms that they couldn't work.

Earlier, Steve had told me that about half of the DBSA members receive either an SSI or SSDI check because they are, in the government's eyes, disabled by their mental illness. This is the patient type that has been swelling the SSI and SSDI rolls for the past fifteen years, while the DBSA has grown into the largest mental health patient organization in the country during that time. Psychiatry now has three classes of medications it uses to treat affective disorders—antidepressants, mood stabilizers, and atypical antipsychotics—but for whatever reason, an ever greater number of people are showing up at DBSA meetings around the country, telling of their persistent and enduring struggles with depression or mania or both.

Four Stories

In medicine, the personal stories of patients diagnosed with a disease are known as "case studies," and it is understood that these anecdotal accounts, while they might provide insight into a disease and the treatments for it, cannot prove whether a treatment works. Only scientific studies that look at outcomes in the aggregate can do that, and even then the picture that emerges is often a cloudy one. The reason that anecdotal accounts can't provide such proof is that people may have widely varying reactions to medical treatments, and that is particularly true in psychiatry. You can find people who will tell of how psychiatric medications have helped them immensely; you can find people who will tell of how the drugs have ruined their lives; and you can find people—and this seems to be the majority in my experience—who don't know what to think. They can't quite decide whether the drugs have helped them or not. Still, as we set out to solve this puzzle of a modern-day epidemic of disabling mental illness in the United States, anecdotal accounts can help us identify questions that we will want to see answered in our search of the scientific literature.

Here are four such life stories.

Cathy Levin

I first met Cathy Levin in 2004, not too long after I had published my first book on psychiatry, *Mad in America*. I immediately came to admire her fierce spirit. The last part of that book explored whether antipsychotic medications might be worsening the long-term course of schizophrenia (a topic that is explored in Chapter 6 of this book), and Cathy, in some ways, objected to that thought. Although she had initially been diagnosed with bipolar disorder (in 1978), her diagnosis had later been changed to "schizoaffective," and she had, by her own reckoning, been "saved" by an atypical antipsychotic, Risperdal. The history that I had related in *Mad in America* threatened, in some way, her own personal experience, and she called me several times to tell me how helpful that drug had been to her.

Born in 1960 in a Boston suburb, Cathy grew up in what she remembers as a "male-dominated" world. Her father, a professor at a college in the Boston area, was a veteran of World War II, and her stay-at-home mom saw such men as the "backbone of the social order." Her two older brothers, she recalls, "bullied her," and on more than one occasion, starting when she was quite young, several boys in her neighborhood molested her. "I cried all the time when I was a child," she says, and often she pretended to be sick so that she wouldn't have to go to school, preferring instead to spend her days alone in her room, reading books.

Although she did fine academically in high school, she was "a difficult teenager, hostile, angry, withdrawn." During her second year in college, at Earlham in Richmond, Indiana, her emotional troubles worsened. She began partying with the young men on the football team, eager, she says, "to have sex" but, at the same time, worried about losing her virginity. "I was confused about being involved with a guy. I went to a lot of parties and I couldn't concentrate anymore on my studies. I started to flunk out of school."

Cathy was smoking a lot of marijuana, too, and soon she began acting in an eccentric manner. She borrowed other people's clothes to wear, trekking around campus in "oversized clogs, a pair of overalls thrown over my regular clothes, a bomber jacket, and a funny hat I got from the Army-Navy store." One night, on her way home from a party, she threw away her glasses for no reason. Her thoughts about sex gradually bloomed into a fantasy about Steve Martin, the comedian. Unable to sleep through the night, she would awaken at four a.m. and go for walks, and at times, it seemed that Steve Martin was there on campus, stalking her. "I thought he was in love with me and was running through the bushes just out of sight," she says. "He was looking for me."

Mania and paranoia were combining into a volatile mix. The breaking point came one evening when she threw a glass object against the wall in her dorm room. "I didn't clean it up, but instead was walking around in it. I was, you know, taking the glass out of my feet. I was completely out of my mind." School officials called police and she was rushed off to a hospital, and it was then, a few days before her eighteenth birthday, that Cathy's medicated life began. She was diagnosed with manic-depressive illness, informed that she suffered from a chemical imbalance in the brain, and put on Haldol and lithium.

For the next sixteen years, Cathy cycled in and out of hospitals. She "hated the meds"—Haldol stiffened her muscles and caused her to drool, while the lithium made her depressed—and often she would abruptly stop taking them. "It feels so great to go off medication," she says, and even now, when she remembers that feeling, she seems to get lost in the pure deliciousness of a memory from the distant past. "When you go off meds it is like taking off a wet wool coat, which you have been wearing even though it's a beautiful spring day, and suddenly feeling so much better, freer, nicer." The problem was that off the drugs, she would "start to decompensate and become disorganized."

In early 1994, she was hospitalized for the fifteenth time. She was seen as chronically mentally ill, occasionally heard voices now, had a new diagnosis (schizoaffective), and was on a cocktail of drugs: Haldol, Ativan, Tegretol, Halcion, and Cogentin, the last drug an antidote to Haldol's nasty side effects. But after she was released that spring, a psychiatrist told her to try Risperdal, a new antipsychotic that had just been approved by the FDA. "Three weeks later, my mind was much clearer," she says. "The voices were going away. I got off the other meds and took only this one drug. I got better. I could start to plan. I wasn't talking to the devil anymore. Jesus and God weren't battling it out in my head." Her father put it this way: "Cathy is back."

Although several studies funded by the NIMH and the British government have found that patients, on the whole, don't do any better on Risperdal and the other atypicals than on the older antipsychotics, Cathy clearly responded very well to this new agent. She went back to school and earned a degree in radio, film, and television from the University of Maryland. In 1998, she began dating the man she lives with today, Jonathan. In 2005, she took a part-time job as editor of *Voices for Change,* a newsletter published by M-Power, a consumer group in Massachusetts, a position she held for three years. In the spring of 2008, she helped lead an M-Power campaign to get the Massachusetts legislature to pass a law that would protect the rights of psychiatric patients in emergency rooms. Still, she remains on SSDI—"I am a kept woman," she jokes—and although there are many reasons for that, she believes that Risperdal, the very drug that has helped her so much, nevertheless has proven to be a barrier to full-time work. Although she is usually energetic by the early afternoon, Risperdal makes her so sleepy that she has trouble getting up in the morning. The other problem is that she has always had trouble getting along with other people, and Risperdal exacerbates that problem, she says. "The meds isolate you. They interfere with your empathy. There is a flatness to you, and so you are uncomfortable with people all the time. They make it hard for you to get along. The drugs may take care of aggression and anxiety and some paranoia, those sorts of symptoms, but they don't help with the empathy that helps you get along with people."

Risperdal has also taken a physical toll. Cathy is five feet, two inches tall, with curly brown hair, and although she is fairly physically fit, she is probably sixty pounds heavier than what would be considered ideal. She has also developed some of the metabolic problems, such as high cholesterol, that the atypical antipsychotics regularly cause. "I can go toe-to-toe with an old lady with a recital of my physical problems," she says. "My feet, my bladder, my heart, my sinuses, the weight gain—I have it all." Even more alarming, in 2006 her tongue began rolling over in her mouth, a sign that she may be developing tardive dyskinesia. When this side effect appears, it means that the basal ganglia, the part of the brain that controls motor movement, is becoming permanently dysfunctional, having been damaged by years of drug treatment. But she can't do well without Risperdal, and in the summer of 2008, this led to a moment of deep despair. "I will, of course, look pretty creepy in a few years, with the involuntary mouth movements," she says.

Such has been her life's course on medications. Sixteen terrible years, followed by fourteen pretty good years on Risperdal. She believes that this drug is essential to her mental health today, and indeed, she could be seen as a local poster child for promoting the wonders of that drug. Still, if you look at the long-term course of her illness, and you go all the way back to her first hospitalization at age eighteen, you have to ask: Is hers a story of a life made better by our drug-based paradigm of care for mental disorders, or a story of a life made worse? How might her life have unfolded if when she suffered her first manic episode in the fall of 1978, she had not been immediately placed on lithium and Haldol, the doctors instead trying other means—rest, psychological therapies, etc.—to restore her sanity? Or if, once she had been stabilized on those medications, she had been encouraged to wean herself from the drugs? Would she have spent sixteen years cycling through hospitals? Would she have gone on SSDI and remained on it ever since? What would her physical health be like now? What would her *subjective* experience of life through those years have been like? And if she had been able to fare well without drugs, how much more might she have accomplished in her life?

This is a question that Cathy, given her experience with Risperdal, had not thought much about before our interviews. But once I raised it, she seemed haunted by this possibility, and she brought it up again and again when we met. "I would have been more productive without the meds," she said the first time. "It would break my heart" to think about that, she said later. Another time she lamented that with a life on antipsychotics, "you lose your soul and you never get it back. I got stuck in the system and the struggle to take meds." Finally, she told me this: "The thing I remember, looking back, is that I was not really that sick early on. I was really just confused. I had all these issues, but nobody talked to me about that. I wish I could go off meds even now, but there is nobody to help me do it. I can't even start a dialogue."

There is, of course, no way of knowing what a life without meds might have been like for Cathy Levin. However, later in this book we will see what science has to reveal about the possible course her illness might have taken if, at that fateful moment in 1978, after her initial psychotic episode, she had not been medicated and told that she would have to take drugs for life. Science should be able to tell us whether psychiatrists have reason to believe that their paradigm of drug-based care alters long-term outcomes for the better or for the worse. But Cathy believes that this is a question that psychiatrists never contemplate.

"They don't have any sense about how these drugs affect you over the long term. They just try to stabilize you for the moment, and look to manage you from week to week, month to month. That's all they ever think about."

George Badillo

Today, George Badillo lives in Sound Beach on Long Island, his neatly kept home only a short drive away from the water. Nearly fifty years old, he is physically fit, with slightly graying hair swept back off his forehead, and he has a quick, warm smile. His thirteen-year-old son, Brandon, lives with him—"He is on the foot-ball team, the wrestling team, the baseball team, and the honor roll," George says, with understandable pride—and his twenty-year-old daughter, Madelyne, who is a student at the College of Staten Island, is visiting him on this day. Even at first glance, you can see both are happy to have this time together.

Like many who have been diagnosed with schizophrenia, George remembers being "different" as a child. As a young boy growing up in Brooklyn, he felt isolated from the other kids, partly because his Puerto Rican parents spoke only Spanish. "I remember all the other kids talking and being so friendly and outgoing, mingling with each other, and I couldn't do that. I'd want to talk with them, but I was always apprehensive," he recalls. He also had an alcoholic father who often beat him, and because of that, he began to think that "people were always plotting and wanting to hurt me."

Still, George did okay in school, and it wasn't until his late teens, when he was a student at Baruch College, that his life began going awry. "I got into the disco life," he explains. "I started doing am-phetamines, marijuana, and cocaine, and I liked it. The drugs re-laxed me. Only then it got out of hand and the cocaine started making me think all crazy. I got real paranoid. I felt there were con-spiracies and all that. People were after me, and the government was in on it." Eventually he ran off to Chicago, where he lived with his aunt and withdrew from the world that he felt was chasing him. Alarmed, his family coaxed him back home and took him to the psychiatric unit at Long Island Jewish Hospital, where he was diag-nosed as a paranoid schizophrenic. "They are all telling me that my brain is broken, and that I will be sick for the rest of my life," he says.

The next nine years passed in a chaotic whirl. Like Cathy Levin, George hated Haldol and the other antipsychotics he was told to take, and partly because of that drug-induced despair, he tried to kill himself multiple times. He fought with his family about the medications, went on and off the drugs, cycled through several hos-pitalizations, and, in 1987, became a father after his eighteen-year-old girlfriend gave birth to Madelyne. He married his girlfriend, intent on being a good father, but Madelyne was a sickly child and George and his wife both suffered breakdowns trying to care for her. His grandmother took Madelyne to Puerto Rico, and George ended up divorced and living in a home for the disabled. There he met and married a woman also diagnosed with paranoid schizophrenia, and after a series of adventures and misadventures in San Francisco, they, too, got divorced. Despondent and paranoid once again, in early 1991 George landed in Kings Park Psychiatric Center, a run-down state hospital on Long Island.

Now came his descent into total hopelessness. After he tried to have a pistol smuggled into the hospital so that he could kill himself, he was given a two-year sentence in the locked facility. Then, as Christmas neared that year, he grew upset when several of his fellow patients weren't allowed to go home for the holiday, and so he helped them escape, breaking a window in his room and tying sheets together so they could clamber to the ground. The hospital responded by moving him to a ward for people who had been institutionalized for decades. "Now I am on a ward with people urinating on themselves," he recalls. "I'm a danger to society and drugged out. You sit down all day and watch television. You can't even go outside. I thought my life was over."

George spent eight months on that ward for the hopelessly mentally ill, lost in a haze of drugs. However, at last he was moved to a unit where he could go outside, and suddenly there was blue sky to be seen and fresh air to breathe. He felt a spark of hope, and then he took a very risky step: He began tonguing the antipsychotic medication and spitting it out when the staff weren't looking. "I could think again," he says. "The antipsychotic drugs weren't letting me think. I was like a vegetable, and I couldn't do anything. I had no emotions. I sat there and watched television. But now I felt more in control. And it felt great to feel alive again."

Luckily, George didn't experience a return of psychotic symptoms, and with his body no longer slowed by drugs, he began to jog and lift weights. He fell in love with another patient in the hospital, Tara McBride, and in 1995, after they were both discharged from the hospital to a nearby community residence, she gave birth to Brandon. George, who had never completely lost touch with his daughter, Madelyne, now had a new goal in life. "I realize I have a second chance. I want to be a good parent."

At first, it didn't go well. Like Madelyne, Brandon had been born with health problems—he had an intestinal abnormality that required surgery—and Tara broke down from that stress and was rehospitalized. Since George was still living in a residence for the mentally ill, the state did not deem him fit to care for Brandon and he was given to Tara's sister to raise. However, in 1998 George began working part-time as a peer specialist for the New York State Office of Mental Health, counseling hospitalized patients about their rights, and three years later, he was able to present himself in court as someone who could be a good father to Brandon. "My sister Madeline and I got custody," he says. "That was the best feeling. I was just jumping for joy. It was like the first time that someone in the system got custody of their kids."

The following year, one of George's sisters bought him the house he lives in today. Although he still receives SSDI, he does contract work for the federal Substance Abuse and Mental Services Health Administration and does volunteer work with hospitalized youth in Long Island. His is a life filled with meaning, and as Brandon's success in school will attest, he is proving to be the good father he dreamed of becoming. Madelyne, meanwhile, is unabashedly proud of him. "He wanted to have Brandon and me in his life," she says. "That made him want to turn around his situation. He wanted to be a father to us. He is proof that someone can recover from mental illness."

Although George's story is clearly an inspiring one, it doesn't prove anything one way or another about the overall merits of antipsychotics. But it does prompt a clinical question: Given that his recovery began when he *stopped* taking antipsychotics, is it possible that some people ill with a serious mental disorder, like schizophrenia or bipolar illness, might recover in the absence of medication? Is his story an anomaly, or does it provide insight into what could be a fairly common path to recovery? George, who today occasionally takes Ambien or a low dose of Seroquel to sleep at night, believes that, at least in his case, getting off the drugs was what enabled him to get well. "If I had stayed on those drugs, I wouldn't be where I am today. I would be stuck in an adult home somewhere, or in the hospital. But I'm recovered. I still have some strange ideas, but now

I keep them to myself. And I weather whatever emotional stress comes up. It stays with me for a few weeks and then it goes away."

Monica Briggs

Monica Briggs is a tall, intense woman and, like so many people active in the "peer recovery" movement, immensely likeable. On the day that I have lunch with her, at a restaurant in South Boston, she comes hobbling over to the booth leaning on a cane, as she recently injured herself, and when I ask how she traveled here, she smiles, slightly pleased with herself. "On my bike," she says.

Monica, who was born in 1967, is from Wellesley, Massachusetts, and as a teenager growing up in that affluent community, she seemed like the last person who might have a life of mental illness awaiting her. She came from an accomplished family—her mother was a professor at Wellesley, while her father taught at several Boston-area colleges—and Monica was a child who excelled at whatever she chose to do. She was a good athlete, earned top grades, and showed a particular talent for art and writing. Upon graduating from high school, she received several scholarship awards, and when she entered Middlebury College in Vermont in the fall of 1985, she believed that her life would follow a very conventional path. "I thought I'd go to school, marry, have a chocolate Labrador, and a home in the suburbs, with the SUV. . . . I thought it would all happen like that."

A month into her freshman year at Middlebury, Monica was blindsided by a severe depressive episode that seemed to have no cause. She'd never had emotional problems before, nothing bad had happened at Middlebury, and yet the depression hit her with such force that she had to leave school and return home. "I was someone who had never quit anything before," she says. "I thought my life was over. I thought this was a failure I could never recover from."

A few months later, she returned to Middlebury. She was taking an antidepressant (desipramine), and as spring neared, her spirits began to lift. However, they didn't just rise to a "normal" level. Instead, they soared beyond to what seemed a much better place. She now had energy to burn. She took long runs and threw herself into her art, dashing off accomplished self-portraits in charcoals and pastels. She had so little need for sleep that she started a T-shirt business. "It was fantastic, great," she says. "I am not thinking that I am God, or anything, but I am thinking I am pretty close to God at that point. This goes on for several weeks, and then I crash for what seems like forever."

This was the start of Monica's long battle with bipolar disorder. Depression had given way to mania followed by worse depression. Although she managed to complete her freshman year, with an A-minus average, she began cycling through depressive and manic episodes, and in May of her sophomore year, she gulped down handfuls of sleeping spills, intending to kill herself. Over the next fifteen years, she was hospitalized thirty times. While lithium kept her mania in check, the suicidal depression always came back, her doctors prescribing one antidepressant after another in an attempt to find the magic pill that would help her stay well.

There were times, between the hospitalizations, when she was fairly stable, and she made the most of them. In 1994, she earned a bachelor's degree from Massachusetts College of Art and Design, and after that she worked for various advertising agencies and publishing houses. She became active in the Depressive and Manic-Depressive Association and developed its logo, the "bipolar bear." But in 2001, after she was fired from her job for having stayed home for a week due to her depression, her suicidal impulses returned with a vengeance. She bought a gun, only to have it misfire six times when she tried to shoot herself. She spent three nights on a bridge that crossed a highway, desperately wanting to fling herself onto the roadway below, but refraining from doing so because she thought she might cause a crash that would hurt others. She was hospitalized several times, and then, in 2002, her mother died from pancreatic cancer, and her mental struggles took an even worse turn. "I am psychotic, hallucinating, seeing things. I think I have super powers and can change the way time flows. I think I have ten-feet wings and that I can fly."

That was the year she went on SSDI. Seventeen years after her initial manic episode, she had officially become disabled by bipolar disorder. "I hate it," she says. "I am a Wellesley girl on welfare, and that's not what Wellesley girls are supposed to do. It is so corrosive to your self-esteem."

As might be guessed, given that she arrived at the diner on a bicycle, having pedaled there during her lunch break at work, Monica's life eventually took a turn for the better. In 2006, she stopped taking an antidepressant, and that triggered a "dramatic change." Her depression lifted, and she began working part-time at the Transformation Center, a Boston peer-run organization that helps people with psychiatric diagnoses. Although the lithium she has continued to take has its drawbacks—"my ability to create artwork is gone," she says—it hasn't exacted too great a physical toll. While she has a thyroid problem and suffers from tremors, her kidneys are fine. "I'm in recovery now," she says, and as we get up to leave the diner, she makes it clear that she would like to secure a full-time job and get off SSDI. "Being on welfare is a phase in my life," she says emphatically, "not an end."

Such has been the long arc of her illness. As a clinical study, her story appears to tell simply of the benefits of lithium. That drug apparently kept her mania in check for decades, and as a monotherapy, it has helped keep her stable since 2006. Still, after years of drug treatment, she ended up on SSDI, and as such, her story illustrates one of the core mysteries of this disability epidemic. How did someone so smart and accomplished end up on that governmental program? And if we wind the clock back to the spring of 1986, a perplexing question appears: Did she suffer her first manic episode because she was "bipolar," or did the antidepressant induce the mania? Is it possible that the drug *converted* her from someone who had suffered a depressive episode into a bipolar patient, and thus put her onto a path of chronic illness? And did the subsequent use of antidepressants alter the course of her "bipolar illness," for one reason or another, for the worse?

To put it another way, in the world of people who attend DBSA meetings, how often do they tell of becoming bipolar *after* initial treatment with an antidepressant?

. . .

Dorea Vierling-Claassen

If you had met Dorea Vierling-Claassen in 2002, when she was twenty-five years old, she would have told you that she was "bipolar." She'd been so diagnosed in 1998, her psychiatrist explaining that she suffered from a chemical imbalance in the brain, and by 2002 she was on a cocktail of drugs that included an antipsychotic, Zyprexa. But by the fall of 2008, she was off all psychiatric medications (and had been for two years), she was thriving in a life that revolved around marriage, motherhood, and postdoctoral research at Massachusetts General Hospital, and she was convinced that her "bipolar" years had all been a big mistake. She believes that she was one of the millions of Americans caught up in a frenzy to diagnose the disorder, and it very nearly ended with her becoming a mental patient for life.

"I escaped by the skin of my teeth," she says.

Dorea tells me her story while sitting in the kitchen of her condominium in Cambridge, Massachusetts. Her spouse, Angela, is here, and their two-year-old daughter is sleeping in the next room. With her freckles and slightly frizzy hair, and evident zest for life, Dorea seems like someone who might have been a bit of a mischievous child, and to a certain extent, that is how she remembers herself. "I was extremely smart, at the far end of that spectrum, and so I was the geeky kid. But I had friends. I was skillful at social navigation—I was also the funny kid." If there was one thing amiss in her life as a child, it was that she was overly emotional, prone to "angry outbursts" and "crying" jags. "Delightful, but odd" is how she sums up her seven-year-old self.

Like many bright "odd" kids, Dorea found pursuits she excelled at. She developed a passion for the trumpet and became an accomplished musician. A top student, she had a particular talent for mathematics. In high school, she ran on the track team and had many friends. However, she remained quite emotional—that part of her personality did not go away—and there was a very real source of distress in her life: She was coming to understand that she was a lesbian. Her parents were "extremely conservative Christians," and while she loved them and deeply admired their devotion to social justice—her father, a physician, volunteered half of his time to work in a clinic he'd founded in Denver's tough "Five Points" neighborhood—she feared that because of their religious beliefs, they wouldn't accept her homosexuality. After Dorea's freshman year at Peabody Institute, a prestigious music conservatory in Baltimore, she took a deep breath and told them her secret. "It went pretty much as awfully as could be expected," she says. "There were tears, a gnashing of teeth. It was so desperately ingrained in their religious thinking."

Dorea barely spoke to her parents for the next two years. She dropped out of Peabody and fell in with a punk crowd that lived in downtown Denver. The once aspiring trumpeter now ran around town with a shaved head and wearing combat boots. After working for a year at a shop that restored rugs, she enrolled at Metro State College, a commuter school. There she struggled constantly with her emotions, often crying in public, and soon she began seeing a therapist, who diagnosed her as depressed. Talk therapy didn't provide much relief, and then, during finals week in the spring of 1998, she found that she couldn't sleep. When she showed up at her therapist's office agitated and a little manic, he had a new explanation for all that bedeviled her: bipolar illness. "I was told it was chronic and that my episodes would increase in frequency, and that I would need to be on drugs for the rest of my life," she recalls.

Although this foretold a bleak future, Dorea took comfort in the diagnosis. It explained why she was so emotional. This also was a diagnosis common to many great artists. She read Kay Jamison's book *Touched with Fire* and thought, "I am just like all these famous writers. This is great." She now had a new identity, and as she resumed her academic career, she arrived at each new institution—first at the University of Nebraska for an undergraduate degree and then at Boston University for a Ph.D. in math and biology—with a "giant box of pills." The cocktail she took usually included a mood stabilizer, an antidepressant, and a benzodiazepine for anxiety, although the exact combination was always changing. One drug would make her sleepy, another would give her tremors, and none of the cocktails seemed to bring her emotional tranquility. Then, in

2001, she was put on an antipsychotic, Zyprexa, which, in a sense, worked like a charm.

"You know what?" she says today, amazed by what she is about to confess. "I loved the stuff. I felt like I finally found the answer. Because what do you know. I have no emotions. It was great. I wasn't crying anymore."

Although Dorea did well academically at Boston University, she still felt "really stupid" on Zyprexa. She slept ten, twelve hours a day, and like so many people on the drug, she began to blimp up, putting on thirty pounds. Angela, who had met and fallen in love with Dorea prior to her going on Zyprexa, felt a sense of loss: "She wasn't as lively anymore, she didn't laugh," she says. But they both understood that Dorea needed to be on the medications, and they began organizing their lives—and their plans for the future— around her bipolar illness. They attended DBSA meetings, and they began to think that Dorea should scale back her career goals. She probably wouldn't be able to handle the stress of postdoctoral research; her previous work in a rug shop seemed about right. "That sounds insane now," says Angela, who is a professor of mathematics at Lesley College. "But at the time, she wasn't a very resilient person, and she was becoming more and more dependent. I had to bear the weight of caretaking."

Dorea's possibilities were diminishing, and she might have continued down that path except for the fact that in 2003 she stumbled across some literature that raised questions about Zyprexa's long-term safety and the merits of antipsychotic drugs. That led her to wean herself from that drug, and while that process was "pure hell"—she suffered terrible anxiety, severe panic attacks, paranoia, and horrible tremors—she eventually did get off that medication. She then decided to see if she could get off the benzodiazepine she was taking, Klonopin, and that turned into another horrible withdrawal experience, as she suffered such severe headaches she'd be in bed by noon. Still, she was gradually undoing her drug cocktail, and that caused her to question her bipolar diagnosis. She had first seen a therapist because she *cried too much*. There had been no mania— her sleeplessness and agitation hadn't arisen until after she had been placed on an antidepressant. Could she just have been a moody teenager who had some growing up to do?

"I had always thought before that I was one of those cases where the illness was clearly biological," she says. "It couldn't have been situational. Nothing had gone terribly wrong in my life. But then I thought, well, I came out as a lesbian, and I had no family support. Duh. That could have been kind of stressful."

The mood stabilizers were the last to go, and on November 22, 2006, Dorea pronounced herself drug free. "It was fabulous. I was surprised to find out who I was after all these years," she says, adding that having shed the bipolar label in her own mind, her sense of personality responsibility changed, too. "When I was 'bipolar,' I had an excuse for any unpredictable or unstable behavior. I had permission to behave in that way, but now I am holding myself to the same behavioral standards as everyone else, and it turns out I can meet them. This is not to say that I don't have bad days. I do, and I may still worry more than the average Joe, but not that much more."

Dorea's research at Massachusetts General Hospital focuses on how vascular activity affects brain function, and given that her struggles with "mental illness" can seemingly be chalked up as a case of misdiagnosis—"I have this fantasy of being undiagnosed as bipolar," she says—it may seem that her story is irrelevant to this book. But, in fact, her story raises a possibility that could go a long way toward explaining the epidemic of disabling mental illness in the United States. If you expand the boundaries of mental illness, which is clearly what has happened in this country during the past twenty-five years, and you treat the people so diagnosed with psychiatric medications, do you run the risk of turning an angst-ridden teenager into a lifelong mental patient? Dorea, who is an extremely smart and capable person, barely escaped going down that path. Hers is a story of a possible *iatrogenic* process at work, of an otherwise normal person being made chronically sick by diagnosis and subsequent treatment. And thus we have to wonder: Do we have a paradigm of care that can, at times, *create* mental illness?

The Parents' Dilemma

Early during the course of my reporting for this book, I met with two families in the Syracuse area who, a few years back, had been faced with deciding whether to put their children on a psychiatric medication. The reason that I had paired these two families up in my mind was that they had come to opposite conclusions about what was best for their child, and I was curious to know what information they had at their disposal when they made their decisions.

I first went to see Gwendolyn and Sean Oates. They live on the south side of Syracuse, in a pleasant house perched on a slight hill. A gracious, biracial couple, they have two children, Nathan and Alia, and as we spoke, Nathan—who was then eight years old— spent most of the time sprawled out in the living room, drawing pictures in a sketchbook with colored pencils.

"We began to worry about him when he was three," his mother says. "We noticed that he was hyperactive. He couldn't sit through a meal, he couldn't even sit down. Dinnertime consisted of him running around the table. It was the same thing in his preschool—he couldn't sit still. He wasn't sleeping either. It would take us until nine thirty or ten p.m. to get him down. He would be kicking and screaming. These were not normal temper tantrums."

They first took Nathan to his pediatrician. However, she was reluctant to diagnose him, and so they took him to a psychiatrist, who quickly concluded that Nathan suffered from "attention deficit hyperactivity disorder." His problem, the psychiatrist explained, was "chemical" in kind. Although they were nervous about putting Nathan on Ritalin—"We were going through this on our own, and we didn't know anything about ADHD," his mother says— kindergarten was looming, and they reasoned that it would be the best thing for him. "The hyperactivity was holding him back from learning," his mother says. "The school didn't even want us to send him to kindergarten, but we said, 'No, we are going to.' We made the decision to keep him moving forward."

At first, there was a period of "trial and error" with the medications. Nathan was put on a high dose of Ritalin, but "he was like a zombie," his mother recalls. "He was calm but he didn't move. He stared off into space." Nathan was then switched to Concerta, a long-lasting stimulant, and he stabilized well on it. However, at some point, Nathan began to exhibit obsessive behaviors, such as refusing to step on the grass or constantly needing to have something in his hands, and he was put on Prozac to control those symptoms. While on that two-drug combo, he started having terrible "rages." He kicked out his bedroom window during one episode, and he repeatedly threatened to kill his sister and even his mother. He was taken off the Prozac, and although his behavior improved somewhat, he continued to be quite aggressive, and he was diagnosed as suffering from both bipolar and ADHD.

"They say that ADHD and bipolar go hand in hand," his mother says. "And now that we know that he is bipolar, too, we think he will probably be on drugs for the rest of his life."

Since that time, Nathan has been on a drug cocktail. When I visited, he was taking Concerta in the morning, Ritalin in the afternoon, and three low doses of Risperdal—an antipsychotic—at various times during the day. This combo, his parents say, works fairly well for him. While Nathan is still moody, he doesn't fly off into total rages, and his hostility toward his younger sister has abated. He does struggle with his schoolwork, but he is moving ahead from grade to grade, and he gets along fairly well with his classmates. The biggest worry that his parents have about the medications is that they may be stunting his growth. Nathan is smaller than his sister, even though he is three years older. However, the physician's assistant and others who are treating Nathan don't talk much about how the drugs may affect him over the long term. "They don't worry about that," his father says. "It's helping him now."

At the end of the interview, Nathan shows me his drawings. He is into sharks and dinosaurs, and after I tell him how much I like his artwork, he seems almost to blush. He has been quiet most of the time I have been there, and even a little subdued, but we shake hands as I get ready to leave, and he seems, at that particular moment, to be a very sweet and gentle kid.

· · ·

Jason and Kelley Smith live on the west side of Syracuse, about thirty minutes distant from the Oates family, and when I knocked on their door, it was their seven-year-old daughter, Jessica, who answered. It appeared that she had been waiting for me, and once I had my tape recorder on, she plunked down on the couch between her mother and me, ready to pipe in with her side of the story. "Jessica," her father says a short while later, "has a lot of charisma."

Jessica's behavioral problems began at age two when she was sent to day care. When she got angry, she would hit and bite the other children. At home, she started having "night terrors" and all-out meltdowns. "The mildest thing would trigger her and she would be off," her mother says.

The Smiths turned to their local school district for help. The district recommended that Jessica go to a "special ed" preschool in north Syracuse, and when she continued to behave aggressively at that school, they were told to take Jessica to the Health Sciences Center at the State University of New York for a psychiatric evaluation. There they saw a nurse practitioner, who immediately concluded that Jessica was "bipolar." The practitioner explained that Jessica had a chemical imbalance and recommended that Jessica be put on a cocktail of three drugs: Depakote, Risperdal, and lithium.

"It blew my mind, especially the thought of putting her on antipsychotics," Jason says. "She was *four* years old."

He and his wife left that consultation not knowing what to do. Kelley works for Oswego County's family service agency, and she knew of many troubled children who had been put on psychiatric medications. In that setting, the county expected parents to comply with medical advice. "There was part of me that thought maybe Jessica is bipolar, that's what it is," Kelley says. Moreover, SUNY Health Sciences told the Smiths that the center wouldn't see Jessica again if she weren't medicated. All of this pointed to following the center's advice—the "experts are telling you that you need to do this, and that it is biological," Jason says—but he had previously worked as a pharmacy technician and knew that drugs could have powerful side effects. "I was scared out of my mind."

Kelley used the Internet to research the drugs that had been recommended. However, she couldn't find any study that told of good long-term outcomes for children placed on such drug cocktails, and even the short-term side effects, she remembers, "were scary." Meanwhile, Jessica's pediatrician told them she thought it would be "absurd" to put Jessica on psychiatric drugs; Jason and Kelley's families also thought it would be a mistake. Jason remembered how a few years earlier talk therapy had helped him address his own "anger management" issues, and if he had been able to change without the use of medications, couldn't Jessica change her behavior too?

"We just didn't want to accept [the bipolar diagnosis]. Jessica is such an outgoing child, and we like to think she is gifted," Kelley says. "And she had made so much progress from the time she was two years old. We just couldn't see giving her the medications."

They made that decision in 2005, and three years later, they say, Jessica is doing well. She gets mostly A's in school; her teachers now think that her earlier bipolar diagnosis was "crazy." While she does sometimes quarrel with other kids and will lash back verbally if another child teases her, she knows that she can't hit anyone. At home, she still has the occasional meltdown, but her emotional outbursts are not so extreme as before. Jessica even has her own advice on how all parents should handle such tirades: "They should say [to their child] 'come here,' and then they should rub them on the back so they feel better and so they can't have a meltdown, and so when they stop having a meltdown, that's what they will remember."

Before I leave, Jessica reads to me the book *The Little Old Lady Who Was Not Afraid of Anything,* and more than once she jumps to the floor to act out a scene. "Even with her behavioral issues, everybody loves her," her father says. "And that's what we were afraid of, with the medication, was that it would totally change her, and her personality. We didn't want to impair her faculties. We just want her to grow up to be healthy and to succeed in life."

Two different families, two different decisions. Both families now saw their decision as the right one, and both believed that their child was on a better path than he or she otherwise would have been. That was heartening, and I promised to check in with both families later, toward the end of my reporting for this book. Still, Nathan and Jessica were clearly on different paths, and as I drove back to Boston, all I could think about was how both sets of parents had needed to make their decision, on whether to medicate their child, in a *scientific vacuum*. Did their child really suffer from a chemical imbalance? Were there studies showing that drug treatment for ADHD or juvenile bipolar illness is beneficial over the long term? If you put a young child on a drug cocktail that includes an antipsychotic, how will it affect his or her physical health? Can the child expect to become a healthy teenager, a healthy adult?

part two

The Science of
Psychiatric Drugs

3

The Roots of an Epidemic

*"Americans have come to believe that science is
capable of almost everything."*
—DR. LOUIS M. ORR, AMA PRESIDENT (1958)[1]

It may seem odd to begin an investigation of a modern-day epidemic with a visit back to one of the great moments in medical history, but if we are going to understand how our society came to believe that Thorazine kicked off a psychopharmacological revolution, we need to go back to the laboratory of German scientist Paul Ehrlich. He was the originator of the notion that "magic bullets" could be found to fight infectious diseases, and when he succeeded, society thought that the future would bring miracle cures of every kind.

Born in East Prussia in 1854, Ehrlich spent his early years as a scientist researching the use of aniline dyes as biological stains. He and others discovered that the dyes, which were used in the textile industry to color cloth, had a selective affinity for staining the cells of different organs and tissues. Methyl blue would stain one type of cell, while methyl red stained a different type. In an effort to explain this specificity, Ehrlich hypothesized that cells had molecules that protruded into the surrounding environment, and that a chemical dye fit into these structures, which he called receptors, in the same way that a key fits into a lock. Every type of cell had a different lock, and that was why methyl blue stained one type of cell and methyl red another—they were keys specific to those different locks.

Ehrlich began doing this research in the 1870s, while he was a doctoral student at the University of Leipzig, and this was the same period that Robert Koch and Louis Pasteur were proving that microbes caused infectious diseases. Their findings led to a thrilling thought: If the invading organism could be killed, the disease could be cured. The problem, most scientists at the time concluded, was that any drug that was toxic to the microbe would surely poison the host. "Inner disinfection is impossible," declared scientists at an 1882 Congress of Internal Medicine in Germany. But Ehrlich's studies with aniline dyes led him to a different conclusion. A dye could stain a single tissue in the body and leave all others uncolored. What if he could find a toxic chemical that would interact with the invading microbe but not with the patient's tissues? If so, it would kill the germ without causing any harm to the patient.

Ehrlich wrote:

> If we picture an organism as infected by a certain species of bacterium, it will be easy to effect a cure if substances have been discovered which have a specific affinity for these bacteria and act on these alone. (If) they possess no affinity for the normal constituents of the body, such substances would then be magic bullets.[2]

In 1899, Ehrlich was appointed director of the Royal Institute of Experimental Therapy in Frankfurt, and there he began his search for a magic bullet. He focused on finding a drug that would selectively kill trypanosomes, which were one-celled parasites that caused sleeping sickness and a number of other illnesses, and he soon settled on an arsenic compound, atoxyl, as the best magic-bullet candidate. This would be the chemical he would have to manipulate so it fit into the parasite's "lock" while not opening the lock on any human cells. He systematically created hundreds of atoxyl derivatives, testing them again and again against trypanosomes, but time and time again he met with failure. Finally, in 1909, after Ehrlich had tested more than nine hundred compounds, one of his assistants decided to see if compound number 606 would kill another recently discovered microbe, *Spirocheta pallida*, which caused syphilis. Within days, Ehrlich had his triumph. The drug, which came to be known as salvarsan, eradicated the syphilis microbe from infected rabbits without harming the rabbits at all. "This was the magic bullet!" wrote Paul de Kruif in a 1926 best-seller. "And what a safe bullet!" The drug, he added, produced "healing that could only be called biblical."[3]

Ehrlich's success inspired other scientists to search for magic bullets against other disease-causing microbes, and although it took twenty-five years, in 1935 Bayer chemical company provided medicine with its second miracle drug. Bayer discovered that sulfanilamide, which was a derivative of an old coal-tar compound, was fairly effective in eradicating staphylococcal and streptococcal infections. The magic bullet revolution was now truly under way, and next came penicillin. Although Alexander Fleming had discovered this bacteria-killing mold in 1928, he and others had found it difficult to culture, and even when they'd succeeded in growing it, they hadn't been able to extract and purify sufficient quantities of the active ingredient (penicillin) to turn it into a useful drug. But in 1941, with World War II raging, both England and the United States saw a desperate need to surmount this hurdle, for wound infections had always been the big killer during war. The United States asked scientists from Merck, Squibb, and Pfizer to jointly work on this project, and by D-Day in 1944, British and American sources were able to produce enough penicillin for all of the wounded in the Normandy invasion.

"The age of healing miracles had come at last," wrote Louis Sutherland, in his book *Magic Bullets,* and indeed, with the war over, medicine continued its great leap forward.[4] Pharmaceutical companies discovered other broad-acting antibiotics—streptomycin, Chloromycetin, and Aureomycin, to name a few—and suddenly physicians had pills that could cure pneumonia, scarlet fever, diphtheria, tuberculosis, and a long list of other infectious diseases. These illnesses had been the scourge of mankind for centuries, and political leaders and physicians alike spoke of the great day at hand. In 1948, U.S. secretary of state George Marshall confidently predicted that infectious diseases might soon be wiped from the face of the earth. A few years later, President Dwight D. Eisenhower called for the "unconditional surrender" of all microbes.[5]

As the 1950s began, medicine could look back and count numerous other successes as well. Pharmaceutical firms had developed improved anesthetics, sedatives, antihistamines, and anticonvulsants, evidence of how scientists were getting better at synthesizing chemicals that acted on the central nervous system in helpful ways. In 1922, Eli Lilly had figured out how to extract the hormone insulin from the pancreas glands of slaughterhouse animals, and this provided doctors with an effective treatment for diabetes. Although replacement insulin didn't rise to the level of a magic-bullet cure for the illness, it came close, for it provided a biological fix for what was missing in the body. In 1950, British scientist Sir Henry Dale, in a letter to the *British Medical Journal,* summed up this extraordinary moment in medicine's long history: "We who have been able to watch the beginning of this great movement may be glad and proud to have lived through such a time, and confident that an even wider and more majestic advance will be seen by those living through the fifty years now opening."[6]

The United States geared up for this wondrous future. Prior to the war, most basic research had been privately funded, with Andrew Carnegie and John D. Rockefeller the most prominent benefactors, but once the war ended, the U.S. government established the National Science Foundation to federally fund this endeavor. There were still many diseases to conquer, and as the nation's leaders looked around for a medical field that had lagged behind, they quickly found one that seemed to stand above all the rest. Psychiatry, it seemed, was a discipline that could use a little help.

Imagining a New Psychiatry

As a medical specialty, psychiatry had its roots in the nineteenth-century asylum, its founding moment occurring in 1844, when thirteen physicians who ran small asylums met in Philadelphia to form the Association of Medical Superintendents of American Institutions for the Insane. At that time, the asylums provided a form of environmental care known as moral therapy, which had been introduced into the United States by Quakers, and for a period, it produced good results. At most asylums, more than 50 percent of newly admitted patients would be discharged within a year, and a significant percentage of those who left never came back. A nineteenth-century long-term study of outcomes at Worcester State Lunatic Asylum in Massachusetts found that 58 percent of the 984 patients discharged from the asylum remained well throughout the rest of their lives. However, the asylums mushroomed in size in the latter part of the 1800s, as communities dumped the senile elderly and patients with syphilis and other neurological disorders into the institutions, and since these patients had no chance of recovering, moral therapy came to be seen as a failed form of care.

At their 1892 meeting, the asylum superintendents vowed to leave moral therapy behind and instead utilize physical treatments. This was the dawn of a new era in psychiatry, and in very short order, they began announcing the benefits of numerous treatments of this kind. Various water therapies, including high-pressure showers and prolonged baths, were said to be helpful. An injection of extract of sheep thyroid was reported to produce a 50 percent cure rate at one asylum; other physicians announced that injections of metallic salts, horse serum, and even arsenic could restore lucidity to a mad mind. Henry Cotton, superintendent at Trenton State Hospital in New Jersey, reported in 1916 that he cured insanity by removing his patients' teeth. Fever therapies were said to be beneficial, as were deep-sleep treatments, but while the initial reports of all these somatic therapies told of great success, none of them stood the test of time.

In the late 1930s and early 1940s, asylum psychiatrists embraced a trio of therapies that acted directly on the brain, which the popular media—at least initially—reported as "miracle" cures. First came insulin coma therapy. Patients were injected with a high dose of insulin, which caused them to lapse into hypoglycemic comas, and when they were brought back to life with an injection of glucose, the *New York Times* explained, the "short circuits of the brain vanish, and the normal circuits are once more restored and bring back with them sanity and reality."[7] Next came the convulsive therapies. Either a poison known as Metrazol or electroshock was used to induce a seizure in the patient, and when the patient awoke, he or she would be free of psychotic thoughts and happier in spirit—or so the asylum psychiatrists said. The final "breakthrough" treatment was frontal lobotomy, the surgical destruction of the frontal lobes apparently producing an instant cure. This "surgery of the soul," the *New York Times* explained, "transforms wild animals into gentle creatures in the course of a few hours."[8]

With such articles regularly appearing in major newspapers and magazines like *Harper's, Reader's Digest,* and the *Saturday Evening Post,* the public had reason to believe that psychiatry was making great strides in treating mental illness, participating in medicine's great leap forward, but then, in the wake of World War II, the public was forced to confront a very different reality, one that produced a great sense of horror and disbelief. There were 425,000 people locked up in the country's mental hospitals at that time, and first *Life* magazine and then journalist Albert Deutsch, in his book *The Shame of the States,* took Americans on a photographic tour of the decrepit facilities. Naked men huddled in barren rooms, wallowing in their own feces. Barefoot women clad in coarse tunics sat strapped to wooden benches. Patients slept on threadbare cots in sleeping wards so crowded that they had to climb over the foot of their beds to get out. These images told of unimaginable neglect and great suffering, and at last, Deutsch drew the inevitable comparison:

> As I passed through some of Byberry's wards, I was reminded of the Nazi concentration camps at Belsen and Buchenwald. I entered buildings swarming with naked humans herded like cattle and treated with less concern, pervaded by a fetid odor so heavy, so nauseating, that the stench seemed to have almost a physical existence of its own. I saw hundreds of patients living under leaking roofs, surrounded by moldy, decaying walls, and sprawling on rotting floors for want of seats or benches.[9]

The nation clearly needed to remake its care of the hospitalized mentally ill, and even as it contemplated that need, it found reason to worry about the mental health of the general population. During the war, psychiatrists had been charged with screening draftees for psychiatric problems, and they had deemed 1.75 million American men mentally unfit for service. While many of the rejected draftees may have been feigning illness in order to avoid conscription, the numbers still told of a societal problem. Many veterans returning from Europe were also struggling emotionally, and in September 1945, General Lewis Hershey, who was the director of the Selective Service System, told Congress that the nation badly needed to address this problem, which had remained hidden for so long. "Mental illness was the greatest cause of noneffectiveness and loss of manpower that we met" during the war, he said.[10]

With mental illness now a primary concern for the nation—and this awareness coming at the very time that antibiotics were taming bacterial killers—it was easy for everyone to see where a long-term solution might be found. The country could put its faith in the transformative powers of science. The existing "medical" treatments said to be so helpful—insulin coma, electroshock, and lobotomy—would have to be provided to more patients, and then long-term solutions could arise from the same process that had produced such astonishing progress in fighting infectious diseases. Research into the biological causes of mental illnesses would lead to better treatments, both for those who were seriously ill and those who were only moderately distressed. "I can envisage a time arriving when we in the field of Psychiatry will entirely forsake our ancestry, forgetting that we had our beginnings in the poorhouse, the workhouse and the jail," said Charles Burlingame, director of the Institute of the Living in Hartford, Connecticut. "I can envisage a time when we will be doctors, think as doctors, and run our psychiatric institutions in much the same way and with much the same relationships as obtain in the best medical and surgical institutions."[11]

In 1946, Congress passed a National Mental Health Act that put the federal government's economic might behind such reform. The government would sponsor research into the prevention, diagnosis, and treatment of mental disorders, and it would provide grants to states and cities to help them establish clinics and treatment centers. Three years later, Congress created the National Institute of Mental Health (NIMH) to oversee this reform.

"We must realize that mental problems are just as real as physical disease, and that anxiety and depression require active therapy as much as appendicitis or pneumonia," wrote Dr. Howard Rusk, a professor at New York University who penned a weekly column for the *New York Times*. "They are all medical problems requiring medical care."[12]

The stage had now been set for a transformation of psychiatry and its therapeutics. The public believed in the wonders of science, the nation saw a pressing need to improve its care of the mentally ill, and the NIMH had been created to make this happen. There was the *expectation* of great things to come and, thanks to the sales of antibiotics, a rapidly growing pharmaceutical industry ready to capitalize on that expectation. And with all those forces lined up, perhaps it is no surprise that wonder drugs for both severe and not-so-severe mental illnesses—for schizophrenia, depression, and anxiety—soon arrived.

4

Psychiatry's Magic Bullets

*"It was the first drug cure in all of
psychiatric history."*
— NATHAN KLINE
DIRECTOR OF RESEARCH AT ROCKLAND STATE
HOSPITAL IN NEW YORK (1974)[1]

The "magic bullet" model of medicine that had led to the discovery of the sulfa drugs and antibiotics was very simple in kind. First, identify the cause or nature of the disorder. Second, develop a treatment to counteract it. Antibiotics killed known bacterial invaders. Eli Lilly's insulin therapy was a variation on the same theme. The company developed this treatment after researchers came to understand that diabetes was due to an insulin deficiency. In each instance, knowledge of the disease came first—that was the magic formula for progress. However, if we look at how the first generation of psychiatric drugs was discovered, and look too at how they came to be called *antipsychotics, anti-anxiety* agents, and *antidepressants*—words that indicate they were antidotes to specific disorders—we see a very different process at work. The psychopharmacology revolution was born from one part science and two parts wishful thinking.

Neuroleptics, Minor Tranquilizers, and Psychic Energizers

The story of the discovery of Thorazine, the drug that is remembered today as having kicked off the psychopharmacology "revolution," begins in the 1940s, when researchers at Rhône-Poulenc, a French pharmaceutical company, tested a class of compounds known as phenothiazines for their magic-bullet properties. Phenothiazines had first been synthesized in 1883 for use as chemical dyes, and Rhône-Poulenc's scientists were trying to synthesize phenothiazines that were toxic to the microbes that caused malaria, African sleeping sickness, and worm-borne illnesses. Although that research didn't pan out, they did discover in 1946 that one of their phenothiazines, promethazine, had antihistaminic properties, which suggested it might have use in surgery. The body releases histamine in response to wounds, allergies, and a range of other conditions, and if this histaminic response is too strong, it can lead to a precipitous drop in blood pressure, which at the time occasionally proved fatal to surgical patients. In 1949, a thirty-five-year-old surgeon in the French Navy, Henri Laborit, gave promethazine to several of his patients at the Maritime Hospital at Bizerte in Tunisia, and he discovered that in addition to its antihistaminic properties, it induced a "euphoric quietude. . . . Patients are calm and somnolent, with a relaxed and detached expression."[2]

Promethazine, it seemed, might have use as an *anesthetic*. At that time, barbiturates and morphine were regularly employed in medicine as general sedatives and painkillers, but those drugs suppressed overall brain function, which made them quite dangerous. But promethazine apparently acted only on selective regions of the brain. The drug "made it possible to disconnect certain brain functions," Laborit explained. "The surgical patient felt no pain, no anxiety, and often did not remember his operation."[3] If the drug was used as part of a surgical cocktail, Laborit reasoned, it would be possible to use much lower doses of the more dangerous anesthetic agents. A cocktail that included promethazine—or an even more potent derivative of it, if such a compound could be synthesized—would make surgery much safer.

Chemists at Rhône-Poulenc immediately went to work. To assess a compound, they would give it to caged rats that had learned, upon hearing the sound of a bell, to climb a rope to a resting platform in order to avoid being shocked (the floor of the cage was electrified). They knew they had found a successor to promethazine when they injected compound 4560 RP into the rats: Not only were the rats physically unable to climb the rope, they weren't emotionally interested in doing so either. This new drug, chlorpromazine, apparently disconnected brain regions that controlled both motor movement and the mounting of emotional responses, and yet it did so without causing the rats to lose consciousness.

Laborit tested chlorpromazine as part of a drug cocktail in surgical patients in June of 1951. As expected, it put them into a "twilight state." Other surgeons tested it as well, reporting that it served to "potentiate" the effects of the other anesthetic agents, the cocktail inducing an "artificial hibernation." In December of that year, Laborit spoke of this new advance in surgery at an anesthesiology conference in Brussels, and there he made an observation that suggested chlorpromazine might also be of use in psychiatry. It "produced a veritable medicinal lobotomy," he said.[4]

Although today we think of lobotomy as a mutilating surgery, at that time it was regarded as a useful operation. Only two years earlier, the Nobel Prize in Medicine had been awarded to the Portuguese neurologist, Egas Moniz, who had invented it. The press, in its most breathless moments, had even touted lobotomy as an operation that plucked madness neatly from the mind. But what the surgery most reliably did, and this was well understood by those who performed the operation, was change people in a profound way. It made them lethargic, disinterested, and childlike. That was seen by the promoters of lobotomy as an improvement over what the patients had been before—anxious, agitated, and filled with psychotic thoughts—and now, if Laborit was to be believed, a pill had been discovered that could transform patients in a similar way.

In the spring of 1952, two prominent French psychiatrists, Jean

Delay and Pierre Deniker, began administering chlorpromazine to psychotic patients at St. Anne's Hospital in Paris, and soon use of the drug spread to asylums throughout Europe. Everywhere the reports were the same: Hospital wards were quieter, the patients easier to manage. Delay and Deniker, in a series of articles they published in 1952, described the "psychic syndrome" induced by chlorpromazine:

> Seated or lying down, the patient is motionless on his bed, often pale and with lowered eyelids. He remains silent most of the time. If questioned, he responds after a delay, slowly, in an indifferent monotone, expressing himself with few words and quickly becoming mute. Without exception, the response is generally valid and pertinent, showing that the subject is capable of attention and of reflection. But he rarely takes the initiative of asking a question; he does not express his preoccupations, desires, or preference. He is usually conscious of the amelioration brought on by the treatment, but he does not express euphoria. The apparent indifference or the delay of the response to external stimuli, the emotional and affective neutrality, the decrease in both initiative and preoccupation without alteration in conscious awareness or in intellectual faculties constitute the psychic syndrome due to the treatment.[5]

U.S. psychiatrists dubbed chlorpromazine, which was marketed in the United States as Thorazine, as a "major tranquilizer." Back in France, Delay and Deniker coined a more precise scientific term: This new drug was a "neuroleptic," meaning it took hold of the nervous system. Chlorpromazine, they concluded, induced deficits similar to those seen in patients ill with encephalitis lethargica. "In fact," Deniker wrote, "it would be possible to cause true encephalitis epidemics with the new drugs. Symptoms progressed from reversible somnolence to all types of dyskinesia and hyperkinesia, and finally to parkinsonism."[6] Physicians in the United States similarly understood that this new drug was not fixing any known pathology. "We have to remember that we are not treating diseases with this drug," said psychiatrist E. H. Parsons, at a 1955 meeting in Philadelphia on chlorpromazine. "We are using a neuropharmacologic agent to produce a specific effect."[7]

At the same time that Rhône-Poulenc was testing phenothiazines for their possible magic-bullet properties against malaria, Frank Berger, a Czech-born chemist, was doing research of a somewhat similar kind in London, and his work led, in 1955, to the introduction of "minor tranquilizers" to the market.

During the war, Berger had been one of the scientists in Britain who had helped develop methods to produce medically useful quantities of penicillin. But penicillin was effective only against grampositive bacteria (microbes that took up a stain developed by Danish scientist Hans Christian Gram), and after the war ended, Berger sought to find a magic bullet that could kill gram-negative microbes, the ones that caused a host of troubling respiratory, urinary, and gastrointestinal illnesses. At that time, there was a commercial disinfectant sold in Britain, called Phenoxetol, that was advertised as effective against gram-negative bacteria in the environment, and Berger, who worked for British Drug Houses, Ltd., tinkered with the active ingredient in that product, a phenylglycerol ether, in an effort to produce a product with superior antibacterial effects. When a compound called mephenesin proved promising, he gave it to mice to test its toxicity. "The compound, much to my surprise, produced reversible flaccid paralysis of the voluntary skeletal muscles unlike that I had ever seen before," Berger wrote.[8]

Berger had stumbled on a potent muscle-relaxing agent. That was curious enough, but what was even more surprising, the drug-paralyzed mice didn't show any signs of being stressed by their new predicament. He would put the animals on their backs and they would be unable to right themselves, and yet their "heart beat was regular, and there were no signs suggesting an involvement of the autonomic nervous system." The mice remained quiet and tranquil, and Berger found that even when he administered low doses of this amazing new compound to mice—the doses too small to cause muscle paralysis—they displayed this odd tranquility.

Berger realized that a drug of this sort might have commercial possibilities as an agent that allayed anxiety in people. However, mephenesin was a very short-acting drug, providing only a few minutes of peace. In 1947, Berger moved to the United States and went to work for Wallace Laboratories in New Jersey, where he synthesized a compound, meprobamate, that lasted eight times as long in the body as mephenesin. When Berger gave it to animals, he discovered that it also had powerful "taming" effects. "Monkeys after being given meprobamate lost their viciousness and could be more easily handled," he wrote.[9]

Wallace Laboratories brought meprobamate to market in 1955, selling it as Miltown. Other pharmaceutical companies scrambled to develop competitor drugs, and as they did so, they looked for compounds that would make animals less aggressive and numb to pain. At Hoffmann-La Roche, chemist Leo Sternbach identified chlordiazepoxide as having a "powerful and unique" tranquilizing effect after he gave it to mice that ordinarily could be prompted to fight by the application of electric shocks to their feet.[10] Even with a low dose of the drug, the mice remained noncombative when shocked. This compound also proved to have potent taming effects in larger animals—it turned tigers and lions into pussycats. The final proof of chlordiazepoxide's merits involved another electric-shock exam. Hungry rats were trained to press a lever for food, and then they were taught that if they did so while a light in the cage blinked on, they would be shocked. Although the rats quickly learned not to press the lever while the light was on, they nevertheless exhibited signs of extreme stress—defecating, etc.—whenever it lit up their cage. But if they were given a dose of chlordiazepoxide? The light would flash and they wouldn't be the least bit bothered. Their "anxiety" had vanished, and they would even press the lever to get something to eat, unworried about the shock to come. Hoffmann-La Roche brought chlordiazepoxide to market in 1960, selling it as Librium.

For obvious reasons, the public heard little about the animal tests that had given rise to the minor tranquilizers. However, an article published in the *Science News Letter* was the exception to the rule, as its reporter put the animal experiments into a human frame of reference. If you took a minor tranquilizer, he explained, "this would mean that you might still feel scared when you see a car speeding toward you, but the fear would not make you run."[11]

Psychiatry now had a new drug for quieting hospitalized patients and a second one for easing anxiety, the latter a drug that could be marketed to the general population, and by the spring of 1957, it gained a medicine for depressed patients, iproniazid, which was marketed as Marsilid. This drug, which was dubbed a "psychic energizer," could trace its roots back to a poetically apt source: rocket fuel.

Toward the end of World War II, when Germany ran low on the liquid oxygen and ethanol it used to propel its V-2 rockets, its scientists developed a novel compound, hydrazine, to serve as a substitute fuel. After the war ended, chemical companies from the Allied countries swooped in to grab samples of it, their pharmaceutical divisions eager to see if its toxic properties could be harnessed for magic-bullet purposes. In 1951, chemists at Hoffmann-La Roche created two hydrazine compounds, isoniazid and iproniazid, that proved effective against the bacillus that caused tuberculosis. The novel medicines were rushed into use in several TB hospitals, and soon there were reports that the drug seemed to "energize" patients. At Staten Island's Sea View Hospital, *Time* magazine reported, "patients who had taken the drugs danced in the wards, to the delight of news photographers."[12]

The sight of TB patients doing a jig suggested that these drugs might have a use in psychiatry as a treatment for depression. For various reasons, iproniazid was seen as having the greater potential, but initial tests did not find it to be particularly effective in lifting spirits, and there were reports that it could provoke mania. Tuberculosis patients treated with iproniazid were also developing so many nasty side effects—dizziness, constipation, difficulty urinating, neuritis, perverse skin sensations, confusion, and psychosis—that its use had to be curtailed in sanitariums. However, in the spring of 1957, Nathan Kline, a psychiatrist at Rockland State Hospital in Orangeburg, New York, rescued iproniazid with a report that if depressed patients were kept on the drug long enough, for at least five weeks, it worked. Fourteen of the sixteen patients he'd treated with iproniazid had improved, and some had a "complete remission of all symptoms."[13]

On April 7, 1957, the *New York Times* summed up iproniazid's strange journey: "A side effect of an anti-tuberculosis drug may have led the way to chemical therapy for the unreachable, severely depressed mental patient. Its developers call it an energizer as opposed to a tranquilizer."[14]

Such were the drugs that launched the psychopharmacology revolution. In the short span of three years (1954–1957), psychiatry gained new medicines for quieting agitated and manic patients in asylums, for anxiety, and for depression. But none of these drugs had been developed after scientists had identified any disease process or brain abnormality that might have been causing these symptoms. They arrived out of the post–World War II search for magic bullets against infectious diseases, with researchers, during that process, stumbling on compounds that affected the central nervous system in novel ways. The animal tests of chlorpromazine, meprobamate, and chlordiazepoxide revealed that these agents sharply curbed normal physical and emotional responses, but did so without causing a loss of consciousness. That was what was so novel about the major and minor tranquilizers. They curbed brain function in a selective manner. It was unclear how iproniazid worked—it seemed to rev up the brain in some way—but, as the *New York Times* had noted, its mood-lifting properties were properly seen as a "side effect" of an anti-tuberculosis agent.

The drugs were best described as "tonics." But in the media, a story of a much different sort was being told.

An Unholy Alliance

The storytelling forces in American medicine underwent a profound shift in the 1950s, and to see how that is so, we need to briefly recount the history of the American Medical Association prior to that time. At the turn of the century, the AMA set itself up as the organization that would help the American public distinguish the good from the bad. At that time, there were fifty thousand or so medicinal products sold in the United States, and they were of two basic types. There were thousands of small companies that sold syrups, elixirs, and herbal remedies directly to the public (or as packaged goods in stores), with these "patent" medicines typically made from "secret" ingredients. Meanwhile, Merck and other "drug houses" sold their chemical preparations, which were known as "ethical" drugs, to pharmacists, who then acted as the retail vendors of these products. Neither group needed to prove to a government regulatory agency that its products were safe or effective, and the AMA, eager to establish a place for doctors in this freewheeling marketplace, set itself up as the organization that would do this assessment. It established a "propaganda department" to investigate the patent medicines and thus protect Americans from "quackery," and it established a Council on Pharmacy and Chemistry to conduct chemical tests of the ethical drugs. The AMA published the results of these tests in its journals and provided the best ethical drugs with its "seal of approval." The AMA also published each year a "useful drugs" book, and its medical journals would not allow advertisements for any drug that had not passed its vetting process.

With this work, the AMA turned itself into a watchdog of the pharmaceutical industry and its products. By doing so, the organization was both providing a valuable service to the public and furthering its members' financial interests, for its drug evaluations provided patients with a good reason to visit a doctor. A physician, armed with his book of useful drugs, could prescribe an appropriate one. And it was this *knowledge,* as opposed to any government-authorized prescribing power, that provided physicians with their value in the marketplace (in terms of providing access to medicines).

The selling of drugs in the United States began to change with the passage of the 1938 Food and Drug Cosmetics Act. The law required drug firms to prove to the Food and Drug Administration that their products were safe (they still did not have to prove that their drugs were helpful), and in its wake, the FDA began decreeing that certain medicines could be purchased only with a doctor's prescription.* In 1951, Congress passed the Durham-Humphrey Amendment to the act, which decreed that most new drugs would be available by prescription only, and that prescriptions would be needed for refills, too.

Physicians now enjoyed a very privileged place in American society. They controlled the public's access to antibiotics and other new medicines. In essence, they had become the retail vendors of these products, with pharmacists simply fulfilling their orders, and as vendors, they now had financial reason to tout the wonders of their products. The better the new drugs were perceived to be, the more inclined the public would be to come to their offices to obtain a prescription. "It would appear that a physician's own market position is strongly influenced by his reputation for using the latest drug," explained *Fortune* magazine.[15]

The financial interests of the drug industry and physicians were lined up in a way they never had been before, and the AMA quickly adapted to this new reality. In 1952, it stopped publishing its yearly book on "useful drugs." Next, it began allowing advertisements in its journals for drugs that had not been approved by its Council on Pharmacy and Chemistry. In 1955, the AMA abandoned its famed "seal of acceptance" program. By 1957, it had cut the budget for its Council on Drugs to a paltry $75,000, which was understandable, given that the AMA was no longer in the business of assessing the merits of these products. Three years later, the AMA even lobbied against a proposal by Tennessee senator Estes Kefauver that drug companies prove to the FDA that their new drugs were effective. The AMA, in its relationship to the pharmaceutical industry, had "become what I would call sissy," confessed Harvard Medical School professor Maxwell Finland, in testimony to Congress.[16]

But it wasn't just that the AMA had given up its watchdog role. The AMA and physicians were also now working with the

---

* In 1914, the Harrison Narcotics Act required a doctor's prescription for opiates and cocaine. The 1938 Food and Drug Cosmetics Act extended that prescription-only requirement to a larger number of drugs.

pharmaceutical industry to promote new drugs. In 1951, the year that the Durham-Humphrey Act was passed, Smith Kline and French and the American Medical Association began jointly producing a television program called *The March of Medicine,* which, among other things, helped introduce Americans to the "wonder" drugs that were coming to market. Newspaper and magazine articles about new medications inevitably included testimonials from doctors touting their benefits, and as Pfizer physician Haskell Weinstein later confessed to a congressional committee, "much of what appears [in the popular press] has in essence been placed by the public relations staffs of the pharmaceutical firms."[17] In 1952, an industry trade publication, *FDC Reports,* noted that the pharmaceutical industry was enjoying a "sensationally favorable press," and a few years later, it commented on why this was so. "Virtually all important drugs," it wrote, receive "lavish praise by the medical profession on introduction."[18]

This new marketplace for drugs proved profitable for all involved. Drug industry revenues topped $1 billion in 1957, the pharmaceutical companies enjoying earnings that made them "the darlings of Wall Street," one writer observed.[19] Now that physicians controlled access to antibiotics and all other prescription drugs, their incomes began to climb rapidly, doubling from 1950 to 1970 (after adjusting for inflation). The AMA's revenues from drug advertisements in its journals rose from $2.5 million in 1950 to $10 million in 1960, and not surprisingly, these advertisements painted a rosy picture. A 1959 review of drugs in six major medical journals found that 89 percent of the ads provided no information about the drugs' side effects.[20]

Such was the environment in the 1950s when the first psychiatric drugs were brought to market. The public was eager to hear of wonder drugs, and this was just the story that the pharmaceutical industry and the nation's physicians were eager to tell.

Miracle Pills

Smith Kline and French, which obtained a license from Rhône-Poulenc to sell chlorpromazine in the United States, secured FDA approval for Thorazine on March 26, 1954. A few days later, the company used its *March of Medicine* show to launch the product. Although Smith Kline and French had spent only $350,000 developing Thorazine, having administered it to fewer than 150 psychiatric patients prior to submitting its application to the FDA, the company's president, Francis Boyer, told viewers that this was a product that had gone through the most rigorous testing imaginable. "It was administered to well over five thousand animals and proved active and safe for human administration," he said. "We then placed the compound in the hands of physicians in our great American medical centers to explore its clinical value and possible limitations. In all, over two thousand doctors in this country and Canada have used it. . . . The development of a new medicine is difficult and costly, but it is a job our industry is privileged to perform."[21]

Boyer's was a story of rigorous science at work, and less than three months later, *Time,* in an article titled "Wonder Drug of 1954?", pronounced Thorazine a "star performer." After a dose of Thorazine, the magazine explained, patients "sit up and talk sense with [the doctor], perhaps for the first time in months."[22] In a follow-up article, *Time* reported that patients "willingly took [the] pills" and that once they did, they "fed themselves, ate heartily and slept well." Thorazine, the magazine concluded, was as important "as the germ-killing sulfas discovered in the 1930s."[23]

This was a magic-bullet reference that was impossible to miss, and other newspapers and magazines echoed that theme. Thanks to chlorpromazine, *U.S. News and World Report* explained, "patients who were formerly untreatable within a matter of weeks or months become sane, rational human beings."[24] The *New York Times,* in a series of articles in 1954 and 1955, called Thorazine a "miracle" pill that brought psychiatric patients "peace of mind" and "freedom from confusion." Thorazine, newspapers and magazines agreed, had ushered in a "new era of psychiatry."[25]

With such stories being told about Thorazine, it was little wonder that the public went gaga when Miltown, in the spring of 1955, was introduced into the market. This drug, *Time* reported, was for "walk-in neurotics rather than locked-in psychotics," and according to what psychiatrists were telling newspaper and magazine reporters, it had amazing properties.[26] Anxiety and worries fled so quickly, *Changing Times* explained, that it could be considered a "happy pill." *Reader's Digest* likened it to a "Turkish bath in a tablet." The drug, explained *Consumer Reports,* "does not deaden or dull the senses, and it is not habit forming. It relaxes the muscles, calms the mind, and gives people a renewed ability to enjoy life."[27]

The public rush to obtain this new drug was such that Wallace Laboratories and Carter Products, which were jointly selling meprobamate, struggled to keep up with the demand. Drugstores lucky enough to have a supply put out signs that screamed: YES, WE HAVE MILTOWN! The comedian Milton Berle said that he liked the drug so much that he might change his first name to Miltown. Wallace Laboratories hired Salvador Dalí to help stoke Miltown fever, paying the great artist $35,000 to create an exhibit at an AMA convention that was meant to capture the magic of this new drug. Attendees walked into a darkened claustrophobic tunnel that represented the interior of a caterpillar—this was what it was like to be anxious—and then, as they emerged back into the light, they came upon a golden "butterfly of tranquility," this metamorphosis due to meprobamate. "To Nirvana with Miltown" is how *Time* described Dalí's exhibit.[28]

There was one slightly hesitant note that appeared in newspaper and magazine articles during the introduction of Thorazine and Miltown. In the 1950s, many of the psychiatrists at top American medical schools were Freudians, who believed that mental disorders were caused by psychological conflicts, and their influence led Smith Kline and French, in its initial promotion of Thorazine, to caution reporters that "there is no thought that chlorpromazine is a cure for mental illness, but it can have great value if it relaxes patients and makes them accessible to treatment."[29] Both Thorazine and Miltown, explained the *New York Times,* should be considered as "adjuncts to psychotherapy, not the cure."[30] Thorazine was called a "major tranquilizer" and Miltown a "minor tranquilizer," and when Hoffmann-La Roche brought iproniazid to market, it was described as a "psychic energizer." These drugs, although they may have been remarkable in kind, were not antibiotics for the mind. As *Life* magazine noted in a 1956 article titled "The Search Has Only Started," psychiatry was still in the early stages of its revolution, for the "bacteria" of mental disorders had yet to be discovered.[31]

Yet, in very short order, even this note of caution went by the wayside. In 1957, the *New York Times* reported that researchers now believed that iproniazid might be a "potent regulator of unbalanced cerebral metabolism."[32] This suggested that the drug, which had been developed to fight tuberculosis, might be fixing something that was wrong in the brains of depressed patients. A second drug for depressed patients, imipramine, arrived on the market during this time, and in 1959 the *New York Times* called them "antidepressants" for the first time. Both appeared to "reverse psychic states," the paper said.[33] These drugs were gaining a new status, and finally psychiatrist Harold Himwich, in a 1958 article in *Science,* explained that they "may be compared with the advent of insulin, which counteracts symptoms of diabetes."[34] The antidepressants were fixing something wrong in the brain, and when Hoffmann-La Roche brought Librium to market in 1960, it picked up on this curative message. Its new drug was not just another tranquilizer, but rather "the successor to this entire group. . . . Librium is the biggest step yet toward *'pure' anxiety relief* as distinct from central sedation or hypnotic action."[35] Merck did the same, marketing its drug Suavitil as "a mood normalizer. . . . Suavitil offers a new and specific type of neurochemical treatment for the patient who is disabled by anxiety, tension, depression, or obsessive-compulsive manifestations."[36]

The final step in this image makeover of the psychiatric drugs came in 1963. The NIMH had conducted a six-week trial of Thorazine and other neuroleptics, and after these drugs were shown to be more effective than a placebo in knocking down psychotic symptoms, the researchers concluded that that the drugs should be regarded "as antischizophrenic in the broad sense. In fact, it is questionable whether the term 'tranquilizer' should be retained."[37]

With this pronouncement by the NIMH, the transformation of the psychiatric drugs was basically complete. In the beginning, Thorazine and other neuroleptics had been viewed as agents that made patients quieter and emotionally indifferent. Now they were "antipsychotic" medications. Muscle relaxants that had been developed for use in psychiatry because of their "taming" properties were now "mood normalizers." The psychic energizers were "antidepressants." All of these drugs were apparently antidotes to specific disorders, and in that sense, they deserved to be compared to antibiotics. They were disease-fighting agents, rather than mere tonics. All that was missing from this story of magic-bullet medicine was an understanding of the biology of mental disorders, but with the drugs reconceived in this way, once researchers came to understand how the drugs affected the brain, they developed two hypotheses that, at least in theory, filled in this gap.

Chemicals in the Brain

At the start of the 1950s, there was an ongoing debate among neurologists about how signals crossed the tiny synapses that separated neurons in the brain. The prevailing view was that the signaling was electrical in kind, but others argued for chemical transmission, a debate that historian Elliot Valenstein, in his book *Blaming the Brain*, characterized as the "war between the sparks and the soups." However, by the mid-1950s, researchers had isolated a number of possible chemical messengers in the brains of rats and other mammals, including acetylcholine, serotonin, norepinephrine, and dopamine, and soon the "soup" model had prevailed.

With that understanding in place, an investigator at the NIMH, Bernard Brodie, planted the intellectual seed that grew into the theory that depression was due to a chemical imbalance in the brain. In 1955, in experiments with rabbits, Brodie reported that reserpine, an herbal drug used in India to quiet psychotic patients, lowered brain levels of serotonin. It also made the animals "lethargic" and "apathetic." Arvid Carlsson, a Swedish pharmacologist who had worked for a time in Brodie's lab, soon reported that reserpine also reduced brain levels of norepinephrine and dopamine (which jointly are known as catecholamines). Thus, a drug that depleted serotonin, norepinephrine, and dopamine in the brain seemed to make animals "depressed." However, investigators discovered that if animals were pretreated with iproniazid or imipramine before they were given reserpine, they didn't become lethargic and apathetic. The two "antidepressants," in one manner or another, apparently blocked reserpine's usual depletion of serotonin and the catecholamines.[38]

During the 1960s, scientists at the NIMH and elsewhere figured out how iproniazid and imipramine worked. The transmission of signals from the "presynaptic" neuron to the "postsynaptic" neuron needs to be lightning fast and sharp, and in order for the signal to be terminated, the chemical messenger must be removed from the synapse. This is done in one of two ways. Either the chemical is metabolized by an enzyme and shuttled off as waste, or else it flows back into the presynaptic neuron. Researchers discovered that iproniazid thwarts the first process. It blocks an enzyme, known as monoamine oxidase, that metabolizes norepinephrine and serotonin. As a result, the two chemical messengers remain in the synapse longer than normal. Imipramine inhibits the second process. It blocks the "reuptake" of norepinephrine and serotonin by the presynaptic neuron, and thus, once again, the two chemicals remain in the synapse longer than normal. Both drugs produce a similar end result, although they do so by different means.

In 1965, the NIMH's Joseph Schildkraut, in a paper published in the *American Journal of Psychiatry,* reviewed this body of research and set forth a chemical imbalance theory of affective disorders:

> Those drugs [like reserpine] which cause depletion and inactivation of norepinephrine centrally produce sedation or depression, while drugs which increase or potentiate norepinephrine are associated with behavioral stimulation or excite-

ment and generally exert an antidepressant effect in man. From these findings a number of investigators have formulated a hypothesis about the pathophysiology of the affective disorders. This hypothesis, which has been designated the "catecholamine hypothesis of affective disorders," proposes that some, if not all depressions are associated with an absolute or relative deficiency of catecholamines, particularly norepinephrine.[39]

Although this hypothesis had its obvious limitations—it was, Schildkraut said, "at best a reductionistic oversimplification of a very complex biological state"—the first pillar in the construction of the doctrine known today as "biological psychiatry" had been erected. Two years later, researchers erected the second pillar: the dopamine hypothesis of schizophrenia.

Evidence for this theory arose from investigations into Parkinson's disease. In the late 1950s, Sweden's Arvid Carlsson and others suggested that Parkinson's might be due to a deficiency in dopamine. To test this possibility, Viennese neuropharmacologist Oleh Hornykiewicz applied iodine to the brain of a man who'd died from the illness, as this chemical turns dopamine pink. The basal ganglia, an area of the brain that controls motor movements, was known to be rich in dopaminergic neurons, and yet in the basal ganglia of the Parkinson's patient, there was "hardly a tinge of pink discoloration," Hornykiewicz reported.[40]

Psychiatric researchers immediately understood the possible relevance of this to schizophrenia. Thorazine and other neuroleptics regularly induced Parkinsonian symptoms—the same tremors, tics, and slowed gait. And if Parkinson's resulted from the death of dopaminergic neurons in the basal ganglia, then it stood to reason that antipsychotic drugs, in some manner or another, thwarted dopamine transmission in the brain. The death of dopaminergic neurons and the blocking of dopamine transmission would both produce a dopamine malfunction in the basal ganglia. Carlsson soon reported that Thorazine and the other drugs for schizophrenia did just that.

This was a finding, however, that told of drugs that "disconnected" certain brain regions. They weren't normalizing brain function; they were creating a profound pathology. However, at this same time, researchers reported that amphetamines—drugs known to trigger hallucinations and paranoid delusions—elevated dopamine activity in the brain. Thus, it appeared that psychosis might be caused by too much dopamine activity, which the neuroleptics then curbed (and thus brought back into balance). If so, the drugs could be said to be antipsychotic in kind, and in 1967, Dutch scientist Jacques Van Rossum explicitly set forth the dopamine hypothesis of schizophrenia. "When the hypothesis of dopamine blockade by neuroleptic agents can be further substantiated, it may have fargoing consequences for the pathophysiology of schizophrenia. Overstimulation of dopamine receptors could then be part of the aetiology" of the disease.[41]

Expectations Fulfilled

The revolution in mental health care that Congress had hoped for when it created the NIMH twenty years earlier was now—or so it seemed—complete. Psychiatric drugs had been developed that were antidotes to biological disorders, and researchers believed that the drugs worked by countering chemical imbalances in the brain. The horrible mental hospitals that had so shamed the nation at the end of World War II could now be shuttered, as schizophrenics—thanks to the new drugs—could be treated in the community. Those suffering from a milder disorder, like depression or anxiety, simply needed to reach into their medicine cabinets for relief. In 1967, one in three American adults filled a prescription for a "psychoactive" medication, with total sales of such drugs reaching $692 million.[42]

This was a narrative of a scientific triumph, and in the late 1960s and early 1970s, the men who had been the pioneers in this new field of "psychopharmacology" looked back with pride at their handiwork. "It was a revolution and not just a transition period," said Frank Ayd Jr., editor of the *International Drug Therapy Newsletter*. "There was an actual revolution in the history of psychiatry and one of the most important and dramatic epics in the history of medicine itself."[43] Roland Kuhn, who had "discovered" imipramine, reasoned that the development of antidepressants could properly be seen as "an achievement of the progressively developing human intellect."[44] Anti-anxiety medicines, said Frank Berger, the creator of Miltown, were "adding to happiness, human achievement, and the dignity of man."[45] Such were the sentiments of those who had led this revolution, and finally, at a 1970 symposium on biological psychiatry in Baltimore, Nathan Kline summed up what most of those in attendance understood to be true: They all had earned a place in the pantheon of great medical men.

"Medicine and science will be *just that much different* because we have lived," Kline told his colleagues. "Treatment and understanding of [mental] illness will forever be altered . . . and in our own way we will persist for all time in that small contribution we have made toward the Human Venture."[46]

A Scientific Revolution . . . or a Societal Delusion?

Today, by retracing the discovery of the first generation of psychiatric drugs and following their transformation into magic bullets, we can see that by 1970 two possible histories were unfolding. One possibility is that psychiatry, in a remarkably fortuitous turn of events, had stumbled on several types of drugs that, although they produced abnormal behaviors in animals, nevertheless fixed various abnormalities in the brain chemistry of those who were mentally ill. If so, then a true revolution was indeed under way, and we can expect that when we review the long-term outcomes produced by these drugs, we will find that they help people get well and stay well. The other possibility is that psychiatry, eager to have its own magic pills and eager to take its place in mainstream medicine, turned the drugs into something they were not. These first-generation drugs were simply agents that perturbed normal brain function in some way, which is what the animal research had shown, and if that is so, then it stands to reason that the *long-term* outcomes produced by the drugs might be problematic in kind.

Two possible histories were under way, and in the 1970s and 1980s, researchers investigated the critical question: Do people diagnosed with depression and schizophrenia suffer from a chemical imbalance that is then corrected by the medication? Were the new drugs truly *antidotes* to something chemically amiss in the brain?

5

The Hunt for Chemical Imbalances

"The great tragedy of science—the slaying of a
beautiful hypothesis by an ugly fact."
—THOMAS HUXLEY (1870)[1]

The adult human brain weighs about three pounds, and when you see it close up, removed from the skull, it is a bit larger than you imagined it to be. I had thought a brain could rest fairly easily in the palm of one's hand, but you really need both hands to lift it securely into the air. If the brain is fresh, not yet pickled in formaldehyde, a spiderweb of blood vessels pinkens the surface, and the tissue feels soft, almost gelatinous. It is definitely "biological" in kind, and yet somehow it gives rise to all of the mysterious and remarkable talents of the human mind. At the invitation of a friend, Jang-Ho Cha, who is a neuroscientist at Massachusetts General Hospital, I attended a brain-cutting seminar at the hospital, with the thought that seeing a human brain would help me better visualize the neurotransmitter pathways that are said to give rise to depression and psychosis, but naturally my visit turned into something more than that. The human brain up close takes your breath away.

The mechanics of its messaging system are fairly well understood. There are, Cha noted, 100 billion neurons in the human brain. The cell body of a "typical" neuron receives input from a vast web of dendrites, and it sends out a signal via a single axon that may project to a distant area of the brain (or down the spinal cord). At its end, an axon branches into numerous terminals, and it is from these terminals that chemical messengers—dopamine, serotonin, etc.—are released into the synaptic cleft, which is a gap about twenty nanometers wide (a nanometer is one-billionth of a meter). A single neuron has between one thousand and ten thousand synaptic connections, with the adult brain as a whole having perhaps 150 trillion synapses.

The axons of neurons that use the same neurotransmitter are regularly bundled together, almost like the strands of a telecommunications cable, and once scientists discovered that dopamine, norepinephrine, and serotonin fluoresced different colors when exposed to formaldehyde vapors, it became possible to track those neurotransmitter pathways in the brain. Although Joseph Schildkraut, when he formulated his theory of affective disorders, thought that norepinephrine was the neurotransmitter most likely to be in short supply in those who were depressed, researchers fairly quickly turned much of their attention to serotonin, and so for our purposes, in regard to our investigation of the chemical imbalance theory of mental disorders, we need to look at that pathway in the

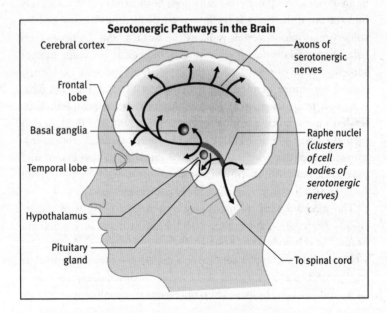

Serotonergic Pathways in the Brain

Cerebral cortex

Frontal lobe

Basal ganglia

Temporal lobe

Hypothalamus

Pituitary gland

Axons of serotonergic nerves

Raphe nuclei *(clusters of cell bodies of serotonergic nerves)*

To spinal cord

brain for depression, and at the dopaminergic pathway for schizophrenia.

The serotonergic pathway is one with ancient evolutionary roots. Serotonergic neurons are found in the nervous systems of all vertebrates and most invertebrates, and in humans their cell bodies are located in the brain stem, in an area known as the raphe nuclei. Some of these neurons send long axons down the spinal cord, a system that is involved in the control of respiratory, cardiac, and gastrointestinal activities. Other serotonergic neurons have axons that ascend into all areas of the brain—the cerebellum, the hypothalamus, the basal ganglia, the temporal lobes, the limbic system, the cerebral cortex, and the frontal lobes. This pathway is involved in

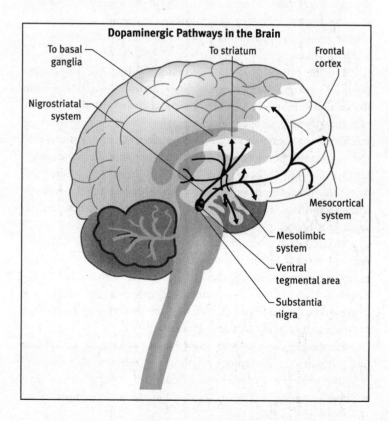

memory, learning, sleep, appetite, and the regulation of moods and behaviors. As Efrain Azmitia, a professor of biology at NYU, has noted, "the brain serotonin system is the single largest brain system known and can be characterized as a 'giant' neuronal system."[2]

There are three major dopaminergic pathways in the brain. The cell bodies of all three systems are located atop the brain stem, in either the substantia nigra or the ventral tegmentum. Their axons project to the basal ganglia (nigrostriatal system), the limbic region (mesolimbic system), and the frontal lobes (mesocortical system). The basal ganglia initiates and controls movement. The limbic structures—the olfactory tubercle, the nucleus accumbens, and the amygdala, among others—are located behind the frontal lobes and help regulate our emotions. It is here that we feel the world, a process that is vital to our sense of self and our conceptions of reality. The frontal lobes are the most distinguishing feature of the human brain, and provide us with the godlike capacity to monitor our own selves.

All of this physiology—the 100 billion neurons, the 150 trillion synapses, the various neurotransmitter pathways—tell of a brain that is almost infinitely complex. Yet the chemical imbalance theory of mental disorders boiled this complexity down to a simple disease mechanism, one easy to grasp. In depression, the problem was that the serotonergic neurons released too little serotonin into the synaptic gap, and thus the serotonergic pathways in the brain were "underactive." Antidepressants brought serotonin levels in the synaptic gap up to normal, and that allowed these pathways to transmit messages at a proper pace. Meanwhile, the hallucinations and voices that characterized schizophrenia resulted from overactive dopaminergic pathways. Either the presynaptic neurons pumped out too much dopamine into the synapse or the target neurons had an abnormally high density of dopamine receptors. Antipsychotics put a brake on this system, and this allowed the dopaminergic pathways to function in a more normal manner.

That was the chemical imbalance theory put forth by Schildkraut and Jacques Van Rossum, and the very research that had led Schildkraut to his hypothesis also provided investigators with a method for testing it. The studies of iproniazid and imipramine had shown that neurotransmitters were removed from the synapse in one of two ways. Either the chemical was taken back up into the presynaptic neuron and restored for later use, or it was metabolized by an enzyme and carted off as waste. Serotonin is metabolized into 5-hydroxyindole acetic acid (5-HIAA); dopamine is turned into homovanillic acid (HVA). Researchers could comb the cerebrospinal fluid for these metabolites, and the amounts found would serve as an indirect gauge of the synaptic levels of the neurotransmitters. Since low serotonin was theorized to cause depression, anyone in that emotional state should have lower-than-normal levels of 5-HIAA in his or her cerebrospinal fluid. Similarly, since an overactive dopamine system was theorized to cause schizophrenia, people who heard voices or were paranoid should have abnormally high cerebrospinal levels of HVA.

This line of research kept scientists busy for nearly fifteen years.

The Serotonin Hypothesis Is Put to the Test

In 1969, Malcolm Bowers at Yale University became the first to report on whether depressed patients had low levels of serotonin metabolites in their cerebrospinal fluid. In a study of eight depressed patients (all of whom had been previously exposed to antidepressants), he announced that their 5-HIAA levels were lower than normal, but not "significantly" so.[3] Two years later, investigators at McGill University said that they, too, had failed to find a "statistically significant" difference in the 5-HIAA levels of depressed patients and normal controls, and that they also had failed to find any correlation between 5-HIAA levels and the severity of depressive symptoms.[4] In 1974, Bowers was back with a more finely tuned follow-up study: Depressed patients who had not been exposed to antidepressants had perfectly normal 5-HIAA levels.[5]

The serotonin theory of depression did not seem to be panning out, and in 1974, two researchers at the University of Pennsylvania, Joseph Mendels and Alan Frazer, revisited the evidence that had led Schildkraut to advance his theory in the first place. Schildkraut had noted that reserpine, which depleted monoamines in the brain (norepinephrine, serotonin, and dopamine), regularly made people depressed. But when Mendels and Frazer looked closely at the scientific literature, they found that when hypertensive patients were given reserpine, only 6 percent in fact got the blues. Furthermore, in 1955, a group of physicians in England had given the herbal drug to their depressed patients, and it had *lifted* the spirits of many. Reserpine, Mendels and Frazer concluded, didn't reliably induce depression at all.[6] They also noted that when researchers had given other monoamine-depleting drugs to people, those agents hadn't induced depression either. "The literature reviewed here strongly suggests that the depletion of brain norepinephrine, dopamine or serotonin is in itself not sufficient to account for the development of the clinical syndrome of depression," they wrote.[7]

It seemed that the theory was about to be declared dead and buried, but then, in 1975, Marie Asberg and her colleagues at the Karolinska Institute in Stockholm breathed new life into it. Twenty of the sixty-eight depressed patients they had tested suffered from low 5-HIAA levels, and these low-serotonin patients were somewhat more suicidal than the rest, with two of the twenty eventually committing suicide. This was evidence, the Swedish researchers said, that there might be "a biochemical subgroup of depressive disorder characterized by a disturbance of serotonin turnover."[8]

Soon prominent psychiatrists in the United States were writing that "nearly 30 percent" of depressed patients had been found to have low serotonin levels. The serotonin theory of depression seemed at least partly vindicated. But today, if we revisit Asberg's study and examine her data, we can see that her finding of a "biological subgroup" of depressed patients was mostly a story of wishful thinking.

In her study, Asberg reported that 25 percent of her "normal" group had cerebrospinal 5-HIAA levels below fifteen nanograms per milliliter. Fifty percent had fifteen to twenty-five nanograms of 5-HIAA per milliliter, and the remaining 25 percent had levels above twenty-five nanograms. The bell curve for her "normals" showed that 5-HIAA levels were quite variable. But what she failed to note in her discussion was that the bell curve for the sixty-eight depressed patients in her study was almost exactly the same. Twenty-nine percent (twenty of the sixty-eight) had 5-HIAA counts below fifteen nanograms, 47 percent had levels between fifteen and twenty-five nanograms, and 24 percent had levels above twenty-five nanograms. Twenty-nine percent of depressed patients may have had "low" levels of serotonin metabolites in their cerebrospinal fluid (this was her "biological subgroup"), but then so did 25 percent of "normal" people. The median level for normals was twenty nanograms, and, it so turned out, more than half of the depressed patients—thirty-seven of sixty-eight—had levels *above* that amount.

Viewed in this way, her study had not provided any new reason to believe in the serotonin theory of depression. Japanese investigators soon revealed, in an unwitting way, the faulty logic at work. They reported that some antidepressants (used in Japan) blocked serotonin receptors, inhibiting the firing of those pathways, and thus they reasoned that depression might be caused by an "excess of free serotonin in the synaptic cleft."[9] They had applied the same backwards reasoning that had given rise to the low-serotonin theory of depression, and if the Japanese scientists had wanted to, they could have pointed to Asberg's study for support of their theory, as the Swedes had found that 24 percent of depressed patients had "high" levels of serotonin.

In 1984, NIMH investigators studied the low-serotonin theory of depression one more time. They wanted to see whether the "biological subgroup" of depressed patients with "low" levels of serotonin were the best responders to an antidepressant, amitriptyline, that selectively blocked its reuptake. If an antidepressant was an antidote to a chemical imbalance in the brain, then amitriptyline should be most effective in that subgroup. But, lead investigator James Maas wrote, "contrary to expectations, no relationships between cerebrospinal 5-HIAA and response to amitriptyline were found."[10] Moreover, he and the other NIMH researchers discovered—just as Asberg had—that 5-HIAA levels varied widely in depressed patients. Some had high levels of serotonin metabolites in their cerebrospinal fluid, while others had low levels. The NIMH scientists drew the only possible conclusion: "Elevations or decrements in the functioning of serotonergic systems per se are not likely to be associated with depression."*

Even after this report, the serotonin theory of depression did not completely go away. The commercial success of Prozac, a "selective serotonin reuptake inhibitor" brought to market in 1988 by Eli Lilly, fueled a new round of public claims that depression was due to low levels of this neurotransmitter, and once again any number of investigators conducted experiments to see if that were so. But this second round of studies produced the same results as the first. "I spent the first several years of my career doing full-time research on brain serotonin metabolism, but I never saw any convincing evidence that any psychiatric disorder, including depression, results from a deficiency of brain serotonin," said Stanford psychiatrist David Burns in 2003.[11] Numerous others made this same point. "There is no scientific evidence whatsoever that clinical depression is due to any kind of biological deficit state," wrote Colin Ross, an associate professor of psychiatry at Southwest Medical Center in Dallas, in his 1995 book, *Pseudoscience in Biological Psychiatry*.[12] In 2000, the authors of *Essential Psychopharmacology* told medical students "there is no clear and convincing evidence that monoamine deficiency accounts for depression; that is, there is no 'real' monoamine deficit."[13] Yet, fueled by pharmaceutical advertisements, the belief lived on, and it caused Irish psychiatrist David Healy, who has written a number of books on the history of psychi-

---

* The NIMH researchers also looked at a number of other possible associations between variable neurotransmitter levels and response to an antidepressant. They measured norepinephrine metabolites and dopamine metabolites; they divided their depressed patients into bipolar and unipolar groups; and they evaluated their response to two antidepressants, imipramine and amitriptyline. They found mild associations between several of these subgroups and their response to one or other of the drugs; I have focused here on their findings regarding whether (a) depression is due to low levels of serotonin, and (b) if the subgroup of patients with low levels of serotonin responds better to a drug that selectively blocks the reuptake of this neurotransmitter.

atry, to quip in 2005 that this theory needed to be put into the medical dustbin, where other such discredited theories can be found. "The serotonin theory of depression," he wrote, with evident exasperation, "is comparable to the masturbatory theory of insanity."[14]

Dopamine Deja Vu

When Van Rossum set forth his dopamine hypothesis of schizophrenia, he noted that the first thing that investigators needed to do was "further substantiate" that antipsychotic drugs did indeed thwart dopamine transmission in the brain. This took some time, but by 1975, Solomon Snyder at Johns Hopkins Medical School and Philip Seeman at the University of Toronto had fleshed out how the drugs achieved that effect. First, Snyder identified two distinct types of dopamine receptors, known as D_1 and D_2. Next, both investigators found that antipsychotics blocked 70 to 90 percent of the D_2 receptors.[15] Newspapers now told of how these drugs might be correcting a chemical imbalance in the brain.

"Too much dopamine function in the brain could account for the overwhelming flood of sensations that plagues the schizophrenic," the New York Times explained. "By blocking the brain's receptor sites for dopamine, neuroleptics put an end to sights and sounds that are not really there."[16]

However, even as Snyder and Seeman were reporting their results, Malcolm Bowers was announcing findings that cast a cloud over the dopamine hypothesis. He had measured the level of dopamine metabolites in the cerebrospinal fluid of unmedicated schizophrenics and found them to be quite normal. "Our findings," he wrote, "do not furnish neurochemical evidence for an over-arousal in these patients emanating from a midbrain dopamine system."[17] Others soon reported similar results. In 1975, Robert Post at the NIMH determined that HVA levels in the cerebrospinal fluid of twenty unmedicated schizophrenics "were not significantly different from controls."[18] Autopsy studies also revealed that the brain tissue of drug-free schizophrenics did not have abnormal levels of dopamine. In 1982, UCLA's John Haracz reviewed this body of research and drew the obvious bottom-line conclusion: "These findings do not support the presence of elevated dopamine turnover in the brains of [unmedicated] schizophrenics."[19]

Having discovered that dopamine levels in never-medicated schizophrenics were normal, researchers turned their attention to a second possibility. Perhaps people with schizophrenia had an over-abundance of dopamine receptors. If so, the postsynaptic neurons would be "hypersensitive" to dopamine, and this would cause the dopaminergic pathways to be overstimulated. In 1978, Philip Seeman at the University of Toronto announced in *Nature* that this was indeed the case. At autopsy, the brains of twenty schizophrenics had 70 percent more D_2 receptors than normal. At first glance, it seemed that the cause of schizophrenia had been found, but Seeman cautioned that all of the patients had been on neuroleptics prior to their deaths. "Although these results are apparently compatible with the dopamine hypothesis of schizophrenia in general," he wrote, the increase in D_2 receptors might "have resulted from the long-term administration of neuroleptics."[20]

A variety of studies quickly proved that the drugs were indeed the culprit. When rats were fed neuroleptics, their D_2 receptors quickly increased in number.[21] If rats were given a drug that blocked D_1 receptors, that receptor subtype increased in density.[22] In each instance, the increase was evidence of the brain trying to compensate for the drug's blocking of its signals. Then, in 1982, Angus MacKay and his British colleagues reported that when they examined brain tissue from forty-eight deceased schizophrenics, "the increases in [D_2] receptors were seen only in patients in whom neuroleptic medication had been maintained until the time of death, indicating that they were entirely iatrogenic [drug-caused]."[23] A few years later, German investigators reported the same results from their autopsy studies.[24] Finally, investigators in France, Sweden, and Finland used positron emission topography to study D_2-receptor densities in living patients who had never been exposed to neuroleptics, and all reported "no significant differences" between the schizophrenics and "normal controls."[25]

Since that time, researchers have continued to study whether there might be something amiss with the dopaminergic pathways in people diagnosed with schizophrenia, and now and then someone reports having found an abnormality of some type in a subset of patients. But by the end of the 1980s, it was clear that the chemical-imbalance hypothesis of schizophrenia—that this was a disease characterized by a hyperactive dopamine system that was then put somewhat back into balance by the drugs—had come to a crashing end. "The dopaminergic theory of schizophrenia retains little credibility for psychiatrists," observed Pierre Deniker in 1990.[26] Four years later, John Kane, a well-known psychiatrist at Long Island Jewish Medical Center, echoed the sentiment, noting that there was "no good evidence for any perturbation of the dopamine function in schizophrenia."[27] Still, the public continued to be told that people diagnosed with schizophrenia had overactive dopamine systems, with the drugs likened to "insulin for diabetes," and thus former NIMH director Steve Hyman, in his 2002 book, *Molecular Neuropharmacology,* was moved to once again remind readers of the truth. "There is no compelling evidence that a lesion in the dopamine system is a primary cause of schizophrenia," he wrote.[28]

Requiem for a Theory

The low-serotonin hypothesis of depression and the high-dopamine hypothesis of schizophrenia had always been the twin pillars of the chemical-imbalance theory of mental disorders, and by the late 1980s, both had been found wanting. Other mental disorders have also been touted to the public as diseases caused by chemical imbalances, but there was never any evidence to support those claims. Parents were told that children diagnosed with attention deficit hyperactivity disorder suffered from low dopamine levels, but the only reason they were told that was because Ritalin stirred neurons to release extra dopamine. This became the storytelling formula that was relied upon by pharmaceutical companies again and again:

Researchers would identify the mechanism of action for a class of drugs, how the drugs either lowered or raised levels of a brain neurotransmitter, and soon the public would be told that people treated with those medications suffered from the opposite problem.

From a scientific point of view, it is apparent today that the chemical imbalance hypothesis was always wobbly in kind, and many of the scientists who watched its rise and fall have looked back on it with a bit of embarrassment. As early as 1975, Joseph Mendels and Alan Frazer had concluded that Schildkraut's hypothesis of depression had arisen out of "tunnel thinking" that relied on an "inadequate evaluation of certain findings not consistent with the initial assumption."[29] In 1990, Deniker said that the same was true of the dopamine hypothesis of schizophrenia. When psychiatric researchers recast the drugs as "antischizophrenic" agents, he noted, they had gone "a bit far . . . one can say that neuroleptics diminish certain phenomena of schizophrenia, but [the drugs] do not pretend to be an etiological treatment of these psychoses."[30] The chemical-imbalance theory of mental disorders, wrote David Healy, in his book *The Creation of Psychopharmacology*, was embraced by psychiatrists because it "set the stage" for them "to become real doctors."[31] Doctors in internal medicine had their antibiotics, and now psychiatrists could have their "anti-disease" pills too.

Yet a societal belief in chemical imbalances has remained (for reasons that will be explored later), and it has led those who have investigated and written about this history to emphasize, time and again, the same bottom-line conclusion. "The evidence does not support any of the biochemical theories of mental illness," concluded Elliot Valenstein, a professor of neuroscience at the University of Michigan, in his 1998 book *Blaming the Brain*.[32] Even U.S. surgeon general David Satcher, in his 1999 report *Mental Health*, confessed that "the precise causes [etiologies] of mental disorders are not known."[33] In *Prozac Backlash*, Joseph Glenmullen, an instructor of psychiatry at Harvard Medical School, noted that "in every instance where such an imbalance was thought to be found, it was later proved to be false."[34] Finally, in 2005, Kenneth Kendler, coeditor in chief of *Psychological Medicine*, penned an admirably succinct epitaph for this whole story: "We have hunted for big simple neurochemical explanations for psychiatric disorders and have not found them."[35]

This brings us to our next big question: If psychiatric drugs don't fix abnormal brain chemistry, what do they do?

Prozac on My Mind

During the 1970s and 1980s, investigators put together detailed accounts of how the various classes of psychiatric drugs act on the brain, and how the brain in turn reacts to the drugs. We could relate the history of antidepressants, neuroleptics, benzodiazepines, or stimulants, and all of those histories would tell of a somewhat common process at work. But since the story of chemical imbalances in the public mind really took off after Eli Lilly brought Prozac (fluoxetine) to market, it seems appropriate to review what Eli Lilly scientists and other investigators, in reports published in scientific journals, had to say about how this "selective serotonin reuptake inhibitor" actually worked.

As was noted earlier, once a presynaptic neuron has released serotonin into the synaptic gap, it must be quickly removed so that the signal can be crisply terminated. An enzyme metabolizes a small amount; the rest is pumped back into the presynaptic neuron, entering via a channel known as SERT (serotonin reuptake transport). Fluoxetine blocks this reuptake channel, and as a result, Eli Lilly scientist James Clemens wrote in 1975, it causes a "pile-up of serotonin at the synapse."[36]

However, as the Eli Lilly investigators discovered, a feedback mechanism then kicks in. The presynaptic neuron has "autoreceptors" on its terminal membrane that monitor the level of serotonin in the synapse. If serotonin levels are too low, one scientist quipped, these autoreceptors scream "turn on the serotonin machine." If serotonin levels are too high, they scream "turn it off." This is a feedback loop designed by evolution to keep the serotonergic system in balance, and fluoxetine triggers the latter message. With serotonin no longer being whisked away from the synapse, the autoreceptors tell the presynaptic neurons to fire at a dramatically lower rate. They begin to release lower-than-normal amounts of serotonin into the synapse.

Feedback mechanisms also change the postsynaptic neurons. Within four weeks, the density of their serotonin receptors drops 25 percent below normal, Eli Lilly scientists reported in 1981.[37] Other investigators subsequently reported that "chronic fluoxetine treatment" may lead to a 50 percent reduction in serotonin receptors in certain areas of the brain.[38] As a result, the postsynaptic neurons become "desensitized" to the chemical messenger.

At this point, it may seem that the brain has successfully adapted to the drug. Fluoxetine blocks the normal reuptake of serotonin from the synapse, but the presynaptic neurons then begin releasing less serotonin and the postsynaptic neurons become less sensitive to serotonin and thus don't fire so readily. The drug was designed to accelerate the serotonergic pathway; the brain responded by putting on the brake. It has kept its serotonergic pathway more or less in balance, an adaptive response that researchers have dubbed "synaptic resilience."[39] However, there is one other change that occurs during this initial two-week period, and it ultimately short-circuits the brain's compensatory response. The autoreceptors for serotonin on the presynaptic neurons decline in number. As a result, this feedback mechanism becomes partially disabled, and the "turn off the serotonin machine" message dims. The presynaptic neurons begin to fire at a normal rate again, at least for a while, and to release more serotonin than normal each time.*[40]

As the Eli Lilly scientists and others put together this picture of fluoxetine's effects on the brain, they speculated as to what part of this process was responsible for the drug's antidepressant properties. Psychiatrists had long observed that antidepressants took two or three weeks to "work," and thus the Eli Lilly researchers reasoned in 1981 that it was the decline in serotonin receptors, which took several weeks to occur, that was "the underlying mechanism associated with the therapeutic response."[41] If so, the drug could be

---

* Over the long term, it appears that serotonin release falls to an abnormally low level, at least in certain regions of the brain.

said to work because it drove the serotonergic system into a less responsive state. But once researchers discovered that fluoxetine partially disabled the feedback mechanism, Claude de Montigny at McGill University argued that this was what allowed the drug to begin working. This disabling process also took two or three weeks to occur, and it allowed the presynaptic neurons to begin pumping higher amounts of serotonin than normal into the synapse. At that point, with fluoxetine continuing to block serotonin's removal, the neurotransmitter could now indeed "pile up" in the synapse, and that would lead "to an enhancement of central serotonergic neuro-transmission," de Montigny wrote.[42]

That is the scientific story of how fluoxetine alters the brain, and it may be that this process helps depressed people get well and stay well. Only the outcomes literature can reveal whether that is so. But the medicine clearly doesn't *fix* a chemical imbalance in the brain. Instead, it does precisely the opposite. Prior to being medicated, a depressed person has no known chemical imbalance. Fluoxetine then gums up the normal removal of serotonin from the synapse, and that triggers a cascade of changes, and several weeks later the serotonergic pathway is operating in a decidedly *abnormal* manner. The presynaptic neuron is putting out more serotonin than usual. Its serotonin reuptake channels are blocked by the drug. The system's feedback loop is partially disabled. The postsynaptic neurons are "desensitized" to serotonin. Mechanically speaking, the sero-tonergic system is now rather mucked up.

Eli Lilly's scientists were well aware that this was so. In 1977, Ray Fuller and David Wong observed that fluoxetine, since it dis-rupted serotonergic pathways, could be used to study "the role of serotonin neurons in various brain functions—behavior, sleep, reg-ulation of pituitary hormone release, thermoregulation, pain re-sponsiveness and so on." To conduct such experiments, researchers could administer fluoxetine to animals and observe which functions became compromised. They would look for *pathologies* to appear. This type of research in fact was already being done: Fuller and Wong reported in 1977 that the drug stirred "stereotyped hyper-activity" in rats and "suppressed REM sleep" in both rats and cats.[43]

In 1991, in a paper published in the *Journal of Clinical Psychiatry*, Princeton neuroscientist Barry Jacobs made this very point about SSRIs. He wrote:

> These drugs "alter the level of synaptic transmission beyond the physiologic range achieved under [normal] environmental/biological conditions. Thus, any behavioral or physiologic change produced under these conditions might more appropriately be considered pathologic, rather than reflective of the normal biological role of 5-HT [serotonin.]"[44]

During the 1970s and 1980s, researchers studying the effects of neuroleptics fleshed out a similar story. Thorazine and other standard antipsychotics block 70 to 90 percent of all D_2 receptors in the brain. In response, the presynaptic neurons begin pumping out more dopamine and the postsynaptic neurons increase the density of their D_2 receptors by 30 percent or more. In this manner, the brain is trying to "compensate" for the drug's effects so that it can maintain the transmission of messages along its dopaminergic pathways. However, after about three weeks, the pathway's feedback mechanism begins to fail, and the presynaptic neurons begin to fire in irregular patterns or turn quiescent. It is this "inactivation" of dopaminergic pathways that "may be the basis for the antipsychotic action," explains the American Psychiatric Association's *Textbook of Psychopharmacology*.[45]

Once again, this is a story of neurotransmitter pathways that have been transformed by the medication. After several weeks, their feedback loops are partially disabled, the presynaptic neurons are releasing less dopamine than normal, the drug is thwarting dopamine's effects by blocking D_2 receptors, and the postsynaptic neurons have an abnormally high density of these receptors. The drugs do not normalize brain chemistry, but disturb it, and if Jacob's reasoning is followed, to a degree that could be considered "pathological."

A Paradigm for Understanding Psychotropic Drugs

Today, as provost of Harvard University, Steve Hyman is mostly engaged in the many political and administrative tasks that come with leading a large institution. But he is a neuroscientist by training, and in 1996 to 2001, when he was the director of the NIMH, he wrote a paper, one both memorable and provocative in kind, that summed up all that had been learned about psychiatric drugs. Titled "Initiation and Adaptation: A Paradigm for Understanding Psychotropic Drug Action," it was published in the *American Journal of Psychiatry*, and it told of how all psychotropic drugs could be understood to act on the brain in a common way.[46]

Antipsychotics, antidepressants, and other psychotropic drugs, he wrote, "create perturbations in neurotransmitter functions." In response, the brain goes through a series of compensatory adaptations. If a drug blocks a neurotransmitter (as an antipsychotic does), the presynaptic neurons spring into hyper gear and release more of it, and the postsynaptic neurons increase the density of their receptors for that chemical messenger. Conversely, if a drug increases the synaptic levels of a neurotransmitter (as an antidepressant does), it provokes the opposite response: The presynaptic neurons decrease their firing rates and the postsynaptic neurons decrease the density of their receptors for the neurotransmitter. In each instance, the brain is trying to nullify the drug's effects. "These adaptations," Hyman explained, "are rooted in homeostatic mechanisms that exist, presumably, to permit cells to maintain their equilibrium in the face of alterations in the environment or changes in the internal milieu."

However, after a period of time, these compensatory mechanisms break down. The "chronic administration" of the drug then causes "substantial and long-lasting alterations in neural function," Hyman wrote. As part of this long-term adaptation process, there are changes in intracellular signaling pathways and gene expression. After a few weeks, he concluded, the person's brain is functioning in a manner that is "qualitatively as well as quantitatively different from the normal state."

His was an elegant paper, and it summed up what had been learned from decades of impressive scientific work. Forty years earlier, when Thorazine and the other first-generation psychiatric drugs were discovered, scientists had little understanding of how neurons communicated with one another. Now they had a remarkably detailed understanding of neurotransmitter systems in the brain and of how drugs acted on them. And what science had revealed was this: Prior to treatment, patients diagnosed with schizophrenia, depression, and other psychiatric disorders do not suffer from any known "chemical imbalance." However, once a person is put on a psychiatric medication, which, in one manner or another, throws a wrench into the usual mechanics of a neuronal pathway, his or her brain begins to function, as Hyman observed, *abnormally*.

Back to the Beginning

While Dr. Hyman's paper may seem startling, it serves as a coda to a scientific narrative that is, in fact, consistent from beginning to end. His was not a conclusion that should be seen as unexpected, but rather one that was predicted by psychopharmacology's opening chapter.

As we saw, Thorazine, Miltown, and Marsilid were all derived from compounds that had been developed for other purposes—for use in surgery or as possible "magic bullets" against infectious diseases. Those compounds were then found to cause alterations in mood, behavior, and thinking that were seen as helpful to psychiatric patients. The drugs, in essence, were perceived as having beneficial *side effects*. They perturbed normal function, and that understanding was reflected in the initial names given to them. Chlorpromazine was a "major tranquilizer," and it was said to produce a change in being similar to frontal lobotomy. Meprobamate was a "minor tranquilizer," and in animal studies, it had been shown to be a powerful muscle relaxant that blocked normal emotional response to environmental stressors. Iproniazid was a "psychic stimulator," and if the report of TB patients dancing in the wards was truthful, it was a drug that could provoke something akin to mania. However, psychiatry then reconceived the drugs as "magic bullets" for mental disorders, the drugs hypothesized to be antidotes to chemical imbalances in the brain. But that theory, which arose as much from wishful thinking as from science, was investigated and it did not pan out. Instead, as Hyman wrote, psychotropics are drugs that perturb the normal functioning of neuronal pathways in the brain. Psychiatry's first impression of its new drugs turned out to be the scientifically accurate one.

With this understanding of psychiatric medications now in mind, it is possible to pose the scientific question at the heart of this book: Do these drugs help or harm patients over the long term? What do fifty years of outcomes research show?

part three

Outcomes

6

A Paradox Revealed

"If we wish to base psychiatry on evidence-based medicine, we run a genuine risk in taking a closer look at what has long been considered fact."
—EMMANUEL STIP, EUROPEAN PSYCHIATRY (2002)[1]

The basement in Harvard Medical School's Countway Library is one of my favorite places in Boston. After stepping off the elevator, you enter a huge, somewhat dingy room, filled with the musty smell of old books. I often stop a few feet inside the doorway and take in the grand sight: row after row of bound copies of medical journals from the early 1800s to 1986. The place is almost always empty, and yet there are rich histories to be discovered here, and soon, as you begin to piece together a particular narrative of medicine, you are hopping from one journal to the next, the pile of books on your desk growing ever higher. There is the thrill of the chase, and it seems too that this part of the library never disappoints. All of the journals are organized in alphabetical order, and whenever in one article you find a citation that interests you, all you have to do is walk a few feet and inevitably you find the journal you need. At least up until recently, the Countway Library seems to have purchased nearly every medical journal that was published.

This is where we can begin our quest to find out how psychiatric drugs affect long-term outcomes. The research method we'll need to follow is straightforward. First, to the best we can, we'll have to flesh out the natural spectrum of outcomes for each particular disorder. In the absence of antipsychotic medications, how would people diagnosed with schizophrenia likely fare over time? What chance—if any—would they have of recovering? How well might they fare in society? The same questions can be asked in regard to anxiety, depression, and bipolar illness. What would outcomes look like in the absence of anti-anxiety drugs, antidepressants, and mood stabilizers? Once we have a sense of a baseline for a disorder, we can trace the outcomes literature for that illness, and we can hope that it will tell a consistent, coherent story. Do the drug treatments alter the *long-term* course of a mental disorder—in the patient population as a whole—for the better? Or for the worse?

Since chlorpromazine (Thorazine) was the drug that launched the psychopharmacology revolution, it seems appropriate to investigate schizophrenia outcomes first.

The Natural History of Schizophrenia

Schizophrenia today is regularly thought of as a lifelong, chronic illness, and that is an understanding that originated with the work of German psychiatrist Emil Kraepelin. In the late 1800s, he systematically tracked the outcomes of patients at an asylum in Estonia, and he observed that there was an identifiable group that reliably deteriorated into dementia. These were patients who, upon entry to the asylum, showed a lack of emotion. Many were catatonic, or lost hopelessly in their own worlds, and they often had gross physical problems. They walked oddly, suffered from facial tics and muscle spasms, and were unable to complete willed physical acts. In his 1899 textbook *Lehrbuch der Psychiatrie,* Kraepelin wrote that these patients suffered from *dementia praecox,* and in 1908, Swiss psychiatrist Eugen Bleuler coined the term "schizophrenia" as a substitute diagnostic term for patients in this dilapidated condition.

However, as British historian Mary Boyle convincingly argued in a 1990 article, "Is Schizophrenia What It Was? A Re-analysis of Kraepelin's and Bleuler's Population," many of Kraepelin's *dementia praecox* patients were undoubtedly suffering from a viral disease, *encephalitis lethargica,* which in the late 1800s had yet to be identified. This disease caused people to turn delirious, or to drop into a stupor, or to start walking in a jerky manner, and once Austrian neurologist Constantin von Economo described the illness in 1917, the *encephalitis lethargica* patients were no longer part of the "schizophrenia" pool, and after that happened, the patient group that remained was quite different from Kraepelin's *dementia praecox* group. "The inaccessible, the stuporous catatonic, the intellectually deteriorated"—those types of schizophrenia patients, Boyle noted, largely disappeared. As a result, the descriptions of schizophrenia in psychiatric textbooks during the 1920s and 1930s changed. All of the old physical symptoms—the greasy skin, the odd gait, the muscle spasms, the facial tics—disappeared from the diagnostic manuals. What remained were the mental symptoms— the hallucinations, the delusions, and the bizarre thoughts. "The referents of schizophrenia," Boyle wrote, "gradually changed until the diagnosis came to be applied to a population who bore only a slight, and possibly superficial, resemblance to Kraepelin's."[2]

So now we have to ask: What is the natural spectrum of outcomes for *that* group of psychotic patients? Here, unfortunately, we run into a second problem. From 1900 until the end of World War II, eugenic attitudes toward the mentally ill were quite popular in the United States, and that social philosophy dramatically affected their outcomes. Eugenicists argued that the mentally ill needed to be sequestered in hospitals to keep them from having children and spreading their "bad genes." The goal was to keep them confined in asylums, and in 1923, an editorial in the *Journal of Heredity* concluded, with an air of satisfaction, that "segregation of the insane is fairly complete."[3] As a result, many people diagnosed with schizophrenia in the first half of the century were hospitalized and never discharged, but that social policy was then misperceived as outcomes data. The fact that schizophrenics never left the hospital was seen as proof that the disease was a chronic, hopeless illness.

However, after World War II, eugenics fell into disrepute. This was the very "science" that Hitler and Nazi Germany had embraced, and after Albert Deutsch's exposé of the abysmal conditions in U.S. mental hospitals, in which he likened them to concentration camps, many states began talking about treating the mentally ill in the community. Social policy changed and discharge rates soared. As a result, there is a brief window of time, from 1946 to 1954, when we can look at how newly diagnosed schizophrenia patients fared and thereby get a sense of the "natural outcomes" of schizophrenia prior to the arrival of Thorazine.*

Here's the data. In a study conducted by the NIMH, 62 percent of first-episode psychotic patients admitted to Warren State Hospital in Pennsylvania from 1946 to 1950 were discharged within twelve months. At the end of three years, 73 percent were out of the hospital.[4] A study of 216 schizophrenia patients admitted to Delaware State Hospital from 1948 to 1950 produced similar results. Eighty-five percent were discharged within five years, and on January 1, 1956—six years or more after initial hospitalization—70 percent were successfully living in the community.[5] Meanwhile, Hillside Hospital in Queens, New York, tracked 87 schizophrenia patients discharged in 1950 and determined that slightly more than half never relapsed in the next four years.[6] During this period, outcomes studies in England, where schizophrenia was more narrowly defined, painted a similarly encouraging picture: Thirty-three percent of the patients enjoyed a "complete recovery," and another 20 percent a "social recovery," which meant they could support themselves and live independently.[7]

These studies provide a rather startling view of schizophrenia outcomes during this time. According to the conventional wisdom, it was Thorazine that made it possible for people with schizophrenia to live in the community. But what we find is that the majority of people admitted for a first episode of schizophrenia during the late 1940s and early 1950s recovered to the point that within the first twelve months, they could return to the community. By the end of three years, that was true for 75 percent of the patients. Only a small percentage—20 percent or so—needed to be continuously hospitalized. Moreover, those returning to the community weren't

---

* During this period, schizophrenia was a diagnosis being broadly applied to those being hospitalized. Many of these patients would be diagnosed as bipolar or schizoaffective today. Still, this was the diagnosis for the most "seriously disturbed" people in American society at that time.

living in shelters and group homes, as facilities of that sort didn't yet exist. They were not receiving federal disability payments, as the SSI and SSDI programs had yet to be established. Those discharged from hospitals were mostly returning to their families, and judging by the social recovery data, many were working. All in all, there was reason for people diagnosed with schizophrenia during that postwar period to be optimistic that they could get better and function fairly well in the community.

It is also important to note that the arrival of Thorazine did not improve discharge rates in the 1950s for people newly diagnosed with schizophrenia, nor did its arrival trigger the release of chronic patients. In 1961, the California Department of Mental Hygiene reported on discharge rates for all 1,413 first-episode schizophrenia patients hospitalized in 1956, and it found that 88 percent of those who weren't prescribed a neuroleptic were discharged within eighteen months. Those treated with a neuroleptic—about half of the 1,413 patients—had a *lower* discharge rate; only 74 percent were discharged within eighteen months. This is the only large-scale study from the 1950s that compared discharge rates for first-episode patients treated with and without drugs, and the investigators concluded that "drug-treated patients tend to have longer periods of hospitalization. . . . The untreated patients consistently show a somewhat lower retention rate."[8]

The discharge of *chronic* schizophrenia patients from state mental hospitals—and thus the beginning of deinstitutionalization—got under way in 1965 with the enactment of Medicare and Medicaid. In 1955, there were 267,000 schizophrenia patients in state and county mental hospitals, and eight years later, this number had barely budged. There were still 253,000 schizophrenics residing in the hospitals.[9] But then the economics of caring for the mentally ill changed. The 1965 Medicare and Medicaid legislation provided federal subsidies for nursing home care but no such subsidy for care in state mental hospitals, and so the states, seeking to save money, naturally began shipping their chronic patients to nursing homes. That was when the census in state mental hospitals began to noticeably drop, rather than in 1955, when Thorazine was introduced. Unfortunately, our societal belief that it was this medication that emptied the asylums, which is so central to the "psychopharma-cology revolution" narrative, is belied by the hospital census data.

Through a Lens Darkly

In 1955, pharmaceutical companies were not required to prove to the FDA that their new drugs were effective (that requirement was added in 1962), and thus it fell to the NIMH to assess the merits of Thorazine and the other new "wonder drugs" coming to market. Much to its credit, the NIMH organized a conference in September 1956 to "consider carefully the entire psychotropic question," and ultimately the conversation at the conference focused on a very particular question: How could psychiatry adapt, for its own use, a scientific tool that had recently proven its worth in infectious medicine: the placebo-controlled, double-blind, randomized clinical trial?[10]

As many speakers noted, this tool wasn't particularly well suited for assessing outcomes of a psychiatric drug. How could a study of a neuroleptic possibly be "double-blind"? The psychiatrist would quickly see who was on the drug and who was not, and any patient given Thorazine would know he was on a medication as well. Then there was the problem of diagnosis: How would a researcher know if the patients randomized into a trial really had "schizophrenia"? The diagnostic boundaries of mental disorders were forever chang-ing. Equally problematic, what defined a "good outcome"? Psychi-atrists and hospital staff might want to see drug-induced behavioral changes that made the patient "more socially acceptable" but weren't to the "ultimate benefit of the patient," said one conference speaker.[11] And how could outcomes be measured? In a study of a drug for a known disease, mortality rates or laboratory results could serve as objective measures of whether a treatment worked. For instance, to test whether a drug for tuberculosis was effective, an X-ray of the lung could show whether the bacillus that caused the disease was gone. What would be the measurable endpoint in a trial of a drug for schizophrenia? The problem, said NIMH physician Edward Evarts at the conference, was that "the goals of therapy in schizophrenia, short of getting the patient 'well,' have not been clearly defined."[12]

All of these questions bedeviled psychiatry, and yet the NIMH, in the wake of that conference, made plans to mount a trial of the neuroleptics. The push of history was simply too great. This was the scientific method now used in internal medicine to assess the merits of a therapy, and Congress had created the NIMH with the thought that it would transform psychiatry into a more modern, scientific discipline. Psychiatry's adoption of this tool would prove that it was moving toward that goal. The NIMH established a Psychopharmacology Service Center to head up this effort, and Jonathan Cole, a psychiatrist from the National Research Council, was named its director.

Over the next couple of years, Cole and the rest of psychiatry settled on a trial design for testing psychotropic drugs. Psychiatrists and nurses would use "rating scales" to measure numerically the characteristic symptoms of the disease that was to be studied. Did a drug for schizophrenia reduce the patient's "anxiety"? His or her "grandiosity"? "Hostility"? "Suspiciousness"? "Unusual thought content"? "Uncooperativeness"? The severity of all of those symptoms would be measured on a numerical scale and a total "symptom" score tabulated, and a drug would be deemed effective if it reduced the total score significantly more than a placebo did within a six-week period.

At least in theory, psychiatry now had a way to conduct trials of psychiatric drugs that would produce an "objective" result. Yet the adoption of this assessment put psychiatry on a very particular path: The field would now see short-term reduction of symptoms as evidence of a drug's efficacy. Much as a physician in internal medicine would prescribe an antibiotic for a bacterial infection, a psychiatrist would prescribe a pill that knocked down a "target symptom" of a "discrete disease." The six-week "clinical trial" would prove that this was the right thing to do. However, this tool wouldn't provide any insight into how patients were faring over the long term.

Were they able to work? Were they enjoying life? Did they have friends? Were they getting married? None of those questions would be answered.

This was the moment that magic-bullet medicine shaped psychiatry's future. The use of the clinical trial would cause psychiatrists to see their therapies through a very particular prism, and even at the 1956 conference, New York State Psychiatric Institute researcher Joseph Zubin warned that when it came to evaluating a therapy for a psychiatric disorder, a six-week study induced a kind of scientific myopia. "It would be foolhardy to claim a definite advantage for a specified therapy without a two- to five-year follow-up," he said. "A two-year follow-up would seem to be the very minimum for the long-term effects."[13]

The Case for Neuroleptics

The Psychopharmacology Service Center launched its nine-hospital trial of neuroleptics in 1961, and this is the study that marks the beginning of the scientific record that serves today as the "evidence base" for these drugs. In the six-week trial, 270 patients were given Thorazine or another neuroleptic (which were also known as "phenothiazines,") while the remaining 74 were put on a placebo. The neuroleptics did help reduce some target symptoms—unrealistic thinking, anxiety, suspiciousness, auditory hallucinations, etc.—better than the placebo, and thus, according to the rating's scales cumulative score, they were effective. Furthermore, the psychiatrists in the study judged 75 percent of the drug-treated patients to be "much improved" or "very much improved," versus 23 percent of the placebo patients.

After that, hundreds of smaller trials produced similar results, and thus the evidence that these drugs reduce symptoms over the short term better than placebo is fairly robust.* In 1977, Ross Baldessarini

---

* In 2007, the Cochrane Collaboration, an international group of scientists that doesn't take funding from pharmaceutical companies, raised questions

at Harvard Medical School reviewed 149 such trials and found that the antipsychotic drug proved superior to a placebo in 83 percent of them.[14] The "Brief Psychiatric Rating Scale" (BPRS) was regularly employed in such trials, and the American Psychiatric Association eventually decided that a 20 percent reduction in total BPRS score represented a clinically significant response to a drug.[15] Based on this measurement, an estimated 70 percent of all schizophrenia patients suffering from an acute episode of psychosis "respond," over a six-week period, to an antipsychotic medication.

Once the NIMH investigators determined that the antipsychotics were efficacious over the short term, they naturally wanted to know how long schizophrenia patients should stay on the medication. To investigate this question, they ran studies that, for the most part, had this design: Patients who were good responders to the medication were either maintained on the drug or abruptly withdrawn from it. In 1995, Patricia Gilbert at the University of California at San Diego reviewed sixty-six relapse studies, involving 4,365 patients, and she found that 53 percent of the drug-withdrawn patients relapsed within ten months versus 16 percent of those maintained on the medications. "The efficacy of these medications in reducing the risk of psychotic relapse has been well documented," she concluded.*[16]

This is the scientific evidence that supports the use of anti-psychotic medications for schizophrenia, both in the hospital and long-term. As John Geddes, a prominent British researcher, wrote in

---

about this short-term efficacy record. They conducted a meta-analysis of all chlorpromazine-versus-placebo studies in the scientific literature, and after identifying fifty of decent quality, they concluded that the advantage of drug over placebo was smaller than commonly thought. They calculated that seven patients had to be treated with chlorpromazine to produce a net gain of one "global improvement," and that "even this finding may be an overestimate of the positive and an underestimate of the negative effects of giving chlorpromazine." The Cochrane investigators, somewhat startled by their results, wrote that "reliable evidence about [chlorpromazine's] short-term efficacy is surprisingly weak."

* There is an evident flaw with Gilbert's meta-analysis. She didn't determine whether the speed with which drugs were withdrawn affected the relapse rate.

a 2002 article in the *New England Journal of Medicine,* "Antipsychotic drugs are effective in treating acute psychotic symptoms and preventing relapse."[17] Still, as many investigators have noted, there is a hole in this evidence base, and it's the very hole that Zubin predicted would arise. "Little can be said about the efficacy and effectiveness of conventional antipsychotics on nonclinical outcomes," confessed Lisa Dixon and other psychiatrists at the University of Maryland School of Medicine in 1995. "Well-designed long-term studies are virtually nonexistent, so the longitudinal impact of treatment with conventional antipsychotics is unclear."[18]

This doubt prompted an extraordinary 2002 editorial in *European Psychiatry,* penned by Emmanuel Stip, a professor of psychiatry at the Université de Montréal. "After fifty years of neuroleptics, are we able to answer the following simple question: Are neuroleptics effective in treating schizophrenia?" There was, he said, "no compelling evidence on the matter, when 'long-term' is considered."[19]

A Conundrum Appears

Although Dixon's and Stip's comments suggest that there is no long-term data to be reviewed, it is in fact possible to piece together a story of how antipsychotics alter the course of schizophrenia, and this story begins, quite appropriately, with the NIMH's follow-up study of the 344 patients in its initial nine-hospital trial. In some ways, the patients—regardless of what treatment they had received in the hospital—were not faring so badly. At the end of one year,

---

After her study appeared, Adele Viguera at Harvard Medical School reanalyzed the same sixty-six studies and determined that when the drugs were gradually withdrawn, the relapse rate was only one-third as high as in the abrupt-withdrawal studies. The abrupt-withdrawal design in the majority of the relapse studies dramatically increased the risk that the schizophrenia patients would become sick again. Indeed, the relapse rate for gradually withdrawn patients was similar to what it was for the drug-maintained patients.

254 were living in the community, and 58 percent of those who—according to their age and gender—could be expected to work were in fact employed. Two-thirds of the "housewives" were functioning OK in that domestic role. Although the researchers didn't report on the medication use of patients during the one-year follow-up, they were startled to discover that "patients who received placebo treatment [in the six-week trial] were *less* likely to be rehospitalized than those who received any of the three active phenothiazines."[20]

Here, at this very first moment in the scientific literature, there is the hint of a paradox: While the drugs were effective over the short term, perhaps they made people more vulnerable to psychosis over the long term, and thus the higher rehospitalization rates for drug-treated patients at the end of one year. Soon, NIMH investigators were back with another surprising result. In two drug withdrawal trials, both of which included patients who weren't on any drug at the start of the study, relapse rates *rose* in correlation with drug dosage. Only 7 percent of those who had been on a placebo at the start of the study relapsed, compared to 65 percent of those taking more than five hundred milligrams of chlorpromazine before the drug was withdrawn. "Relapse was found to be significantly related to the dose of the tranquilizing medication the patient was receiving before he was put on placebo—the higher the dose, the greater the probability of relapse," the researchers wrote.[21]

Something was amiss, and clinical observations deepened the suspicion. Schizophrenia patients discharged on medications were returning to psychiatric emergency rooms in such droves that hospital staff dubbed it the "revolving door syndrome." Even when patients reliably took their medications, relapse was common, and researchers observed that "relapse is greater in severity during drug administration than when no drugs are given."[22] At the same time, if patients relapsed after quitting the medications, Cole noted, their psychotic symptoms tended to "persist and intensify," and, at least for a time, they suffered from a host of new symptoms as well: nausea, vomiting, diarrhea, agitation, insomnia, headaches, and weird motor tics.[23] Initial exposure to a neuroleptic seemed to be setting patients up for a future of severe psychotic episodes, and that was true regardless of whether they stayed on the medications.

These poor results prompted two psychiatrists at Boston Psychopathic Hospital, J. Sanbourne Bockoven and Harry Solomon, to revisit the past. They had been at the hospital for decades, and in the period after World War II ended, when they treated psychotic patients with a progressive form of psychological care, they had seen the majority regularly improve. That led them to believe that "the majority of mental illnesses, especially the most severe, are largely self-limiting in nature if the patient is not subjected to a demeaning experience or loss of rights and liberties." The antipsychotics, they reasoned, should speed up this natural healing process. But were the drugs improving long-term outcomes? In a retrospective study, they found that 45 percent of the patients treated in 1947 at their hospital hadn't relapsed in the next five years and that 76 percent were successfully living in the community at the end of that follow-up period. In contrast, only 31 percent of the patients treated at the hospital in 1967 with neuroleptics remained relapse-free for five years, and as a group they were much more "socially dependent"—on welfare and needing other forms of support. "Rather unexpectedly, these data suggest that psychotropic drugs may not be indispensable," Bockoven and Solomon wrote. "Their extended use in aftercare may prolong the social dependency of many discharged patients."[24]

With debate over the merits of neuroleptics rising, the NIMH funded three studies during the 1970s that reexamined whether schizophrenia patients—and in particular those suffering a first episode of schizophrenia—could be successfully treated without medications. In the first study, which was conducted by William Carpenter and Thomas McGlashan at the NIMH's clinical research facility in Bethesda, Maryland, those treated without drugs were discharged *sooner* than the drug-treated patients, and only 35 percent of the nonmedicated group relapsed within a year after discharge, compared to 45 percent of the medicated group. The off-drug patients also suffered less from depression, blunted emotions, and retarded movements. Indeed, they told Carpenter and McGlashan that they had found it "gratifying and informative" to have gone through their psychotic episodes without having their feelings numbed by the drugs. Medicated patients didn't have that same learning experience, and as a result, Carpenter and Mc-Glashan concluded, over the long term they "are less able to cope with subsequent life stresses."[25]

A year later, Maurice Rappaport at the University of California in San Francisco announced results that told the same story, only more strongly so. He had randomized eighty young newly diagnosed male schizophrenics admitted to Agnews State Hospital into drug and non-drug groups, and although symptoms abated more quickly in those treated with antipsychotics, both groups, on average, stayed only six weeks in the hospital. Rappaport followed the patients for three years, and it was those who weren't treated with antipsychotics in the hospital and who stayed off the drugs after discharge that had—by far—the best outcomes. Only two of the twenty-four patients in this never-exposed-to-antipsychotics group relapsed during the three-year follow-up. Meanwhile, the patients that arguably fared the worst were those on drugs throughout the study. The very standard of care that, according to psychiatry's "evidence base," was supposed to produce the best outcomes had instead produced the worst.

"Our findings suggest that antipsychotic medication is not the treatment of choice, at least for certain patients, if one is interested in long-term clinical improvement," Rappaport wrote. "Many unmedicated-while-in-hospital patients showed greater long-term

Rappaport's Study: Three-Year Schizophrenia Outcomes

Medication Use (In hospital/ after discharge)	Number of Patients	Severity Illness Scale (1=best outcome; 7=worst outcome)	Rehospitalization
Placebo/off	24	1.70	8%
Antipsychotic/off	17	2.79	47%
Placebo/on	17	3.54	53%
Antipsychotic/on	22	3.51	73%

In this study, patients were grouped according to both their in-hospital care (placebo or drug) and whether they used antipsychotics after they were discharged. Thus, 24 of the 41 patients treated with placebo in the hospital remained off the drugs during the follow-up period. This never-exposed group had the best outcomes by far. Rappaport, M. "Are there schizophrenics for whom drugs may be unnecessary or contraindicated." *International Pharmacopsychiatry* 13 (1978): 100-11.

improvement, less pathology at follow-up, fewer rehospitalizations, and better overall functioning in the community than patients who were given chlorpromazine while in the hospital."[26]

The third study was led by Loren Mosher, head of schizophrenia studies at the NIMH. Although he may have been the nation's top schizophrenia doctor at the time, his vision of the illness was at odds with many of his peers, who had come to think that schizophrenics suffered from a "broken brain." He believed that psychosis could arise in response to emotional and inner trauma and, in its own way, could be a coping mechanism. As such, he believed there was the possibility that people could grapple with their hallucinations and delusions, struggle through a schizophrenic break, and regain their sanity. And if that was so, he reasoned that if he provided newly psychotic patients with a safe house, one staffed by people who had an evident empathy for others and who wouldn't be frightened by strange behavior, many would get well, even though they weren't treated with antipsychotics. "I thought that sincere human involvement and understanding were critical to healing interactions," he said. "The idea was to treat people as people, as human beings, with dignity and respect."

The twelve-room Victorian house he opened in Santa Clara, California, in 1971 could shelter six patients at a time. He called it Soteria House, and eventually he started a second home as well, Emanon. All told, the Soteria Project ran for twelve years, with eighty-two patients treated at the two homes. As early as 1974, Mosher began reporting that his Soteria patients were faring better than a matched cohort of patients being treated conventionally with drugs in a hospital, and in 1979, he announced his two-year results. At the end of six weeks, psychotic symptoms had abated as much in his Soteria patients as in the hospitalized patients, and at the end of two years, the Soteria patients had "lower psychopathology scores, fewer [hospital] readmissions, and better global adjustment."[27] Later, he and John Bola, an assistant professor at the University of Southern California, reported on their medication use: Forty-two percent of the Soteria patients had never been exposed to drugs, 39 percent had used them on a temporary basis, and only 19 percent had needed them throughout the two-year follow-up.

"Contrary to popular views, minimal use of antipsychotic medications combined with specially designed psychosocial intervention for patients newly identified with schizophrenia spectrum disorder is not harmful but appears to be advantageous," Mosher and Bola wrote. "We think that the balance of risks and benefits associated with the common practice of medicating nearly all early episodes of psychosis should be re-examined."[28]

Three NIMH-funded studies, and all pointed to the same conclusion.* Perhaps 50 percent of newly diagnosed schizophrenia patients, if treated without antipsychotics, would recover and stay well through lengthy follow-up periods. Only a minority of patients seemed to need to take the drugs continuously. The "revolving door" syndrome that had become so familiar was due in large part to the drugs, even though, in clinical trials, the drugs had proven to be effective in knocking down psychotic symptoms. Carpenter and McGlashan neatly summarized the scientific conundrum that psychiatry now faced:

> There is no question that, once patients are placed on medication, they are less vulnerable to relapse if maintained on neuroleptics. But what if these patients had never been treated with drugs to begin with? . . . We raise the possibility that

* In the early 1960s, Philip May conducted a study that compared five forms of in-hospital treatment: drug, electroconvulsive therapy (ECT), psychotherapy, psychotherapy plus drug, and milieu therapy (a supportive environment). Over the short term, the drug-treated patients did much better. As a result, the study came to be cited as proof that schizophrenia patients could not be treated without drugs. However, the two-year results told a more nuanced story. Fifty-nine percent of patients initially treated with milieu therapy but no drugs were successfully discharged in the initial study period, and this group "functioned over the follow-up at least as well, if not better, than the successes from the other treatments." Thus, the May study, which is usually cited as proving that all psychotic patients should be medicated, in fact suggested that a majority of first-episode patients would fare best over the long term if initially treated with milieu therapy rather than drugs. Source: P. May, "Schizophrenia: a follow-up study of the results of five forms of treatment," *Archives of General Psychiatry* 38 (1981): 776–84.

antipsychotic medication may make some schizophrenic patients more vulnerable to future relapse than would be the
case in the natural course of the illness.[29]

And if that was so, these drugs were increasing the likelihood
that a person who suffered a psychotic break would become chronically ill.

A Cure Worse Than the Disease?

All drugs have a risk-benefit profile, and the usual thought within
medicine is that a drug should provide a benefit that outweighs the
risks. A drug that curbs psychotic symptoms clearly provides a
marked benefit, and that was why antipsychotics could be viewed as
helpful even though the list of negatives with these drugs was a long
one. Thorazine and other first-generation neuroleptics caused
Parkinsonian symptoms and extraordinarily painful muscle spasms.
Patients regularly complained that the drugs turned them into emotional "zombies." In 1972, researchers concluded that neuroleptics
"impaired learning."[30] Others reported that even if medicated patients stayed out of the hospital, they seemed totally unmotivated
and socially disengaged. Many lived in "virtual solitude" in group
homes, spending most of the time "staring vacantly at television,"
wrote one investigator.[31] None of this told of medicated schizophrenia patients faring well, and here was the quandary that psychiatry
now faced: If the drugs *increased* relapse rates over the long term,
then where was the benefit? This question was made all the more
pressing by the fact that many patients maintained on the drugs
were developing tardive dyskinesia (TD), a gross motor dysfunction
that remained even after the drugs were withdrawn, evidence of permanent brain damage.

All of this required psychiatry to recalculate the risks and benefits
of antipsychotics, and in 1977 Jonathan Cole did so in an article
provocatively titled "Is the Cure Worse Than the Disease?" He
reviewed all of the long-term harm the drugs could cause and

observed that studies had shown that at least 50 percent of all schizophrenia patients could fare well without the drugs. There was only one moral thing for psychiatry to do: "Every schizophrenic outpatient maintained on antipsychotic medication should have the benefit of an adequate trial without drugs." This, he explained, would save many "from the dangers of tardive dyskinesia as well as the financial and social burdens of prolonged drug therapy."[32]

The evidence base for maintaining schizophrenia patients on antipsychotics had collapsed. "Are the antipsychotics to be withdrawn?" asked Pierre Deniker, the French psychiatrist who, in the early 1950s, had first promoted their use.[33]

Supersensitivity Psychosis

In the late 1970s, two physicians at McGill University, Guy Chouinard and Barry Jones, stepped forward with a biological explanation for why the drugs made schizophrenia patients more biologically vulnerable to psychosis. Their understanding arose, in large part, from the investigations into the dopamine hypothesis of schizophrenia, which had detailed how the drugs perturbed this neurotransmitter system.

Thorazine and other standard antipsychotics block 70 to 90 percent of all D_2 receptors in the brain. In an effort to compensate for this blockade, the postsynaptic neurons increase the density of their D_2 receptors by 30 percent or more. The brain is now "supersensitive" to dopamine, Chouinard and Jones explained, and this neurotransmitter is thought to be a mediator of psychosis. "Neuroleptics can produce a dopamine supersensitivity that leads to both dyskinetic and psychotic symptoms," they wrote. "An implication is that the tendency toward psychotic relapse in a patient who has developed such a supersensitivity is determined by more than just the normal course of the illness."[34]

A simple metaphor can help us better understand this drug-induced biological vulnerability to psychosis and why it flares up when the drug is withdrawn. Neuroleptics put a brake on dopamine transmission, and in response the brain puts down the dopamine accelerator (the extra D_2 receptors). If the drug is abruptly withdrawn, the brake on dopamine is suddenly released while the accelerator is still pressed to the floor. The system is now wildly out of balance, and just as a car might careen out of control, so too the dopaminergic pathways in the brain. The dopaminergic neurons in the basal ganglia may fire so rapidly that the patient withdrawing from the drugs suffers weird tics, agitation, and other motor abnormalities. The same out-of-control firing is happening with the dopaminergic pathway to the limbic region, and that may lead to "psychotic relapse or deterioration," Chouinard and Jones wrote.[35]

This was an extraordinary piece of scientific detective work by the two Canadian investigators. They had—at least in theory—identified the reason that relapse rates were so high in the medication-withdrawal trials, which psychiatry had mistakenly interpreted as proving that the drugs prevented relapse. The severe relapse suffered by many patients withdrawn from antipsychotics was not necessarily the result of the "disease" returning, but rather was drug-related. Chouinard and Jones's work also revealed that both psychiatrists and their patients would regularly suffer from a clinical delusion: They would see the return of psychotic symptoms upon drug withdrawal as proof that the antipsychotic was necessary and that it "worked." The relapsed patient would then go back on the drug and often the psychosis would abate, which would be further proof that it worked. Both doctor and patient would experience this to be "true," and yet, in fact, the reason that the psychosis abated with the return of the drug was that the brake on dopamine transmission was being reapplied, which countered the stuck dopamine accelerator. As Chouinard and Jones explained: "The need for continued neuroleptic treatment may itself be drug-induced."

In short, initial exposure to neuroleptics put patients onto a path where they would likely need the drugs for life. Yet—and this was the second haunting aspect to this story of medicine—staying on the drugs regularly led to a bad end. Over time, Chouinard and Jones noted, the dopaminergic pathways tended to become permanently dysfunctional. They became *irreversibly* stuck in a hyperactive state, and soon the patient's tongue was slipping rhythmically in and out of his mouth (tardive dyskinesia) and psychotic symptoms were worsening (tardive psychosis). Doctors would then need to prescribe higher doses of antipsychotics to tamp down those tardive symptoms. "The most efficacious treatment is the causative agent itself, the neuroleptic," Chouinard and Jones said.

Over the next few years, Chouinard and Jones continued to flesh out and test their hypothesis. In 1982, they reported that 30 percent of 216 schizophrenia outpatients they studied showed signs of tardive psychosis.[36] They also observed that it tended to afflict those patients who, at initial diagnosis, had a "good prognosis," and thus would have had a chance to fare well over the long term if they had never been exposed to neuroleptics. These were the "placebo responders" who had fared best in the studies conducted by Rappaport and Mosher, and now Chouinard and Jones were reporting that they were becoming chronically psychotic after years of taking antipsychotics. Finally, Chouinard quantified the risk, reporting that tardive psychosis seemed to develop at a slightly slower rate than tardive dyskinesia. It afflicted 3 percent of patients a year, with the result that after fifteen years on the drugs, perhaps 45 percent suffered from it. When tardive psychosis sets in, Chouinard added, "the illness appears worse" than ever before. "New schizophrenic or original symptoms of greater severity will appear."[37]

Animal studies confirmed this picture too. Philip Seeman reported that antipsychotics caused an increase in D_2 receptors in rats, and while the density of these receptors could revert to normal if the drug was withdrawn (he reported that for every month of exposure, it took two months for renormalization to occur), at some point the increase in receptors became irreversible.[38]

In 1984, Swedish physician Lars Martensson, in a presentation at the World Federation of Mental Health Conference in Copenhagen, summed up the devastating bottom line. "The use of neuroleptics is a trap," he said. "It is like having a psychosis-inducing agent built into the brain."[39]

A Crazy Idea . . . Or Not?

This was the view of neuroleptics that came together in the early 1980s, and it was a story of science at its best. Psychiatrists saw that the drugs "worked." They saw that antipsychotics knocked down psychotic symptoms, and they observed that patients who stopped taking their medications regularly became psychotic again. Scientific tests reinforced their clinical perceptions. Six-week trials proved the drugs were effective. Relapse studies proved that patients should be maintained on the drugs. Yet once researchers came to understand how the drugs acted on the brain, and once they began investigating why patients were developing tardive dyskinesia and why they were becoming so chronically ill, then this *counterintuitive* picture of the drugs—that they were increasing the likelihood that patients would become chronically ill—emerged. It was Chouinard and Jones who explicitly connected all the dots, and for a time, their work did stir up a hornet's nest within psychiatry. One physician, at a meeting where the two McGill University doctors spoke, asked in astonishment: "I put my patients on neuroleptics because they're psychotic. Now you're saying that the same drug that controls their schizophrenia also causes a psychosis?"[40]

But what was psychiatry supposed to do with this information? It clearly imperiled the field's very foundation. Could it really now confess to the public, or even admit to itself, that the very class of drugs said to have "revolutionized" the care of the mentally ill was in fact making patients chronically ill? That antipsychotics made patients—at least in the aggregate—more psychotic over time? Psychiatry desperately needed this discussion to go away. Soon the articles by Chouinard and Jones on "supersensitivity psychosis" were filed away in the "interesting hypothesis" category, and everyone in the field breathed a sigh of relief when Solomon Snyder, who knew as much about dopamine receptors as any scientist in the world, assured everyone in his 1986 book *Drugs and the Brain* that it had all turned out to be a false alarm. "If dopamine receptor sensitivity is greater in patients with tardive dyskinesia, one might wonder whether they would also suffer a corresponding increase in schizophrenia symptoms. Interestingly, though researchers have looked carefully for any possible exacerbation of schizophrenic symptoms in patients who begin to develop tardive dyskinesia, none has ever been found."[41]

That moment of crisis within psychiatry, when it briefly worried about supersensitivity psychosis, occurred nearly thirty years ago, and today the notion that antipsychotics increase the likelihood that a person diagnosed with schizophrenia will become chronically ill seems, on the face of it, absurd. Ask psychiatrists at top medical schools, staff at a mental hospital, NIMH officials, leaders of the National Alliance for the Mentally Ill, science writers at major newspapers, or the ordinary person in the street, and everyone will attest that antipsychotics are essential for treating schizophrenia, the very cornerstone of care, and that anyone who touts a different idea is, well, a bit *loony*. Still, we started down this path of research, I've invited readers into this loony bin, and so now we need to move up one floor in the Countway Library. The volumes in the basement end in 1986, and now we need to comb the scientific literature since that date, and see what story it has to tell. Was it all a false alarm . . . or not?

The most efficient way to answer that question is to summarize, one by one, the relevant studies and avenues of research.

The Vermont longitudinal study
In the late 1950s and early 1960s, Vermont State Hospital discharged 269 chronic schizophrenics, most of whom were middle-aged, into the community. Twenty years later, Courtenay Harding interviewed 168 patients from this cohort (those who were still alive), and found that 34 percent were recovered, which meant they were "asymptomatic and living independently, had close relationships, were employed or otherwise productive citizens, were able to care for themselves, and led full lives in general."[42] This was a startling good long-term outcome for patients who had been seen as hopeless in the 1950s, and those who had recovered, Harding told the *APA Monitor,* had one thing in common: They all "had long since stopped taking medications."[43] She concluded that it was a

"myth" that schizophrenia patients "must be on medication all their lives," and that, in fact, "it may be a small percentage who need medication indefinitely."[44]

The World Health Organization cross-cultural studies

In 1969, the World Health Organization launched an effort to track schizophrenia outcomes in nine countries. At the end of five years, the patients in the three "developing" countries—India, Nigeria, and Colombia—had a "considerably better course and outcome" than patients in the United States and five other "developed countries." They were much more likely to be asymptomatic during the follow-up period, and even more important, they enjoyed "an exceptionally good social outcome."

These findings stung the psychiatric community in the United States and Europe, which protested that there must have been a design flaw in the study. Perhaps the patients in India, Nigeria, and Colombia had not really been schizophrenic. In response, WHO launched a ten-country study in 1978, and this time they primarily enrolled patients suffering from a first episode of schizophrenia, all of whom were diagnosed by Western criteria. Once again, the results were much the same. At the end of two years, nearly two-thirds of the patients in the "developing countries" had had good outcomes, and slightly more than one-third had become chronically ill. In the rich countries, only 37 percent of the patients had good outcomes, and 59 percent became chronically ill. "The findings of a better outcome of patients in developing countries was confirmed," the WHO scientists wrote. "Being in a developed country was a strong predictor of not attaining a complete remission."[45]

Although the WHO investigators didn't identify a reason for the stark disparity in outcomes, they had tracked antipsychotic usage in the second study, having hypothesized that perhaps patients in the poor countries fared better because they more reliably took their medication. However, they found the opposite to be true. Only 16 percent of the patients in the poor countries were regularly maintained on antipsychotics, versus 61 percent of the patients in the rich countries. Moreover, in Agra, India, where patients arguably fared the best, only 3 percent of the patients were kept on an antipsychotic. Medication usage was highest in Moscow, and that city had the highest percentage of patients who were constantly ill.[46]

In this cross-cultural study, the best outcomes were clearly associated with low medication use. Later, in 1997, WHO researchers interviewed the patients from the first two studies once again (fifteen to twenty-five years after the initial studies), and they found that those in the poor countries continued to do much better. The "outcome differential" held up for "general clinical state, symptomatology, disability, and social functioning." In the developing countries, 53 percent of the schizophrenia patients were simply "never psychotic" anymore, and 73 percent were employed.[47] Although the WHO investigators didn't report on medication usage in their follow-up study, the bottom line is clear: In countries where patients hadn't been regularly maintained on antipsychotics earlier in their illness, the majority had recovered and were doing well fifteen years later.

Tardive dyskinesia and global decline

Tardive dyskinesia and tardive psychosis occur because the dopaminergic pathways to the basal ganglia and limbic system become dysfunctional. But there are *three* dopaminergic pathways, and so it stands to reason that the third one, which transmits messages to the frontal lobes, also becomes dysfunctional over time. If so, researchers could expect to find a global decline in brain function in patients diagnosed with tardive dyskinesia, and from 1979 to 2000, more than two dozen studies found that to be the case. "The relationship appears to be linear," reported Medical College of Virginia psychiatrist James Wade in 1987. "Individuals with severe forms of the disorder are most impaired cognitively."[48] Researchers determined that tardive dyskinesia was associated with a worsening of the negative symptoms of schizophrenia (emotional disengagement); psychosocial impairment; and a decline in memory, visual retention, and the capacity to learn. People with TD lose their "road map of consciousness," concluded one investigator.[49] Investigators have dubbed this long-term cognitive deterioration tardive dementia; in 1994, researchers found that three-fourths of medicated schizophrenia patients seventy years and older suffer from a brain pathology associated with Alzheimer's disease.[50]

MRI studies

The invention of magnetic resonance imaging technology provided researchers with the opportunity to measure volumes of brain structures in people diagnosed with schizophrenia, and while they hoped to identify abnormalities that might characterize the illness, they ended up documenting instead the effect of antipsychotics on brain volumes. In a series of studies from 1994 to 1998, investigators reported that the drugs caused basal ganglion structures and the thalamus to swell, and the frontal lobes to shrink, with these changes in volumes "dose related."[51] Then, in 1998, Raquel Gur at the University of Pennsylvania Medical Center reported that the swelling of the basal ganglia and thalamus was "associated with greater severity of both negative and positive symptoms."[52]

This last study provided a very clear picture of an iatrogenic process. The antipsychotic causes a change in brain volumes, and as this occurs, the patient becomes more psychotic (known as the "positive symptoms" of schizophrenia) and more emotionally disengaged ("negative symptoms"). The MRI studies showed that antipsychotics worsen the very symptoms they are supposed to treat, and that this worsening begins to occur during the first three years that patients are on the drugs.

Modeling psychosis

As part of their investigations of schizophrenia, researchers have sought to develop biological "models" of psychosis, and one way they have done that is to study the brain changes induced by various drugs—amphetamines, angel dust, etc.—that can trigger delusions and hallucinations. They also have developed ways to induce psychotic-like behaviors in rats and other animals. Lesions to the hippocampus can cause such disturbed behaviors; certain genes can be "knocked out" to produce such symptoms. In 2005, Philip

Seeman reported that *all* of these psychotic triggers cause an increase in D_2 receptors in the brain that have a "HIGH affinity" for dopamine, and by that, he meant that the receptors bound quite easily with the neurotransmitter. These "results imply that there may be many pathways to psychosis, including multiple gene mutations, drug abuse, or brain injury, all of which may converge via D_2 HIGH to elicit psychotic symptoms," he wrote.[53]

Seeman reasoned that this is why antipsychotics work: They block D_2 receptors. But in his research, he also found that these drugs, including the newer ones like Zyprexa and Risperdal, double the density of "high affinity" D_2 receptors. They induce the same abnormality that angel dust does, and thus this research confirms what Lars Martensson observed in 1984: Taking a neuroleptic is like having a "psychosis inducing agent built into the brain."

Nancy Andreasen's longitudinal MRI study

In 1989, Nancy Andreasen, a psychiatry professor at the University of Iowa who was editor in chief of the *American Journal of Psychiatry* from 1993 to 2005, began a long-term study of more than five hundred schizophrenia patients. In 2003, she reported that at the time of initial diagnosis, the patients had slightly smaller frontal lobes than normal, and that over the next three years, their frontal lobes continued to shrink. Furthermore, this "progressive reduction in frontal lobe white matter volume" was associated with a worsening of negative symptoms and functional impairment, and thus Andreasen concluded that this shrinkage is evidence that schizophrenia is a "progressive neurodevelopmental disorder," one which antipsychotics unfortunately fail to arrest. "The medications currently used cannot modify an injurious process occurring in the brain, which is the underlying basis of symptoms."[54]

Hers was a picture of antipsychotics as therapeutically ineffective, rather than harmful, and two years later, she fleshed out this picture. Her patients' cognitive abilities began to "worsen significantly" five years after initial diagnosis, a decline tied to the "progressive brain volume reductions after illness onset."[55] In other words, as her patients' frontal lobes shrank in size, their ability to think declined. But other researchers conducting MRI studies had found that the shrinkage of the frontal lobes was *drug-related,* and in a 2008 interview with the *New York Times,* Andreasen conceded that the "more drugs you've been given, the more brain tissue you lose." The shrinkage of the frontal lobes may be part of a disease process, which the drugs then *exacerbate.* "What exactly do these drugs do?" Andreasen said. "They block basal ganglia activity. The prefrontal cortex doesn't get the input it needs and is being shut down by drugs. That reduces the psychotic symptoms. It also causes the prefrontal cortex to slowly atrophy."[56]

Once again, Andreasen's investigations revealed an iatrogenic process at work. The drugs block dopamine activity in the brain and this leads to brain shrinkage, which in turn correlates with a worsening of negative symptoms and cognitive impairment. This was yet another disturbing finding, and it prompted Yale psychiatrist Thomas McGlashan, who three decades earlier had wondered whether antipsychotics were making patients "more biologically vulnerable to psychosis," to once again question this entire paradigm of care. He put his troubled thoughts into a scientific context:

> In the short term, acute D_2 [receptor] blockade detaches salience and the patient's investment in positive symptoms. In the long term, chronic D_2 blockade dampens salience for all events in everyday life, inducing a chemical anhedonia that is sometimes labeled postpsychotic depression or neuroleptic dysphoria. . . . Do we free patients from the asylum with D_2 blocking agents only to block incentive, engagement with the world, and the *joie de vivre* of everyday life? Medication can be lifesaving in a crisis, but it may render the patient more psychosis-prone should it be stopped and more deficit-ridden should it be maintained.[57]

His comments appeared in a 2006 issue of the *Schizophrenia Bulletin,* and at that moment it seemed like the late 1970s all over again. The "cure," it seemed, had once again been proven to be "worse than the disease."

The Clinician's Illusion

I attended the 2008 meeting of the American Psychiatric Association for a number of reasons, but the person I most wanted to hear speak was Martin Harrow, who is a psychologist at the University of Illinois College of Medicine. From 1975 to 1983, he enrolled sixty-four young schizophrenics in a long-term study funded by the NIMH, recruiting the patients from two Chicago hospitals. One was private and the other public, as this ensured that the group would be economically diverse. Ever since then, he has been periodically assessing how well they are doing. Are they symptomatic? In recovery? Employed? Do they take antipsychotic medications? His results provide an up-to-date look at how schizophrenia patients in the United States are faring, and thus his study can bring our investigation of the scientific literature to a fitting climax. If the conventional wisdom is to be believed, then those who stayed on antipsychotics should have had better outcomes. If the scientific literature we have just reviewed is to be believed, then it should be the reverse.

Here is Harrow's data. In 2007, he published a report on the patients' fifteen-year outcomes in the *Journal of Nervous and Mental Disease,* and he further updated that review in his presentation at the APA's 2008 meeting.[58] At the end of two years, the group not on antipsychotics were doing slightly better on a "global assessment scale" than the group on the drugs. Then, over the next thirty months, the collective fates of the two groups began to dramatically diverge. The off-med group began to improve significantly, and by the end of 4.5 years, 39 percent were "in recovery" and more than 60 percent were working. In contrast, outcomes for the medication group *worsened* during this thirty-month period. As a group, their global functioning declined slightly, and at the 4.5-year mark, only 6 percent were in recovery and few were working. That stark divergence in outcomes remained for the next ten years. At the fifteen-year follow-up, 40 percent of those off drugs were in recovery, more than half were working, and only 28 percent suffered from psychotic symptoms. In contrast, only 5 percent of those taking anti-

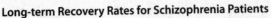

Long-term Recovery Rates for Schizophrenia Patients

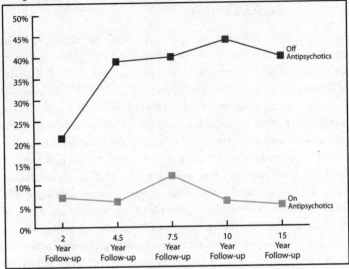

Source: Harrow, M. "Factors involved in outcome and recovery in schizophrenia patients not on antipsychotic medications." *The Journal of Nervous and Mental Disease,* 195 (2007): 406–14.

psychotics were in recovery, and 64 percent were actively psychotic. "I conclude that patients with schizophrenia not on antipsychotic medication for a long period of time have significantly better global functioning than those on antipsychotics," Harrow told the APA audience.

Indeed, it wasn't just that there were more recoveries in the unmedicated group. There were also fewer terrible outcomes in this group. There was a shift in the entire *spectrum* of outcomes. Ten of the twenty-five patients who stopped taking antipsychotics recovered, eleven had so-so outcomes, and only four (16 percent) had a "uniformly poor outcome." In contrast, only two of the thirty-nine patients who stayed on antipsychotics recovered, eighteen had so-so outcomes, and nineteen (49 percent) fell into the "uniformly poor" camp. Medicated patients had one-eighth the recovery rate of unmedicated patients, and a threefold higher rate of faring miserably over the long term.

This is the outcomes picture revealed in an NIMH-funded study,

Spectrum of Outcomes in Schizophrenia Patients

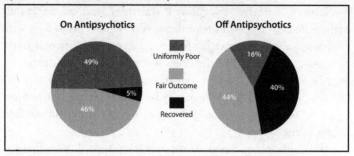

The spectrum of outcomes for medicated versus unmedicated patients. Those on antipsychotics had a much lower recovery rate, and were much more likely to have a "uniformly poor" outcome. Source: Harrow, M. "Factors involved in outcome and recovery in schizophrenia patients not on antipsychotic medications." *The Journal of Nervous and Mental Disease,* 195 (2007): 406–14.

the most up-to-date one we have today. It also provides us with insight into how *long* it takes for the better outcomes for nonmedicated patients, as a group, to become apparent. Although this difference began to show up at the end of two years, it wasn't until the 4.5-year mark that it became evident that the nonmedicated group, as a whole, was doing much better. Furthermore, through his rigorous tracking of patients, Harrow discovered why psychiatrists remain blind to this fact. Those who got off their antipsychotic medications left the system, he said. They stopped going to day programs, they stopped seeing therapists, they stopped telling people they had ever been diagnosed with schizophrenia, and they disappeared into society. A few of the nonmedicated people in Harrow's study even got "high-level jobs"—one became a college professor and another a lawyer—and several had "mid-level jobs." Explained Harrow: "We [clinicians] get our experience from seeing those who leave us, and then come back because they relapse. We don't see the ones who don't relapse. They don't come back. They are quite happy."

Afterward, I asked Dr. Harrow why he thought the nonmedicated patients did so much better. He did not attribute it to their being off antipsychotics, but rather said it was because this group "had a stronger internal sense of self," and once they initially stabilized on the medications, this "better personhood" gave them the confidence to go off the drugs. "It's not that those who went off medications did better, but rather it was those who did better [initially] who then went off the medications." When I pressed on with a question about whether his findings supported a different interpretation, which was that the drugs worsened long-term outcomes, he grew a bit testy. "That's a possibility, but I'm not advocating it," he said. "People recognize there may be side effects. . . . I'm not just trying to avoid the question. I'm one of the few people in the field without drug money."

I asked one last question. At the very least, shouldn't his findings be worked into the paradigm of care used in our society to treat those diagnosed with schizophrenia? "There is no question about that," he replied. "Our data is overwhelming that not all schizophrenic patients need to be on antipsychotics all their lives."

Reviewing the Evidence

We have followed a trail of documents to a surprising end, and thus I think we need to ask one final question: Does the evidence refuting the common wisdom all hang together? In other words, does the outcomes literature tell a coherent and consistent story? We need to double-check to make sure we are not missing something, for it is always discomforting to arrive at a conclusion so at odds with what society "knows" to be true.

First, as researchers Lisa Dixon and Emmanuel Stip acknowledged, there is no good evidence that antipsychotics improve long-term schizophrenia outcomes. As such, we can be confident that we haven't missed any such studies in our survey. Second, evidence that the drugs might worsen long-term outcomes showed up in the very first follow-up study conducted by the NIMH, and then it appears again and again over the next fifty years. We can link the authors of this research into a lengthy chain: Cole, Bockoven, Rappaport, Carpenter, Mosher, Harding, the World Health Organization, and Harrow. Third, once researchers came to understand how antipsychotics affected the brain, Chouinard and Jones stepped forward with a biological explanation for why the drugs made patients more vulnerable to psychosis over the long term. They were also able to explain why the drug-induced brain changes made it so risky for people to go off the medications, and thus they revealed why the drug-withdrawal studies misled psychiatrists into believing that the drugs prevented relapse. Fourth, evidence that long-term recovery rates are higher for nonmedicated patients appears in studies and investigations of many different types. It shows up in the randomized studies conducted by Rappaport, Carpenter, and Mosher; in the cross-cultural studies conducted by the World Health Organization; and in the naturalistic studies conducted by Harding and Harrow. Fifth, we see in the tardive dyskinesia studies evidence that the drugs induce global brain dysfunction in a high percentage of patients over the long term. Sixth, once a new tool for studying brain structures came along (MRIs), investigators discovered that antipsychotics cause morphological changes in the brain and that these changes are associated with a worsening of both positive and negative symptoms, and with cognitive impairment as well. Finally, for the most part, the psychiatric researchers who conducted these studies hoped and expected to find the reverse. They wanted to tell a story of drugs that help schizophrenia patients fare well over the long term—their bias was in that direction.

We are trying to solve a puzzle in this book—why have the number of disabled mentally ill soared over the past fifty years—and I think we now have our first puzzle piece in hand. We saw that in the decade before the introduction of Thorazine, 65 percent or so of first-episode schizophrenics would be discharged within twelve months, and the majority of those discharged would not be rehospitalized in follow-up periods of four and five years. This was what we saw in Bockoven's study, too: Seventy-six percent of the psychotic patients treated with a progressive form of psychosocial care in 1947 were living successfully in the community five years later. But, as we saw in Harrow's study, only 5 percent of schizophrenia patients who stayed on their drugs long-term ended up recovered. That is a dramatic decline in recovery rates in the modern era, and older psychiatrists, who can still remember what it was like to work with unmedicated patients, can personally attest to this difference in outcomes.

"In the nonmedication era, my schizophrenic patients did far better than do those in the more modern era," said Maryland psychiatrist Ann Silver, in an interview. "They chose careers, pursued them, and married. One patient, who had been called the sickest admitted to the adolescent division [of her hospital], is raising three children and works as a registered nurse. In the later [medicated] era, none chose a career, although many held various jobs, and none married or even had lasting relationships."

We can also see how this drug-induced chronicity has contributed to the rise in the number of disabled mentally ill. In 1955, there were 267,000 people with schizophrenia in state and county mental hospitals, or one in every 617 Americans. Today, there are an estimated 2.4 million people receiving SSI or SSDI because they are ill with schizophrenia (or some other psychotic disorder), a disability rate of one in every 125 Americans.[59] Since the arrival of Thorazine, the disability rate due to psychotic illness has increased fourfold in our society.

Cathy, George, and Kate

In the second chapter, we met two people—Cathy Levin and George Badillo—who had been diagnosed with schizoaffective disorder (Cathy) or schizophrenia (George). We can now see how their stories fit into the outcomes literature.

As I said, Cathy Levin is one of the best responders to atypical antipsychotics that I've ever met. She could be Janssen's poster girl for promoting Risperdal. Still, she remains on SSDI and she perceives the medications as a barrier to her working full-time. Now let's go back to that moment when she had her first psychotic episode at Earlham College. What might her life have been like if she had not been immediately placed on neuroleptics, but instead had been treated with some form of psychosocial care? Or if, at some point early on, she had been encouraged to withdraw gradually from the antipsychotic medication? Would she have cycled in and out of hospitals for the next twelve years? Would she have ended up on SSDI? Although we can't really answer those questions, we can say that the drug treatment increased the likelihood that she would suffer that long period of constant hospitalizations, and decreased the likelihood that she would fully recover from her initial crackup. As Cathy said: *"The thing I remember, looking back, is that I was not really that sick early on. I was really just confused."*

Meanwhile, George Badillo's story illustrates how getting off meds can be the key to recovery, at least for some people diagnosed with schizophrenia. His journey out of the back wards of a state hospital began when he started tonguing his antipsychotic medication. He is healthy today, he has an evident zest for life, and he revels in being a good father to his son and having his daughter Madelyne back in his life. He is an example of the many recovered people who showed up in the long-term studies by Harding and Harrow—former patients who have quit taking antipsychotics and are doing well.

Here is a third story of a young woman I'll call Kate, as she did not want her real name used. Diagnosed with schizophrenia at age nineteen, she did well on antipsychotics. In Harrow's study, she would have been among the 5 percent on meds who recovered. But she also knows what it is like to be off meds and doing well, and from her perspective, the latter type of recovery is totally unlike the first.

Before I met Kate in person, I knew from a phone conversation the bare outlines of her story, of how she had spent ten years on antipsychotics, and given that those drugs can take such a physical toll, I was a bit startled by her appearance when she showed up at my office. To be blunt, the words "drop dead gorgeous" popped into my head. A dark-haired woman, she wore jeans, a roseate top, and light makeup, and she introduced herself in a confident, warm way. Soon, she was showing me a "before" picture taken three years earlier. "I was well over two-hundred pounds," she says. "I was very slow, my face was droopy. I smoked a lot of cigarettes. . . . It was very inhibiting to any sort of professional look."

Kate's story about her childhood is a familiar one. Her parents divorced when she was eight, and she remembers herself as socially awkward and horribly shy. "I only had social skills enough to interact with my family members," she says, and that awkwardness followed her to college. During her freshman year at the University of Massachusetts at Dartmouth, she found it difficult to make friends, and she felt so isolated that she cried constantly. Early in her sophomore year she dropped out and went to live with her mother in Boston, hoping to find a "purpose in life." Instead, "my sense of reality started to disintegrate," she recalls. "I started worrying about God versus the devil, and I started becoming afraid of everything. I'd say to my mom's friend, 'Is the food poisoned?' I was acting quite bizarre, and I couldn't make sense of the conversations around me. I would say these very odd things, and I would speak very slowly, very deliberately, and weird."

When she began talking about seeing wolves in her bedroom, her mother put her in the hospital. Although she stabilized pretty well on the antipsychotic medication, she hated how it made her feel, and not long after she was discharged, she abruptly went off it, which triggered a florid psychotic break. During her second hospitalization, in February 1997, she was diagnosed with schizophrenia, and this time she accepted the fact that she would have to take antipsychotics for life. Eventually, she found a two-drug combination that worked well for her, and she began rebuilding a life. In 2001, she graduated from UMass Boston, and a year later she married a man she had met in a day treatment program. "We both had a psychiatric disability, and we both smoked heavily," she says. "We both saw therapists daily. This is what we had in common."

Kate took a job in a group home for the mentally handicapped, and although at times she had trouble staying awake, a side effect of her medications, she earned enough to get off SSDI. For a person with schizophrenia, she was doing extremely well. Yet she wasn't happy. She had gained nearly one hundred pounds, and her husband often cruelly taunted her, telling her that she was "ugly" and had a "fat ass." She chafed too over how everybody in the system treated her. "Recovery on the med model requires you to be obedient, like a child," she explains. "You are obedient to your doctors, you are compliant with your therapist, and you take your meds. There's no striving toward greater intellectual concerns."

In 2005, she grew closer to a longtime friend, who was twenty years older and belonged to a fundamentalist religious community. She began attending their meetings, and they in turn began advising her to dress, speak, and present herself to the world in a more formal way. "They told me, 'You are representing God, and you don't want to bring shame to God," she says. Kate's older friend also urged her to stop thinking of herself as schizophrenic. "He's making me think outside the box, and to think in ways that before I never would have accepted. I would always defend my therapist, defend my psychiatrist, defend the drugs, and defend my illness. He was asking me to give up my identity as a mentally impaired person."

Soon, her old life fell completely apart. She discovered that her husband had been sleeping with one of her friends, and after she moved out of their apartment, she had to sleep for a time in her car. Although at first, during that desperate time, she clung to her meds, the nonschizophrenic vision of herself also beckoned, and in February of 2006, she decided to take the leap: She would stop smoking, she would stop drinking coffee, and she would wean herself from her psychiatric medications. "Now I have no drugs, no nicotine, and no coffee, and my body is going into shock. I am coming down from all of this, and I am almost vibrating because I need my cigarettes, my drugs."

This decision also put her at odds with most everyone in her life. "I stopped talking to my family, because I didn't want to go back into that identity [of a disabled person]. My mind was very delicate. So I had to disengage from what I knew, and disengage from my therapist." Soon, she was losing so much weight that her friends thought she must be sick. As she struggled to stay sane, she clung to the advice from her religious group, speaking to others in a very formal manner, and this behavior convinced her mother that she was relapsing. "Strange ain't the word, honey" is how her mother puts it, and even Kate privately feared that she was becoming psychotic again. "But I had this hope, this faith, and so I said to myself, 'I am going to walk this tightrope across this horrible canyon, and hopefully when I get to the other side, there will be a mountain ridge I can stand on.' I had to focus on going forward regardless of where it took me, because if I fell off the tightrope, I was back in the hospital."

It was at that perilous moment, when it seemed that she was about to crash, that Kate agreed to meet her mother for dinner. "I think she is having a breakdown," her mother says. "She sat very proper, and looked scattered and disorganized. Her body was stiff. I was seeing a lot of the same symptoms as before. Her eyes were dilated and she seemed paranoid." As they drove away from the restaurant, Kate's mother started to turn toward the hospital, but at the last second she changed her mind. Kate "wasn't so crazy" that she needed to be locked up. "I went home and cried," her mother remembers. "I didn't know what was happening."

By her mother's reckoning, it took Kate six months to get through this withdrawal process. But she emerged on the other side *transformed*. "I see that her face is so alive now and she is more connected to her body," her mother says. "She feels comfortable in her own skin and more at peace with herself than ever. She is physically healthy. I didn't know that this kind of recovery was possible." In 2007, Kate married the older man who had encouraged her to go this route; she also has thrived in her job as the manager of a home for people with psychiatric problems, the company recognizing her for her "outstanding" performance in 2008, an award that came with a cash prize.

Kate does still struggle at times. The home she manages provides shelter to several men who are sexual deviants—"I've had people say they are going to set me on fire, or they are going to pee in my mouth," she says—and she no longer is having her emotional responses to such stress numbed by medication. "I've been off the drugs for two years, and sometimes I find it very, very difficult to deal with my emotions. I tend to have these rages of anger. Did the drugs bring such a cloud over my mind, make me so comatose, that I never gained skills on how to deal with my emotions? Now I'm finding myself getting angrier than ever and getting happier than ever too. The circle with my emotions is getting wider. And yes, it's easy to deal with when you're happy, but how do you deal with it when you are mad? I'm working on not getting overly defensive, and trying to take things in stride."

Kate's story, of course, is idiosyncratic in kind. Her success at getting off meds does not mean that everyone can successfully withdraw from them. Kate is an *amazing* person—incredibly willful and incredibly brave. Indeed, what the scientific literature reveals is that once a person is on an antipsychotic, it can be very difficult and risky to withdraw from the medication, and that many people suffer severe relapses. But the literature also reveals that there are people who can successfully withdraw from the medications and that it is this group that fares best in the long term. Kate made it into that group.

"That day in 2005 when I decided to get better, that's the dividing line in my life," she says. "I was a completely different person then. I was very heavy, I smoked all the time, I had flat affect. Today I run into people who knew me then, and they don't even recognize me. Even my mother says, 'You are not the same person.' "

7

The Benzo Trap

"What seemed so good about the benzodiazepines when I was playing with them was that it seemed like we really did have a drug that didn't have many problems. But in retrospect it's difficult to put a spanner into a wristwatch and expect that it won't do any harm."

—ALEC JENNER, BRITISH PHYSICIAN WHO CONDUCTED FIRST TRIALS OF A BENZODIAZEPINE IN THE UK (2003)[1]

Fans of the cable television series *Mad Men,* which tells of the lives of Don Draper and other Madison Avenue advertising men in the early 1960s, may recall a scene from the last episode of season two, when a friend of Draper's wife, Betty, says to her: "Do you want a Miltown? It's the only thing keeping me from chewing my nails off." That was a nice, historically accurate touch, and if the creators of *Mad Men* retain this period accuracy in season three and beyond, which will tell the story of the ad men and their families during the turbulent years of the mid-1960s, viewers can expect Betty Draper and her friends to reach into their purses and make sly references to "mother's little helper." Hoffmann-La Roche brought Valium to market in 1963, advertising it in particular to women, and from 1968 to 1981, it was the bestselling drug in the Western world. Yet, as Americans gobbled up this pill designed to keep them tranquil, something very odd happened: The number of people admitted to mental hospitals, psychiatric emergency rooms, and mental health outpatient clinics soared.

The scientific literature can explain why the two were linked.

Anxiety Before Miltown

Although anxiety is a regular part of the human psyche, our minds fashioned by evolution to worry and fret, there are some people who are more anxious than others, and the notion that such emotional distress is a diagnosable condition can be traced back to a New York nerve doctor, George Beard. In 1869, he announced that dread, worry, fatigue, and insomnia resulted from "tired nerves," a physical illness he dubbed "neurasthenia." The diagnosis proved to be a popular one, this illness thought to be a by-product of the industrial revolution that was sweeping America in the wake of the Civil War, and naturally the market created a variety of therapies that could restore a person's "tired" nerves. Makers of patent medicines sold "nerve revitalizers" laced with opiates, cocaine, and alcohol. Neurologists touted the restorative powers of electricity, and this led those diagnosed with neurasthenia to buy electric belts, suspenders, and handheld massagers. Those who were wealthier could head to spas that offered "rest cures," the patients' nerves restored through the healing touch of soothing baths, massages, and various electric gadgets.

Sigmund Freud provided psychiatry with a rationale for treating this group of patients and, in so doing, enabled psychiatry to move out of the asylum and into the office. Born in 1856, Freud set out his shingle as a nerve doctor in Vienna in 1886, which meant that many of his patients were women suffering from neurasthenia (Beard's disease had become popular in Europe, too). After hours of conversation with his clients, Freud became convinced that their feelings of dread and worry were psychological in origin, rather than the result of tired nerves. In 1895, he wrote about "anxiety neurosis" in women, which he theorized arose in large part from their unconscious repression of sexual desires and fantasies. Those suffering from such psychological conflicts could find relief through psychoanalysis, the patient on the couch led by the doctor into an exploration of her unconscious mind.

At this time, psychiatry was a profession for those who treated mad patients in the asylum. People with tired nerves went to see a nerve doctor or a general practitioner for help. But if anxiety arose from a psychological disorder in the brain, rather than from a frazzling of the nerves, then it made sense that psychiatrists could tend to these patients, and after Freud visited America in 1909, psychoanalytic societies began to form, with New York City the hub of this new therapy. Nationwide, only 3 percent of psychiatrists were in private practice in 1909; thirty years later, 38 percent were seeing patients in private settings.[2] Moreover, Freudian theory made nearly everyone a candidate for the psychiatrist's couch. "Neurotics," Freud explained during his 1909 tour, "fall ill of the same complexes with which we sound people struggle."[3]

Thanks to Freudian theories, psychiatric disorders were now divided into two basic categories: psychotic and neurotic. In 1952, the American Psychiatric Association published the first edition of its *Diagnostic and Statistical Manual,* and it described the neurotic patient in this way:

> The chief characteristic of [neurotic] disorders is "anxiety," which may be directly felt and expressed or which may be unconsciously and automatically controlled by the utilization of various psychological defense mechanisms. . . . In contrast to those with psychoses, patients with psychoneurotic disorder do not exhibit gross distortion or falsification of external reality (delusions, hallucinations, illusions) and they do not present gross disorganization of the personality.[4]

Such was the understanding of anxiety when Miltown came to market. Anxious people had their feet firmly planted in reality, and rarely was anxiety a condition that required hospitalization. In 1955, there were only 5,415 "psychoneurotic" patients in state mental hospitals.[5] As Stanford psychiatrist Leo Hollister confessed after the benzodiazepines were introduced, these drugs were "designed to treat what many would regard as a 'minor disorder.'"[6] The drugs were a balm for the "walking wounded," and thus, as we review the outcomes literature for the benzodiazepines, we should expect this patient group to function well. After all, that was the future promised by Miltown inventor Frank Berger: "Tranquilizers, by attenuating the disruptive influence of anxiety on the mind, open the way to a better and more coordinated use of the existing gifts," he said.[7]

The Minor Tranquilizers Fall from Grace

When Miltown first appeared, there were a number of studies published in medical journals that told—as two Harvard Medical School researchers, David Greenblatt and Richard Shader, later recalled—of how it "was almost magically effective in reducing anxiety." But as has often been the case in psychiatry, once a successor pill appeared on the market (Librium, in 1960), the efficacy of the old drug suddenly began to fade. In their review of the Miltown literature in 1974, Greenblatt and Shader found that in twenty-six well-controlled trials, there were only five in which Miltown "was more effective than placebo" as a treatment for anxiety. Nor was there any evidence that Miltown was better than a barbiturate in calming the nerves. The initial popularity of this drug, they wrote, "illustrates how factors other than scientific evidence may determine physicians' patterns of drug use."[8]

However, Miltown's fall from favor with the public arose from a different problem than lack of scientific efficacy. Many who tried the drug found that they became sick when they stopped taking it, and in 1964, Carl Essig, a scientist at the Addiction Research Center in Lexington, Kentucky, reported that it "could induce physical dependence in man."[9] *Science News* quickly announced that the happy pill could be "addictive," and on April 30, 1965, *Time* all but buried Miltown. There is "a growing disillusionment with Miltown on the part of many doctors," the magazine wrote. "Some doubt that it has any more tranquilizing effect than a dummy sugar pill. . . . A few physicians have reported that in some patients, Miltown may cause a true addiction, followed by withdrawal symptoms like those of narcotics users 'kicking the habit.' "[10]

Publicly, the benzodiazepines mostly escaped this opprobrium during the 1960s. When Hoffmann-La Roche brought Librium to market in 1960, it claimed that its drug provided "pure anxiety relief," and unlike Miltown and the barbiturates, was "safe, harmless and non-addicting." That belief took hold and the FDA did little to counter it, even though very early on it started receiving letters from people who were experiencing odd and quite distressing symptoms when they tried to quit a benzodiazepine. They told of awful insomnia, anxiety more severe than they had known before, and a rash of physical symptoms—tremors, headaches, and nerves that "jangled like crazy." As one man wrote the FDA, "I was not sleeping and in general felt horrible. Sometimes I thought I would die and other times wished I had."[11] Although the FDA held a hearing on the matter, it did not impose any legal control on benzodiazepines similar to what had been placed on amphetamines and barbiturates, and so the public's belief that the drugs were relatively nonaddictive and harmless survived until 1975, when the U.S. Justice Department demanded that they be classified as schedule IV drugs under the Controlled Substances Act. This designation limited the number of refills a patient could obtain without a new prescription, and revealed to the public that the government had concluded that benzodiazepines were, in fact, addictive.

"Danger ahead! Valium—The Pill You Love Can Turn on You," a *Vogue* headline screamed. A benzodiazepine, the magazine explained, could lead to a "far worse addiction than heroin."[12] The Valium backlash had begun, particularly in the pages of women's magazines, and soon *Ms.* magazine provided readers with first-person accounts of the horrors of withdrawing from it. "My withdrawal symptoms are a double-dose of the anxiety, irritableness, and insomnia I used to feel," one user said. Confessed another: "I can't begin to describe the physical and mental anguish that accompanied my withdrawal."[13] The happiness pill of the 1950s was turning into the misery pill of the 1970s, with the *New York Times* reporting in 1976 that "some critics go so far to say that [Valium] is doing more harm than good, or even deny that it is doing any good at all for the great majority of patients. Some cry with alarm that it is far from being as safe as it is proclaimed, that it can be hideously and dangerously addictive, and may be the direct cause of addicts' deaths."[14] Two million Americans were said to be addicted to benzodiazepines, four times the number of heroin addicts in the country, and one of the pill takers turned out to be former first lady Betty Ford, who checked herself into an alcohol and drug rehab center in 1978. Abuse of tranquilizers, said her physician Joseph Pursch, was "the nation's number one health problem."[15]

Over the next few years, the benzodiazepines officially fell from grace. In 1979, Senator Edward Kennedy held a Senate Health Subcommittee hearing on the dangers of benzodiazepines, which he said had "produced a nightmare of dependence and addiction, both very difficult to treat and recover from."[16] After reviewing the scientific literature, the White House Office of Drug Policy and the National Institute of Drug Abuse concluded that the drugs' sleep-promoting effects didn't last more than two weeks, and this finding was soon seconded by the Committee on the Review of Medicines in the United Kingdom, which found that the drugs' anti-anxiety effects didn't last beyond four months. As such, the committee recommended that "patients receiving benzodiazepine therapy be carefully selected and monitored and that prescriptions be limited to short-term use."[17] As an editorial in the *British Medical Journal* put it: "Now that benzodiazepines have been shown to cause drug dependence should their use be more closely controlled—or even banned?"[18]

The ABCs of Benzodiazepines

This story of the benzodiazepines' fall from grace might seem like ancient history, a footnote in our quest to understand why there has been such a rise in the number of disabled mentally ill in the United States over the past fifty years, except for the fact that the benzodiazepines never really went away. Although the number of prescriptions for benzodiazepines dropped after they were classified as schedule IV drugs, from 103 million in 1975 to 71 million in 1980, the following year Upjohn brought Xanax to market, and this helped stabilize sales of benzodiazepines.[19] Psychiatrists continued to prescribe benzodiazepines to many of their nervous patients, and in 2002, Stephen Stahl, a well-known psychopharmacologist at the

University of California in San Diego, confessed to psychiatry's dirty little secret in an article titled "Don't Ask, Don't Tell, But Benzodiazepines Are Still the Leading Treatments for Anxiety Disorders."[20] Since that time, the prescribing of benzodiazepines in the United States has increased, from 69 million prescriptions in 2002 to 83 million in 2007, which isn't all that far below the number written at the height of the Valium craze in 1973.[21]

So, given that benzodiazepines have been widely used for fifty years, we need to look at what science has to tell about these drugs, and whether their use may be contributing in some way to the increase in the number of disabled mentally ill in the United States.

Short-term efficacy

As anyone who has taken a benzodiazepine can attest, it acts rapidly, and if a person hasn't become habituated to the drug, it will numb his or her emotional distress. As such, a benzodiazepine has an obvious utility in helping people through a situational crisis. The writer Andrea Tone, in her book *The Age of Anxiety,* relates how a benzodiazepine enabled her to get on an airplane after she somewhat mysteriously developed a fear of flying. But as clinical trials revealed, that immediate efficacy quickly begins to fade and pretty much disappears by the end of four to six weeks.

In 1978, Kenneth Solomon at Albany Medical College in New York reviewed seventy-eight double-blind trials of benzodiazepines and determined that the drugs had proved to be significantly better than a placebo in only forty-four of them. At best, the collective results could be said to "hint at therapeutic efficacy," he wrote.[22] Five years later, Arthur Shapiro at Mt. Sinai School of Medicine in New York City fleshed out this efficacy picture a bit more, reporting that in a trial of 224 anxious patients, Valium proved superior to a placebo for the first week, but then this advantage began to lessen. Based on the patients' self-assessment of their symptoms, by the end of the second week there was no difference between the drug and a placebo, and by the end of six weeks, the placebo group was faring slightly better. "It is unlikely in our opinion that carefully controlled

studies would consistently show significant benzodiazepine therapeutic antianxiety effects," Shapiro wrote.[23]

That picture of the short-term efficacy of benzodiazepines has
not markedly changed since then. The drugs show clear efficacy for
the first week, and then their advantage over a placebo abates. But,
as British investigators noted in 1991, this brief period of efficacy
comes at a fairly high cost. "Both psychomotor and cognitive functioning may be impaired, and amnesia is a common effect of all benzodiazepines," they said.[24] In 2007, researchers in Spain looked at
whether these adverse events negated the small "efficacy benefit"
provided by the drugs, and found that the drop-out rates in clinical
trials, a measure often used to assess the overall "effectiveness" of a
drug, were the same for benzodiazepine and placebo patients. "This
systematic review did not find convincing evidence of the short-term
effectiveness of the benzodiazepines in the treatment of generalized
anxiety disorder," they reported.[25]

Malcolm Lader, a psychiatrist at the Institute of Psychiatry in
London who is one of the world's leading experts on benzodi-
azepines, explained the importance of this finding in an interview:
"Effectiveness is a measure of what it's like in real practice."[26]

Withdrawal syndromes

Although the first report of benzodiazepine dependence appeared in
the scientific literature in 1961, when Leo Hollister at Stanford University reported that patients withdrawing from Librium were experiencing odd symptoms, it wasn't until the Justice Department
classified benzodiazepines as schedule IV drugs that researchers
began investigating the problem with any vigor. In 1976, physicians
Barry Maletzky and James Kotter jump-started this inquiry, reporting that when their patients stopped taking Valium, many
complained of "extreme anxiety."[27] Two years later, physicians at
Pennsylvania State University announced that patients withdrawing
from benzodiazepines often experienced "an increase in anxiety
above baseline levels . . . a condition that we term 'rebound anxiety.' "[28] In Britain, Lader reported similar findings. "Anxiety rose

Rebound Anxiety with Valium

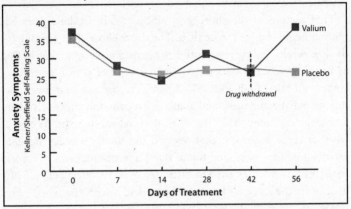

In this 1985 study by British investigators, the patients treated with Valium did not fare better than the placebo patients during the first six weeks. The Valium patients were then withdrawn from the drug and their anxiety symptoms soared, to a much higher level than the symptoms in placebo patients. Source: Power, K. "Controlled study of withdrawal symptoms and rebound anxiety after six week course of diazepam for generalised anxiety." *British Medical Journal* 290 (1985): 1246–48.

sharply during withdrawal, and to a point of panic in several patients. Patients commonly experienced bodily symptoms of anxiety, such as a choking feeling, dry mouth, hot and cold, legs like jelly, etc."[29]

Patients withdrawing from benzodiazepines, it seemed, were becoming more anxious than they had ever been. Over the course of the next decade, Lader and other British physicians (most notably Heather Ashton, a doctor at the University of Newcastle upon Tyne who ran a withdrawal clinic) continued to investigate this problem, and they compiled a long list of symptoms that could bedevil those quitting a benzodiazepine. In addition to rebound anxiety, patients could experience insomnia, seizures, tremors, headaches, blurred vision, a ringing in the ears, extreme sensitivity to noise, a feeling that insects were crawling over them, nightmares, hallucinations, extreme depression, depersonalization, and derealization (a sense that the external world is unreal). Withdrawal, one patient told Heather Ashton, was like "living death . . . I thought I had gone mad."

"These findings show very clearly that benzodiazepine withdrawal

is a severe illness," Ashton wrote. "The patients were usually frightened, often in intense pain, and genuinely prostrated. . . . Through
no fault of their own, the patients suffered considerable physical as
well as mental distress."[30]

Not all people withdrawn from benzodiazepines suffer in this
way. The risk of suffering withdrawal symptoms varies according to
how long a person has been on the drug, the potency of the benzodiazepine, and the speed of the drug-tapering process. A majority of
patients who've taken a benzodiazepine for a relatively short time,
such as a month or two, may be able to withdraw from it with little
difficulty. However, some people experience withdrawal symptoms
after taking a benzodiazepine for only a few weeks, and it can take a
longtime user a year or longer to taper from the drug. Moreover, a
small percentage of people suffer a "protracted withdrawal syndrome," their anxiety remaining at elevated levels "for many months
after benzodiazepine withdrawal," Ashton observed.[31] Depression
may deepen, and the odd perceptual symptoms—the depersonalization, the derealization, the sensation of insects crawling on the
skin—can haunt a person for an extended period. Most alarming, a
small percentage of long-term users never fully recover. "It is very
worrying," Lader said, in an interview. "Somehow there has been a
change [in the brain]. I cannot say that everybody is going to recover
back to normality when they come off long-term usage."

The biology of benzodiazepine withdrawal

In 1977, researchers discovered that benzodiazepines affect a neurotransmitter in the brain known as GABA. Unlike dopamine and
serotonin, which transmit an "excitatory" message telling a neuron
to fire, GABA (gamma-aminobutyric acid) inhibits neuronal activity. A neuron receiving the GABA message either fires at a slower
rate or stops firing for a period of time. A majority of neurons in the
brain have GABA receptors, which means that this neurotransmitter acts as the brain's brake on neuronal activity. A benzodiazepine
binds to the GABA receptor and, in so doing, amplifies GABA's in-
hibitory effects. It pushes down on the GABA brake, so to speak,
and as a result, it suppresses central nervous system activity.

In response, the brain decreases its output of GABA and decreases the density of its GABA receptors. It is trying to "restore normal GABA transmission," British scientists explained in 1982.[32] However, as a result of these adaptive changes, the brain's braking system is now in a physiologically impaired state. Its braking fluid is low (GABA output), and its brake pads are worn (GABA receptors). As a result, when the benzodiazepine is withdrawn, the brain is no longer able to properly inhibit neuronal activity, and its neurons may begin firing at a helter-skelter pace. This overactivity, Heather Ashton concluded, may "account for many of the effects of withdrawal."[33] The anxiety, the insomnia, the sensation of insects crawling across the skin, the paranoia, the derealization, the seizures—all of these vexing symptoms may arise from neuronal hyperactivity.

If a person gradually tapers off from a benzodiazepine, the GABA system may slowly revert to normal, and thus withdrawal symptoms may be mild. However, the fact that some long-term users suffer "protracted symptoms" is probably "due to the failure of the [GABA] receptors to revert to their normal state," Ashton said.[34] Long-term benzodiazepine use, she explained, may "give rise not only to slowly reversible functional changes in the central nervous system, but may also occasionally cause structural neuronal damage."[35] In such cases, the GABA brake never again functions like it should.

Long-term effects

Once researchers in the United States and the United Kingdom determined that benzodiazepines did not provide any durable relief from anxiety, an obvious question arose: Do these drugs, when taken on a continual basis, *worsen* the very symptom they are supposed to treat? In 1991, Karl Rickels at the University of Pennsylvania School of Medicine reported on a group of anxious patients who had tried to quit benzodiazepines three years earlier, and he found that those who had successfully gotten off the drugs were doing "significantly" better than those who had failed to do so.[36] A few years later, he was back with a new study: When long-term users withdrew from benzodiazepines, they "became more alert, more relaxed, and less anxious, and this change was accompanied by improved psychomotor functions."[37] Those who stayed on the benzodiazepines were more emotionally distressed than those who got off.

Others told of similar long-term results. Canadian investigators found that benzodiazepine usage led to a fourfold increase in depressive symptoms.[38] In England, Ashton observed that those who stay on the drugs tend to became more ill: "Many patients find that anxiety symptoms gradually increase over the years despite continuous benzodiazepine use, and panic attacks and agoraphobia may appear for the first time."[39] These studies and observations told of a very problematic long-term course, and in 2007, French researchers surveyed 4,425 long-term benzodiazepine users and found that 75 percent were "markedly ill to extremely ill . . . a great majority of the patients had significant symptomatology, in particular major depressive episodes and generalized anxiety disorder, often with marked severity and disability."[40]

In addition to causing emotional distress, long-term benzodiazepine usage also leads to cognitive impairment. Early on, researchers recognized that memory problems were associated with short-term use, and this led David Knott, a physician at the University of Tennessee, to warn in 1976 that "I am very convinced that Valium, Librium and other drugs of that class cause damage to the brain. I have seen damage to the cerebral cortex that I believe is due to the use of these drugs, and I am beginning to wonder if the damage is permanent."[41] Over the next twenty-five years, reports of cognitive impairment in long-term benzodiazepine users regularly appeared in scientific journals. These studies told of people who were having trouble focusing, remembering things, learning new material, and solving problems. However, the patients "are not aware of their reduced ability," Lader wrote, evidence that their self-insight was impaired as well.[42] In 2004, a group of Australian scientists, after reviewing the relevant literature, concluded that "long-term benzodiazepine users were consistently more impaired than controls across all cognitive categories," with these deficits "moderate to large" in magnitude. The studies showed the "higher the intake, dose and period of use [of a benzodiazepine], the greater the risk of impairment."[43]

Increased anxiety, increased depression, and cognitive impairment—all of these factors contribute to a decline in a person's ability to function in society. In 1983, the World Health Organization noted a "striking deterioration in personal care and social interactions" in long-term benzodiazepine users.[44] Another investigator reported that they end up with poor coping skills.[45] In a study funded by Hoffmann-La Roche, the manufacturer of Valium, University of Michigan investigators determined that taking this drug was "associated with poor quality of life, poor performance in work and personal life, low social support, perceived lack of internal control, poor perceived health and high levels of stress."[46] Ashton determined that long-term use led to "malaise, ill-health, and elevated scores for neuroticism."[47] Benzodiazepines, she said, contribute to "job loss, unemployment, and loss of work through illness."[48]

Such is the history told about benzodiazepines in the scientific literature. Moreover, it is a story easily traced, as Dr. Stevan Gressitt, who today is the medical director for Adult Mental Health Services in Maine, can attest. In 2002, he helped form the Maine Benzo Study Group, which was comprised of physicians and other health-care professionals, and it concluded that "there is no evidence supporting the long-term use of benzodiazepines for any mental health condition." Benzodiazepines, Gressitt and his colleagues wrote, may "aggravate" both "medical and mental health problems." In an interview, I asked Dr. Gressitt whether those "problems" included increased anxiety, cognitive impairment, and functional decline. Was his understanding of the scientific literature, I wondered, the same as mine?

"Your words I don't contradict or argue with," he replied.[49]

Geraldine, Hal, and Liz

The scientific literature reveals that benzodiazepines—much as the neuroleptics do—act like a trap. The drugs ameliorate anxiety for a short period of time, and thus they can provide a distressed person much needed relief. However, they work by *perturbing* a neurotransmitter system, and in response, the brain undergoes compensatory adaptations, and as a result of this change, the person becomes vulnerable to relapse upon drug withdrawal. That difficulty in turn may lead some to take the drugs indefinitely, and these patients are likely to become more anxious, more depressed, and cognitively impaired.

Here are the stories of three people who fell into the trap.

Geraldine Burns, a thin woman with dark red hair, still lives in the house she grew up in. She tells me her story while we sit in her kitchen, her elderly mother darting in and out.

Born in 1955, Geraldine was one of six children, and theirs was a happy family. Her father was Irish, her mother Lebanese, and their Boston neighborhood was known as "Little Lebanon," a place where everybody definitely knew your name. Aunts, uncles, and other relatives lived nearby. At age eighteen, Geraldine started dating a boy who lived down the block, Joe Burns. "I've been with him ever since," she says, and for a time their life unfolded just as Geraldine had hoped. She had a job that she enjoyed in human resources at a rehabilitation center, she and Joe had a healthy son (Garrett) in 1984, and they basked in their close-knit neighborhood. Geraldine—outgoing and energetic—was the constant hostess for gatherings of family and friends. "I loved my life," she says. "I loved working, I loved my family, and I loved this neighborhood. I was the one who organized the reunion of my grammar school. I still had friends from kindergarten. I couldn't have been more normal."

However, in March 1988, Geraldine gave birth to a daughter, Liana, and she felt physically unwell afterward. "I kept telling the doctors and nurses that I felt like I weighed a thousand pounds," she says, and after a doctor ruled out an infection, he figured she must be anxious and prescribed Ativan. Geraldine came home from the hospital with a prescription for that benzodiazepine, and although it helped for a short while, months later she still felt something wasn't right and so she went to see a psychiatrist. "She immediately tells me I have a chemical imbalance," Geraldine recalls. "She says that I should keep taking the Ativan and assures me that it is harmless and nonaddictive. She tells me that I will have to take this drug for the rest of my life. Later, when I questioned her about this, she explained it this way: 'If you were a diabetic you would have to take insulin for the rest of your life, wouldn't you?' "

Soon her psychiatrist added an antidepressant to the Ativan, and as Geraldine struggled to take care of her daughter that first year, her emotions seemed numbed, her mind fogged. "I was in a daze half the time. My mother would call and I would tell her something, and she would say, 'You told me that last night.' And I'd say, 'I did?' " Worse, as the months wore on, she found herself becoming ever more anxious, so much so that she started staying inside her house. Going back to her job in human resources at the rehabilitation center was now out of the question. At one point, after she stopped taking Ativan for a day or two, she had a "massive panic attack." The federal government agreed that she was disabled by "anxiety" and thus eligible for a monthly SSDI payment. "Me, who was the most social person on the planet, is not able to go out," Geraldine says, shaking her head in disbelief. "I wouldn't go out unless my husband would take me."

Over the next eight years, Geraldine cycled through an endless combination of anti-anxiety and antidepressant medications. None worked. The anxiety and panic remained, and she suffered from a medley of side effects—rashes, sexual dysfunction, weight gain, tachycardia (from the panic attacks), and excessive menstrual bleeding, the last leading to a hysterectomy. "All of the women I've known who were on Ativan long-term ended up having a hysterectomy, every single one of us," she says, with evident bitterness. At last, in October 1996, she went to a new physician, who, after reviewing her medical history, identified a likely culprit. "He told me, 'You are on one of the most addictive drugs known,' and I thought,

'Thank God.' I was in tears. It was the drugs all along. I had been made iatrogenically ill."

Geraldine spent two nightmarish years withdrawing from Ativan and the other psychiatric drugs she had been taking. Horrible smells came from her body, her muscles twitched, she lost weight, and at one point, she couldn't sleep for weeks. "It was like hell opened up and swallowed me in," she says. Although she did kick the habit, it took several more years for her to feel better physically, and she still suffers from a great deal of anxiety. The gregarious, socially-at-ease person she had always been before that fateful day in March 1988 when she was prescribed Ativan has never returned. "Am I back to my old self? No," she whispers. "I mourn who I used to be. We all mourn. I am still so afraid of so many things."

Three days before I was to meet with Hal Flugman, who lives in South Florida, he called to say that his anxiety had flared up again, and the thought of leaving his house to talk to me was too stressful. "I am not feeling right," he said. "I'm over-breathing, I have these terrible gastrointestinal problems. I think I have to get my Klonopin dose upped. . . . This is what is happening to me."

Hal, whom I'd interviewed by phone a few months earlier, first became anxious when he was thirteen years old. Overweight and small, he didn't get along well with his classmates in middle school. "I had panic attacks, and a slight fear of being around people," he recalls. For the next five years, he went to counseling, but he was not prescribed a medication. "I was living with it, dealing with it," he says, but then one night at a rock concert, the panic hit so hard that he had to call his family and beg that they come get him. The following day a doctor gave him a prescription for Klonopin.

"I remember saying to the doctor, 'Am I going to become ad-dicted and have a really hard time coming off?' I was worried about the side effects, too. But the doctor said that the side effects would go away in a couple of weeks, and didn't that beat living with these unbearable panic attacks? I said, 'Well, of course.' And I knew from the first pill that this was going to solve my anxiety problem. It absolutely worked for me. I felt great."

Hal's life since then is a story of addiction. Shortly after going on the drug, he moved to San Francisco to pursue a career as a musician, and for a time it went well—he even got to hang out with Carlos Santana, the great guitarist. But his music career failed to take off, and today he thinks that the Klonopin was partly to blame, for it stifled his ambition and didn't help his finger dexterity, either. Eventually, he fell into a deep depression—"I felt like a zombie," he says—and at age twenty-nine he returned to Florida to live with his parents. At that point, he was diagnosed with bipolar illness, the government agreeing that he was so disabled by mental illness that he was eligible to receive SSI. The years slid by, his mother passed away, and then, in 2001, he began taking higher doses of Klonopin, as otherwise his depression would become unbearable. His doctor told him he was abusing the drug and sent him to a detox facility, where, over a period of ten days, he was withdrawn from the benzodiazepine he had been taking for sixteen years.

"What happened next was absolutely the worst thing in my life," he says. "I could give you a list of symptoms, but that wouldn't do justice to what I was going through mentally. Month after month I got worse and worse. I couldn't sleep, and the symptoms—the most debilitating one was this feeling that I was dead. I felt that my brain was ripped out of my head, like I wasn't even a living thing. I had depersonalization, my skin felt weird, my body felt weird. I didn't even want to get into the shower. Even room-temperature water felt strange on my skin. If I put on mildly hot water, it felt like it was burning right through me. I couldn't digest food right, I couldn't go to the bathroom for weeks at a time, I couldn't urinate right . . . I was in a constant state of panic attacks, and this doctor is telling me it's all in my mind, that he won't write me a script, and that withdrawal symptoms can last a maximum of thirty days. I was cracking up, going insane."

This went on for ten months. He found Geraldine Burns on the Internet, as she had started a benzodiazepine support group, and she would console him for hours at a time. Ten, twenty times a night he would call his sister Susan, screaming that he was going to kill himself. He desperately sought to get a new prescription for Klonopin, but the doctors he saw didn't believe that his torment was related to benzodiazepine withdrawal. Instead, they figured that he had abused the drug in the past and so they refused to put him back on it. "They don't understand that the drug changes the whole biology of your brain, and that your brain doesn't work right anymore," Hal says. Finally, his sister found a physician who agreed to write him a script, and "within hours, the nightmare was over. Every single side effect, every single withdrawal problem I had been going through was gone. Completely. Like magic. I was jumping up and down I was so excited."

Hal has never tried going off Klonopin again. His brain adapted to the drug, he says, and now it can't adapt back. "Klonopin ruined my life. It takes away your drive, and in the morning, you don't want to get out of bed, because you feel so groggy. I don't even know what it's like to feel normal. This is my world. Things don't get me as excited as most people because I'm in a constant state of sedation. It should never have been prescribed for long-term use."

Susan sees it much the same way. "My sister and I have talked at length about how our brother is very good-looking, and how when he is acting normal, you would not know there is anything wrong," she says. "He is adorable, charming; he carries on conversations. He could have been with a nice woman and had a family. But now? He has no friends. None whatsoever. He stays at home most of the time, except when he has to go to the store. He is trapped. He can't get off Klonopin. I feel terrible for him, and I feel terrible for my dad, who when he dies will never have seen his son do well. It kills us that he could have had a life."

If a picture is worth a thousand words, the photos that an Ohio woman, whom I'll call Liz, sends me tell her story in a very succinct fashion. There is the "before" photo in which she is smiling and looking confidently into the camera, posed like a model in a fashionable black dress. One hand is posed gracefully on her hip, a necklace adds a touch of elegance, and she is a bit dolled up—the makeup and styled black hair tell of a woman who presents herself carefully to the world. And then there is the "after" photo, her eyes hollowed out and bloodshot, her face taut and drawn, her hair thinned—she looks like a somewhat crazed methamphetamine addict who is now getting her photo taken following an arrest.

We first spoke on the phone in July of 2008, three months after she had taken her last dose of a benzodiazepine, a drug she had been on for thirteen years. Here's how she starts her story: "My head is feeling crushed. It's like horses are kicking my skull."

Liz, who is in her mid-thirties, grew up in an affluent suburb of Columbus, Ohio, where she attended private schools and excelled in multiple ways. She sang competitively, won school awards for her art, and was a top student. Petite and pretty, she was asked by a representative of the Miss Ohio pageant to enter that competition. "I was a vibrant, creative, fun person," she says. However, she did occasionally struggle with anxiety and depression, and during her sophomore year at Ohio State University a psychiatrist put her on an antidepressant. Unfortunately, that drug seemed to increase her anxiety, and so eventually the psychiatrist added Klonopin to the mix. "He said it was a gentle little pill used to help old ladies sleep. He said that it wasn't addictive and that if I wanted to stop, at most I'd experience a few nights of bad sleep. But he said I would probably need to take it for life, just like a diabetic needs insulin."

For the next ten years, Liz functioned okay. She graduated summa cum laude from Ohio State University in 1996, earned a master's degree in counseling, and after various adventures, in 2002 she began teaching fourth grade in a public school. However, throughout this period, her anxiety returned again and again, and each time it did, her psychiatrist upped her dose of Klonopin. And as the dose increased, her ability to function declined. "I would wonder, What is wrong with me? Why am I becoming so withdrawn? Why am I losing interest in everything? I was getting sicker and sicker." Then, in late 2004, the anxiety, panic, and depression returned worse than ever, and new symptoms—obsessions and suicidal ideation—appeared too. She was told this meant she was "bipolar" and she was prescribed an antipsychotic, Abilify. "That's when I flipped out. My anxiety went through the roof, it was like being injected with stimulants, and I was teaching one day and I started crying in class. I couldn't take it anymore, and I was hospitalized in a psychiatric ward."

Now came the drug merry-go-round. During the next two years, Liz was put on Lamictal, Lexapro, Seroquel, Neurontin, lithium, Wellbutrin, and other drugs she can't remember, with Klonopin always part of the cocktail. This treatment caused her eyes to swell, her skin to break into rashes, and her eyebrows and hair to fall out. "My poor brain was being treated like a mixing bowl," she says. Only when she asked doctors whether the cocktail might be making her sick, "they would say, 'We have tried the drugs and they are not helping, and so the problem is you.'" Indeed, since the drugs weren't working, her psychiatrists gave her electroshock, which took its toll on her memory.

Growing ever more desperate, toward the end of 2006 Liz concluded that "it was the drugs that were making me sick." She began withdrawing from the medications one by one, and although she was able to get off the antidepressants and antipsychotics, every time she tried tapering off Klonopin she suffered a long list of torments: hallucinations, horrible anxiety, vertigo, painful muscle spasms, perceptual distortions, and derealization, just to name a few. Finally, in the spring of 2008, she adopted a new strategy: She would get off by progressively switching to less potent benzodiazepines. Klonopin was replaced by Valium, the Valium by Librium, and then, in April 2008, she withdrew from Librium. She was now drug free, yet three months later, when I spoke to her on the phone, she was still in withdrawal torment. "What I've been through . . . the trauma," she says, breaking into tears. "I feel dizzy all the time. It is like the floor is tilting one way and I am spinning the other way. It is horrific. I have had hallucinations, I have to wear sunglasses in the house, sometimes I scream from the pain."

At the end of our interview, I asked her to think back to what her life had been like before she was put on a benzodiazepine, and once more she began to cry.

"My anxiety then was like a mild case of asthma, and today it's like I have end-stage lung disease. I'm terrified that I'm not going to make it. I'm so, so scared."

. . .

Those interviews provide a snapshot of three lives, and several months later I spoke to each of the subjects again to see if anything had changed. Geraldine was doing much the same. Hal had become much more distraught. The Klonopin no longer seemed to be working, his anxiety had returned with a vengeance, and he felt physically sick. "I've come to accept this is my life," he said, his voice filled with what seemed like bottomless despair. There was, however, an encouraging postscript to Liz's story. Not long after our phone interview, her withdrawal symptoms began to abate, and in early 2009, she had this to report: The hallucinations, the vertigo, the seizures, the hair loss, and the blurry vision had all disappeared. The muscle spasms, the tinnitus, and the hypersensitivity to light and noise had become less severe. The feeling that her head was "packed in cement" had lessened.

"I have a few good days now, and my bad days are not all that bad anymore," she says. "I think I can see the light at the end of the tunnel. There is no doubt I am going to be better. I am going to move to a new city, and although I'll have to start from scratch, I know it will be okay. I now value life like nobody else I know. I enjoy being able to walk in a straight line again, and being able to see again, and even having a normal heartbeat. My hair is beginning to come back. I am getting better; I am just waiting for the cement to completely leave my brain."

The Disability Numbers

At least to a degree, we can track the toll that the anti-anxiety drugs have taken over the past fifty years. As was noted at the beginning of this chapter, once the Miltown craze erupted, the number of people turning up at mental hospitals, outpatient centers, and residential facilities for the mentally ill began to sharply rise. The U.S. Department of Health and Human Services dubs this number "patient care episodes," and it soared from 1.66 million in 1955 to 6.86

million in 1975, when Valiumania was near its peak.[50] On a per-capita basis, that was an increase from 1,028 patient-care episodes per 100,000 people to 3,182 per 100,000, a threefold jump in twenty years. While many factors may have contributed to that increase (the emotional struggles that some Vietnam veterans experienced is one possibility that comes to mind, and illicit drug use is a second), Valiumania was clearly a major one. In the late 1970s, Betty Ford's physician, Joseph Pursch, concluded that benzodiazepines were the "nation's number one health problem," and that was because he knew they were driving people to detox centers, emergency rooms, and psychiatric wards.

As the personal stories of Geraldine, Hal, and Liz attest, benzodiazepines continue to be a pathway to disability for many. These three are part of the surge of people with an "affective disorder" who have swelled the SSI and SSDI rolls in the past twenty years. Although the Social Security Administration doesn't detail the number of disabled mentally ill who have anxiety as a primary diagnosis, a 2006 report by the U.S. General Accountability Office provides a proxy for estimating that number. It noted that 8 percent of the younger adults (eighteen to twenty-six years old) on the SSI and SSDI rolls were disabled by anxiety, and if that percentage holds true for all ages, then there were more than 300,000 adults in the United States who received government support in 2006 due to an anxiety disorder.[51] That is roughly sixty times the number of psychoneurotics hospitalized in 1955.

Although it was thirty years ago that governmental review panels in the United States and the United Kingdom concluded that the benzodiazepines shouldn't be prescribed long-term, with dozens of studies subsequently confirming the wisdom of that advice, the prescribing of benzodiazepines for continual use goes on. Indeed, a 2005 study of anxious patients in the New England area found that more than half regularly took a benzodiazepine, and many bipolar patients now take a benzodiazepine as part of a drug cocktail.[52] The scientific evidence simply doesn't seem to affect the prescribing habits of many doctors. "The lesson has either never been learned, or it has passed people by," Malcolm Lader said.[53]

8

An Episodic Illness Turns Chronic

"With the range of available treatments for depression, one might wonder why depression-related disability is on the rise."
—CAROLYN DEWA,
CENTRE FOR ADDICTION AND MENTAL HEALTH,
ONTARIO (2001)[1]

M-Power in Boston is a peer-run advocacy group for the mentally ill, and while I was at one of their meetings in April 2008, a young, quiet woman came up to me and whispered, "I'd be willing to talk to you." Red hair fell about her shoulders, and she seemed so shy as to almost be frightened. Yet when Melissa Sances told me her story a few days later, she spoke in the most candid manner possible, her shyness transformed into an introspective honesty so intense that when she was recounting her struggles growing up in Sandwich on Cape Cod, she suddenly stopped and said: "I was unhappy, but I didn't have an awareness that I was depressed." It was important that I understood the difference between those two emotions.

Her unhappiness as a child was comprised of familiar ingredients. She felt socially awkward and "different" from other kids at school, and after her parents divorced when she was eight, she and her brothers lived with their mother, who struggled with depression. In middle school, Melissa began to come out of her shell, making friends and feeling "more normal," only then she ran head-on into the torments of puberty. "When I was fourteen, I was overweight, I had acne. I felt like a social outcast, and the kids at high school were very cruel. I was called a freak and ugly. I would sit at my desk with my head down, and my hair pulled over my face, trying to hide from the world. Every day I woke up feeling like I wanted to die."

Today, Melissa is an attractive woman, and so it is a bit surprising to learn of this ugly-duckling moment from her past. But with her schoolmates taunting her, her childhood unhappiness metamorphosed into a deep depression, and when she was sixteen, she tried to commit suicide by gulping down handfuls of Benadryl and Valium. She woke up in the hospital, where she was told that she had a mental illness and was prescribed an antidepressant. "The psychiatrist tells me that it adjusts serotonin levels, and that I will probably have to be on it for the rest of my life. I cried when I heard that."

For a time, Zoloft worked great. "I was like a new person," Melissa recalls. "I became open to people, and I made a lot of friends. I was the pitcher on the softball team." During her senior year, she began making plans to attend Emerson College in Boston, thinking that she would study creative writing. Only then, slowly but surely, Zoloft's magic started to fade. Melissa began to take higher doses to keep her depression at bay, and eventually her psychiatrist switched her to a very high dose of Paxil, which left her feeling like a zombie. "I was out of it. During a softball game, someone hit a ground ball to me and I just held the ball. I didn't know what to do with it. I told my team I was sorry."

Melissa has struggled with depression ever since. It followed her to college, first to Emerson and then to UMass Dartmouth, and although it did lift somewhat when she became immersed in writing for the UMass newspaper, it never entirely went away. She tried this drug and that drug, but none brought any lasting relief. After graduating, she found a job as an editorial assistant at a magazine, but depression caught up with her there, too, and in late 2007, the government deemed her eligible to receive SSDI because of her illness.

"I have always been told that a person has to accept that the illness is chronic," she says, at the end of our interview. "You can be 'in recovery,' but you can never be 'recovered.' But I don't want to be on disability forever, and I have started to question whether depression is really a chemical thing. What are the origins of my despair? How can I really help myself? I want to honor the other parts of me, other than the sick part that I'm always thinking about.

I think that depression is like a weed that I have been watering, and I want to pull up that weed, and I am starting to look to people for solutions. I really don't know what the drugs did for me all these years, but I do know that I am disappointed in how things have turned out."

Such is Melissa Sances's story. Today it is a fairly common one. A distressed teenager is diagnosed with depression and put on an antidepressant, and years later he or she is still struggling with the condition. But if we return to the 1950s, we will discover that depression rarely struck someone as young as Melissa, and it rarely turned into the chronic suffering that she has experienced. Her course of illness is, for the most part, unique to our times.

The Way Depression Used to Be

Melancholy, of course, visits nearly everyone now and then. "I am a man, and that is reason enough to be miserable," wrote the Greek poet Menander in the fourth century B.C., a sentiment that has been echoed by writers and philosophers ever since.[2] In his seventeenth-century tome *Anatomy of Melancholy,* English physician Robert Burton advised that everyone "feels the smart of it . . . it is most absurd and ridiculous for any mortal man to look for a perpetual tenure of happiness in this life." It was only when such gloomy states became a "habit," Burton said, that they became a "disease."[3]

This was the same distinction that Hippocrates had made more than two thousand years earlier, when he identified persistent melancholy as an illness, attributing it to an excess of black bile (*melaina chole* in Greek). Symptoms included "sadness, anxiety, moral dejection, [and] tendency to suicide" accompanied by "prolonged fear." To curb the excess of black bile and bring the four humors of the body back into balance, Hippocrates recommended the administration of mandrake and hellebore, changes in diet, and the use of cathartic and emetic herbs.[4]

During the Middle Ages, the deeply melancholic person was seen as possessed by demons. Priests and exorcists would be called upon to drive out the devils. With the arrival of the Renaissance in the fifteenth century, the teachings of the Greeks were rediscovered, and physicians once again offered medical explanations for persistent melancholy. After William Harvey discovered in 1628 that blood circulated throughout the body, many European doctors reasoned that this illness arose from a lack of blood to the brain.

Psychiatry's modern conception of depression has its roots in Emil Kraepelin's work. In his 1899 book, *Lehrbuch der Psychiatrie,* Kraepelin divided psychotic disorders into two broad categories—dementia praecox and manic-depressive psychosis. The latter category was mostly comprised of three subtypes—depressive episode only, manic episode only, and episodes of both kinds. But whereas dementia praecox patients deteriorated over time, the manic-depressive group had fairly good long-term outcomes. "Usually all morbid manifestations completely disappear; but where that is exceptionally not the case, only a rather slight, peculiar psychic weakness develops," Kraepelin explained in a 1921 text.[5]

Today, Kraepelin's depression-only group would be diagnosed with unipolar depression, and in the 1960s and early 1970s, prominent psychiatrists at academic medical centers and at the NIMH described this disorder as fairly rare and having a good long-term course. In her 1968 book, *The Epidemiology of Depression,* Charlotte Silverman, who directed epidemiology studies for the NIMH, noted that community surveys in the 1930s and 1940s had found that fewer than one in a thousand adults suffered an episode of clinical depression each year. Furthermore, most who were struck did not need to be hospitalized. In 1955, there were only 7,250 "first admissions" for depression in state and county mental hospitals. The total number of depressed patients in the nation's mental hospitals that year was around 38,200, a disability rate of one in every 4,345 people.[6]

Depression, Silverman and others noted, was primarily an "ailment of middle aged and older persons." In 1956, 90 percent of the first-admissions to public and private hospitals for depression were thirty-five years and older.[7] Depressive episodes, explained Baltimore psychiatrist Frank Ayd Jr., in his 1962 book, *Recognizing the*

Depressed Patient, "occur most often after age thirty, have a peak incidence between age 40 and 60, and taper off sharply thereafter."[8]

Although the manic-depressive patients that Kraepelin studied were severely ill, as their minds were also buffeted by psychotic symptoms, their long-term outcomes were pretty good. Sixty percent of Kraepelin's 450 "depressed-only" patients experienced but a single episode of depression, and only 13 percent had three or more episodes.[9] Other investigators in the first half of the twentieth century reported similar outcomes. In 1931, Horatio Pollock, of the New York State Department of Mental Hygiene, in a long-term study of 2,700 depressed patients hospitalized from 1909 to 1920, reported that more than half of those admitted for a first episode had but a single attack, and only 17 percent had three or more episodes.[10] Thomas Rennie, who investigated the fate of 142 depressives admitted to Johns Hopkins Hospital from 1913 to 1916, determined that 39 percent had "lasting recoveries" of five years or more.[11] A Swedish physician, Gunnar Lundquist, followed 216 patients treated for depression for eighteen years, and he determined that 49 percent never experienced a second attack, and that another 21 percent had only one other episode. In total, 76 percent of the 216 patients became "socially healthy" and resumed their usual work. After a person has recovered from a depressive episode, Lundquist wrote, he "has the same capacity for work and prospects of getting on in life as before the onset of the disease."[12]

These good outcomes spilled over into the first years of the antidepressant era. In 1972, Samuel Guze and Eli Robins at Washington University Medical School in St. Louis reviewed the scientific literature and determined that in follow-up studies that lasted ten years, 50 percent of people hospitalized for depression had no recurrence of their illness. Only a small minority of those with unipolar depression—one in ten—became chronically ill, Guze and Robins concluded.[13]

That was the scientific evidence that led NIMH officials during the 1960s and 1970s to speak optimistically about the long-term course of the illness. "Depression is, on the whole, one of the psychiatric conditions with the best prognosis for eventual recovery with or without treatment. Most depressions are self-limited,"

Jonathan Cole wrote in 1964.[14] "In the treatment of depression," explained Nathan Kline that same year, "one always has as an ally the fact that most depressions terminate in spontaneous remissions. This means that in many cases regardless of what one does the patient eventually will begin to get better."[15] George Winokur, a psychiatrist at Washington University, advised the public in 1969 that "assurance can be given to a patient and to his family that subsequent episodes of illness after a first mania or even a first depression will not tend toward a more chronic course."[16]

Indeed, as Dean Schuyler, head of the depression section at the NIMH explained in a 1974 book, spontaneous recovery rates were so high, exceeding 50 percent within a few months, that it was difficult to "judge the efficacy of a drug, a treatment [electroshock] or psychotherapy in depressed patients." Perhaps a drug or electroshock could shorten the time to recovery, as spontaneous remission often took many months to happen, but it would be difficult for any treatment to improve on the natural long-term course of depression. Most depressive episodes, Schuyler explained, "will run their course and terminate with virtually complete recovery without specific intervention."[17]

Short-Term Blues

The history of trials on the short-term efficacy of antidepressants is a fascinating one, for it reveals much about the capacity of a society and a medical profession to cling to a belief in the magical merits of a pill, even though clinical trials produce, for the most part, dispiriting results. The two antidepressants developed in the 1950s, iproniazid and imipramine, gave birth to two broad types of drugs for depression, known as monamine oxidase inhibitors (MAOIs) and tricyclics, and studies in the late 1950s and early 1960s found both kinds to be wonderfully effective. However, the studies were of dubious quality, and in 1965, the British Medical Council put both types through a more rigorous test. While the tricyclic (imipramine) was modestly superior to placebo, the MAOI (phenelzine) was not. Treatment with this drug was "singularly unsuccessful."[18]

Four years later, the NIMH conducted a review of all anti-depressant studies, and it found that the "more stringently controlled the study, the lower the improvement rate reported for a drug." In well-controlled studies, 61 percent of the drug-treated patients improved versus 46 percent of the placebo patients, a net benefit of only 15 percent. "The differences between the effectiveness of anti-depressant drugs and placebo are not impressive," it said.[19] The NIMH then conducted its own trial of imipramine, and it was only in *psychotically* depressed patients that this tricyclic showed any significant benefit over a placebo. Only 40 percent of the drug-treated patients completed the seven-week study, and the reason so many dropped out was that their condition "deteriorated." For many depressed patients, the NIMH concluded in 1970, "drugs play a minor role in influencing the clinical course of their illness."[20]

The minimal efficacy of imipramine and other antidepressants led some investigators to wonder whether the placebo response was the mechanism that was helping people feel better. What the drugs did, several speculated, was amplify the placebo response, and they did so because they produced physical side effects, which helped convince patients that they were getting a "magic pill" for depression. To test this hypothesis, investigators conducted at least seven studies in which they compared a tricyclic to an "active" placebo, rather than an inert one. (An active placebo is a chemical that produces an unpleasant side effect of some kind, like dry mouth.) In six of the seven, there was no difference in outcomes.[21]

That was the efficacy record racked up by tricyclics in the 1970s: slightly better than inactive placebo, but no better than an active placebo. The NIMH visited this question of imipramine's efficacy one more time in the 1980s, comparing it to two forms of psychotherapy and placebo, and found that nothing had changed. At the end of sixteen weeks, "there were no significant differences among treatments, including placebo plus clinical management, for the less severely depressed and functionally impaired patients." Only the severely depressed patients fared better on imipramine than on a placebo.[22]

Societal belief in the efficacy of antidepressants was reborn with the arrival of Prozac in 1988. Eli Lilly, it seemed, had come up with a very good pill for the blues. This selective serotonin reuptake inhibitor (SSRI) was said to make people feel "better than well." Unfortunately, once researchers began poking through the clinical trial data submitted to the FDA for Prozac and the other SSRIs that were subsequently brought to market, the "wonder drug" story fell apart.

The first blow to the SSRIs' image came from Arif Khan at the Northwest Clinical Research Center in Washington. He reviewed the study data submitted to the FDA for seven SSRIs and concluded that symptoms were reduced 42 percent in patients treated with tricyclics, 41 percent in the SSRI group, and 31 percent in those given a placebo.[23] The new drugs, it turned out, were no more effective than the old ones. Next, Erick Turner from Oregon Health and Science University, in a review of FDA data for twelve antidepressants approved between 1987 and 2004, determined that thirty-six of the seventy-four trials had failed to show any statistical benefit for the antidepressants. There were just as many trials that had produced negative or "questionable" results as positive ones.[24] Finally, in 2008, Irving Kirsch, a psychologist at the University of Hull in the United Kingdom, found that in the trials of Prozac, Effexor, Serzone, and Paxil, symptoms in the medicated patients dropped 9.6 points on the Hamilton Rating Scale of Depression, versus 7.8 points for the placebo group. This was a difference of only 1.8 points, and the National Institute for Clinical Excellence in Britain had previously determined that a three-point drug-placebo difference was needed on the Hamilton scale to demonstrate a "clinically significant benefit." It was only in a small subgroup of patients—those most severely depressed—that the drugs had been shown to be of real use. "Given these data, there seems little evidence to support the prescription of antidepressant medication to any but the most severely depressed patients, unless alternative treatments have failed to provide benefit," Kirsch and his collaborators concluded.[25]

All of this provoked some soul-searching by psychiatrists in their journals. Randomized clinical trials, admitted a 2009 editorial in the *British Journal of Psychiatry,* had generated "limited valid evidence" for use of the drugs.[26] A group of European psychiatrists affiliated with the World Health Organization conducted their own review of Paxil's clinical data and concluded that "among adults with moderate to severe major depression," this popular SSRI "was not superior to placebo in terms of overall treatment effectiveness and acceptability."[27] Belief in these medications' effectiveness, wrote Greek psychiatrist John Ioannidis, who has an appointment at Tufts University School of Medicine in Massachusetts, was a "living myth." A review of the SSRI clinical data had led to a depressing end for psychiatry, and, as Ioannidis quipped, he and his colleagues couldn't even now turn to Prozac and the other SSRIs for relief from this dispiriting news because, alas, "they probably won't work."[28]

There is one other interesting addendum to this research history. In the late 1980s, many Germans who were depressed turned to *Hypericum perforatum,* the plant known as Saint-John's-wort, for relief. German investigators began conducting double-blind trials of this herbal remedy, and in 1996, the *British Medical Journal* summarized the evidence: In thirteen placebo-controlled trials, 55 percent of the patients treated with Saint-John's-wort significantly improved, compared with 22 percent of those given a placebo. The herbal remedy also bested antidepressants in head-to-head competition: In those trials, 66 percent given the herb improved compared to 55 percent of the drug-treated patients. In Germany, Saint-John's-wort was effective. But would it work similar magic in Americans? In 2001, psychiatrists at eleven medical centers in the United States reported that it wasn't effective at all. Only 15 percent of the depressed outpatients treated with the herb improved in their eight-week trial. Yet—and this was the curious part—only 5 percent of the placebo patients got better in this study, far below the usual placebo response. American psychiatrists, it seemed, were not eager to see anyone as having gotten better, lest the herb prove effective. But then the NIH funded a second trial of Saint-John's-wort that had a design that complicated matters for any researcher who wanted to play favorites. It compared Saint-John's-wort to both Zoloft and a placebo. Since the herb causes side effects, such as dry mouth, it would act at the very least as an active placebo. As such, this truly was a blinded trial, the psychiatrists unable to rely on side effects as a clue to which patients were getting what, and here were the results: Twenty-four percent of the patients treated with Saint-John's-wort had a "full response," 25 percent of the Zoloft patients, and 32 percent of the placebo group. "This study fails to support the efficacy of *H perforatum* in moderately severe depression," the investigators concluded, glossing over the fact that their drug had failed this test too.[29]

The Chronicity Factor, Yet Again

The antidepressants' relative lack of short-term efficacy was not, by itself, a reason to think that the drugs were causing harm. After all, most of those treated with antidepressants were seeing their symptoms abate. Medicated patients in the short-term trials were getting better. The problem was that they were not improving significantly more than those treated with a placebo. However, during the 1960s, several European psychiatrists reported that the long-term course of depression in their drug-treated patients seemed to be worsening.

Exposure to antidepressants, wrote German physician H. P. Hoheisel in 1966, appeared to be "shortening the intervals" between depressive episodes in his patients. These drugs, wrote a Yugoslavian doctor four years later, were causing a "chronification" of the disease. The tricyclics, agreed Bulgarian psychiatrist Nikola Schipkowensky in 1970, were inducing a "change to a more chronic course." The problem, it seemed, was that many people treated with antidepressants were only "partially cured."[30] Their symptoms didn't entirely remit, and then, when they stopped taking the antidepressant, their depression regularly got much worse again.

With this concern having surfaced in a few European journals, a Dutch physician, J. D. Van Scheyen, examined the case histories of ninety-four depressed patients. Some had taken an antidepressant and some had not, and when Van Scheyen looked at how the two groups had fared over a five-year period, the difference was startling: "It was evident, particularly in the female patients, that more systematic long-term antidepressant medication, with or without ECT [electroconvulsive therapy], exerts a paradoxical effect on the recurrent nature of the vital depression. In other words, this therapeutic approach was associated with an increase in recurrent rate and a decrease in cycle duration. . . . Should [this increase] be regarded as an untoward long-term side effect of treatment with tricyclic antidepressants?"[31]

Over the next twenty years, investigators reported again and again that people treated with an antidepressant were very likely to relapse once they stopped taking the drug. In 1973, investigators in Britain wrote that 50 percent of drug-withdrawn patients relapsed within six months;[32] a few years later, investigators at the University of Pennsylvania announced that 69 percent of patients withdrawn from antidepressants relapsed within this time period. There was, they confessed, "rapid clinical deterioration in most of the patients."[33] In 1984, Robert Prien at the NIMH reported that 71 percent of depressed patients relapsed within eighteen months of drug withdrawal.[34] Finally, in 1990, the NIMH added to this gloomy picture when it reported the long-term results from its study that had compared imipramine to two forms of psychotherapy and to a placebo. At the end of eighteen months, the stay-well rate was best for the cognitive therapy group (30 percent) and lowest for the imipramine-exposed group (19 percent).[35]

Everywhere, the message was the same: Depressed people who were treated with an antidepressant and then stopped taking it regularly got sick again. In 1997, Ross Baldessarini from Harvard Medical School, in a meta-analysis of the literature, quantified the relapse risk: Fifty percent of drug-withdrawn patients relapsed within fourteen months.[36] Baldessarini also found that the longer a person was on an antidepressant, the greater the relapse rate following drug withdrawal. It was as though a person treated with the drug gradually became less and less able, in a physiological sense, to do without it. Investigators in Britain came to the same sobering realization: "After stopping an antidepressant, symptoms tend to build up gradually and become chronic."[37]

Do All Psychotropics Work This Way?

Although a handful of European physicians may have sounded the alarm about the changing course of depression in the late 1960s and early 1970s, it wasn't until 1994 that an Italian psychiatrist, Giovanni Fava, from the University of Bologna, pointedly announced that it was time for psychiatry to confront this issue. Neuroleptics had been found to be quite problematic over the long term, the benzodiazepines had, too, and now it looked like the antidepressants were producing a similar long-term record. In a 1994 editorial in *Psychotherapy and Psychosomatics,* Fava wrote:

> Within the field of psychopharmacology, practitioners have been cautious, if not fearful, of opening a debate on whether the treatment is more damaging [than helpful]. . . . I wonder if the time has come for debating and initiating research into the likelihood that psychotropic drugs actually worsen, at least in some cases, the progression of the illness which they are supposed to treat.[38]

In this editorial and several more articles that followed, Fava offered a biological explanation for what was going on with the antidepressants. Like antipsychotics and benzodiazepines, these drugs perturb neurotransmitter systems in the brain. This leads to compensatory "processes that oppose the initial acute effects of a drug. . . . When drug treatment ends, these processes may operate unopposed, resulting in appearance of withdrawal symptoms and increased vulnerability to relapse," he wrote.[39] Moreover, Fava noted, pointing to Baldessarini's findings, it was evident that the longer one stayed on antidepressants, the worse the problem. "Whether one treats a depressed patient for three months, or three years, it does not matter when one stops the drugs. A statistical trend suggested that the longer the drug treatment, the higher the likelihood of relapse."[40]

But, Fava also wondered, what was the outcome for people who stayed on antidepressants indefinitely? Weren't they also relapsing with great frequency? Perhaps the drugs cause "irreversible receptor modifications," Fava said, and, as such, "sensitize" the brain to depression. This could explain the "bleak long term outcome of depression." He summed up the problem in this way:

> Antidepressant drugs in depression might be beneficial in the short term, but worsen the progression of the disease in the long term, by increasing the biochemical vulnerability to depression. . . . Use of antidepressant drugs may propel the illness to a more malignant and treatment unresponsive course.[41]

This possibility was now front and center in psychiatry. "His question and the several related matters . . . are not pleasant to contemplate and may seem paradoxical, but they now require open-minded and serious clinical and research consideration," Baldessarini said.[42] Three physicians from the University of Louisville School of Medicine echoed the sentiment. "Long-term antidepressant use may be depressogenic," they wrote, in a 1998 letter to the *Journal of Clinical Psychiatry*. "It is possible that antidepressant agents modify the hardwiring of neuronal synapses [which] not only render antidepressants ineffective but also induce a resident, refractory depressive state."[43]

It's the Disease, Not the Drug

Once again, psychiatry had reached a moment of crisis. The specter of supersensitivity psychosis had stirred up a hornets' nest in the early 1980s, and now, in the mid-1990s, a concern very similar in kind had appeared. This time, the stakes were perhaps even higher. Fava was raising this issue even as U.S. sales of SSRIs were soaring. Prominent psychiatrists at the best medical schools in the United States had told newspaper and magazine reporters of their wonders. These drugs were now being prescribed to an ever-larger group of people, including to more than a million American children. Could the field now confess that these medications might be making people chronically depressed? That they led to a "malignant" long-term course? That they caused biological changes in the brain that "sensitized" a person to depression? And if that were so, how could they possibly be prescribed to young children and teenagers? Why would doctors do that to children? This concern of Fava's needed to be hushed up, and hushed up fast. Early in 1994, after Fava first broached the subject, Donald Klein from Columbia University told *Psychiatric News* that this subject was not going to be investigated.

"The industry is not interested [in this question], the NIMH is not interested, and the FDA is not interested," he said. "Nobody is interested."[44]

Indeed, by this time, leaders of American psychiatry were already coming up with an alternative explanation for the "bleak" long-term outcomes, one that spared their drugs any blame. The old epidemiological studies from the pre-antidepressant era, which had shown that people regularly recovered from a severe depressive episode and that a majority then stayed well, were "flawed." A panel of experts convened by the NIMH put it this way: "Improved approaches to the description and classification of [mood] disorders and new epidemiologic studies [have] demonstrated the recurrent and chronic nature of these illnesses, and the extent to which they represent a continual source of distress and dysfunction for affected individuals."[45] Depression was at last being understood, that was the story that psychiatry embraced, and textbooks were rewritten to tell of this advance in knowledge. Not long ago, noted the 1999 edition of the American Psychiatric Association's *Textbook of Psychiatry*, it was believed that "most patients would eventually recover from a major depressive episode. However, more extensive studies have disproved this assumption."[46] It was now known, the APA said, that "depression is a highly recurrent and pernicious disorder."

Depression, it seemed, had never been the relatively benign illness described by Silverman and others at the NIMH in the late 1960s and early 1970s. And with depression reconceived in this way, as a chronic illness, psychiatry now had a rationale for long-term use of antidepressants. The problem wasn't that exposure to an antidepressant caused a biological change that made people more vulnerable to depression; the problem was that once the drug was withdrawn, the disease returned. Moreover, psychiatry did have studies proving the merits of keeping people on antidepressants. After all, relapse rates were higher for patients withdrawn from the medications than for those maintained on the drugs. "Antidepressants reduce the risk of relapse in depressive disorder, and continued treatment with antidepressants would benefit many patients with recurrent depressive disorder," explained a group of psychiatrists who reviewed this literature.[47]

During the 1990s, psychiatrists in the United States and elsewhere fleshed out the spectrum of outcomes achieved with this new paradigm of care, which emphasized "maintaining" people on the medications. One-third of all unipolar patients, researchers concluded, are "non-responders" to antidepressants. Their symptoms do not abate over the short term, and this group is said to have a poor long-term outcome. Another third of unipolar patients are "partial responders" to antidepressants, and in short-term trials, they show up as being helped by the drugs. The problem, NIMH investigators discovered, in a long-term study called the Collaborative Program on the Psychobiology of Depression, was that these drug-maintained patients fared poorly over the long term. "Resolution of major depressive episode with residual subthreshold depressive symptoms, even the first lifetime episode, appears to be the first step of a more severe, relapsing, and chronic future course," explained Lewis Judd, a former director of the NIMH, in a 2000 report.[48] The final third of patients see their symptoms remit over the short term, but only about half of this group, when maintained on an antidepressant, stay well for long periods of time.[49]

In short, two-thirds of patients initially treated with an antidepressant can expect to have recurrent bouts of depression, and only a small percentage of people can be expected to recover and stay well. "Only 15% of people with unipolar depression experience a single bout of the illness," the APA's 1999 textbook noted, and for the remaining 85 percent, with each new episode, remissions become "less complete and new recurrences develop with less provocation."[50] This outcomes data definitely told of a pernicious disorder, but then John Rush, a prominent psychiatrist at Texas

Southwestern Medical Center in Dallas, suggested that "real-world outcomes" were even worse. Those outcome statistics arose from clinical trials that had cherry-picked patients most likely to respond *well* to an antidepressant, he said. "Longer-term clinical outcomes of representative outpatients with nonpsychotic major depressive disorder treated in daily practice in either the private or public sectors are yet to be well defined."[51]

In 2004, Rush and his colleagues filled in this gap in the medical literature. They treated 118 "real world" patients with antidepressants and provided them with a wealth of emotional and clinical support "specifically designed to maximize clinical outcomes." This was the best care that modern psychiatry could provide, and here were their real-world results: Only 26 percent of the patients even responded to the antidepressant (meaning that their symptoms decreased at least 50 percent on a rating scale), and only about half of those who responded stayed better for any length of time. Most startling of all, only 6 percent of the patients saw their depression fully remit and stay away during the yearlong trial. These "findings reveal remarkably low response and remission rates," Rush said.[52]

This dismal picture of real-world outcomes was soon confirmed by a large NIMH study known as the STAR*D trial, which Rush helped direct. Most of the 4,041 real-world outpatients enrolled in the trial were only moderately ill, and yet fewer than 20 percent remitted and stayed well for a year. "Most individuals with major depressive disorders have a chronic course, often with considerable symptomatology and disability even between episodes," the investigators concluded.[53]

In the short span of forty years, depression had been utterly transformed. Prior to the arrival of the drugs, it had been a fairly rare disorder, and outcomes generally were good. Patients and their families could be reassured that it was unlikely that the emotional problem would turn chronic. It just took time—six to twelve months or so—for the patient to recover. Today, the NIMH informs the public that depressive disorders afflict one in ten Americans every year, that depression is "appearing earlier in life" than it did in the past, and that the long-term outlook for those it strikes is glum. "An episode of major depression may occur only once in a person's lifetime, but more often, it recurs throughout a person's life," the NIMH warns.[54]

Unmedicated v. Medicated Depression

We've now arrived at an intellectual place similar to what we experienced with the antipsychotics: Can it really be that antidepressants, which are so popular with the public, worsen long-term outcomes? All of the data we've reviewed so far indicates that the drugs do just that, but there is one piece of evidence that we are still missing: What does unmedicated depression look like today? Does it run a better long-term course? Unfortunately, as researchers from the University of Ottawa discovered in 2008, there aren't good-quality randomized trials comparing long-term outcomes in antidepressant-treated and never-medicated patients. As such, they concluded, randomized trials "provide no guidance for longer treatment."[55] However, we can search for "naturalistic" studies that might help us answer this question.*

Researchers in the UK, the Netherlands, and Canada investigated this question by looking back at case histories of depressed patients whose medication use had been tracked. In a 1997 study of outcomes at a large inner-city facility, British scientists reported that ninety-five never-medicated patients saw their symptoms decrease by 62 percent in six months, whereas the fifty-three drug-treated patients experienced only a 33 percent reduction in symptoms. The medicated patients, they concluded, "continued to have depressive symptoms throughout the six months."[56] Dutch investigators, in a retrospective study of the ten-year outcomes of 222 people who had

---

* The caveat with the naturalistic studies is that the unmedicated cohort, at the moment of initial diagnosis, may not be as depressed as those who go on drugs. Furthermore, those who eschew drugs may also have a greater "inner resilience." Even given these caveats, we should be able to gain a sense of the course of unmedicated depression from the naturalistic studies, and see how it compares to the course of depression treated with antidepressants.

suffered a first episode of depression, found that 76 percent of those not treated with an antidepressant recovered and never relapsed, compared to 50 percent of those prescribed an antidepressant.[57] Finally, Scott Patten, from the University of Calgary, plumbed a large Canadian health database to assess the five-year outcomes of 9,508 depressed patients, and he determined that the medicated patients were depressed on average nineteen weeks each year, versus eleven weeks for those not taking the drugs. These findings, Patten wrote, were consistent with Giovanni Fava's hypothesis that "antidepressant treatment may lead to a deterioration in the long-term course of mood disorders."[58]

A study conducted by the World Health Organization in fifteen cities around the world to assess the value of screening for depression led to similar results. The researchers looked for depression in patients who showed up at health clinics for other complaints, and then, in a fly-on-the-wall manner, followed those they had identified as depressed for the next twelve months. They reasoned that the general practitioners in the clinics would detect depression in some of the patients but not all, and hypothesized that outcomes would fall into four groups: those diagnosed and treated with antidepressants would fare the best, those diagnosed and treated with benzodiazepines would fare the second best, those diagnosed and treated without psychotropics the third best, and those undetected and untreated the worst. Alas, the results were the opposite. Altogether, the WHO investigators identified 740 people as depressed, and it was the 484 who weren't exposed to psychotropic medications (whether diagnosed or not) that had the best outcomes. They enjoyed much better "general health" at the end of one year, their depressive symptoms were much milder, and a lower percentage were judged to still be "mentally ill." The group that suffered most from "continued depression" were the patients treated with an antidepressant. The "study does not support the view that failure to recognize depression has serious adverse consequences," the investigators wrote.[59]

Next, researchers in Canada and the United States studied whether antidepressant use affected disability rates. In Canada, Carolyn Dewa and her colleagues at the Centre for Addiction and

One-Year Outcomes in WHO Screening Study for Depression

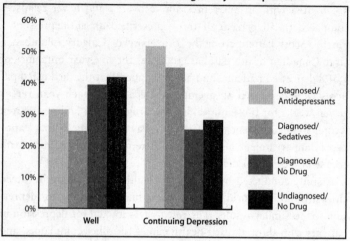

The WHO investigators reported that a higher percentage of the unmedicated group recovered, and that "continuing depression" was highest in those treated with an antidepressant. Source: Goldberg, D. "The effects of detection and treatment of major depression in primary care." *British Journal of General Practice* 48 (1998): 1840–44.

Mental Health in Ontario identified 1,281 people who went on short-term disability between 1996 and 1998 because they missed ten consecutive days of work due to depression. The 564 people who subsequently didn't fill a prescription for an antidepressant returned to work, on average, in 77 days, while the medicated group took 105 days to get back on the job. More important, only 9 percent of the unmedicated group went on to long-term disability, compared to 19 percent of those who took an antidepressant.* "Does the lack of antidepressant use reflect a resistance to adopting a sick role and consequently a more rapid return to work?" Dewa won-

---

* This study powerfully illustrates why we, as a society, may be deluded about the merits of antidepressants. Seventy-three percent of those who took an antidepressant returned to work (another 8 percent quit or retired), and undoubtedly many in that group would tell of how the drug treatment helped them. They would become societal voices attesting to the benefits of this paradigm of care, and without a study of this kind, there would be no way to know that the medications were, in fact, increasing the risk of long-term disability.

The Risk of Disability for Depressed Patients

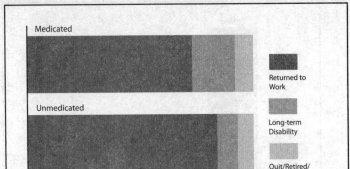

This was a study of 1,281 employees in Canada who went on short-term disability due to depression. Those who took an antidepressant were more than twice as likely to go on to long-term disability. Source: Dewa, C. "Pattern of antidepressant use and duration of depression-related absence from work." *British Journal of Psychiatry* 183 (2003): 507–13.

dered.[60] In a similar vein, University of Iowa psychiatrist William Coryell and his NIMH-funded colleagues studied the six-year "naturalistic" outcomes of 547 people who suffered a bout of depression, and they found those who were treated for the illness were three times more likely than the untreated group to suffer a "cessation" of their "principal social role" and nearly seven times more likely to become "incapacitated." Moreover, while many of the treated patients saw their economic status markedly decline during the six years, only 17 percent of the unmedicated group saw their incomes drop, and 59 percent saw their incomes *rise*. "The untreated individuals described here had milder and shorter-lived illnesses [than those who were treated], and, despite the absence of treatment, did not show significant changes in socioeconomic status in the long term," Coryell wrote.[61]

Several countries also observed that following the arrival of the SSRIs, the number of their citizens disabled by depression dramatically increased. In Britain, the "number of days of incapacity" due to depression and neurotic disorders jumped from 38 million in 1984 to 117 million in 1995, a threefold increase.[62] Iceland reported that the percentage of its population disabled by depression

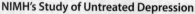

NIMH's Study of Untreated Depression

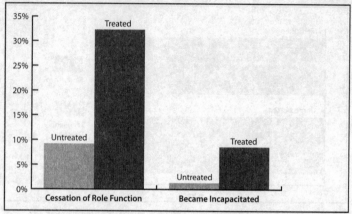

In this study, the NIMH investigated the naturalistic outcomes of people diagnosed with major depression who got treatment and those who did not. At the end of six years, the treated patients were much more likely to have stopped functioning in their usual societal roles and to have become incapacitated. Source: Coryell, W. "Characteristics and significance of untreated major depressive disorder." *American Journal of Psychiatry* 152 (1995): 1124–29.

nearly doubled from 1976 to 2000. If antidepressants were truly helpful, the Iceland investigators reasoned, then the use of these drugs "might have been expected to have a public health impact by reducing disability, morbidity, and mortality due to depressive disorders."[63] In the United States, the percentage of working-age Americans who said in health surveys that they were disabled by depression tripled during the 1990s.[64]

There is one final study we need to review. In 2006, Michael Posternak, a psychiatrist at Brown University, confessed that "unfortunately, we have little direct knowledge regarding the untreated course of major depression." The poor long-term outcomes detailed in APA textbooks and the NIMH studies told the story of *medicated* depression, which might be a very different beast. To study what untreated depression might be like in modern times, Posternak and his collaborators identified eighty-four patients enrolled in the NIMH's Psychobiology of Depression program who, after recovering from an initial bout of depression, subsequently relapsed but did not then go back on medication. Although these patients were not a "never-exposed" group, Posternak could still track their "untreated" recovery from this second episode of depression. Here were the results: Twenty-three percent recovered in one month, 67 percent in six months, and 85 percent within a year. Kraepelin, Posternak noted, had said that untreated depressive episodes usually cleared up within six to eight months, and these results provided "perhaps the most methodologically rigorous confirmation of this estimate."[65]

The old epidemiological studies were apparently not so flawed after all. This study also showed why six-week trials of the drugs had led psychiatry astray. Although only 23 percent of the unmedicated patients were recovered after one month, spontaneous remissions continued after that at the rate of about 2 percent per week, and thus at the end of six months, two-thirds were depression free. It takes *time* for unmedicated depression to lift, and that is missed in short-term trials. "If as many as 85% of depressed individuals who go without somatic treatment spontaneously recover within one year, it would be extremely difficult for any intervention to demonstrate a superior result to this," Posternak said.[66]

It was just as Joseph Zubin had warned in 1955: "It would be foolhardy to claim a definite advantage for a specified therapy without a two- to five-year follow-up."[67]

Nine Million and Counting

We can now see how the antidepressant story all fits together, and why the widespread use of these drugs would contribute to a rise in the number of disabled mentally ill in the United States. Over the short term, those who take an antidepressant will likely see their symptoms lessen. They will see this as proof that the drugs work, as will their doctors. However, this short-term amelioration of symptoms is not markedly greater than what is seen in patients treated with a placebo, and this initial use also puts them onto a problematic long-term course. If they stop taking the medication, they are at high risk of relapsing. But if they stay on the drugs, they will also likely suffer recurrent episodes of depression, and this chronicity increases the risk that they will become disabled. The SSRIs, to a certain extent, act like a trap in the same way that neuroleptics do.

We can also track the rise in the number of people disabled by depression during the antidepressant era. In 1955, there were 38,200 people in the nation's mental hospitals due to depression, a per-capita disability rate of 1 in 4,345. Today, major depressive disorder is the leading cause of disability in the United States for people ages fifteen to forty-four. According to the NIMH, it affects 15 million American adults, and researchers at Johns Hopkins School of Public Health reported in 2008 that 58 percent of this group is "severely impaired."[68] That means nearly nine million adults are now disabled, to some extent, by this condition.

It's also important to note that this disability doesn't arise solely from the fact that people treated with antidepressants are at high risk of suffering recurrent episodes of depression. SSRIs also cause a multitude of troubling side effects. These include sexual dysfunction, suppression of REM sleep, muscle tics, fatigue, emotional blunting, and apathy. In addition, investigators have reported that long-term use is associated with memory impairment, problem-solving difficulties, loss of creativity, and learning deficiencies. "Our field," confessed Maurizio Fava and others at Massachusetts General Hospital in 2006, "has not paid sufficient attention to the presence of cognitive symptoms emerging or persisting during long-term antidepressant treatment. . . . These symptoms appear to be quite common."[69]

Animal studies have also produced alarming results. Rats fed high doses of SSRIs for four days ended up with neurons that were swollen and twisted like corkscrews. "We don't know if the cells are dying," the researchers from Jefferson Medical College in Philadelphia wrote. "These effects may be transient and reversible. Or they may be permanent."[70] Other reports have suggested that the drugs may reduce the density of synaptic connections in the brain, cause cell death in the hippocampus, shrink the thalamus, and trigger abnormalities in frontal-lobe function. None of these possibilities has been well studied or documented, but something is clearly going amiss if symptoms of cognitive impairment in long-term users of antidepressants are "quite common."

Melissa

I interviewed a number of people who receive SSI or SSDI due to depression, and many told stories similar to Melissa Sances's. They first took an antidepressant when they were in their teens or early twenties, and the drug worked for a time. But then their depression returned, and they have struggled with depressive episodes ever since. Their stories fit to a remarkable degree with the long-term chronicity detailed in the scientific literature. I also caught up with Melissa a second time, nine months after our first interview, and her struggles remained much the same. In the fall of 2008, she started taking a high dose of a monoamine oxidase inhibitor, which provided a few weeks of relief, and then her depression returned with a vengeance. She was now considering electroshock therapy, and as we ate lunch at a Thai restaurant, she spoke, in a wistful manner, of how she wished her treatment could have been different.

"I do wonder what might have happened if [at age sixteen] I could have just talked to someone, and they could have helped me learn about what I could do on my own to be a healthy person. I never had a role model for that. They could have helped me with my eating problems, and my diet and exercise, and helped me learn how to take care of myself. Instead, it was you have this problem with your neurotransmitters, and so here, take this pill Zoloft, and when that didn't work, it was take this pill Prozac, and when that didn't work, it was take this pill Effexor, and then when I started having trouble sleeping, it was take this sleeping pill," she says, her voice sounding more wistful than ever. "I am so tired of the pills."

9

The Bipolar Boom

*"I would like to point out that in the history of
medicine, there are many examples of situations
where the vast majority of physicians did something
that turned out to be wrong. The best example is
bloodletting, which was the most common medical
practice from the first century* A.D. *until the
nineteenth century."*
—NASSIR GHAEMI, TUFTS MEDICAL CENTER,
APA CONFERENCE (2008)

At the American Psychiatric Association's 2008 annual meeting in
Washington, D.C., there were press conferences each day, and during the presentations that told of the great advances that lay ahead,
the leaders of the APA regularly urged the reporters and science
writers in attendance to help "get out the message that [psychiatric]
treatment works and is effective, and that our diseases are real diseases just like cardiovascular diseases and cancer," said APA president Carolyn Robinowitz. "We need to work together as partners
so we can get the word out to patients and families." The press had
an important role to play, explained incoming president Nada
Logan Stotland, because "the public is vulnerable to misinformation." She urged the reporters to "help us inform the public that
psychiatric illnesses are real, psychiatric treatments work, and that
our data is as solid as in other areas of medicine."

I scribbled all of these quotes in my notebook, even though it
didn't seem that *Anatomy of an Epidemic* was going to quite fit the
partnership model that the APA had in mind, and then each day I
would go for a stroll in the great exhibit hall, which I always enjoyed. Eli Lilly, Pfizer, Bristol-Myers Squibb, and the other leading
vendors of psychiatric drugs all had huge welcoming centers, where,

if you were a doctor, you could collect various trinkets and gifts. Pfizer's seemed to be the most popular, as the psychiatrists could pick up a new personalized gift each day, their names printed on a mini-flashlight one day and a mobile phone charger the next. They could also win a gift by playing a video game called the *Physician's Race Challenge,* the pace of their virtual self racing toward the finish line governed by how well they answered questions about the wonders of Geodon as a treatment for bipolar illness. After playing that game, many lined up to have their photo taken and stamped on a campaign button that said: "Best Doctor on Earth."

The best-attended events of the conference were the industry-sponsored symposiums. At every breakfast, lunch, and dinner hour, the doctors could enjoy a sumptuous free meal, which was then followed by talks on the chosen topic. There were symposiums on depression, ADHD, schizophrenia, and the prescribing of antipsychotics to children and adolescents, and nearly all of the speakers hailed from top academic schools. The fact that they all were being paid by the drug companies was openly acknowledged, as the APA, as part of a new disclosure policy, had published a chart listing all the ways that pharmaceutical money flowed to these "thought leaders." In addition to receiving research monies, most of the "experts" served as consultants, on "advisory boards," and as members of "speakers' bureaus." Thus, you could see that Joseph Biederman, a psychiatrist at Massachusetts General Hospital in Boston who, during the 1990s, led the way in popularizing juvenile bipolar disorder, received research grants from eight firms, acted as a "consultant" to nine, and served as a "speaker" for eight. His long list of pharmaceutical clients was not all that unusual, and at times, speakers had to update their information in the disclosure guide when they strode to the podium, as they had recently added yet another pharmaceutical company to their list of clients. After Harvard Medical School's Jean Frazier dutifully relayed such information, at a symposium devoted to the merits of putting children on multiple psychiatric drugs, she said, without any apparent hint of irony, "I hope you find my presentation unbiased."

The speakers put on very polished presentations, evidence of the training in public speaking they had received from the pharmaceutical firms. They regularly opened with a joke before moving on to their PowerPoint slides, which were splashed on ballroom screens larger than those found in most theaters. Often the diners were given handheld remote devices to answer multiple-choice questions during the presentations, with dramatic music playing as they keyed in their responses, much as it might during "Final Jeopardy," and when their collective wisdom was splashed on the screens, most usually got the answer right. "You guys are so smart," one speaker said.

Patty Duke provided the 2008 APA meeting with its celebrity patient story. AstraZeneca sponsored her talk, and the company spokesman who introduced her, apparently worried that somehow the audience might miss the point of what she had to say, informed everyone that "the take-home message is that mental illness is diagnosable and recognizable, and that treatment works." Then the Oscar-winning actress, clad in a pumpkin orange dress, told of how she had suffered from undiagnosed bipolar illness for twenty years, during which time she drank excessively and was sexually promiscuous. Diagnosis and medication "made me marriage material," she said, and whenever she speaks to patient groups around the country, she hammers this point home. "I tell them, 'Take your medicines!'" she said. The drugs fix the disease "with very little downside!" The audience clapped loudly at that, and then America's favorite identical cousin offered the psychiatrists a final benediction: "We are beyond blessed to have people like you who have chosen to take care of us and to lead us to a balanced life. . . . I get my information from you and NAMI [National Alliance on Mental Illness], and if I resisted such information, I would deserve to have a net thrown over me. When I hear someone say, at one of my talks, 'I don't need the medication, I don't take it,' I tell them to 'sit down, you are making a fool of yourself.'"

That led to a standing ovation, and so, as I put away my notebook, it seemed certain that this was a meeting where the bottom-line message, no matter where you went, would be quite well controlled. Nearly everything was set up and organized in a way that told of a profession quite confident in its therapeutics, and while I knew that Martin Harrow would be giving a talk on his long-term study of schizophrenia outcomes, he had been allotted only twenty minutes, and his session had been assigned to one of the convention center's smallest rooms. His presentation would be the one exception to the rule, and so I didn't expect to hear anything startling on the Tuesday afternoon that I squeezed my way into a crowded, slightly larger room for a forum titled "Antidepressants in Bipolar Disorder." I figured that the speakers would simply present trial results that justified, in one way or another, the use of these drugs, but soon I was writing furiously away. The discussion, which was led by the top bipolar experts in the country, including the two grand old men of biological psychiatry in the United States, Frederick Goodwin and Robert Post, focused on this question: Do antidepressants *worsen* the long-term course of bipolar disorder? And notably so?

"The illness has been altered," said Goodwin, who in 1990 coauthored the first edition of his text *Manic-Depressive Illness,* which is considered the bible in the field. Today "we have a lot more rapid cycling than we described in the first edition, a lot more mixed states than we described in the first edition, a lot more lithium resistance, and a lot more lithium treatment failure than there was in the first edition. The illness is not what Kraepelin described anymore, and the biggest factor, I think, is that most patients who have the illness get an antidepressant before they ever get exposed to a mood stabilizer."

This was the opening salvo in what turned into an hour-long confessional. Although not all the speakers agreed that antidepressants had been disastrous for bipolar patients, that was the general theme, and nobody questioned Goodwin's bottom-line summary that bipolar outcomes had noticeably worsened in the past twenty years. Antidepressants, said Nassir Ghaemi, from Tufts Medical Center, can cause manic switches and turn patients into "rapid cyclers," and may increase the amount of time they spend in depressive episodes. Rapid cycling, Post added, led to a very bad end.

"The number of episodes, and it's a very rich literature [documenting this], is associated with more cognitive deficits," he said. "We are building more episodes, more treatment resistance, more cognitive dysfunction, and there is data showing that if you have four depressive episodes, unipolar or bipolar, it doubles your late-life risk of dementia. And guess what? That isn't even the half of it. . . . In the United States, people with depression, bipolar, and schizophrenia are losing twelve to twenty years in life expectancy compared to people not in the mental health system."

These were words that told of a paradigm of care that had completely failed, of treatment that made patients constantly symptomatic and cognitively impaired, and led to their early death as well. "Now you just heard that one of the things we do doesn't work very well in the long term," Post practically screamed. "So what the hell should we be doing?"

The confessions came fast and furious. Psychiatry, of course, had its "evidence base" for using antidepressants in bipolar disorder, but, Post said, the clinical trials conducted by pharmaceutical companies "are virtually useless for us as clinicians. . . . They don't tell us what we really need to know, what our patients are going to respond to, and if they don't respond to that first treatment, what should be the next iteration, and how long they should stay on things." Only a small percentage of people, he added, actually "respond to these crummy treatments, like antidepressants." As for recent pharma-funded trials that had shown that bipolar patients withdrawn from antipsychotic medications relapsed at high rates, which theoretically served as evidence that patients needed to take these drugs long-term, those studies "were designed to get relapse [in the placebo group]," Goodwin said. "It isn't evidence that the drug is still needed; it's evidence that if you suddenly change a brain that has adapted to the drug, you are going to get relapse." Added Post: "Right now, fifty years after the advent of antidepressant drugs, we still don't really know how to treat bipolar depression. We need new treatment algorithms that aren't just made up."

This was all much like the moment in *The Wizard of Oz* when the curtain is pulled back and the mighty wizard is revealed as a frail old man. For anyone in the audience who had spent his or her morning in Pfizer's welcoming center, answering video-game questions about the wonders of Geodon for bipolar illness, it must have been crushing. Thirty years earlier, Guy Chouinard and Barry Jones had rattled the profession with their talks on drug-induced "supersensitivity psychosis," and now the profession was being asked to confront the fact that bipolar outcomes were worse today than they had been thirty years earlier, and that antidepressants were a likely culprit. Stimulants, it seemed, could make bipolar patients worse too, and at last Ghaemi told the audience that psychiatry needed to adopt a "Hippocratic" approach to the use of psychiatric medications, which would require them to stop prescribing them unless they had good evidence they were truly beneficial over the long term. "Diagnosis, not druggery," he said, and at one point, several in the audience—which had grown increasingly agitated by this discussion—booed him.

"Can fifty thousand psychiatrists be wrong?" he asked, speaking about the profession's use of antidepressants as a treatment for bipolar disorder. "I think that the answer is yes, probably."

Bipolar Before Lithium

Readers of this book, having come this far in the text, cannot be surprised to learn that outcomes for bipolar disorder have dramatically worsened in the pharmacotherapy era. The only surprising thing is that this failure was so openly discussed at the APA meeting. Given what the scientific literature revealed about the long-term outcomes of medicated schizophrenia, anxiety, and depression, it stood to reason that the drug cocktails used to treat bipolar illness were not going to produce good long-term results. The increased chronicity, the functional decline, the cognitive impairment, and the physical illness—all of these can be expected to show up in people treated with a cocktail that often includes an antidepressant, an antipsychotic, a mood stabilizer, a benzodiazepine, and perhaps a stimulant, too. This was a medical train wreck that could have been anticipated, and unfortunately, as we trace the history of this story, the details will seem all too familiar.

Although "bipolar" illness is a diagnosis of recent origin, first showing up in the APA's *Diagnostic and Statistical Manual* in 1980 (DSM-III), medical texts dating back to Hippocrates contain descriptions of patients suffering from alternating episodes of mania and melancholia. "Melancholia," wrote German physician Christian Vater in the seventeenth century, "often passes into mania and vice versa. The melancholics now laugh, now are saddened, now express numberless other absurd gestures and forms of behaviour." The English mad doctor John Haslam told of how "the most furious maniacs suddenly sink into a profound melancholy, and the most depressed and miserable objects become violent and raving." In 1854, a French asylum doctor, Jules Baillarger, dubbed this illness *la folie à double forme*. It was an uncommon, but recognizable form of insanity.[1]

When Emil Kraepelin published his diagnostic texts, he put these patients into his manic-depressive group. This diagnostic category also included patients who suffered from depression or mania only (as opposed to both), and Kraepelin reasoned that these varied emotional states all arose from the same underlying disease. The splitting of manic-depressive disorder into separate unipolar and bipolar factions got its start in 1957, when a German psychiatrist, Karl Leonhard, determined that the manic form of the illness seemed to run more in families than the depressive form did. He called the manic patients "bipolar," and other researchers then identified additional differences between the unipolar and bipolar forms of manic-depressive illness. Onset occurred earlier in bipolar patients, often when they were in their twenties, and it also appeared that bipolar patients were at somewhat higher risk of becoming chronically ill.

In his 1969 book, *Manic Depressive Illness*, George Winokur at Washington University in St. Louis treated unipolar depression and bipolar illness as separate entities, and with this distinction having been made, he and others began reviewing the literature on manic-depressive illness to isolate the data on the "bipolar" patients. On average, in the older studies, about one-fourth of the manic-depressive group had suffered from manic episodes and thus were "bipolar." By all accounts, this was a rare disorder. There were perhaps 12,750 people hospitalized with bipolar illness in 1955, a disability rate of one in every 13,000 people.[2] That year there were only about 2,400 "first admissions" for bipolar illness in the country's mental hospitals.[3]

As Winokur discovered, the long-term outcomes of the manic patients in the pre-drug era had been pretty good. In his 1931 study, Horatio Pollock reported that 50 percent of the patients admitted to New York State mental hospitals for a first attack of mania never suffered a second attack (during an eleven-year follow-up), and only 20 percent experienced three or more episodes.[4] F. I. Wertham, from Johns Hopkins Medical School, in a 1929 study of two thousand manic-depressive patients, determined that 80 percent of the manic group recovered within a year, and that fewer than 1 percent required long-term hospitalization.[5] In Gunnar Lundquist's study, 75 percent of the 103 manic patients recovered within ten months, and during the following twenty years, half of the patients never had another attack, and only 8 percent developed a chronic course. Eighty-five percent of the group "socially recovered" and resumed their former positions.[6] Finally, Ming Tsuang, at the University of Iowa, studied how eighty-six manic patients admitted to a psychiatric hospital between 1935 and 1944 fared over the next thirty years, and he found that nearly 70 percent had good outcomes, which meant they married, lived in their own homes, and worked. Half were asymptomatic during this lengthy follow-up. All in all, the manic patients had fared as well as the unipolar patients in Tsuang's study.[7]

These results, Winokur wrote, revealed that there "was no basis to consider that manic depressive psychosis permanently affected those who suffered from it. In this way it is, of course, different from schizophrenia." While some people suffered multiple episodes of mania and depression, each episode was usually only "a few months in duration," and "in a significant number of patients, only one episode of illness occurs." Most important of all, once patients recovered from their bipolar episodes, they usually had "no difficulty resuming their usual occupations."[8]

Gateways to Bipolar

Today, according to the NIMH, bipolar illness affects one in every forty adults in the United States, and so, before we review the outcomes literature for this disorder, we need to try to understand this astonishing increase in its prevalence.[9] Although the quick-and-easy explanation is that psychiatry has greatly expanded the diagnostic boundaries, that is only part of the story. Psychotropic drugs—both legal and illegal—have helped fuel the bipolar boom.

In studies of first-episode bipolar patients, investigators at McLean Hospital, the University of Pittsburgh, and the University of Cincinnati Hospital found that at least one-third had used marijuana or some other illegal drug prior to their first manic or psychotic episode.[10] This substance abuse, the University of Cincinnati investigators concluded, may "initiate progressively more severe affective responses, culminating in manic or depressive episodes, that then become self-perpetuating."[11] Even the one-third figure may be low; in 2008, researchers at Mt. Sinai Medical School reported that nearly two-thirds of the bipolar patients hospitalized at Silver Hill Hospital in Connecticut in 2005 and 2006 experienced their first bout of "mood instability" after they had abused illicit drugs.[12] Stimulants, cocaine, marijuana, and hallucinogens were common culprits. In 2007, Dutch investigators reported that marijuana use "is associated with a fivefold increase in the risk of a first diagnosis of bipolar disorder" and that one-third of new bipolar cases in the Netherlands resulted from it.[13]

Antidepressants have also led many people into the bipolar camp, and to understand why, all we have to do is return to the discovery of this class of drugs. We see tuberculosis patients treated with iproniazid dancing in the wards, and while that magazine report was probably a bit exaggerated, it told of lethargic patients suddenly behaving in a manic way. In 1956, George Crane published the first report of antidepressant-induced mania, and this problem has remained present in the scientific literature ever since.[14] In 1985, Swiss investigators tracking changes in the patient mix at Burghölzli psychiatric hospital in Zurich reported that the percentage with manic symptoms jumped dramatically following the introduction of antidepressants. "Bipolar disorders increased; more patients were admitted with frequent episodes," they wrote.[15] In a 1993 practice guide to depression, the APA confessed that "all antidepressant treatments, including ECT [electroconvulsive therapy], may provoke manic or hypomanic episodes."[16] A few years later, researchers at Yale University School of Medicine quantified this risk. They reviewed the records of 87,290 patients diagnosed with depression or anxiety between 1997 and 2001 and determined those treated with antidepressants converted to bipolar at the rate of 7.7 percent per year, which was three times greater than for those not exposed to the drugs.[17] As a result, over longer periods, 20 to 40 percent of all patients initially diagnosed with unipolar depression today eventually convert to bipolar illness.[18] Indeed, in a recent survey of members of the Depressive and Manic-Depressive Association, 60 percent of those with a bipolar diagnosis said they had initially fallen ill with major depression and had turned bipolar after exposure to an antidepressant.[19]

This is data that tells of a process that routinely *manufactures* bipolar patients. "If you create iatrogenically a bipolar patient," explained Fred Goodwin, in a 2005 interview in *Primary Psychiatry,* "that patient is likely to have recurrences of bipolar illness even if the offending antidepressant is discontinued. The evidence shows that once a patient has had a manic episode, he or she is more likely to have another one, even without the antidepressant stimulation."[20] Italy's Giovanni Fava put it this way: "Antidepressant-induced mania is not simply a temporary and fully reversible phenomenon, but may trigger complex biochemical mechanisms of illness deterioration."[21]

With illegal and legal drugs greasing the road to bipolar illness, it is little wonder that a rare disorder in 1955 has become commonplace today. SSRIs took the country by storm in the 1990s, and from 1996 to 2004, the number of adults diagnosed with bipolar illness rose 56 percent. At the same time, psychiatry's steady expansion of diagnostic boundaries over the past thirty-five years has helped fuel the bipolar boom too.

When bipolar disorder was first separated from manic-depressive illness, the diagnosis required a person to have suffered bouts of mania and depression so severe that each type had resulted in hospitalization. Then, in 1976, Goodwin and others at the NIMH suggested that if a person had been hospitalized for depression but not for mania, and yet had experienced a mild episode of mania (hypomania), he or she could be diagnosed with bipolar II, a less severe form of the disease. Then the bipolar II diagnosis was expanded so that it included people who had never been hospitalized for either depression or mania, but simply had experienced episodes of both. Next, in the 1990s, the psychiatric community decided that a diagnosis of hypomania no longer required four days of "elevated, expansive, or irritable mood," but rather simply two days of such moodiness. Bipolar illness was on the march, and with the diagnostic boundaries expanded in this way, researchers were suddenly announcing that it affected up to 5 percent of the population. But even that didn't end the bipolar boom: In 2003, former NIMH director Lewis Judd and others argued that many people suffer "subthreshold" symptoms of depression and mania, and thus could be diagnosed with "bipolar spectrum disorder."[22] There was now bipolar I, bipolar II, and a "bipolarity intermediate between bipolar disorder and normality," one bipolar expert explained.[23] Judd calculated that 6.4 percent of American adults suffer from bipolar symptoms; others have argued that one in every four adults now falls into the catchall bipolar bin, this once-rare illness apparently striking almost as frequently as the common cold.[24]

The Lithium Years

With the psychopharmacology revolution in full bloom during the 1960s, it seemed that every major psychiatric disorder should have its own magic bullet, and once bipolar disorder was separated from manic-depressive illness, psychiatry found a suitable candidate in lithium. Salts made from this alkali metal had been hanging around the fringes of medicine for more than 150 years, and then suddenly, during the early 1970s, lithium was touted as a cure of sorts for this newly identified disease. "I have not found another treatment in psychiatry that works so quickly, so specifically, and so permanently as lithium for recurrent manic and depressive mood states," said Columbia University psychiatrist Ronald Fieve, in his 1975 book, *Moodswing*.[25]

Nature's lightest metal, lithium was discovered in 1818, found in rocks off the Swedish coast. It was reported to dissolve uric acid and thus was marketed as a therapy that could break up kidney stones and the uric crystals that gathered in the joints of people who suffered from gout. In the late 1800s and early 1900s, lithium became a popular ingredient in elixirs and tonics, and it would even be added to beers and other beverages. However, lithium was eventually found to have no uric-acid–dissolving properties, and in 1949, the FDA banned it after it was found to cause cardiovascular problems.[26]

Its revival as a psychiatric drug began in Australia, where the physician John Cade fed it to guinea pigs and observed that it made them docile. In 1949, he reported that he had successfully treated ten manic patients with lithium; however, he neglected to mention in his published article that the treatment killed one person and made two others severely ill. As makers of lithium tonics had long known, lithium can be toxic even in fairly small doses. Both intellectual function and motor movement may become impaired, and if too high of a dose is given, a person may lapse into a coma and die.

As a group, psychiatrists in the United States showed little interest in lithium until bipolar made its appearance as a distinct illness. Prior to that time, Thorazine and other neuroleptics were used to curb manic episodes and thus there was no need for another drug that seemed to have similar brain-dampening effects. But once George Winokur published his book in 1969 dividing manic-depressive illness into unipolar and bipolar forms, psychiatry had a new disease in need of its own antidote.

Since no pharmaceutical company could patent lithium, the APA took the lead in getting the FDA to approve it. Only a few placebo-controlled trials of the drug were ever conducted. In 1985, UK researchers who scoured the scientific literature could only find four of any merit. However, in those studies, lithium produced a good response in 75 percent of the patients, which was much higher than the response rate in the placebo group.[27] The second part of the evidence base for lithium came, as usual, from withdrawal studies. Investigators who analyzed nineteen such trials in 1994 found that 53.5 percent of the patients withdrawn from lithium relapsed, versus 37.5 percent of the lithium-maintained patients. That was taken as evidence that lithium prevented relapse, although the researchers noted that in the few studies where patients had been *gradually* withdrawn from the drug, only 29 percent relapsed (which was lower than the rate among the drug-maintained patients).[28]

All in all, this was not particularly robust evidence that lithium benefited patients, and during the 1980s, several investigators began raising concerns about its long-term effects. They noted that readmission rates for mania in both the United States and the United Kingdom had risen since lithium was introduced, and eventually it became clear why bipolar patients were turning up at hospital emergency rooms with such great frequency.

Various studies found that more than 50 percent of lithium-treated patients would quit taking the drug in fairly short order, usually because they objected to how the drug dulled their minds and slowed their physical movements, and when they did, they relapsed at astonishingly high rates. In 1999, Ross Baldessarini reported that half of all patients relapsed within five months of quitting lithium, even though in the absence of exposure to the drug, it took nearly three years for 50 percent of bipolar patients to relapse. The time between episodes following lithium withdrawal was *seven times shorter* than it was naturally.[29] "The risk of recurrence after discontinuation of lithium therapy . . . especially of mania, is much higher than predicted by a patient's course before treatment or by general knowledge of the natural history of the illness," Baldessarini wrote.[30] Other investigators noted the same phenomenon: "Manic relapse is readily triggered [by lithium withdrawal], probably by the release of supersensitized receptors or membrane pathways," explained Jonathan Himmelhoch from the University of Pittsburgh.[31]

This meant that bipolar patients who were treated with lithium and then stopped taking it ended up "worse than if they had never had any drug treatment," wrote UK psychiatrist Joanna Moncrieff.[32] A Scottish psychiatrist, Guy Goodwin, concluded in 1993 that if patients were exposed to lithium and then quit taking it within the first two years, the risk of relapse was so great that the drug may be "harmful to bipolar patients." The higher hospitaliza-tion readmission rates for bipolar patients since the introduction of lithium "could be explained entirely" by this drug-induced worsen-ing, he said.[33]

Yet the patients who stayed on lithium weren't faring particularly well either. Roughly 40 percent relapsed within two years of their initial hospitalization, and by the end of five years, more than 60 percent fell sick again.[34] There was a core group of good, long-term lithium responders—perhaps 20 percent of those initially treated with the drug—but for the majority of patients, it provided little long-term relief. In 1996, Martin Harrow and Joseph Goldberg, from the University of Illinois, reported that at the end of 4.5 years, 41 percent of the patients on lithium had "poor outcomes," nearly one-half had been rehospitalized, and as a group they weren't "functioning" any better than those not taking the drug.[35] This was a dismal finding, and then Michael Gitlin at UCLA reported similar five-year results for his lithium-treated bipolar patients. "Even ag-gressive pharmacological maintenance treatment does not prevent relatively poor outcome in a significant number of bipolar pa-tients," he wrote.[36]

Although lithium is still in use today, it lost its place as a first-line therapy once "mood stabilizers" were brought to the market in the late 1990s. As Moncrieff wrote in 1997, summing up lithium's record of efficacy: "There are indications that it is ineffective in the long-term outlook of bipolar disorders, and it is known to be associ-ated with various forms of harm."[37]

Bipolar All the Time

There are really two narratives to be dug out of the scientific litera-ture regarding the treatment of bipolar illness with psychiatric drugs. The first tells of lithium's rise and fall as a magic bullet for the disorder. The second tells of how bipolar outcomes have dra-matically worsened during the psychopharmacology era, with experts in the field documenting this at every turn.

As early as 1965, before lithium had made its triumphant entry into American psychiatry, German psychiatrists were puzzling over the change they were seeing in their manic-depressive patients. Patients treated with antidepressants were relapsing frequently, the drugs "transforming the illness from an episodic course with free intervals to a chronic course with continuous illness," they wrote. The German physicians also noted that in some patients, "the drugs produced a destabilization in which, for the first time, hypomania was followed by continual cycling between hypomania and depression."[38]

This was obviously alarming, for the good outcomes in manic-depressive patients arose from the fact that they spent a large part of their lives in symptom-free intervals between episodes, during which time they functioned well. Antidepressants were destroying those asymptomatic interludes, or at least dramatically shortening them. Prior to the drug era, Kraepelin and others reported that only about one-third of manic patients suffered three or more episodes in their lives. Yet studies of bipolar patients in the 1960s and 1970s told of two-thirds who were becoming chronically ill. "The administration of tricyclics may account for artificially high relapse rate estimates," Fred Goodwin wrote in 1979. "Induction of mania, breakdown of otherwise long episodes into multiple ones . . . induction of rapid cycling . . . are some of the mechanisms by which the administration of tricyclics may contribute to an increase in the number of episodes."[39]

Once again, it was becoming apparent that psychiatric medications were worsening the course of a mental illness. In 1983, Athanasious Koukopoulos, director of a mood disorders clinic in Rome, said that he and his colleagues were observing the same thing in their Italian patients. "The general impression of clinicians today is that the course of recurrences of manic-depressive illness has substantially changed in the last 20 years," he wrote. "The recurrences of many patients have become more frequent. One sees more manias and hypomanias . . . more rapid cyclers, and more chronic depressions." Whereas in the pre-drug era rapid cyclers were unknown, 16 percent of Koukopoulos's manic-depressive patients were now in this predicament, and they were suffering an astonishing 6.5

mood episodes annually, up from less than one episode a year prior to being treated with an antidepressant. "It certainly seems paradoxical," he admitted, "that a treatment that is therapeutic for depression can worsen the further course of the disease."[40]

In spite of such information, antidepressants continued to be prescribed to bipolar patients, and even today, 60 to 80 percent are exposed to an SSRI or some other antidepressant. As a result, investigators have continued to document the harm done. In 2000, Nassir Ghaemi reported that in a study of thirty-eight bipolar patients treated with an antidepressant, 55 percent developed mania (or hypomania) and 23 percent turned into rapid cyclers. This antidepressant-treated group also spent "significantly more time depressed" than a second group of bipolar patients who weren't exposed to this class of medication.[41] "There are significant risks of mania and long-term worsening with antidepressants," Ghaemi wrote a few years later, repeating a message that had been uttered many times before.[42] At the University of Louisville, Rif El-Mallakh similarly concluded that antidepressants may "destabilize the illness, leading to an increase in the number of both manic and depressive episodes." The drugs, he added, "increase the likelihood of a mixed state," in which feelings of depression and mania occur simultaneously.[43]

In 2003, Koukopoulos chimed in again, reporting that antidepressant-induced rapid cycling fully abates in only one-third of patients over the long term (even after the offending antidepressant is withdrawn), and that 40 percent of patients continue to "cycle rapidly with unmodified severity" for years on end.[44] Soon, in 2005, El-Mallakh pointed out yet another problem: Antidepressants could induce a "chronic, dysphoric, irritable state" in bipolar patients, meaning that they were almost continually depressed and miserable.[45] Finally, in 2008, in a large NIMH study called the Systematic Treatment Enhancement Program for Bipolar Disorder (STEP-BD), "the major predictor of worse outcome was antidepressant use, which about 60 percent of patients received," Ghaemi noted.[46] The antidepressant users were nearly four times more likely than the non-exposed patients to develop rapid cycling, and twice as likely to have multiple manic or depressive episodes.[47] "This study," wrote Ghaemi, in an editorial that appeared in the *American Journal of Psychiatry,* "may be one more nail in the coffin of antidepressant use in bipolar disorder."

During the past ten years, several large studies have documented just how constantly symptomatic bipolar patients are today. In a long-term follow-up of 146 bipolar I patients who enrolled in an NIMH study in 1978–81, Lewis Judd found that they were depressed 32 percent of the time, manic or hypomanic 9 percent of the time, and suffering from mixed symptoms 6 percent of the time.[48] The bipolar II patients in that study arguably fared even worse: They were depressed 50 percent of the time. "The nature of this deceptively 'milder' form of manic-depressive illness is so chronic as to seem to fill the entire life," Judd wrote.[49] Russell Joffe, at the New Jersey Medical School, reported in 2004 that 33 percent of the bipolar I patients and 22 percent of the bipolar II patients he studied were rapid cyclers, and both groups were symptomatic nearly half of the time.[50] Meanwhile, Robert Post announced that nearly two-thirds of the 258 bipolar patients he studied had four or more episodes per year.[51]

All of these studies showed the same bottom-line result: "It is now well established that bipolar disorders are chronic, with a course characterized by frequent affective episode recurrence," Judd said.[52]

The Harm Done

In a 2000 paper published in the *Psychiatric Quarterly,* a Harvard Medical School psychiatrist, Carlos Zarate, and a psychiatrist who worked for Eli Lilly, Mauricio Tohen, opened up a new line of concern: Bipolar patients today aren't just much more symptomatic than in the past, they also don't function as well. "In the era prior to pharmacotherapy, poor outcome in mania was considered a relatively rare occurrence," Zarate and Tohen wrote. "However, modern outcome studies have found that a majority of bipolar patients evidence high rates of functional impairment." What, they wondered, could explain "these differences"?[53]

The remarkable decline in the functional outcomes of bipolar patients is easy to document. In the pre-lithium era, 85 percent of mania patients would return to work or to their "pre-morbid" social role (as a housewife, for example). As Winokur wrote in 1969, most patients had "no difficulty resuming their usual occupations." But then bipolar patients began cycling through emergency rooms more frequently, employment rates began to decline, and soon investigators were reporting that fewer than half of all bipolar patients were employed or otherwise "functionally recovered." In 1995, Michael Gitlin at UCLA reported that only 28 percent of his bipolar patients had a "good occupational outcome" at the end of five years.[54] Three years later, psychiatrists at the University of Cincinnati announced that only 24 percent of their bipolar patients were "functionally recovered" at the end of one year.[55] David Kupfer at the University of Pittsburgh School of Medicine, in a study of 2,839 bipolar patients, discovered that even though 60 percent had attended college and 30 percent had graduated, two-thirds were unemployed.[56] "In summary," wrote Ross Baldessarini in a 2007 review article, "functional status is far more impaired in type I bipolar patients than previously believed, [and] remarkably, there is some evidence that functional outcome in type II bipolar patients may be even worse than in type I."[57]

The antidepressants, by increasing the frequency of episodes that bipolar patients suffer, naturally reduce their ability to return to work. But, as has become evident in recent years, the problem runs much deeper than that. One of the hallmarks of manic-depressive illness, dating back to Kraepelin, was that once people recovered from their episodes of mania and depression, they were as smart as they had been before they became ill. As Zarate and Tohen noted in their 2000 paper, "studies conducted prior to 1975 found no consistent findings in cognitive deficits in bipolar patients." But lithium was known to slow thinking, and suddenly researchers began reassessing this belief. In 1993, NIMH investigators compared cognitive function in bipolar and schizophrenia patients, and they concluded that while the bipolar patients showed signs of impairment, the deficits were "more severe and extensive in schizophrenia."[58]

This was something of a glass-half-full finding. You could interpret it to mean that cognitive impairment was not that bad in bipolar patients, or, if you remembered the pre-lithium days, you might wonder why these patients were suddenly showing signs of mental decline. But this was just the beginning salvo of a tragic story. Once lithium monotherapy fell from favor, psychiatrists began to turn to "drug cocktails" to treat their patients, and soon investigators had this to report: "Cognitive impairments [that] exist in schizophrenia and affective disorders . . . cannot be qualitatively distinguished with sufficient reliability."[59] The degree of impairment in these two illnesses was suddenly converging, and in 2001, Faith Dickerson at the Sheppard Pratt Health System in Baltimore provided a more detailed picture of that convergence. She ran seventy-four medicated schizophrenia patients and twenty-six medicated bipolar patients through a series of tests that assessed forty-one cognitive and social-functioning variables, and found that the bipolar patients were as impaired as the schizophrenia patients on thirty-six of the forty-one measures. There was "a similar pattern of cognitive functioning in patients with bipolar disorder as compared to those with schizophrenia," she wrote. "On most measures of social functioning, our patients with bipolar disorder were not significantly different from those in the schizophrenia group."[60]

After that, reports of significant cognitive decline in bipolar patients seemed to pour in from psychiatric researchers around the globe—English, Swedish, German, Australian, and Spanish investigators all told of it. The Australians reported in 2007 that even when bipolar patients are only mildly symptomatic, they are "neuropsychologically scarred"—impaired in their decision-making skills, their verbal fluency, and their ability to remember things.[61] Meanwhile, Spanish investigators, after noting that cognitive function in their bipolar and schizophrenia patients "did not differ over time in any test," concluded that both groups suffered from dysfunction in the "prefrontal cortex and temporolimbic structures." They also observed that "the more medications the patients received, the greater the psychosocial functioning impairment."[62]* Finally, English researchers who looked at the daily lives of bipolar patients found that more than two-thirds "rarely or never engaged in social activities with friends," their social lives nearly as impoverished as those diagnosed with schizophrenia.[63]

This was an astonishing convergence in long-term outcomes between the two diagnostic groups, and while the psychiatrists in the United States and abroad who documented it mostly tried, in their discussion of the phenomenon, to ignore the medication elephant in the room, several did confess that it was *possible* that psychiatric drugs were to blame. Conventional antipsychotics, said Zarate in one of his papers, "may have a negative impact on the overall course of the illness."[64] Later, he and Tohen wrote that "medication induced changes may be yet another factor in explaining the discrepancies in recovery rates between earlier and more recent studies." The antidepressants, they noted, might cause a "worsening of the course of illness," while the antipsychotics might lead to more "depressive episodes" and "lower functional recovery rates." Cognitive impairment was a primary reason that medicated schizophrenia patients fared so poorly over the long term, they said, and "it has been suggested that drug side effects may in part explain the cognitive deficits in bipolar disorder patients."[65] Baldessarini, in his 2007 review, also acknowledged that "neuropharmacological-neurotoxic factors" might be causing "cognitive deficits in bipolar disorder patients." Finally, Kupfer threw one more concern into the mix. He detailed all the physical illnesses that now struck bipolar patients—cardiovascular problems, diabetes, obesity, thyroid dysfunction, etc.—and wondered whether "treatment factors such as toxicity from medications" could be causing these devastating ailments, or at least contributing to them.[66]

All of these writers put their concerns into a conditional context,

---

* In this study, the investigators reported that cognitive impairment, from least to most, was as follows, according to drug treatment received: lithium monotherapy, untreated, neuroleptic monotherapy, and then combination drug therapy. However, no details are given about the "untreated" group and whether they had previous exposure to psychiatric medications.

stating that the drugs *might* be causing this mental and physical deterioration in their patients. But it's easy to see that their hesitancy was scientifically unwarranted. Schizophrenia and manic-depressive illness had been diagnostically born as distinct in kind precisely because those with schizophrenia deteriorated cognitively over time, into dementia, while the manic-depressive group did not.* The convergence in outcomes developed once both groups were treated with similar drug cocktails (which usually included an antipsychotic). "The field is witnessing a convergence of pharmacological approaches to the treatment of schizophrenia and bipolar disorder," wrote Stephen Stahl, author of *Antipsychotics and Mood Stabilizers*, in 2005. It was adopting "similar blended treatments for these two disease states."[67] Psychiatric drugs, of course, perturb various neurotransmitter pathways in the brain, and thus once schizophrenia and bipolar patients are on similar drug cocktails, they suffer from similar abnormalities in brain function. The convergence of outcomes in the two groups reflects an iatrogenic process at work: The two groups, apart from whatever "natural" problems they may have, both end up suffering from what could be dubbed "polypharmacy psychiatric drug illness."

Today, bipolar illness is a far cry from what it once was. Prior to the psychopharmacology era, it had been a rare disorder, affecting perhaps one in ten thousand people. Now it affects one in forty (or by some counts, one in twenty). And even though most patients today—at initial diagnosis—are not nearly as ill as the hospitalized patients of the past, their long-term outcomes are almost incomprehensibly worse. In his 2007 review, Baldessarini even detailed, step by step, this remarkable deterioration in outcomes. In the pre-drug

* The schizophrenia patients who routinely deteriorated into dementia were Kraepelin's dementia praecox patients. That group of patients presented with symptoms very different in kind from schizophrenia patients today, and as we saw in Martin Harrow's fifteen-year study, many unmedicated schizophrenia patients recover. Courtenay Harding reported the same thing in her long-term study—many of the unmedicated patients had completely recovered. So it's unclear what percentage of people diagnosed with schizophrenia today, if not continually medicated, would deteriorate cognitively over time.

The Transformation of Bipolar Disorder in the Modern Era

	Pre-Lithium Bipolar	Medicated Bipolar Today
Prevalence	1 in 5,000 to 20,000	1 in 20 to 50
Good long-term functional outcomes	75% to 90%	33%
Symptom course	Time-limited acute episodes of mania and major depression with recovery to euthymia and a favorable functional adaptation between episodes	Slow or incomplete recovery from acute episodes, continued risk of recurrences, and sustained morbidity over time
Cognitive function	No impairment between episodes or long-term impairment	Impairment even between episodes; long-term impairment in many cognitive domains; impairment is similar to what is observed in medicated schizophrenia

This information is drawn from multiple sources. See in particular Huxley, N. "Disability and its treatment in bipolar disorder patients." *Bipolar Disorders* 9 (2007): 183–96.

era, there was "recovery to euthymia [no symptoms] and a favorable functional adaptation between episodes." Now there is "slow or incomplete recovery from acute episodes, continued risk of recurrences, and sustained morbidity over time." Before, 85 percent of bipolar patients would regain complete "premorbid" functioning and return to work. Now only a third achieve "full social and occupational functional recovery to their own premorbid levels." Before, patients didn't show cognitive impairment over the long term. Now they end up nearly as impaired as those with schizophrenia. This all tells of an astonishing medical disaster, and then Baldessarini penned what might be considered a fitting epitaph for the entire psychopharmacology revolution:

> Prognosis for bipolar disorder was once considered relatively favorable, but contemporary findings suggest that disability and poor outcomes are prevalent, despite major therapeutic advances.[68]

The Graphic That Tells It All

We are now coming to the close of our examination of the outcomes literature for the major psychiatric disorders (for adults), and a return to Martin Harrow's fifteen-year study on schizophrenia outcomes brings it to a climactic end. In addition to following schizophrenia patients, Harrow studied a group of eighty-one patients with "other psychotic disorders" that would have been described by Kraepelin as a manic-depressive cohort. There were thirty-seven bipolar and twenty-eight unipolar patients in this group, and the remaining sixteen had various milder psychotic disorders. Nearly half of this group stopped taking psychiatric medications during the study, and thus Harrow really had four groups he followed: schizophrenia patients on and off meds and manic-depressive patients on and off meds. Before we review the results, we can run a quick check of our own thoughts: How should we expect the long-term outcomes of all four groups to stack up?

Go ahead—take out a pencil and jot down what you believe the results will be.

Here are his findings. Over the long term, the manic-depressive patients who stopped taking psychiatric drugs fared pretty well. But their recovery took *time*. At the end of two years, they were still struggling with their illness. Then they began to improve, and by the end of the study their collective scores fell into the "recovered" category (a score of one or two on Harrow's global assessment scale). The recovered patients were working at least part-time, they had "acceptable" social functioning, and they were largely asymptomatic. Their outcomes fit with Kraepelin's understanding of manic-depressive illness.

The manic-depressive patients who stayed on their psychiatric medications did not fare so well. At the end of two years, they remained quite ill, so much so they were now a little bit *worse* than the schizophrenia patients off meds. Then, over the next two-and-one-half years, while the manic-depressive and schizophrenia patients who were off meds improved, the manic-depressive patients who kept taking their pills did not, such that by the end of 4.5

years, they were doing markedly worse than the schizophrenia off-med group. That disparity remained through the rest of the study, and thus here is how the long-term outcomes stacked up, from best to worst: manic-depressive off meds, schizophrenia off meds, manic-depressive on meds, and then schizophrenia on meds.[69]

Schizophrenia, of course, has long been the psychiatric diagnosis with the worst long-term prognosis. It is the most severe mental illness that nature has to offer. But in this NIMH-funded study, two groups of medicated patients fared worse than the unmedicated schizophrenia patients. The results tell of a medical treatment gone horribly awry, and yet they do not come as a surprise. Anyone who knew the history of the outcomes literature in psychiatry, a history that began to unfold more than fifty years ago, could have predicted that the outcomes would stack up in this way.

In terms of contributing to our modern-day epidemic of disabling mental illness, the bipolar numbers are staggering. In 1955, there were about 12,750 people hospitalized with bipolar illness. Today, according to the NIMH, there are nearly six million adults in the

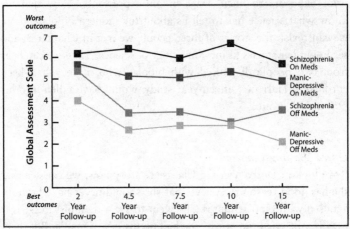

15-Year Outcomes for Schizophrenia and Manic-Depressive Patients

In this graphic, the group labeled "manic depressive" consisted of psychotic patients with bipolar illness, unipolar depression, and milder psychotic disorders. Source: Harrow, M. "Factors involved in outcome and recovery in schizophrenia patients not on antipsychotic medications." *The Journal of Nervous and Mental Disease*, 195 (2007): 406–14.

United States with this diagnosis, and according to researchers at the Johns Hopkins School of Public Health, 83 percent are "severely impaired" in some facet of their lives.[70] Bipolar illness is now said to be the sixth leading cause of medical-related disability in the world, right behind schizophrenia, and in the near future, as more and more people are diagnosed with this condition and put on drug cocktails, we can expect that bipolar will climb past schizophrenia and take its place behind major depression as the mental illness that fells the most people in the United States. Such is the fruit, bitter in kind, born from the psychopharmacology revolution.

Bipolar Narratives

I interviewed more than sixty people with psychiatric diagnoses for this book, and roughly half at some point had been diagnosed as bipolar. Yet of the thirty or so who got that diagnosis, only four suffered from what might be called "organic" bipolar illness, and that is to say they were hospitalized for a manic episode and had no prior exposure to illicit drugs or antidepressants. Now that we know what science has to tell us about the modern bipolar boom, we can revisit the stories of three people we met in Chapter 2, and see how their stories fit into that story of science. Then we can hear from two people diagnosed with bipolar who, if they had been enrolled in Harrow's fifteen-year study, would have fallen into his "off-meds" group.

Dorea Vierling-Claassen

If we look at Dorea Vierling-Claassen's story now, we can see that she has good reason to believe that she should never have been diagnosed with bipolar illness. She went to see a therapist in Denver because she cried too much. She had no history of mania. But then, during finals week in college she had trouble sleeping and grew agitated, and soon she had a bipolar diagnosis and a prescription for a drug cocktail that included an antipsychotic. A bright teenager had been turned into a mental patient, and Dorea would have continued to be one for the rest of her life if she had not weaned herself from the drugs. When I last spoke to her, in the spring of 2009, she was aglow with the blush of motherhood, as she had recently given birth to a son, Reuben. She and Angela were busily raising their children, with Dorea planning shortly to resume her postdoctoral research at Massachusetts General Hospital, the memory of her "bipolar" days receding into an ever-more-distant past.

Monica Briggs

During the time that I worked on this book, Monica Briggs was the one person who, after an initial interview, got off SSDI (or SSI). She secured a full-time position with the Transformation Center, a peer-run organization in Boston that focuses on helping people "recover" from mental illness, and if you parse her medical story, it's easy to see that her return to work was related to a change in her medication.

When we first met, I mentioned to Monica the risk of antidepressant-induced mania, and as she remembered back to her breakdown at Middlebury College, a light went on: "I got manic within six weeks of being put on desipramine," she said. "I'm sure that's what happened to me." After that initial manic episode, she was prescribed a drug cocktail that included an antidepressant, and she spent the next twenty years cycling in and out of hospitals, struggling constantly with depression, manic episodes, and suicidal impulses. Psychiatrists put her on eight or nine different antidepressants, and she also went through a series of electroshock treatments. None of this worked. Then, in 2006, she "casually" stopped taking an antidepressant. For the first time, she was on lithium alone, and bingo—the suicidal feelings went away, as did the depression and mania. That symptom relief is what enabled her to work full-time, and now, as she looks back on the horrible twenty years, she is stunned by what she sees: "I have not yet recovered from the immensity of the likelihood that my roulette game with antidepressants exacerbated my illness."

Steve Lappen

Steve Lappen, who is a leader of the Depressive and Bipolar Support Alliance in Boston, was diagnosed with manic-depressive illness in 1969, when he was nineteen years old. He was one of the four people I interviewed whose manic-depressive illness was "organic" in kind, and on the first day we met, he was in something of a hyper state, talking so fast that I quickly put my pen away and took out a tape recorder instead. "OK," I told him, "fire away."

Raised in Newton, Massachusetts, in a family he describes as dysfunctional, Steve got tagged with the "bad apple" label early in life, both by his teachers at school and his parents at home. "I was disruptive in class," he says. "Every day, during the pledge of allegiance to the flag, I would go sharpen my pencil. I would also get up without provocation and just spin around until I was overcome with dizziness. I would announce that I was a tornado." He struggled with mood swings even as a kid, and at age sixteen, while hospitalized for fainting spells, he jumped out of bed one night and donned a white coat. "I went around to patient rooms and had conversations as if I were a doctor. I was manic."

During his first year at Boston College, he was hit by a bout of severe depression. His was a classic case of true manic-depressive illness, and Kraepelin would have recognized the course his illness took over the next five years. "I didn't take medication," he explains, and while he suffered several bouts of depression, he did well in between those episodes, particularly when he was in a slightly hypomanic state. "When I was feeling well, I would read more, and I would write papers that weren't due for two or three months," he says. "When you are hypomanic, your output is remarkable." He graduated with a double major in philosophy and English, with nearly a straight-A average.

However, in his first year of graduate school at Stony Brook in Long Island, he had a full-blown manic episode followed by a plunge into depression that left him suicidal. It was then that he was put on lithium and a tricyclic antidepressant for the first time. "I didn't have mood swings after that, but instead of having a baseline of functioning normally, I was depressed. I was in a state of depression the entire time I was on the medication. I stayed on it for a year and said, 'No more.' "

Over the next two decades, Steve mostly stayed away from psychiatric medications. He married, had two sons, and divorced. He worked, but skipped from job to job. His life was proceeding down a chaotic path, a chaos that was clearly related to his manic-depressive illness, and yet his life was not marked by vocational disability—he always found work. In 1994, seeking relief from the mood swings that plagued him, he began taking psychiatric medications regularly. He cycled through an endless number of anti-depressants and mood stabilizers, none of which worked for long. Those drug failures led to fourteen electroshock treatments, which in turn left his memory so impaired that when he returned to his job as a financial planner, "I could no longer recognize my best client." In 1998, he was put on the tricyclic desipramine, which promptly turned him into a rapid cycler. "I'd wake up and feel great, completely emancipated from the demon of depression, and then two days later, I am back into depression," he explains. "Two days after that, I'm feeling well again. And there is nothing in my external environment that would account for that change in mood."

He has been on SSDI ever since. The good news is that he hasn't been hospitalized since 2000, and, as he rightly points out, in spite of his constant battle with bipolar symptoms, he leads a productive life. Remarried now, he volunteers as a "reader" for people who are physically disabled, gives talks about bipolar illness to community groups, and is one of the leaders of DBSA Boston. He also has published essays and poetry in various small publications. But when I last spoke to him, in the spring of 2009, he was cycling through multiple mood swings every day, his symptoms apparently continuing to worsen.

"I would say in the main, I have been worse when taking medication. The medication I am taking now is neutral at best. I wish I could clone myself. I could be my own control group in a trial. I'd like to know if I'd be better, the same, or worse without it."

Brandon Banks

Brandon Banks can identify the precise moment he became "bipolar," and while it did involve an antidepressant, there was a series of life events that led up to it. He grew up poor in Elizabethtown, Kentucky, without a father at home, and he has painful memories of sexual abuse, physical abuse, and of a horrible car wreck that killed his aunt, uncle, and another relative. At school, other kids regularly taunted him about a facial birthmark, which so traumatized him that he began wearing a hat pulled low on his head to cover it up. After graduating from high school in 2000, he moved to Louisville, where he went to college part-time and worked nights at United Parcel Service. Soon he noticed that he "wasn't feeling right," and when he went back home, his family doctor diagnosed him with "moderate depression" and prescribed an antidepressant. "I went manic in three days," Brandon says. "It was fast."

His doctor explained that since he'd had that reaction to the drug, he must be bipolar, rather than just depressed. The drug had "unmasked" the illness, which Brandon took as a positive thing. "I'm thinking, This isn't so bad, I could have stayed in the system a long time without getting immediate confirmation that I'm bipolar like that." He was put on a cocktail composed of a mood stabilizer, an antidepressant, and an antipsychotic, and then it hit him. "This was a serious shove into seriousness."

Over the next four years, his psychiatrists constantly changed his prescriptions. "It was like musical chairs with the cocktails," he says. "They would tell me, 'Let's take this drug out and put this one in.' " He took Depakote, Neurontin, Risperdal, Zyprexa, Seroquel, Haldol, Thorazine, lithium, and an endless succession of antidepressants, and as time went on he became a rapid cycler who suffered from mixed states. His medical records also document the development of new psychiatric symptoms: worsening anxiety, panic attacks, obsessive-compulsive behaviors, voices, hallucinations. He was hospitalized several times, and at one point he climbed up on top of a parking garage and threatened to jump off. His ability to concentrate declined so severely that Kentucky took away his driver's license. "What my life became was staying at home all day, getting up in the morning and laying my pills out on the counter, taking them, and then going back to sleep because I couldn't stay awake if I tried. Then I would get up, play some video games, and hang out with my family."

Twenty-four years old, he felt like a total failure, and one day, after a fight with his mother, he moved out and stopped taking his meds. "I deteriorated badly," he recalls. "I wasn't bathing and I wasn't eating." However, as the weeks turned into months, his bipolar symptoms lessened, and "I began to think that it's more like I'm just fucked up," he says. This was a thought that gave him hope, because now there was the possibility of change, and he took off traveling around the South. "I might as well be homeless," he told himself, and that journey ultimately turned into a transformative experience. By the time he returned home, he had sworn off eating meat and drinking alcohol, on his way to becoming a "health freak" who practices yoga. "I came back from that trip, and man, I was on top of it. I felt like a million dollars, and everyone in my family—cousins, relatives, aunts and uncles—said that they hadn't seen me glow like this since I was a kid."

Since then, Brandon has stayed off psychiatric medications. But it hasn't been easy, and the up-and-down nature of his life came into sharp relief during his 2008–2009 year at Elizabethtown Community and Technical College. He enrolled there in January of 2008 with dreams of becoming a journalist and a writer, and in the fall, he became managing editor of the school's newspaper. Under his leadership, the newspaper won twenty-four awards from the Kentucky Intercollegiate Press Association during the 2008–2009 year, and Brandon personally garnered ten such honors for the articles he'd written, including first place in a deadline-writing competition. Incredibly, during those nine months, Brandon racked up other successes too. One of his short stories won second place in a competition and was published in a Louisville weekly; one of his photos was picked as cover art for a literary journal; a short film he shot was nominated for a best documentary award in a local film festival. In May of 2009, his school honored him with its "outstanding sophomore" award. Yet, even during this season of remarkable accomplishment, Brandon suffered several hypomanic and depressive episodes that left him feeling deeply suicidal. "I spent several weekends reading depressive authors with a gun in my hand," he says. "My accomplishments at these moments just seem to make everything worse. It never seems like enough."

That is where matters stood in his life in the summer of 2009. He was thriving and struggling at the same time, and his struggles were such that if psychiatric medications had worked for him the first time, he would gladly have turned to them for relief. "I'm still pretty isolated from other people," he explains. "I stick out because of the birthmark. I'm different. I can't blend in. It becomes an issue with people. But I'm trying to integrate myself more into life. I have more people in my life now than I have had in a long time. I'm starting to make more contacts. I had lunch with a friend the other day. Doing this is hard for me, and that's because it's just not easy for me to deal with people and deal with my emotions. I am trying to get better at it."

Greg

A math and science whiz, Greg, who asked that I not use his last name, was the sort of child who, when he was in junior high, built a Van de Graaff generator from scrounged parts (which included a vacuum cleaner and a salad bowl, to be precise). However, he had a troubled relationship with his parents, and at the start of his senior year, he began to slide into a mad state (and without having used illegal drugs). "I was delusional, very paranoid, and full of anxiety," he says. "I was convinced that my parents were trying to kill me."

Hospitalized for six weeks, Greg was told he was schizoaffective with bipolar tendencies (a "manic-depressive" type diagnosis), and he was discharged on a cocktail composed of two antipsychotics and an antidepressant. But the drugs didn't chase away his paranoid thoughts, and after he was hospitalized a second time, his psychiatrists added a mood stabilizer and a benzodiazepine to the cocktail and told him he needed to give up his scholastic dreams. "They told me I would be on medication for the rest of my life, and that I would probably be a ward of the state, and that maybe, by the time I was twenty-five or thirty, I could think about getting a part-time job. And I believed it, and so I began trying to figure out how to live with the crushing hopelessness that they are telling you is going to be your life."

The next five years passed pretty much as his psychiatrists had predicted. Although Greg entered Worcester Polytechnic Institute (WPI) in Massachusetts, he was so heavily medicated that, he says, "I was living in a haze most of the time. Your mind is just a bag of sand. And so I did really poorly in school. I rarely even left my room, and I was kind of out of touch with reality." He petered along in school for a couple of years, not really making much progress, and then, from 2004 to 2006, he dropped out and mostly stayed in his apartment, smoking marijuana constantly, as "it helped me accept the condition I was forced into." Six feet, five inches tall, Greg's weight went from 255 pounds to nearly 500 pounds. "Finally, I said to myself, this is ridiculous. I'd rather be crazy and have a life than not be crazy and not have a life."

He went for a medical checkup, thinking this would be a first step toward reducing his medications, only to be informed that he needed to stop taking Depakote and Geodon right away, as his liver was shutting down. The abrupt withdrawal induced such physical pain—"sweats, joint and muscle pain, nausea, dizziness," he says—that he didn't even pay attention to whether his paranoia was coming back. But in very short order, he was off all of his psychiatric drugs, except for occasional use of a stimulant, and he had also stopped smoking marijuana. "Honestly, it felt like I was waking up for the first time in five years," he says. "It felt like I had been turned off all those years and had just been rolling through life and I was being pushed around in a wheelchair and finally I had woken up and had gotten back to being myself again. I felt like the drugs took away everything that was me, and then when I went off the drugs, my brain woke up and started working again."

In late 2007, Greg went back to school. We met in the spring of 2009, and after he had told me the story of his bout with mental illness, he showed me around his research laboratory at WPI, where he now spent eighty hours a week, designing and constructing a robot capable of conducting brain surgery inside an MRI. In a few weeks, he would receive an undergraduate degree in mechanical engineering, and since he'd entered a master's program while still doing undergraduate work, later that summer he would receive a master's degree in mechatronics, which is a fusion of mechanical and electrical engineering. The day before my visit, his robotics research had won second prize in a competition that featured 187 entries by graduate students at WPI. Already he had published three papers in academic journals on his project, and in a few weeks he was scheduled to fly to Japan to give a talk about it. He was doing this project under the guidance of a WPI professor, and they expected to conduct animal and cadaver trials with the robot in the fall of 2009. If all went well, clinical trials with humans would begin in two years.

While in his laboratory, Greg showed me the robot and the computer drawings of its circuit boards, which seemed impossibly complex. Naturally, I thought of John Nash, the Princeton mathematician whose inspiring story of recovering from schizophrenia, and doing so while off medication, was told in the book *A Beautiful Mind*. "I still feel that I have some bad habits to get out of and some better habits to get into before I get into the professional life, but I really do feel that I have left that [mentally ill] part of my life behind," says Greg, who has lost more than one hundred pounds. "Honestly, I almost never think of it. I now think of myself as a person who is susceptible to building anxiety, but when I start feeling this anxiety, or start feeling negative about things, I stop and say to myself, 'Are these really reasonable feelings to feel, or is it just insecurity?' I just have to take the time to check myself." He is, he concluded, "pretty optimistic about my future now."

An Epidemic Explained

*"With psychiatric medications, you solve one
problem for a period of time, but the next thing you
know you end up with two problems. The treatment
turns a period of crisis into a chronic mental illness."*
—AMY UPHAM (2009)[1]

There is a famous optical illusion called the young lady and the old
hag, and depending on how you look at it, you see either a beautiful
young woman or an old witch. The drawing illustrates how one's
perception of an object can suddenly flip, and in a sense, the dueling
histories that we have fleshed out in this book have that same curious quality. There is the "young woman" picture of the psychopharmacology era that most of American society believes in, which
tells of a revolutionary advance in the treatment of mental disorders, and then there is the "old hag" picture that we have sketched
out in this book, which tells of a form of care that has led to an
epidemic of disabling mental illness.

The young-lady picture of the psychopharmacology era arises
from a powerful combination of history, language, science, and clinical experience. Prior to 1955, history tells us, the state mental hospitals were bulging with raving lunatics. But then researchers
discovered an *antipsychotic* medication, Thorazine, and that drug
made it possible for the states to close their decrepit hospitals and
to treat schizophrenics in the community. Next, psychiatric researchers discovered *anti-anxiety* agents, *antidepressants,* and a
magic bullet—lithium—for bipolar disorder. Science then proved
that the drugs worked: In clinical trials, the drugs were found to

Young or old woman? If you shift your eyes slightly, your perception of the image will change from one to the other. Courtesy of Exploratorium.

ameliorate a target symptom over the short term better than placebo. Finally, psychiatrists regularly saw that their drugs were effective. They gave them to their distressed patients, and their symptoms often abated. If their patients stopped taking the drugs, their symptoms frequently returned. This clinical course—initial symptom reduction and relapse upon drug withdrawal—also gave patients reason to say: "I need my medication. I can't do well without it."

The old-hag picture of the psychopharmacology era arises from a more careful reading of history and a more thorough review of the science. When we reviewed the history of deinstitutionalization, we found that the discharge of chronic schizophrenia patients resulted from the enactment of Medicare and Medicaid legislation in the mid-1960s, as opposed to from Thorazine's arrival in asylum medicine. As for the drugs, we discovered that there was no scientific breakthrough that led to the introduction of Thorazine and other first-generation psychiatric medications. Instead, scientists studying compounds for use as anesthetics and as magic bullets for infectious diseases stumbled upon several agents that had novel *side effects*. Then, over the course of the next thirty years, researchers determined that the drugs work by perturbing the normal functioning of neuronal pathways in the brain. In response, the brain undergoes "compensatory adaptations" to cope with the drug's mucking up of its messaging system, and this leaves the brain functioning in an "abnormal" manner. Rather than fix chemical imbalances in the brain, the drugs *create* them. We then combed through the outcomes literature, and we found that these pills *worsen* long-term outcomes, at least in the aggregate. Researchers even put together biological explanations for why the drugs had this paradoxical long-term effect.

Those are the dueling visions of the psychopharmacology era. If you think of the drugs as "anti-disease" agents and focus on short-term outcomes, the young lady springs into sight. If you think of the drugs as "chemical imbalancers" and focus on long-term outcomes, the old hag appears. You can see either image, depending on where you direct your gaze.

A Quick Thought Experiment

Just for a moment, before we examine whether we have solved the puzzle that we set forth in the opening of this book, here is a quick way to see the old-hag picture a bit more clearly. Imagine that a virus suddenly appears in our society that makes people sleep twelve, fourteen hours a day. Those infected with it move about somewhat slowly and seem emotionally disengaged. Many gain huge amounts of weight—twenty, forty, sixty, and even one hundred pounds. Often, their blood sugar levels soar, and so do their cholesterol levels. A number of those struck by the mysterious illness—including young children and teenagers—become diabetic in fairly short order. Reports of patients occasionally dying from pancreatitis appear in the medical literature. Newspapers and magazines fill their pages with accounts of this new scourge, which is dubbed metabolic dysfunction illness, and parents are in a panic over the thought that their children might contract this horrible disease. The federal government gives hundreds of millions of dollars to scientists at the best universities to decipher the inner workings of this virus, and they report that the reason it causes such global dysfunction is that it blocks a multitude of neurotransmitter receptors in the brain—dopaminergic, serotoninergic, muscarinic, adrenergic, and histaminergic. All of those neuronal pathways in the brain are compromised. Meanwhile, MRI studies find that over a period of several years, the virus shrinks the cerebral cortex, and this shrinkage is tied to cognitive decline. A terrified public clamors for a cure.

Now such an illness has in fact hit millions of American children and adults. We have just described the effects of Eli Lilly's best-selling antipsychotic, Zyprexa.

A Mystery Solved

We began this book by raising a question: Why have we seen such a sharp increase in the number of disabled mentally ill in the United States since the "discovery" of psychotropic medications? At the very least, I think we have identified one major cause. In large part, this epidemic is iatrogenic in kind.

Now there may be a number of social factors contributing to the epidemic. Our society may be organized in a way today that leads to a great degree of stress and emotional turmoil. For instance, we may lack the close-knit neighborhoods that help people stay well. Relationships are the foundation of human happiness, or so it seems, and as Robert Putnam wrote in 2000, we spend too much time "bowling alone." We also may watch too much television and get too little exercise, a combination that is known to be a prescription for becoming depressed. The food we eat—more processed foods and so on—might be playing a role too. And the common use of illicit drugs—marijuana, cocaine, and hallucinogens—has clearly contributed to the epidemic. Finally, once a person goes on SSI or SSDI, there is a tremendous financial disincentive to return to work.

People on disability call it the "entitlement trap." Unless they can get a job that pays health insurance, they will lose that safety net if they go back to work, and once they start working, they may lose their rent subsidy, too.

However, in this book, we have been focusing on the role that psychiatry and its medications may be playing in this epidemic, and the evidence is quite clear. First, by greatly expanding diagnostic boundaries, psychiatry is inviting an ever-greater number of children and adults into the mental illness camp. Second, those so diagnosed are then treated with psychiatric medications that increase the likelihood they will become chronically ill. Many treated with psychotropics end up with new and more severe psychiatric symptoms, physically unwell, and cognitively impaired. That is the tragic story writ large in five decades of scientific literature.

The record of disability produced by psychiatric medications can be easily summarized. With schizophrenia, in the decade prior to the introduction of Thorazine, roughly 70 percent of people suffering a first episode of psychosis were discharged from the hospital within eighteen months, and the majority didn't return to the hospital during fairly lengthy follow-up periods. Researchers in the post-Thorazine era reported similar results for unmedicated patients. Rappaport, Carpenter, and Mosher all found that perhaps half of those diagnosed with schizophrenia would do fairly well if they were not continuously medicated. But that is now the standard of care, and as Harrow's study showed, only 5 percent of medicated patients recover over the long term. Today, there are an estimated 2 million adults disabled by schizophrenia in the United States, and this disability number could perhaps be halved if we adopted a paradigm of care that employed antipsychotic medications in a selective, cautious manner.

With the affective disorders, the iatrogenic effects of our drug-based paradigm of care are even more apparent. Anxiety used to be viewed as a mild disorder, one that rarely required hospitalization. Today, 8 percent of the younger adults on the SSI and SSDI roles due to a psychiatric disability have anxiety as a primary diagnosis. Similarly, outcomes for major depression used to be good. In 1955, there were only thirty-eight thousand people hospitalized with depression, and the illness could be expected to remit. Today, major depression is the leading cause of disability in the United States for people fifteen to forty-four years old. It is said to strike 15 million adults, and according to researchers at Johns Hopkins School of Public Health, 60 percent are "severely impaired." As for bipolar disorder, an extremely rare illness has become a common one. According to the NIMH, nearly 6 million adults suffer from it today. Whereas 85 percent of those struck by it used to recover and go back to work, now only about a third of bipolar patients function this well, and over the long term those bipolar patients who reliably take their medications end up nearly as impaired as those with schizophrenia who stay on neuroleptics. The Johns Hopkins investigators concluded that 83 percent are "severely impaired."

In sum, there were fifty-six thousand people hospitalized with anxiety and manic-depressive illness in 1955. Today, according to the NIMH, at least 40 million adults suffer from one of these affective disorders. More than 1.5 million people are on SSI or SSDI because they are disabled by anxiety, depression, or bipolar illness, and, according to the Johns Hopkins data, more than 14 million people who have these diagnoses are "severely impaired" in their ability to function in society. That is the astonishing bottom-line result produced by a medical specialty that has dramatically expanded diagnostic boundaries in the past fifty years and treated its patients with drugs that perturb normal brain function.

Moreover, the epidemic continues its march. In the eighteen months it took me to research and write this book, the Social Security Administration released its 2007 reports for its SSI and SSDI programs, and the numbers were as expected. There were 401,255 children and adults under sixty-five years old added to the SSI and SSDI rolls in 2007 because of a psychiatric disability. Imagine a large auditorium filling up *every day* with 250 children and 850 adults newly disabled by mental illness, and you get a visual sense of the horrible toll exacted by this epidemic.

Physical Illness, Cognitive Impairment, and Early Death

Fleshing out the nature of a disease usually involves identifying all the symptoms that may develop, and then following their course over time. In the previous chapters, we mostly focused on studies that showed that psychiatric medications worsen target symptoms over the long run, and only briefly noted that the drugs may cause physical problems, emotional numbing, and cognitive impairment. This is also a form of care that leads to early death. The seriously mentally ill are now dying fifteen to twenty-five years earlier than normal, with this problem of early death having become much more pronounced in the past fifteen years.[2] They are dying from cardiovascular ailments, respiratory problems, metabolic illnesses, diabetes, kidney failure, and so forth—the physical ailments tend to pile up as people stay on antipsychotics (or drug cocktails) for years on end.[3]

Here are three stories that bear witness to these various long-term risks.

Amy Upham

Amy Upham lives in a small one-bedroom apartment in Buffalo, and as I enter the living room, she points to a table cluttered with papers. "This is me on psychiatric drugs," she says and hands me a stack of medical documents. They tell of a drug-induced swelling of the brain, faltering kidneys, a swollen liver, a swollen gallbladder, thyroid problems, gastritis, and cognitive abnormalities. A little over five feet tall, with frizzy reddish brown hair, Amy, who is thirty years old, weighs ninety pounds. She squeezes a fold of loose skin near her elbow, the muscle underneath having wasted away. "This is like what you see with heroin users."

Amy first took a psychiatric medication at age sixteen when she contracted Lyme disease and suffered a bout of depression. Twelve years later, she was still on antidepressants, and as she reviews that history, she identifies several instances when the drugs stirred hypomanic episodes and worsened her obsessive-compulsive behaviors. Finally, in 2007, she decided to gradually wean herself from the two-drug combo she was taking, and at first, it went well. However, at the time, she was working for the county mental health department as an advocate for the mentally ill, and eventually someone anonymously informed her bosses that she was going off her medication. This went against what the agency preached, and it all ended with Amy out of a job and paranoid that someone was stalking her. "I had a nervous breakdown," she says. "I went into the hospital to hide."

This was the first time Amy had ever been hospitalized, and she was immediately put on a cocktail that included lithium. Within a few months, her endocrine system began to fail. Her menstrual cycle ceased, her thyroid went haywire, and an EEG revealed that her brain was swollen. Then her kidneys started shutting down. She had to abruptly stop taking the lithium, and that triggered a manic episode. Doctors put her on Ativan to counter the mania, but that drug stirred feelings of horrible rage and left her feeling suicidal. Months passed, and in December 2008, she checked herself into a psych hospital, where she was diagnosed with Ativan toxicity. "I've never seen a drug fuck up a person like Ativan fucks you up," a nurse told her. The hospital switched her from Ativan to Klonopin and prescribed Abilify, which triggered a seizure. Next a doctor discovered something wrong with her heart, which appeared to be related to the Klonopin, and so Amy was put back on Ativan. "Now I start hallucinating for the first time in my life," she says. "I was pacing uncontrollably and crawling out of my skin." Other drug-related complications ensued, and on February 24, 2009, Amy moved into a shelter on the hospital grounds, her thoughts now so scattered that a nurse wondered "if early Alzheimer's runs in the family."

Remarkably, much of that story is documented in the sheaf of papers that Amy has given me. She spent the last four months trying to get off the Ativan, but every time she dropped to a lower dose, she suffered fits of rage and something akin to delirium. "I am feeling scared," she says, as I hand the papers back to her. "The withdrawals are really bad and I live alone. I'm in a constant state of panic, anxiety, and I have some agoraphobia. It's not safe."

Rachel Klein

When I first met Rachel Klein in the spring of 2008, she hobbled into my office with a cane and a service dog by her side, which flopped by her feet while we spoke. She was not yet forty years old, but very quickly she rewound the clock for me, and soon she was telling of a bright fall day in 1984. Only sixteen years old, she was entering the Massachusetts Institute of Technology, a child prodigy with an IQ of 173 and her ears ringing with predictions that one day she would win a Nobel Prize. "I arrived on campus with a teddy bear sticking out of my backpack," she says, smiling slightly at the memory. "That's how ill-equipped emotionally I was."

Rachel's emotional crash at MIT got under way at the end of her sophomore year, when she became involved with an older student who was "totally psychotic" and she began using illicit drugs—Ecstasy, acid, mushrooms, and nitrous oxide. Her sense of self began to crumble, and after a summer of talk therapy left her more confused than ever, she was hospitalized for psychotic depression. When she was released, she had prescriptions for an antipsychotic, an antidepressant, and a benzodiazepine (Xanax). "None of those drugs helped me," she says. "They numbed me out, and trying to get off Xanax was a disaster. That is the evilest drug ever. It is so addictive, and all of the symptoms that caused you to go into the hospital in the first place get one thousand times worse when you try to go off it."

Although Rachel eventually graduated from MIT and was accepted into an M.D.-Ph.D. program at the University of Colorado, she began cycling in and out of hospitals; her crash at MIT transformed into a case of chronic mental illness. "They told me I was hopeless, and that I would never get better," she recalls. She enjoyed a period of stability from 1995 to 2001, when she worked as an assistant house manager at a group home in Boston, but then her brother died suddenly and her psychological problems flared up anew. Her psychiatrist took her off Risperdal and switched her to high doses of Geodon and Effexor, and he gave her an injection of another psychiatric medication as well.

"I had a severe serotonergic reaction, a toxic reaction," Rachel says, shaking her head at the memory. "It caused vasoconstriction in my brain, and this caused brain damage. I ended up in a wheel-chair, and I couldn't think, speak, or walk. Those centers of the brain need a lot of juice."

Since then, her life has had its ups and downs. She takes comfort in her volunteer work with M-Power, the Boston peer advocacy group, and in the spring of 2008, she was working sixteen hours a week for Advocates, Inc., which provides services to the deaf. But she also has battled ovarian cancer, and it's possible that illness was related to the psychiatric medications. She does find such drugs use-ful today, but when she looks back at her life, she sees a paradigm of care that utterly failed her. "It's really a travesty," she says.

Scott Sexton

In the spring of 2005, Scott Sexton received his MBA from Rice University. A bright future lay ahead at that moment, but then he broke up with the woman he had intended to marry, and he was hospitalized for depression. This was his second bout of major de-pression (he'd suffered a first episode five years earlier, when his par-ents divorced), and since Scott's father had suffered from bipolar illness, he was now diagnosed with that disorder. He was put on a cocktail that included Zyprexa.

That fall, he began working as a consultant for Deloitte, the big accounting firm. Although his first few months on the job went fine, by early 2006 he was sleeping twelve to sixteen hours a day, zonked out by the Zyprexa. He soon needed another pill to get up in the morning, and he began "putting on weight like gangbusters," his mother, Kaye, recalls. "He was five feet, ten inches tall and he went from 185 pounds to 250 pounds. He had a beer belly, and his cheeks looked like he was a chipmunk. We knew that Zyprexa caused weight gain, and he was alarmed, and so was I."

By the fall of 2006, Scott was sleeping so much that on weekends he wouldn't get up until the afternoon. He stopped going into the office and told Deloitte he was working from home. On Thanks-giving, he called his mother to tell her that he was suffering severe stomach pains, and the next day he was admitted to St. Luke's

Episcopal Hospital in Houston. His mother flew in from Midland. "Scott is beet red, he's sweating, and his hands are so swollen that they have trouble getting his ring off. He is burning up, and his [laboratory] tests are wacko. They are off the wall. His cholesterol is sky-high. His triglycerides are off the charts."

Scott's pancreas was shutting down. Zyprexa was known to cause pancreatitis, but the doctors at St. Luke's didn't connect the dots. They kept Scott on that drug until his death on December 7. "I had always told him to take his meds," his mother says. "I said, 'Scott, if I ever find out you are off your meds, I will come to Houston and shoot you.' That's what I said to him. And here he is doing everything he thinks he needs to do to be functional in our society, to be a productive member of society, and it kills him."

The Epidemic Spreads to Children

*"For many parents and families, the experience [of
having a child diagnosed with a mental illness] can be
a disaster; we must say that."*
— E. JANE COSTELLO, PROFESSOR OF PSYCHIATRY AT
DUKE UNIVERSITY (2006)[1]

The prescribing of psychiatric drugs to children and adolescents is a
recent phenomenon, as relatively few youth were medicated prior to
1980, and so as we investigate this story, we have an opportunity to
put the thesis of this book to a second test. Do we find, in the scientific literature and in societal data, that the medicating of children and
teenagers is doing more harm than good? Is it putting many children,
who initially may be struggling with a relatively minor problem—a
disinterest in school, or a bout of sadness—onto a path that leads to
lifelong disability? One of the principles of science is that the results from an experiment should be replicable, and in essence the
medicating of children makes for a second experiment. First we
medicated adults diagnosed with mental illness, and as we saw in the
previous chapters, that did not lead to good long-term outcomes.
Next, over the past thirty years, we diagnosed children and adolescents with various disorders and put them on psychiatric drugs, and
now we can see if the results this second time around are the same.

I realize that this frames our investigation of the medicating
of children in a rather cold, analytical way, given the frightening
possibility at stake here. If the outcomes are the same in children
and teenagers as in adults, then the prescribing of psychiatric drugs
to millions of American youth is causing harm on an almost

unfathomable scale. But that possibility lends itself to an emotional review of the medical literature, which is precisely why we are going to conduct our inquiry in the most dispassionate manner possible. We need the facts to speak for themselves.

The story of progress that psychiatry tells about the medicating of children is slightly different in kind from the one it tells about its advances in care for adults. In 1955, when Thorazine arrived, there were hundreds of thousands of adults in mental hospitals, and they were diagnosed with illnesses that had a recognizable past. But when the psychopharmacology era began, very few children were diagnosed as "mentally ill." There were bullies and goof-offs in elementary schools, but they were not diagnosed with attention-deficit/ hyperactivity disorder (ADHD), as that diagnosis had yet to be born. There were moody and emotionally volatile teenagers, but society's expectation was that they would grow up into more-or-less normal adults. However, once psychiatry began treating children with psychotropic medications, it rethought that view of childhood. The story that psychiatry now tells is that during the past fifty years it *discovered* that children regularly suffer from mental illnesses, which are said to be biological in kind. First psychiatry fleshed out ADHD as an identifiable disease, and then it determined that major depression and bipolar illness regularly struck children and adolescents. Here's how Harvard Medical School psychiatrist Ronald Kessler summed up this "history" in 2001:

> Although epidemiological studies of child and adolescent mood disorders have been carried out for many years, progress long was hampered by two misconceptions: that mood disorders are rare before adulthood and that mood disturbance is a normative and self-limiting aspect of child and adolescent development. Research now makes it clear that neither of these beliefs is true. Depression, mania, and mania-like symptoms are all comparatively common among children and adolescents in the general population."[2]

Illnesses that used to go undetected, it seems, have now been identified. The second part of this story of scientific progress tells of how psychiatric medications are both helpful and necessary. Millions of children who used to suffer in silence are now getting treatment that helps them thrive. Indeed, the story now emerging in pediatric psychiatry is that psychotropic medications help create healthy brains. In his 2006 book *Child and Adolescent Psychopharmacology Made Simple,* psychiatrist John O'Neal explained to readers why it was so essential that children with mental illness be treated with medication:

> Increasing evidence shows that some psychiatric disorders are subject to progressive neurobiological impairment if they go untreated. . . . Toxic levels of neurotransmitters, such as glutamates, or stress hormones, such as cortisol, may damage neural tissue or interfere with normal pathways of neuromaturation. Pharmacological treatment of those disorders may be not only successful in improving symptoms, but also neuroprotective (in other words, medical treatments may either protect against brain damage or promote normal neuromaturation)."[3]

If this is true, psychiatry has indeed made a great leap ahead in the past thirty years. The field has learned to diagnose brain illnesses in children that used to go unnoticed, and its "neuroprotective" drugs now turn them into normal adults.

The Rise of ADHD

Although attention-deficit disorder did not show up in psychiatry's *Diagnostic and Statistical Manual* until 1980, the field likes to point out that it didn't just appear out of thin air. This is a disorder that traces its medical roots back to 1902. That year, Sir George Frederick Still, a British pediatrician, published a series of lectures on twenty children who were of normal intelligence but "exhibited violent outbursts, wanton mischievousness, destructiveness, and a lack of responsiveness to punishment."[4] Moreover, he reasoned that their bad behavior arose from a biological problem (as opposed to bad parenting). Children with known diseases—epilepsy, brain tumors, or meningitis—were often aggressively defiant, and thus Still figured that these twenty children suffered from "minimal brain dysfunction," even though there was no obvious illness or trauma that had caused it.

Over the next fifty years, a handful of others advanced the notion that hyperactivity was a marker for brain injury. Children who recovered from encephalitis lethargica, a viral epidemic that swept around the globe from 1917 to 1928, often exhibited antisocial behaviors and severe emotional swings, leading pediatricians to conclude that the illness had caused mild brain damage, even though the nature of that damage couldn't be identified. In 1947, Alfred Strauss, who was the director of a school for disturbed youth in Racine, Wisconsin, called his extremely hyperactive students "normal brain injured children."[5] Psychiatry's first *Diagnostic and Statistical Manual,* published in 1952, said such children suffered from an "organic brain syndrome."

The notion that stimulants might be beneficial for such children arose in 1937, when Charles Bradley gave a newly synthesized amphetamine, Benzedrine, to hyperactive children who complained of headaches. Although the drug didn't cure their head pain, Bradley reported that it "subdued" the children and helped them concentrate better on their schoolwork. The children dubbed Benzedrine the "arithmetic pill."[6] Although his report was mostly forgotten for the next twenty years, in 1956 Ciba-Geigy brought Ritalin (methylphenidate) to market as a treatment for narcolepsy, touting it as a "safe" alternative to amphetamines, and physicians at Johns Hopkins University School of Medicine, who were aware of Bradley's findings, soon deemed this new drug useful for quieting "disturbed" children who were thought to be suffering from a "brain damage syndrome."[7]

There was no great rush by psychiatrists during the 1960s to prescribe Ritalin to fidgety children who went to regular schools. At that time, there was a sense that psychoactive drugs, because of their many risks, should be administered only to hospitalized children, or children in residential facilities. The population of children so hyperactive that they might be diagnosed with "organic brain dysfunction" was small. However, psychiatry's use of Ritalin slowly began to climb during the 1970s, such that by the end of the decade perhaps 150,000 children in the United States were taking the drug. Then, in 1980, the field published a third edition of its *Diagnostic and Statistical Manual* (DSM-III), and it identified "attention-deficit disorder" as a disease for the first time. The cardinal symptoms were "hyperactivity," "inattention," and "impulsivity," and given that many children fidget in their seats and have trouble paying attention in school, the diagnosis of ADD began to take off. In 1987, psychiatry further loosened the diagnostic boundaries, renaming it attention-deficit/hyperactivity disorder in a revised edition of DSM-III. Next, Ciba-Geigy helped fund Children and Adults with Attention Deficit Hyperactivity Disorder (CHADD), a "patient-support group" that immediately began promoting public awareness of this "disease." Finally, in 1991, CHADD successfully lobbied Congress to include ADHD as a disability that would be covered by the Individuals with Disabilities Education Act. Children diagnosed with ADHD were now eligible for special services, which were to be funded with federal money, and schools regularly began identifying children who seemed to have this condition. As the *Harvard Review of Psychiatry* noted in 2009, even today the diagnosis of ADHD arises primarily from teacher complaints, as "only a minority of children with the disorder exhibit symptoms during a physician's office visit."[8]

Suddenly, ADHD children could be found in every classroom. The number of children so diagnosed rose to nearly 1 million in 1990, and more than doubled over the next five years. Today, perhaps 3.5 million American children take a stimulant for ADHD, with the Centers for Disease Control reporting in 2007 that one in every twenty-three American children four to seventeen years old is so medicated. This prescribing practice is mostly a U.S. phenomenon—children here consume three times the quantity of stimulants consumed by the rest of the world's children combined.

Although the public often hears that research has shown that ADHD is a "brain disease," the truth is that its etiology remains unknown. "Attempts to define a biological basis for ADHD have been consistently unsuccessful," wrote pediatric neurologist Gerald

Golden in 1991. "The neuroanatomy of the brain, as demonstrated by imaging studies, is normal. No neuropathologic substrate has been demonstrated."[9] Seven years later, a panel of experts convened by the National Institutes of Health reiterated this same point: "After years of clinical research and experience with ADHD, our knowledge about the cause or causes of ADHD remains largely speculative."[10] During the 1990s, CHADD advised the public that children with ADHD suffered from a chemical imbalance, characterized by an underactive dopamine system, but that was simply a drug-marketing claim. Ritalin and other stimulants increase dopamine levels in the synaptic cleft, and thus CHADD was attempting to make it seem that such drugs "normalized" brain chemistry, but, as the American Psychiatric Press's 1997 *Textbook of Neuropsychiatry* confessed, "efforts to identify a selective neurochemical imbalance [in ADHD children] have been disappointing."[11]

So we see in this history that nothing new was discovered that told of a "mental illness" called ADHD. There was a long record of speculation within medicine that extremely hyperactive children suffered from brain dysfunction of some kind, which was certainly a reasonable thought, but the nature of that dysfunction was never discerned, and then, in 1980, psychiatry simply created, with a stroke of its pen in DSM-III, a dramatically expanded definition of "hyperactivity." The fidgety seven-year-old boy who might have been dubbed a "goof-off" in 1970 was now suffering from a psychiatric disorder.

Given that the biology of ADHD remains unknown, it is fair to say that Ritalin and other ADHD drugs "work" by perturbing neurotransmitter systems. Ritalin could best be described as a dopamine reuptake inhibitor. At a therapeutic dose, it blocks 70 percent of the "transporters" that remove dopamine from the synaptic cleft and bring it back into the presynaptic neuron. Cocaine acts on the brain in the same way. However, methylphenidate clears much more slowly from the brain than cocaine does, and thus it blocks dopamine reuptake for hours, as opposed to cocaine's relatively brief disruption of this function.*

---

* The fact that cocaine is so short-acting is why it is more addictive than methylphenidate, for as soon as it leaves the brain, the addict may want to

In response to methylphenidate, the child's brain goes through a series of compensatory adaptations. Dopamine is now remaining in the synaptic cleft too long, and so the child's brain dials down its dopamine machinery. The density of dopamine receptors on the postsynaptic neurons declines. At the same time, the amount of dopamine metabolites in the cerebrospinal fluid drops, evidence that the presynaptic neurons are releasing less of it. Ritalin also acts on serotonin and norepinephrine neurons, and that causes similar compensatory changes in those two pathways. Receptor densities for serotonin and norepinephrine decline, and the output of those two chemicals by presynaptic neurons is altered as well. The child's brain is now operating, as Steven Hyman said, in a manner that is "qualitatively as well as quantitatively different from the normal state."[12]

Now we can turn our attention to the outcomes data. Does this treatment help children diagnosed with ADHD over the long term? What does the scientific literature show?

Passive, Sitting Still, and Alone

Ritalin and other ADHD drugs do reliably change a child's behavior, and in his 1937 report, Charles Bradley set the stage for the efficacy story that eventually emerged: "Fifteen of the thirty children responded to Benzedrine by becoming distinctly subdued in their emotional responses. Clinically in all cases this was an improvement from the social viewpoint."[13] Ritalin, which the FDA approved for use in children in 1961, was found to have a similar subduing effect. In a 1978 double-blind study, Ohio State University psychologist Herbert Rie studied twenty-eight "hyperactive" children for three months, half of whom were prescribed methylphenidate. Here is what he wrote:

---

experience again the "rush" that comes when dopaminergic pathways are first sent into a hyperactive state.

Children who were retrospectively confirmed to have been on active drug treatment appeared, at the times of evaluation, distinctly more bland or "flat" emotionally, lacking both the age-typical variety and frequency of emotional expression. They responded less, exhibited little or no initiative or spontaneity, offered little indication of either interest or aversion, showed virtually no curiosity, surprise, or pleasure, and seemed devoid of humor. Jocular comments and humorous situations passed unnoticed. In short, while on active drug treatment, the children were relatively but unmistakably affectless, humorless, and apathetic.[14]

Numerous investigators reported similar observations. Children on Ritalin show "a marked drug-related increase in solitary play and a corresponding reduction in their initiation of social interactions," announced Russell Barkley, a psychologist at the Medical College of Wisconsin, in 1978.[15] This drug, observed Bowling Green State University psychologist Nancy Fiedler, reduced a child's "curiosity about the environment."[16] At times, the medicated child "loses his sparkle," wrote Canadian pediatrician Till Davy in 1989.[17] Children treated with a stimulant, concluded a team of UCLA psychologists in 1993, often become "passive, submissive" and "socially withdrawn."[18] Some children on the drug "seem zombie-like," noted psychologist James Swanson, director of an ADHD center at the University of California, Irvine.[19] Stimulants, explained the editors of the *Oxford Textbook of Clinical Psychophamacology and Drug Therapy*, curb hyperactivity by "reducing the number of behavioral responses."[20]

All of these reports told the same story. On Ritalin, a student who previously had been an annoyance in the classroom, fidgeting too much in his or her chair or talking to a nearby classmate while the teacher scribbled on the blackboard, would be stilled. The student wouldn't move around as much and wouldn't engage as much socially with his or her peers. If given a task like answering arithmetic problems, the student might focus intently on it. Charles Bradley thought this change in behavior was "an improvement from the social viewpoint," and it is that perspective that shows up in efficacy trials of Ritalin and other ADHD drugs. Teachers and other observers fill out rating instruments that view a reduction in the child's movements and engagement with others as positive, and when the results are tabulated, 70 to 90 percent of the children are reported to be "good responders" to ADHD medications. These drugs, NIMH investigators wrote in 1995, are highly effective in "dramatically reducing a range of core ADHD symptoms such as task-irrelevant activity (e.g., finger tapping, fidgetiness, fine motor movement, off-task [behavior] during direct observation) and classroom disturbance."[21] ADHD experts at Massachusetts General Hospital summed up the scientific literature in a similar way: "The extant literature clearly documents that stimulants diminish behaviors prototypical of ADHD, including motoric overactivity, impulsivity, and inattentiveness."[22]

However, none of this tells of drug treatment that benefits the child. Stimulants work for the teacher, but do they help the child? Here, right from the start, researchers ran into a wall. "Above all else," wrote Esther Sleator, a physician at the University of Illinois who asked fifty-two children what they thought of Ritalin, "we found a pervasive dislike among hyperactive children for taking stimulants."[23] Children on Ritalin, University of Texas psychologist Deborah Jacobvitz reported in 1990, rated themselves as "less happy and [less] pleased with themselves and more dysphoric." When it came to helping a child make friends and sustain friendships, stimulants produced "few significant positive effects and a high incidence of negative effects," Jacobvitz said.[24] Other researchers detailed how Ritalin harmed a child's self-esteem, as the children felt they must be "bad" or "dumb" if they had to take such a pill. "The child comes to believe not in the soundness of his own brain and body, not in his own growing ability to learn and to control his behavior, but in 'my magic pills that make me into a good boy,' " said University of Minnesota psychologist Alan Sroufe.[25]

All of this told of harm done, of a drug that made a child depressed, lonely, and filled with a sense of inadequacy, and when researchers looked at whether Ritalin at least helped hyperactive children fare well academically, to get good grades and thus succeed as students, they found that it wasn't so. Being able to focus intently on a math test, it turned out, didn't translate into long-term academic achievement. This drug, Sroufe explained in 1973, enhances performance on "repetitive, routinized tasks that require sustained attention," but "reasoning, problem solving and learning do not seem to be [positively] affected."[26] Five years later, Herbert Rie was much more negative. He reported that Ritalin did not produce any benefit on the students' "vocabulary, reading, spelling, or math," and hindered their ability to solve problems. "The reactions of the children strongly suggest a reduction in commitment of the sort that would seem critical for learning."[27] That same year, Russell Barkley at the Medical College of Wisconsin reviewed the relevant scientific literature and concluded "the major effect of stimulants appears to be an improvement in classroom manageability rather than academic performance."[28] Next it was James Swanson's turn to weigh in. The fact that the drugs often left children "isolated, withdrawn and overfocused" could "impair rather than improve learning," he said.[29] Carol Whalen, a psychologist from the University of California at Irvine, noted in 1997 that "especially worrisome has been the suggestion that the unsalutary effects [of Ritalin] occur in the realm of complex, high-order cognitive functions such as flexible problem-solving or divergent thinking."[30] Finally, in 2002, Canadian investigators conducted a meta-analysis of the literature, reviewing fourteen studies involving 1,379 youths that had lasted at least three months, and they determined that there was "little evidence for improved academic performance."[31]

There was one other disappointment with Ritalin. When researchers looked at whether stimulants improved a child's behavior over the long term, they couldn't find any benefit. When a child stopped taking Ritalin, ADHD behaviors regularly flared up, the "excitability, impulsivity, or talkativeness" worse than ever. "It is often disheartening to observe how rapidly behavior deteriorates when medication is discontinued," Whalen confessed.[32] Nor was there evidence that staying on a stimulant led to a sustained improvement in behavior. "Teachers and parents should not expect long-term improvement in academic achievement or reduced anti-social behavior," Swanson wrote in 1993.[33] The 1994 edition of the APA's *Textbook of Psychiatry* admitted to the same bottom-line conclusion: "Stimulants do not produce lasting improvements in aggressivity, conduct disorder, criminality, education achievement, job functioning, marital relationships, or long-term adjustment."[34] Thirty years of research had failed to provide any good-quality evidence that stimulants helped "hyperactive" children thrive, and in the early 1990s, a team of prominent ADHD experts picked to lead a long-term NIMH study, known as the Multisite Multimodal Treatment Study of Children with ADHD, acknowledged that this was so. "The long-term efficacy of stimulant medication has not been demonstrated for *any* domain of child functioning," they wrote.[35]

Stimulants Flunk Out

The NIMH touted its ADHD study as "the first major clinical trial" the institute had ever conducted of "a childhood mental disorder." However, it was a rather flawed intellectual exercise right from the start. Although the investigators, led by Peter Jensen, associate director of child and adolescent research at the NIMH, acknowledged during the planning stages that there was no evidence in the scientific literature that stimulants improved long-term outcomes, they did not include a placebo control in the study, reasoning that it would have been "unethical" to withhold "treatment of known efficacy" for an extended period. The study basically compared drug treatment to behavioral therapy, but in that latter group, 20 percent were on a stimulant at the start of the trial, and there never was a time during the fourteen months that all of the children in that group were off such medication.[36]

Despite this obvious design flaw, the NIMH-funded investigators declared victory for the stimulants at the end of fourteen months. "Carefully crafted medication management" had proven to be "superior" to behavioral treatment in terms of reducing core ADHD symptoms. There was also a hint that the medicated children had fared better on reading tests (although not in other academic subjects), and as a result, psychiatry now had a long-term study that documented the continuing benefits of stimulants. "Since ADHD is now regarded by most experts as a chronic disorder, ongoing treatment often seems necessary," the researchers concluded.[37]

After that initial fourteen-month period of treatment, the investigators followed up periodically with the students, assessing how they were doing and whether they were taking an ADHD medication. This was now a naturalistic study much like the one that Martin Harrow had conducted of schizophrenia outcomes, and readers of this book, having become familiar with the scientific literature, can easily guess what is coming next. At the end of three years, Jensen and the others discovered that "medication use was a significant marker not of beneficial outcome, but of deterioration. That is, participants using medication in the 24-to-36 month period actually showed increased symptomatology during that interval relative to those not taking medication."[38]

In other words, those on medications saw their core ADHD symptoms—the impulsiveness, the inattentiveness, the hyperactivity—*worsen,* at least in comparison to those not on drugs. In addition, those on meds had higher "delinquency scores" at the end of three years, which meant they were more likely to get into trouble in school and with the police.[39] They were also now shorter and weighed less than their off-med counterparts, evidence that the drugs suppressed growth. These results told of a drug therapy causing long-term harm, and when the NIMH-funded investigators reported on six-year outcomes, the findings remained the same. Medication use was "associated with worse hyperactivity-impulsivity and oppositional defiant disorder symptoms" and with greater "overall functional impairment."[40]

Controversy has long raged over whether ADHD is a "real" disease, but this study showed that when it comes to using stimulants to treat it, the controversy is moot. Even if ADHD is real, stimulants aren't going to provide long-term help. "We had thought that children medicated longer would have better outcomes. That didn't happen to be the case," said William Pelham from the State University of New York at Buffalo, who was one of the principal investigators. "There were no beneficial effects, none. In the short term, [medication] will help the child behave better, in the long run it won't. And that information should be made very clear to parents."[41]

Tallying Up the Harm

With any medication, there is a benefit-risk assessment to be made, and the expectation is that the benefit will outweigh the risks. But in this case, the NIMH found that over the long term there was *nothing* to be entered on the benefit side of the ledger. That leaves only risks to be tallied up, and so now we need to look at all the ways that stimulants can harm children.

Ritalin and the other ADHD medications cause a long list of physical, emotional, and psychiatric adverse effects. The physical problems include drowsiness, appetite loss, lethargy, insomnia, headaches, abdominal pain, motor abnormalities, facial and vocal tics, jaw clenching, skin problems, liver disorders, weight loss, growth suppression, hypertension, and sudden cardiac death. The emotional difficulties include depression, apathy, a general dullness, mood swings, crying jags, irritability, anxiety, and a sense of hostility toward the world. The psychiatric problems include obsessive-compulsive symptoms, mania, paranoia, psychotic episodes, and hallucinations. Methylphenidate also reduces blood flow and glucose metabolism in the brain, changes that usually are associated with "neuropathologic states."[42]

Animal studies of stimulants are also cause for alarm. Repeated exposure to amphetamines, scientists at the Yale School of Medicine reported in 1999, caused monkeys to exhibit "aberrant behaviors" that remained long after the drug exposure had stopped.[43] Various rat studies suggested that lengthy exposure to methylphenidate might cause dopaminergic pathways to become permanently desensitized, and since dopamine is the brain's "reward system," medicating the child may produce an adult with a "reduced ability to experience pleasure."[44] Scientists at Texas Southwestern Medical Center in Dallas found that "preadolescent" rats exposed to methylphenidate for fifteen days turned into anxious, depressed "adult" rats. The adult rats moved around less, were less responsive to novel environments, and showed a "deficit in sexual behavior." They concluded that "administration of methylphenidate" while the brain is still developing "results in aberrant behavioral adaptations during adulthood."[45]

Such is the outcomes literature for Ritalin and other ADHD medications. The drugs alter a hyperactive child's behavior over the short term in a manner that teachers and some parents find helpful, but other than that, the medications diminish a child's life in many ways, and they may turn a child into an adult with a reduced physiological capacity to experience joy. And, as we'll see later in this chapter, there is one other heartbreaking risk with stimulants that remains to be explored.

Depressing Results

As recently as 1988, the year that Prozac came to market, only one in 250 children under nineteen years of age in the United States was taking an antidepressant.[46] That was partly due to a cultural belief that youth were naturally moody and recovered quickly from depressive episodes, and partly because study after study had shown that tricyclics worked no better than placebo in this age group. "There is no escaping the fact that research studies certainly have not supported the efficacy of tricyclic antidepressants in treated depressed adolescents," a *Journal of Child and Adolescent Psychopharmacology* editorial acknowledged in 1992.[47]

However, when Prozac and other SSRIs were brought to market and touted as wonder drugs, the prescribing of antidepressants to children took off. The percentage of children so medicated tripled between 1988 and 1994, and by 2002 one in every forty children under nineteen years of age in the United States was taking an antidepressant.[48] Presumably these drugs provide a short-term benefit to children and adolescents that the tricyclics fail to provide, but unfortunately, we can't review the scientific literature to see if that is true because, as is widely acknowledged today, the literature is hopelessly poisoned. The trials were biased by design; the results that were published in the scientific journals didn't square with the actual data; adverse events were downplayed or omitted; and negative studies went unpublished or were spun into positive ones. "The story of research into selective serotonin reuptake inhibitor use in childhood depression is one of confusion, manipulation, and institutional failure," the *Lancet* wrote in a 2004 editorial. The fact that psychiatrists at leading medical schools had participated in this scientific fraud constituted an "abuse of the trust patients place in their physicians."[49]

However, a somewhat accurate picture of the merits of the drugs' efficacy in children has emerged through a roundabout process. During the course of SSRI-related lawsuits, expert witnesses for the plaintiffs—most notably David Healy in England and Peter Breggin in the United States—got a look at some of the trial data, and they observed that the drugs increased the suicide risk. They spoke out about what they had found, and with an increasing number of anguished parents telling of how their children had killed themselves after going on an SSRI, the FDA was forced to hold a hearing in 2004 on this risk. That, in turn, led to a stunning admission by the FDA's Thomas Laughren about the drugs' efficacy in children. Twelve of the fifteen pediatric antidepressant trials that had been conducted had failed. The FDA, in fact, had rejected the applications of six manufacturers seeking approval to sell their antidepressants to children. "These are sobering findings," Laughren confessed.[50]

The FDA did approve Prozac for use in children, as two of the three positive studies reviewed by Laughren had come from trials of this drug. But, as many critics have pointed out, from a scientific perspective, there is no reason to think that Prozac is any better than the other SSRIs. The percentage of children who responded to Prozac in the two positive trials was similar to the drug response rate in the twelve failed trials; Eli Lilly simply had been better at using biased trial designs to make it *appear* that its drug worked. For example, in one of the two Prozac trials, all of the children were initially put on placebo for one week, and if they got better during that period, they were excluded from the study. This helped knock down the placebo response rate. Next, the children who were randomized onto Prozac were evaluated for a week, and only those "who adapted well" to the drug were then enrolled in the study.

This helped increase the drug response rate. "Before the study even started," explained Jonathan Leo, editor in chief of the journal *Ethical Human Psychology and Psychiatry,* "there was a mechanism in place to maximize any difference between the drug and placebo groups—the placebo group was preselected for *nonresponders,* while the drug group was preselected for *responders.*"[51] Yet, even with this extremely biased trial design, the Prozac-treated children still fared no better than the placebo group on self-rating scales or ratings by their parents. In addition, the trial failed to show efficacy for fluoxetine on its "primary endpoint," and thus efficacy arose entirely from a secondary "improvement" scale filled out by the psychiatrists paid by Eli Lilly to run the trial.

Such was the record of efficacy produced by the SSRIs in pediatric trials for depression. Most trials failed to show any benefit, and Eli Lilly had to use a grossly biased trial design to make Prozac appear effective. In 2003, the Medicines and Healthcare Regulatory Agency (MHRA) in the United Kingdom essentially banned the use of SSRIs, except for fluoxetine, in patients under eighteen years old. English scientists then reviewed all the relevant data and reported in the *Lancet* that they supported "the conclusions reached by the MHRA."[52] The truth, explained the *Lancet* editors in an accompanying editorial, was that these drugs "were both ineffective and harmful in children."[53] Australian scientists chimed in with a similar review in the *British Medical Journal,* their article enlivened by descriptions of the shenanigans that American psychiatrists had employed to make the SSRIs look beneficial in the first place. The authors of the positive studies, they said, had "exaggerated the benefits, downplayed the harms, or both." The Australians also reviewed Lilly's fluoxetine trials in children and determined that the "evidence for efficacy is not convincing." As such, they concluded that "recommending [any antidepressant] as a treatment option, let alone as first line treatment, would be inappropriate."[54]

In the absence of any efficacy benefit, we are now left with the unhappy task of tallying up the harm done by the prescribing of antidepressants to children and teenagers. We can start with the physical problems. SSRIs may cause insomnia, sexual dysfunction, headaches, gastrointestinal problems, dizziness, tremors, nervousness, muscle cramps, muscle weakness, seizures, and a severe inner agitation known as akathisia, which is associated with an increased risk of violence and suicide. The psychiatric problems they can trigger are even more problematic. Timothy Wilens and Joseph Biederman at Massachusetts General Hospital conducted a chart review of eighty-two children treated with SSRIs, and determined that 22 percent of the children had suffered an adverse psychiatric event. Ten percent had become psychotic, and another 6 percent manic. "One of the most disturbing adverse outcomes is a worsening of emotional, cognitive or behavioral symptoms," they wrote. "These psychiatric adverse events to medication can be significantly impairing."[55] North Carolina psychiatrist Thomas Gualtieri determined that 28 percent of the 128 children and adolescents he treated with SSRIs developed some type of "behavioral toxicity."[56] Other physicians have told of their SSRI-treated younger patients suffering panic attacks, anxiety, nervousness, and hallucinations.

Those findings tell of children and adolescents being made sick by SSRIs, and that is over the short term. To appreciate the long-term risks, we can look at the problems that have cropped up in adults and in animal studies. If the children go off the medication, they can expect to suffer withdrawal symptoms, both physical and mental. Should they remain on the drugs for years, they are at high risk of becoming chronically depressed. They may also develop—as the American Psychiatric Association warns in one of its textbooks—an "apathy syndrome," which "is characterized by a loss of motivation, increased passivity, and often feelings of lethargy and 'flatness.'"[57] There is also memory loss and cognitive decline to worry about, and, as we saw earlier, animal studies suggest that the drugs may cause serotonergic neurons to become swollen and misshapen.

Yet Another Illness Appears

First there was the ADHD explosion, and then came the news that childhood depression was rampant, and not long after that, in the late 1990s, juvenile bipolar disorder burst into public view. Newspapers and magazines ran features on this phenomenon, and once more psychiatry explained its appearance with a story of scientific discovery. "It has long been thought in the psychiatric community that children could not be given a diagnosis of bipolar disorder until the mid-to-late teens, and that mania in children was extremely rare," wrote psychiatrist Demitri Papolos, in his bestselling book *The Bipolar Child*. "But scientists in the research vanguard are beginning to prove that the disorder can begin very early in life and that it is far more common than was previously supposed."[58] Yet the rise in the number of children and adolescents with this diagnosis was so astonishing—a fortyfold increase from 1995 to 2003—that *Time*, in an article titled "Young and Bipolar," wondered if something else might be going on.[59] "New awareness of the disorder may not be enough to account for the explosion of juvenile bipolar cases," the magazine explained. "Some scientists fear that there may be something in the environment or in modern lifestyles that is driving into a bipolar state children and teens who might otherwise escape the condition."[60]

That speculation made perfect sense. How could a severe mental illness have gone unrecognized for so long, with doctors only now noticing that thousands of kids were going wildly manic? But if there were something new *in the environment* stirring this behavior, as *Time* suggested to its readers, there would be a logical explanation for the epidemic. Infectious agents stir epidemics, and thus, as we trace the rise of juvenile bipolar disorder, this is what we'll want to discover: Can we identify "outside agents" that are causing this modern-day plague?

As we learned earlier, manic-depressive illness was a rare condition prior to the psychopharmacology era, affecting perhaps one in ten thousand people. Although initial onset sometimes occurred in those fifteen to nineteen years old, it usually didn't appear until people were in their twenties. But more to the point, it virtually *never* appeared in children under thirteen years of age, and both pediatricians and medical researchers regularly emphasized this point.

In 1945, Charles Bradley said that pediatric mania was so rare that "it is best to avoid the diagnosis of manic-depressive psychosis in children."[61] An Ohio physician, Louis Lurie, reviewed the literature in 1950 and found that "observers have concluded that mania does not occur in children."[62] Two years later, Barton Hall reviewed the case histories of 2,200 psychiatric patients five to sixteen years old, and found only two instances of manic-depressive illness. In both instances, the patients were over thirteen years of age. "These facts endorse the general belief that manic-depressive states are illnesses of the maturing or matured personality," Hall said.[63] In 1960, Washington University psychiatrist James Anthony scoured the medical literature for case reports of manic-depressive illness in children and could find only three. "Occurrence of manic depression in early childhood *as a clinical phenomenon* has yet to be demonstrated," he wrote.[64]

But then, slowly but surely, such case reports began to appear. In the late 1960s and early 1970s, psychiatrists began prescribing Ritalin to hyperactive children, and suddenly, in 1976, Washington University's Warren Weinberg, a pediatric neurologist, was writing in the *American Journal of Diseases of Childhood* that it was time for the field to realize that children could go manic. "Acceptance of the concept that mania occurs in children is important in order that affected children can be identified, the natural history defined, and appropriate treatment established and offered to these children," he wrote.[65]

This was the moment in the medical literature that pediatric bipolar disorder was, in essence, "discovered." In his article, Weinberg reviewed the case histories of five children suffering from this previously unrecognized illness, but he rushed past the fact that at least three of the five children had been treated with a tricyclic or Ritalin *prior* to becoming manic. Two years later, doctors at Massachusetts General Hospital announced that they had identified nine children with manic-depressive illness, and they, too, skipped over the fact that seven of the nine had been previously treated with amphetamines, methylphenidate, or "other medications to affect behavior."[66] Then, in 1982, Michael Strober and Gabrielle Carlson at the UCLA Neuropsychiatric Institute put a new twist into the juvenile bipolar story. Twelve of the sixty adolescents they had treated with antidepressants had turned "bipolar" over the course of three years, which—one might think—suggested that the drugs had caused the mania. Instead, Strober and Carlson reasoned that their study had shown that antidepressants could be used as a *diagnostic* tool. It wasn't that antidepressants were causing some children to go manic, but rather the drugs were *unmasking* bipolar illness, as only children with the disease would suffer this reaction to an antidepressant. "Our data imply that biologic differences between latent depressive subtypes are already present and detectable during the period of early adolescence, and that pharmacologic challenge can serve as one reliable aid in delimiting specific affective syndromes in juveniles," they said.[67]

The "unmasking" of bipolar illness in children soon speeded up. The prescribing of Ritalin and antidepressants took off in the late 1980s and early 1990s, and as this occurred, the bipolar epidemic erupted. The number of hostile, aggressive, and out-of-control children admitted to psychiatric wards soared, and in 1995 Peter Lewinsohn from the Oregon Research Institute concluded that 1 percent of all American adolescents were now bipolar.[68] Three years later, Carlson reported that 63 percent of the pediatric patients treated at her university hospital suffered from mania, the very symptom that doctors in the pre-psychopharmacologic era almost never saw in children. "Manic symptoms are the rule, rather than the exception," she noted.[69] Indeed, Lewinsohn's epidemiological data was now already out of date. The number of children discharged from hospitals with a bipolar diagnosis rose fivefold between 1996 and 2004, such that this "ferocious mental illness" was now said to strike one in every fifty prepubertal children in America. "We don't have the exact numbers yet," University of Texas psychiatrist Robert Hirschfeld told *Time* in 2002, "except we know it's there, and it's underdiagnosed."[70]

An epidemic had come of age, and history reveals that it rose in lockstep with the prescribing of stimulants and antidepressants to children.

Creating the Bipolar Child

Given that chronology, we should be able to find data that explains why stimulants and antidepressants would have that iatrogenic effect. There should be data showing that if you treat 5 million children and adolescents with these drugs, then 20 percent or so will deteriorate in ways that will lead to a bipolar diagnosis. There should be evidence of iatrogenic harm that adds up mathematically to an epidemic.

We'll start with Ritalin.

Even before the prescribing of Ritalin took hold, it was well known that amphetamines could stir psychotic and manic episodes. Indeed, amphetamines did this with such regularity that psychiatric researchers pointed to this effect as evidence supporting the dopamine hypothesis of schizophrenia. Amphetamines upped dopamine levels in the brain, suggesting that psychosis was caused by too much of this neurotransmitter. In 1974, David Janowsky, a physician at the University of California at San Diego School of Medicine, tested this hypothesis by giving three dopamine-elevating agents—d-amphetamine, l-amphetamine, and methylphenidate—to his schizophrenia patients. While all three drugs made them more psychotic, methylphenidate turned out to be tops in this regard, doubling the severity of their symptoms.[71]

Given this understanding of methylphenidate, psychiatry could expect that giving Ritalin to young children would cause many to suffer a manic or psychotic episode. Although this risk isn't well quantified, Canadian psychiatrists reported in 1999 that nine of ninety-six ADHD children they treated with stimulants for an average of twenty-one months developed "psychotic symptoms."[72] In 2006, the FDA issued a report on this risk. From 2000 to 2005, the agency had received nearly one thousand reports of stimulant-induced psychosis and mania in children and adolescents, and given that these MedWatch reports are thought to represent only 1 percent of the actual number of adverse events, this suggests that 100,000 youths diagnosed with ADHD suffered psychotic and or manic episodes during that five-year period. The FDA determined that these episodes regularly occurred in "patients with no identifiable risk factors" for psychosis, meaning that they were clearly drug-induced, and that a "substantial portion" of the cases occurred in children ten years or less. "The predominance in young children of hallucinations, both visual and tactile, involving insects, snakes and worms is striking," the FDA wrote.[73]

Once this drug-induced psychosis occurs, the children are usually diagnosed with bipolar disorder. Moreover, this diagnostic progression, from medicated ADHD to bipolar illness, is well recognized by experts in the field. In a study of 195 bipolar children and adolescents, Demitri Papolos found that 65 percent "had hypomanic, manic and aggressive reactions to stimulant medications."[74] In 2001, Melissa DelBello, at the University of Cincinnati Medical Center, reported that twenty-one of thirty-four adolescent patients hospitalized for mania had been on stimulants "prior to the onset of an affective episode." These drugs, she confessed, may "precipitate depression and/or mania in children who would not have otherwise developed bipolar disorder."[75]

Yet there is an even bigger problem with stimulants. They cause children to cycle through arousal and dysphoric states on a *daily* basis. When a child takes the drug, dopamine levels in the synapse increase, and this produces an aroused state. The child may show increased energy, an intensified focus, and hyperalertness. The child may become anxious, irritable, aggressive, hostile, and unable to sleep. More extreme arousal symptoms include obsessive-compulsive and hypomanic behaviors. But when the drug exits the brain, dopamine levels in the synapse sharply drop, and this may lead to such dysphoric symptoms as fatigue, lethargy, apathy, social withdrawal, and depression. Parents regularly talk of this daily "crash." But—and this is the key—such arousal and dysphoric symptoms are the very symptoms that the National Institute of Mental Health identifies as characteristic of a bipolar child. Symptoms of mania in children, the NIMH says, include increased energy, intensified goal-directed activity, insomnia, irritability, agitation, and destructive outbursts. Symptoms of depression in children include loss of energy, social isolation, a loss of interest in activities (apathy), and a sad mood.

The ADHD to Bipolar Pathway

Stimulant-Induced Symptoms		Bipolar Symptoms	
Arousal	Dysphoric	Arousal	Dysphoric
Increased energy	Somnolence	Increased energy	Sad mood
Intensified focus	Fatigue, lethargy	Intensified goal-directed activity	Loss of energy
Hyperalertness	Social withdrawal, isolation	Decreased need for sleep	Loss of interest in activities
Euphoria	Decreased spontaneity	Severe mood change	Social isolation
Agitation, anxiety	Reduced curiosity	Irritability	Poor communication
Insomnia	Constriction of affect	Agitation	Feelings of worthlessness
Irritability	Depression	Destructive outbursts	Unexplained crying
Hostility	Emotional lability	Increased talking	
Hypomania		Distractibility	
Mania		Hypomania	
Psychosis		Mania	

Stimulants used to treat ADHD induce both arousal and dysphoric symptoms. These drug-induced symptoms overlap to a remarkable degree the symptoms said to be characteristic of juvenile bipolar disorder.

In short, every child on a stimulant turns a bit bipolar, and the risk that a child diagnosed with ADHD will move on to a bipolar diagnosis after being treated with a stimulant has even been quantified. Joseph Biederman and his colleagues at Massachusetts General Hospital reported in 1996 that 15 of 140 children (11 percent) diagnosed with ADHD developed bipolar symptoms—which were not present at initial diagnosis—within four years.[76] This gives us our first mathematical equation for solving the juvenile bipolar epidemic: If a society prescribes stimulants to 3.5 million children and adolescents, as is the case in the United States today, it should expect that this practice will create 400,000 bipolar youth. As *Time* noted, most children with bipolar illness are diagnosed with a different psychiatric disorder first, with "ADHD the likeliest first call."

Now let's look at the SSRIs.

It is well established that antidepressants can induce manic episodes in adults, and naturally they have this effect on children, too. As early as 1992, when the prescribing of SSRIs to children was just getting started, University of Pittsburgh researchers reported that 23 percent of boys eight to nineteen years old treated with Prozac developed mania or maniclike symptoms, and another 19 percent developed "drug-induced" hostility.[77] In Eli Lilly's first study of Prozac for pediatric depression, 6 percent of the children treated with the drug suffered a manic episode; none in the placebo group did.[78] Luvox, meanwhile, was reported to cause a 4 percent rate of mania in children under 18.[79] In 2004, Yale University researchers assessed this risk of antidepressant-induced mania in young and old, and they found that it is *highest* in those under thirteen years of age.[80]

The incidence rates cited above are from short-term trials; the risk rises when children and teenagers stay on antidepressants for extended periods. In 1995, Harvard psychiatrists determined that 25 percent of children and adolescents diagnosed with depression convert to bipolar illness within two to four years. "Antidepressant treatment may well induce switching into mania, rapid cycling or affective instability in the young, as it almost certainly does in adults," they explained.[81] Washington University's Barbara Geller extended the follow-up period to ten years, and in her study, nearly half of prepubertal children treated for depression ended up bipolar.[82] These findings give us our second mathematical equation for solving the bipolar epidemic: If 2 million children and adolescents are treated with SSRIs for depression, this practice will create 500,000 to 1 million bipolar youth.

We now have numbers that tell of an iatrogenic epidemic: 400,000 bipolar children arriving via the ADHD doorway, and at least another half million through the antidepressant doorway. There is also a way that we can double-check that conclusion: When investigators survey juvenile bipolar patients, do they find that most traveled down one of those two iatrogenic paths?

Here are the results. In a 2003 study of seventy-nine juvenile bipolar patients, University of Louisville psychiatrist Rif El-Mallakh determined that forty-nine (62 percent) had been treated with a stimulant or an antidepressant prior to their becoming manic.[83] That same year, Papolos reported that 83 percent of the 195 bipolar children he studied had been diagnosed with some other psychiatric illness first, and that two-thirds had been exposed to an antidepressant.[84] Finally, Gianni Faedda found that 84 percent of the children treated for bipolar illness at the Luci Bini Mood Disorders Clinic in New York City between 1998 and 2000 had been previously exposed to psychiatric drugs. "Strikingly, *in fewer than 10%* [of the cases] was diagnosis of bipolar disorder considered initially," Faedda wrote.[85]

Not surprisingly, parents bear witness to this iatrogenic course. In May 1999, Martha Hellander, executive director of the Child and Adolescent Bipolar Foundation, and Tomie Burke, founder of Parents of Bipolar Children, jointly wrote this letter to the *Journal of the Academy of Child and Adolescent Psychiatry*:

> Most of our children initially received the ADHD diagnosis, were given stimulants and or antidepressants, and either did not respond or suffered symptoms of mania such as rages, insomnia, agitation, pressured speech, and the like. In lay language, parents call this "bouncing off the wall." First hospitalization occurred often among our children during manic or mixed states (including suicidal gestures and attempts) triggered or exacerbated by treatment with stimulants, tricyclics, or serotonin reuptake inhibitors.[86]

With so many teenagers prescribed SSRIs, an epidemic of mania has erupted on college campuses as well. In a 2002 article titled "Crisis on the Campus," *Psychology Today* reported that an increasing number of students, having arrived at college with an antidepressant prescription in hand, were crashing badly during the school term. "We are seeing more first episodes of mania every year," said Morton Silverman, head of counseling services at the University of Chicago. "It's very disruptive. It generally means hospitalization for the student." The magazine was even able to identify a precise date when this mania epidemic began to emerge: 1988.[87] Readers need only remember when Prozac came to market to connect the dots.

One final bit of evidence comes from the Netherlands. In 2001, Dutch psychiatrists reported only thirty-nine cases of pediatric bipolar illness in their country. Dutch investigator Catrien Reichart then studied the offspring of parents with bipolar disorder in both the

AN EPIDEMIC UNFOLDS

The Iatrogenic Agents Spread

Percentage of American youth younger than 20 on a stimulant or antidepressant

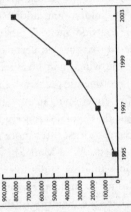

The prescription rates are compiled from three separate reports. See in particular Zito, J. "Psychotropic practice patterns for youth." *Archives of Pediatric Adolescent Medicine* 157 (2003): 17–25.

Juvenile Bipolar Diagnoses Leap

Outpatient office visits by youths under 20 with a diagnosis of bipolar disorder

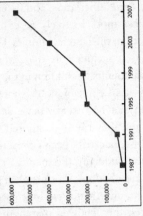

Source: Moreno, C. "National trends in the outpatient diagnosis and treatment of bipolar disorder in youth." *Archives of General Psychiatry* 64 (2007): 1032–39.

And Disability Numbers Soar

SSI recipients under 18 years old disabled by mental illness, 1987–2007

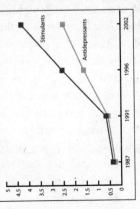

Source: Social Security Administration reports, 1987–2007.

United States and the Netherlands, and determined that the Americans were ten times more to likely to exhibit bipolar symptoms before age twenty than the Dutch children. The likely reason for this difference, Reichart concluded, is that "the prescription of antidepressants and stimulants to children in the U.S. is much higher."[88]

All of this tells of an epidemic that is mostly iatrogenic in kind. Fifty years ago, physicians virtually never saw manic-depressive illness in preteens, and they rarely diagnosed it in adolescents. Then pediatricians and psychiatrists began prescribing Ritalin to hyperactive children, and suddenly the medical journals began running case reports of manic children. This problem grew as the prescribing of Ritalin increased, and then it exploded with the introduction of the SSRIs. Research then showed that both of these drugs trigger bipolar symptoms in children and adolescents on a regular basis. These are the two "outside agents" fueling the epidemic, and it should be remembered that they do perturb normal brain function. The manic children showing up at hospital emergency rooms have dopaminergic and serotonergic pathways that have been altered by the drugs and are now functioning in an "abnormal" manner. There is a step-by-step logic that explains this epidemic.

In addition, there are at least three more pathways to a diagnosis of juvenile bipolar illness. As El-Mallakh, Papolos, and Faedda all found, there are some children and adolescents so diagnosed who have no prior exposure to antidepressants or stimulants, and it's fairly easy to see where the majority of those patients are coming from. First, Harvard psychiatrist Joseph Biederman led the way in expanding the diagnostic boundaries in the 1990s, proposing that extreme "irritability" could be seen as evidence of bipolar illness. The child no longer needs to have gone manic to be diagnosed as bipolar. Second, foster children in many states are now regularly given a bipolar diagnosis, their anger apparently not the result of having been born into a dysfunctional family, but rather due to a biological illness. Finally, teenagers who get into trouble with the law are now regularly funneled into psychiatric roles. Many states have set up "mental health courts" that send them off to hospitals and psychiatric shelters rather than to correctional facilities, and these youth are adding to the bipolar numbers as well.

The Fate That Awaits

As we saw earlier in this book, outcomes for adult bipolar patients have deteriorated dramatically in the past forty years, and the worst outcomes are seen in those with "mixed state" and "rapid cycling" symptoms. That clinical course in adults was virtually never seen prior to the psychopharmacology era, but rather it was one associated with exposure to antidepressants, and, tragically, those are the very symptoms that afflict the overwhelming majority of juvenile bipolar patients. They exhibit symptoms "similar to the clinical picture reported for severely ill, treatment-resistant adults," explained Barbara Geller in 1997.[89]

Thus, this is not just a story of children turned bipolar; it's a story of children afflicted with a particularly severe form of it. Papolos found that 87 percent of his 195 juvenile bipolar patients suffered from "ultra, ultra rapid cycling," which meant that they were constantly switching between manic and depressed mood states.[90] Similarly, Faedda determined that 66 percent of the juvenile bipolar patients treated at the Luci Bini Mood Disorders Clinic were "ultra, ultra rapid-cyclers," and another 19 percent suffered from rapid cycling only a little bit less extreme. "In contrast to a biphasic, episodic and relatively slow cycling course in some adults with bipolar disorder, pediatric forms usually involve mixed mood states and a subchronic, unstable, and unremitting course," Faedda wrote.[91]

Outcome studies have found that the long-term prognosis for these children is grim. The NIMH, as part of its STEP-BD study, charted the outcomes of 542 children and adolescent bipolar patients, and it reported that pre-adult onset "was associated with greater rates of comorbid anxiety disorders and substance abuse, more recurrences, shorter periods of euthymia [normal mood], and greater likelihood of suicide attempts and violence."[92] Boris Birmaher, at the University of Pittsburgh, determined that "early onset" bipolar patients are symptomatic about 60 percent of the time, and that, on average, they shift "polarity"—from depression to mania or vice versa—an astonishing sixteen times a year. The prepubertal patients were "two times less likely than those with postpubertal onset bipolar to recover," he said, and it was "expected that children will be poor responders to treatment when they become adults."[93] DelBello followed a group of adolescents hospitalized for a first bipolar episode and concluded that only 41 percent functionally recovered within a year.[94] This impairment, Birmaher determined, then worsens after the first year. "Functional impairment in bipolar appears to increase during adolescence regardless of age of onset."[95]

Youth diagnosed with bipolar illness are typically put on drug cocktails that include an atypical antipsychotic and a mood stabilizer. This means that they now have multiple neurotransmitter pathways in their brains that are being mucked up, and naturally, this treatment does not lead them back to emotional and physical health. In 2002, Geller reported that lithium, antidepressants, and mood stabilizers all failed to help bipolar youth fare better at the end of two years. Those who were treated with a neuroleptic, she added, "were significantly less likely to recover than those who did not receive a neuroleptic."[96] Six years later, Hayes, Inc., a Pennsylvania consulting firm that conducts "unbiased" assessments of drugs for health-care providers, concluded that there was no good scientific evidence that the mood stabilizers and atypical antipsychotics prescribed for pediatric bipolar were either safe or effective. "Our findings indicate that at this time, anticonvulsants and atypical antipsychotics cannot be recommended for children diagnosed with bipolar disorders," said Elisabeth Houtsmuller, senior analyst for Hayes.[97] These reports attest to a lack of drug efficacy, but as Houtsmuller noted, the side effects from these "pharmacological treatments" are "alarming." In particular, atypical antipsychotics may cause metabolic dysfunction, hormonal abnormalities, diabetes, obesity, emotional blunting, and tardive dyskinesia.* Eventually, the

---

* In a 2008 report published by the European College of Neuropsychopharmacology, Spanish investigators observed that "children and adolescents seem to have a higher risk than adults for experiencing adverse events such as extrapyramidal symptoms [movement disorders], prolactin elevation [high hormone levels], sedation, weight gain, and metabolic effects when taking antipsychotics." Investigators have also reported that these risks may be higher for girls than for boys.

drugs will induce cognitive decline, and the child who stays on the cocktails into adulthood can expect to die early as well.

That is the long-term course of this iatrogenic illness: A child who may be hyperactive or depressed is treated with a drug that triggers a manic episode or some degree of emotional instability, and then the child is put on a drug cocktail that leads to a lifetime of disability.

The Disability Numbers

There are no good studies yet on the percentage of "early onset" bipolar patients who, when they reach adulthood, end up on the SSI and SSDI disability rolls. However, the astonishing jump in the number of "severely mentally ill" children receiving SSI speaks volumes about the havoc that is being wreaked. There were 16,200 psychiatrically disabled youth under eighteen years old on the SSI rolls in 1987, and they comprised less than 6 percent of the total number of disabled children. Twenty years later, there were 561,569 disabled mentally ill children on the SSI rolls, and they comprised 50 percent of the total. This epidemic is even hitting preschool children. The prescribing of psychotropic drugs to two-year-olds and three-year-olds began to become more commonplace about a decade ago, and sure enough, the number of severely mentally ill children under six years of age receiving SSI has *tripled* since then, rising from 22,453 in 2000 to 65,928 in 2007.[98]

Moreover, the SSI numbers only begin to hint at the scope of the harm being done. Everywhere there is evidence of a worsening of the mental health of children and teenagers. From 1995 to 1999, psychiatric-related emergency room visits by children increased 59 percent.[99] The deteriorating mental health of the nation's children, declared U.S. surgeon general David Satcher in 2001, constituted "a health crisis."[100] Next, colleges were suddenly wondering why so many of their students were suffering manic episodes or behaving in disturbed ways; a 2007 survey discovered that one in six college students had deliberately "cut or burned self" in the prior year.[101] All

The Epidemic Hits America's Children
SSI Recipients Under 18 Years Old Disabled by Mental Illness, 1987–2007

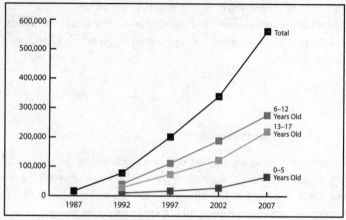

Prior to 1992, the government's SSI reports did not break down children recipients into subgroups by age. Source: Social Security Administration reports, 1987–2007.

of this led the U.S. Government Accountability Office to investigate what was going on, and it reported in 2008 that one in every fifteen young adults, eighteen to twenty-six years old, is now "seriously mentally ill." There are 680,000 in that age group with bipolar disorder and another 800,000 ill with major depression, and, the GAO noted, this was in fact an undercount of the problem, as it didn't include young adults who were homeless, incarcerated, or institutionalized. All of these youth are "functionally impaired" to some degree, the GAO said.[102]

That is where we stand as a nation today. Twenty years ago, our society began regularly prescribing psychiatric drugs to children and adolescents, and now one out of every fifteen Americans enters adulthood with a "serious mental illness." That is proof of the most tragic sort that our drug-based paradigm of care is doing a great deal more harm than good. The medicating of children and youth became commonplace only a short time ago, and already it has put millions onto a path of lifelong illness.

I 2

Suffer the Children

"You wonder all the time:
Are you helping or harming your child?"
—JASMINE'S MOM (2009)

There are an endless number of stories of medicated children that can be told, and as I worked on this book, each visit to a place where such children can be found—to a family's home or to a foster care provider or to a psychiatric hospital—offered at least a brief glimpse of this new society we have created in the past thirty years. There are, of course, many parents who will tell of how their children have been helped by psychiatric drugs, and given the spectrum of outcomes that occur with this paradigm of care, that is undoubtedly true (at least over the short term). But this book is about the epidemic of disabling mental illness that has erupted in our country, and so the stories that follow tell, at best, of ambivalent long-term outcomes, and of how diagnosis and treatment during childhood may lead to a life of disability.

Lost in Seattle

I met the young woman I'll call Jasmine for only a short time, and even that brief encounter left her visibly agitated.* Born in 1988, Jasmine resides today in a somewhat dilapidated group home for the severely mentally ill in a suburb of Seattle, and even as her mother and I approached the facility, we could see Jasmine through a window, pacing back and forth. Once we stepped inside, Jasmine took once glance at me and quickly retreated, huddling next to the wall, very much liked a frightened creature of the wild. She wore jeans and a light blue jacket, and she also kept her distance from her mother—Jasmine won't let anyone hug her now. We drove in two cars to a nearby Dairy Queen, as Jasmine would not have been will-ing to go if I had been in the car with her, and after we got there, Jasmine stayed in the backseat, staring straight ahead and rocking back and forth. "If she ever speaks again," her mother says quietly, "she will have quite the story to tell."

Photos of Jasmine as a young girl are a good place to start her story. Her mother had shown them to me earlier, and they all told of a happy childhood. In one, Jasmine is joyfully lined up next to her two sisters in front of a Disneyland ride; in another, she is showing off a gap-toothed grin; in a third, she is playfully sticking out her tongue. "She was very smart and funny, pretty much the light of our lives," her mother recalls. "She would be outside playing, riding her bike up and down the street, just like a typical kid. She would even go around to the neighbors and tell them she would sing 'Row, Row, Row Your Boat' for fifty cents. She was such a hellion—you can see in these photos how spunky she was."

All was fine in Jasmine's life until the summer after fifth grade. Because she still occasionally wet her bed, she was anxious about going away to camp, and so a doctor prescribed a "bed-wetting"

---

* Since "Jasmine" could not give consent to having her name used, her mother and I agreed to keep her identity hidden. I've also kept her mother unnamed for that same reason.

pill, which happened to be a tricyclic antidepressant. Very quickly, Jasmine became agitated and hostile, and one afternoon she told her mom: "I'm having all these horrible thoughts. I feel like I'm going to kill people."

In hindsight, it is easy to see what was happening to Jasmine. Her extreme agitation was a sign that she was suffering from akathisia, a side effect of antidepressants closely linked to suicide and violence. "But nobody ever asked about whether the drug might have triggered the homicidal ideation," her mother says. "I didn't learn that imipramine could do that until years later when I went on the Internet." Instead, Jasmine was referred to a psychiatrist, who diagnosed her with obsessive-compulsive disorder and bipolar illness. He put her on a drug cocktail composed of Zoloft, Luvox, and Zyprexa, and by the time she entered middle school that fall, she was a changed person.

"It was horrible," her mother says. "She gained over a hundred pounds on Zyprexa, and she is petite, five feet, three inches tall. Kids who knew her from elementary school said, 'What happened to you?' Boys began calling her 'the beast.' She ended up with no friends, and she would cry and cry, and ask to eat lunch in the principal's office to stay out of the cafeteria." Meanwhile, Jasmine's rages at home continued, and her psychiatrist upped her dosage of Zyprexa so high that her eyes would roll up into her head and get stuck. "It was like she was being tortured. She would lie on her bed and scream, 'Why is this happening to me?' "

Eventually, after the Zoloft was finally withdrawn, Jasmine stabilized fairly well on a combination of Zyprexa and Depakote. Although she rarely socialized with classmates, she did well academically, and during her first years in high school, she regularly earned A's and kudos for her photography and artwork. She immersed herself in volunteer work, too, helping out at a humane society, a senior center, and a food bank, her school giving her an "unsung hero" award for this work. She had come to accept that she was bipolar, and even made plans to write a book that would help other teenagers understand it. "She used to tell me, 'Mom, when I graduate from high school, I am going to stand up and ask, Has anybody ever wondered what happened to me?' She was so brave."

Toward the end of her junior year, Jasmine read on the Internet that Zyprexa could cause weight gain, hypoglycemia, and diabetes. She suffered from the first two of those problems, but when she asked her psychiatrist about Zyprexa's side effects, he dismissed her concerns. Enraged, Jasmine "fired" him, and in June of 2005, she took herself off both medications, stopping them rather abruptly. Ten days after she took a final dose of Zyprexa, she was on an excursion with her mother when she suddenly turned ashen, sweat beading up on her lip. "This is really bad," she muttered. "Mom, fight for me."

Jasmine has been more or less lost to the world ever since. By the time they arrived at the hospital, Jasmine was screaming and tearing at her hair. She was deep into a withdrawal psychosis, and doctors began giving her one powerful drug after another, trying to get it to abate. "They put her on eleven medications in thirteen days, which essentially fried her brain," her mother says. Jasmine began cycling in and out of hospitals, and every time she was discharged home, it ended badly. At times, she was so psychotic that she would call the police to tell them that she was being kidnapped or that men were building bombs in her front yard. On several occasions, she "escaped" from her house and ran screaming into the streets. Another time she kicked and punched her mom; afterward, she ripped a soda can open and slashed at her wrist. "This is the most psychotic person we have ever seen in the history of this ER," hospital staff told Jasmine's mom after one such episode.

In late 2006, a doctor put Jasmine on a single antipsychotic, Clozaril, and that led to a brief respite. Although Jasmine rarely spoke, she calmed down and entered a school for disabled children. At night, her mother read to her for hours, seeking to nurture the spark of sanity she now saw in Jasmine. "I also noticed that if I sang to her, like to an Alzheimer's patient, she would sing back, communicating through singing." But in early 2007, Jasmine suffered another severe bout of psychosis, which ended with her screaming in the middle of a busy road. "There is no hope for her," doctors said, and soon Jasmine was placed at the residential facility, where today she passes her days, shying away from contact with other people and, except for an occasional word now and then, mute.

"The doctors tell me she was always going to be schizophrenic," her mother says. "But no doctor ever asked about this history, about what she was like before she was put on drugs. And you know what's so hard to accept? We came in for help that summer when she was eleven years old for a minor problem that had nothing to do with psychiatry. In my mind, I can hear her laughing, like she was back then. But her life has been stolen away. We've lost her, even though her body remains. I see every minute what I've lost."

Ambivalent in Syracuse

Senior year was a good time for Andrew Stevens. Diagnosed with ADHD and put on medication when he was in first grade, he'd had up-and-down times in school until his senior year. But then he took a course in auto mechanics, and bingo, he excelled in a way he never had before. "I'm in the zone," he explains. "I enjoy it. It doesn't feel like school."

On this afternoon, Andrew, who is slight of build and perhaps five feet, six inches tall, looks very much like the skateboarder he is: short-cropped hair, black earring, and wearing a T-shirt, shorts, and tennis shoes splashed with a kaleidoscope of colors. I had met his mother, Ellen, a year earlier, at a conference in Albany, New York, and she had expressed a sentiment that, I thought, neatly summarized the moral aspect of our society's medicating of youth: "Andrew has been a guinea pig for the medical field," she'd said.

Very early on, she and her husband had realized that Andrew was different from their other two children. He had speech problems; his behavior seemed eccentric; he had "rage issues." In first grade, he was so wound up he regularly needed to go into the hallway and bounce on a mini-trampoline in order to refocus. "I remember crying when he was diagnosed with ADHD, and it wasn't because my kid was labeled," his mother says. "It was, 'Thank God, we know something real is going on with him and they know how to help him. It's not our imagination.'"

Although she and her husband worried about putting Andrew on

Ritalin, doctors and school authorities led her to believe that she would be "remiss as a parent" if she didn't give him the medication. And at first, "it was like a miracle," she says. Andrew's fears abated, he learned to tie his shoes, and his teachers praised his improved behavior. But after a few months, the drug no longer seemed to work so well, and whenever its effects wore off, there would be this "rebound effect." Andrew would "behave like a wild man, out of control." A doctor increased his dosage, only then it seemed that Andrew was like a "zombie," his sense of humor reemerging only when the drug's effects wore off. Next, Andrew needed to take clonidine in order to fall asleep at night. The drug treatment didn't really seem to be helping, and so Ritalin gave way to other stimulants, including Adderall, Concerta, and dextroamphetamine. "It was always more drugs," his mother says.

Meanwhile, Andrew's success in the classroom fluctuated according to the talents of his teacher. In fourth and fifth grade, he had teachers who knew how to work with him, and he did fairly well. But his sixth-grade teacher was impatient with him, and Andrew's self-esteem took such a nosedive that his mother homeschooled him the following year. Andrew's anxieties worsened during this period, and often he would be "hyperfocused," worrying all the time that his mother might die. He also was notably smaller than his peers, and his parents thought the drugs were probably curbing his growth. "That has been the most frustrating part. I never know what is my son and what is the drug," his mother says.

Today, her ambivalence about the medications is such that she wishes she could turn back the clock and try a different tack. "My Andrew is not a circle or a square, he is not even a triangle," she explains. "He is a rhombus trapezoid, and he will never fit into those other molds. And I do think that if we had never put him on medicine, he would have learned many more coping mechanisms, because he would have had to. And we should be able to help kids like Andrew without making them feel so different, without suppressing their appetite, and without worrying about the long-term effects of the drugs—all the things I am sitting here worrying about."

When Andrew was younger, he was allowed "medication breaks" now and then, and when I ask him what that was like, he recalls how nice it was to fall asleep without having to take cloni-dine. Being off meds, he says, "feels less constricted, more free." Still, he tells me, he is about to graduate from high school, and he has ended up at a good place. He has a girlfriend, he enjoys skate-boarding and playing the guitar, and thanks to the auto mechanics class, he now has career plans, as he intends to one day open his own garage. "It's hard to think back to a time when it could have been different," he says, shrugging, thinking about his life on med-ications. "I don't think there was a right or wrong choice—this is just how it's been."

If You're a Ward of the State, You Must Be Bipolar

The medicating of foster children in the United States took off in the late 1990s, and so I thought, in order to gain a perspective on this phenomenon, I would visit with Theresa Gately. She and her hus-band, Bill, took ninety-six foster children into their Boston home from 1996 to 2000, and thus she personally witnessed this change in how our society treats foster kids. The first children that Social Services sent them weren't medicated, but by the end, "it felt like all of them were on psych drugs," she says.

Over the course of several hours, we sat on her front porch, which looks out over a busy street in a fairly rough part of Boston, and nearly everyone who walked by waved and affectionately shouted hello, no matter what their ethnicity. Theresa Gately is a thin woman with straw blond hair, and she has her own history as a foster child. Born in 1964, she was sexually abused by her step-father, and she turned so defiant as a teenager that she landed in a Maryland psychiatric hospital. There she was put on Thorazine and other neuroleptics, and, she said, it wasn't until she started "tongu-ing" the drugs—pretending to take them while nurses were watch-ing and then spitting them out—that her head started to clear. However, she isn't "anti-medication" at all, and during a difficult time a few years back, she found an antidepressant and a mood sta-bilizer to be extremely helpful, and she remains on those drugs.

As a foster mother, Gately was required to follow "medical advice" and give psychiatric medications to the children who arrived on them. Most of the children were on cocktails, and it seemed to her that the drugs were primarily being used to make the children quieter and easier to manage. "One young girl, Liz, was so heavily medicated that she couldn't think at all," she recalls. "You would ask her if she wanted a pork chop and she wouldn't answer." Another was "almost mute when she came to me. The last thing you need to do is give somebody who already doesn't talk more drugs." Theresa ran through the histories of several more of her foster children, concluding that "maybe nine to eleven [of the ninety-six children] needed to have the drugs and were being helped."

She has kept track of a number of the ninety-six children, and as could be expected, many have struggled mightily as adults. Had she, I wondered, noticed a difference in the fate of those who stayed on the drug cocktails, versus those who stopped taking them?

"When I look back on the kids that stayed on the drugs and those who got off, it is the ones that are off that are the successes," she says. "Liz should never have been on the drugs. She got off the drugs and is doing great. She is a full-time student in nursing school and almost ready to graduate, and is about to get married. The thing is, if you get off the drugs, you start building these coping mechanisms. You learn internal controls. You start building these strengths. Most of these kids have had very bad stuff happen to them. But they are able to rise above their past once they are off the medications, and then they can move on. The kids who were drugged and continue to be drugged never have that opportunity to build coping skills. And because they never had that opportunity as a teenager, as an adult they don't know what to do with themselves."

Hers isn't a scientific study. But her experience does offer a peek into the toll that the medicating of foster kids is taking. Most of those who stayed on the drugs, she says, ended up "filing for disability."

Like Theresa Gately, Sam Clayborn, who is a social worker in New Rochelle, New York, can tell from personal experience what it is like to have been a foster kid in the United States. When he was born in Harlem in 1965, his mother was unable to take care of him, and by age six he was living in a residential group home. We met in his apartment in Croton-on-Hudson, and very quickly he put things into a historical context. "They weren't so hot on psychiatric diagnoses back then," he explains. "They were more into beating your ass, restraining you, and just throwing you into an empty fucking room. I'm glad I grew up when it was like that rather than what it is like today, because if I grew up now, I'd be fucking drugged up. I'd be doped out and zonked out."

For the past two decades, he and his partner Eva Dech have worked as advocates for foster children and poor youth in Westchester County. She also had a tough childhood, which included a stint in a mental hospital where she was forcibly medicated, and they see a racial aspect to this medicating of foster children. Starting around 2000, rates of black youth diagnosed with bipolar disorder soared, and based on hospital discharges, they are now said to suffer from bipolar disorder at a greater rate than whites.[1] The diagnosis provides a rationale for medicating the kids, and that in turn puts yet one more burden on them, Clayborn believes.

"The Tuskegee syphilis experiments were nothing compared to this. That's mild shit compared to what they are doing to black kids today. The pharmaceutical companies and the government are fucking in cahoots, and they are doing a wicked dance with a lot of people's lives. They don't give a fuck about these kids. It's all about capitalism, and they will sacrifice all the niggers in the hood. We are damaging these kids for life, and the majority of these kids will never rebound. These kids will be destroyed and they are going to make the SSI rolls more overwhelmed."

One of the area youth that Clayborn has mentored is Jonathan Barrow, who had been splayed out on the living room floor during our conversation, half sleeping and half listening. Born in 1985 in Harlem to a mother on crack, Jonathan bounced around as a child, eventually ending up at his grandfather's home in White Plains. At age seven, he was diagnosed with ADHD and put on Ritalin. In junior high, he started becoming rebellious and got into a few fights, and that led to a diagnosis of bipolar disorder and a prescription for Depakote and Risperdal. Up until that time, Jonathan had been an active adolescent who spent most of his free time on the basketball court, but now he began spending most of his time "in his room isolated," Clayborn says. He went onto the SSI disability rolls before he turned eighteen, apparently "severely impaired" by this bipolar illness, and he remains on SSI today. "I'm doped up," Jonathan explains, still somewhat heavy-lidded from his afternoon nap. "I don't like it. It makes me sleepy and feel like a dope fiend."

At this, Clayborn rose from his chair, more agitated than ever. "This is happening to a lot of the brothers today, and once they are on the medication, it takes them away from themselves. They lose all the willpower to struggle, to change, to make something out of themselves and have success. They succumb to the chemical handcuffs of the motherfucking medications. It's medical bondage is what it is."

Not long after that interview, I attended a meeting of the Statewide Youth Advisory Council at Westborough State Hospital in Massachusetts. The council is composed of young adults who entered the mental health system before they were eighteen, and it provides advice to the Massachusetts Department of Mental Health on what it can do to help teenagers with psychiatric problems thrive as adults. In 2008, the coordinator of the council was Mathew McWade, who was first diagnosed when he was in the seventh grade, and it was he who made my visit possible.

At the meeting, I went around the table and asked everyone how they had gotten into the system. I thought I might hear stories of kids who were first put on a stimulant or an antidepressant and then moved on to a bipolar diagnosis, and while there was some of that, several men in this racially mixed group told of yet another societal route to psychiatric disability.

When Cal Jones* was sixteen years old, he had gotten into a violent argument that ended with his being treated in the emergency room at Children's Hospital in Boston. There he told ER staff that

* Cal Jones is a pseudonym. Hospital staff asked that I not reveal the names of the hospitalized patients.

he "wanted to kill the other kid," a sentiment that earned him a trip to a psychiatric facility, where he was diagnosed with bipolar illness. "They didn't run any tests," he says. "They just asked me a bunch of questions and started me on a bunch of medicines." Since then, he has been hospitalized twenty-five times. He doesn't like antipsychotics, and so he regularly stops taking them when he is discharged, preferring to smoke marijuana instead, and inevitably that leads to trouble. "I get arrested and get sent back to the (psych) hospital, and I'm like okay, it's just a business. The more patients they have, the more the doctors make. But I hate it. I can't stand it. I feel like a slave in a Nazi camp."

At least three others at the meeting told similar stories. One young man said that shortly after he graduated from high school in 2002, he got upset over a family matter and smashed the windows of his car. "I was having a bad time. They wanted to label me as mentally ill. I don't know if I am." Another explained that six months earlier, after he had committed a minor criminal act, a judge had given him the choice of going to prison or to Westborough State Hospital. "It's safer in here than in prison," he says, explaining his choice. A third member of the council said that he had been diagnosed with bipolar illness at age thirteen after "I killed somebody."

Their stories bore witness to another pathway into the mental health system for poor youth. Delinquency and crime can get them diagnosed, medicated, and routed into a mental institution. While many of the young men on the council were on heavy-duty cocktails, moving about and speaking in a sluggish manner, the one who had told of having killed somebody was now living in the community and not taking any medications. "If the state really wants to help us, it should put money into a jobs program," he says.

Back to Syracuse

As a last stop, I returned to visit the two Syracuse families—Jason and Kelley Smith and Sean and Gwen Oates—that I had met in the spring of 2008. Families, friends, therapists, and doctors had given the two families conflicting advice about whether they should medicate their child, and faced with such bewildering advice, the two families had come to opposite decisions.

Jessica

I knew from an earlier telephone conversation that Jessica Smith had been doing well, and when I arrived at their home, she bounded to the door to welcome me, much as she had a year earlier. When she was diagnosed with bipolar disorder at age four, her parents had rejected the recommendations of staff at the State University of New York Health Sciences Center that she be put on a cocktail of three drugs that included an antipsychotic. Today, they have an eight-year-old girl reminiscent of Maurice Sendak's endearing "Really Rosie" character on their hands. Jessica, who is very much the extroverted child, had recently starred in a school musical. "She just loves it," her father says, and he pointed to her behavior on opening night as evidence of how much better she had become at controlling her emotions. "She was playing a brainiac, and another girl in the show stole her chair, which she wasn't supposed to do. We could see that Jessica was upset. But then she let it pass. It showed that she is getting better at de-escalating situations."

Although Jessica no longer sees a therapist, "there are still struggles," her mother says. "She still has a hard time with groups, with playing with more than one kid at a time. And she will still lash out if someone hurts her feelings. She wants to be the boss, and she can be loud and boisterous. But the kicking and biting is gone."

Adds her father: "She has a big personality, but that is like others in my family. I was the same way. I was very loud. I wouldn't sit still. And I turned out all right."

Nathan

Nathan Oates had gone through a more topsy-turvy twelve months. I had called his mother several times during the year, and in the summer of 2008, Nathan—who had been diagnosed with ADHD at age four and subsequently with bipolar illness—had been doing well. He took Concerta for the ADHD and Risperdal for the bipolar disorder, and that summer he discovered that he "loves track," his mother told me. "They are teaching him how to do hurdles and the long jump." Even more important, his mood swings had become less severe, his hostility toward his sister had lessened, and he was sleeping better, too. "He said he wants to start being more responsible," his mother said. "He gets up in the morning and makes his bed, and now he is at a point he will take a shower by himself. He is starting to do things without my hounding him. It seems he is kind of maturing on his own."

This was a heartening report, but that relatively peaceful time ended when Nathan returned to school in the fall. He became quite anxious and moody, and started resisting going to school. The physician's assistant overseeing his care upped his Risperdal, hoping that would quiet his anxiety. "They are trying to figure out whether his anxiety is bipolar related or a separate disorder," his mother explained, in a phone interview in early 2009. "The ADHD is fine and under control. If this doesn't work, they will give him an anti-anxiety medication. They want to make sure that he doesn't get too lethargic under the higher dose of Risperdal."

When I returned to Syracuse in the spring, Nathan's parents were close to despair over the difficulties that he was experiencing. Nathan's anxiety hadn't abated, and to make matters worse, he had lost control of his bladder. A few days earlier, his mother had witnessed in heartbreaking fashion how this was affecting her son. "I went to pick him up in school, and he was sitting in the middle of the room at his desk alone," she says. "It was almost like he was invisible to everybody else. The teachers swear he has friends but he never talks about anybody. There is only one classmate who doesn't pick on him." This isolation, his mother adds, followed Nathan into the home. "He stays in his room all the time."

Nathan's father remained hopeful that another "medication adjustment" would help his son. But beyond that, both parents confessed that they were at a loss about what to do. The psychologist who counseled Nathan was running out of ideas; the school wasn't doing much to alleviate Nathan's severe anxiety; and their families and friends didn't appreciate how difficult this all was. "I feel so alone in this," his mother says. "It stinks. It's wearing. It's exhausting. I cry for him. I just don't know what to do anymore. I don't know how to help him."

Before I left, Nathan came down from his room, and he shyly showed me a few of his favorite possessions, including a *Star Wars* helmet. He told me that Zachariah was his best friend (the one classmate who didn't tease him), and then he taught me how to fold a piece of paper into an airplane, which he sent flying around the room. "I like to make movies" with a video recorder, he says, and eventually I quizzed him on a couple of subjects he loves. "The *Titanic* sank in 1912," he informs me, and after that he proudly identified various bones in the human body—he is fascinated with drawings of skeletons. "His teachers all love him," his mother says, and at that moment, it was very easy to see why.

part four

Explication of a Delusion

The Rise of an Ideology

*"It was not surprising that medical students accepted
the dogma of biomedical reductionism in psychiatry
uncritically; they had no time to read and analyze the
original literature. What took me a while to understand,
as I moved through my residency, was that psychiatrists
rarely do the critical reading either."*
—COLIN ROSS, CLINICAL ASSOCIATE PROFESSOR OF
PSYCHIATRY AT SOUTHWEST MEDICAL CENTER IN
DALLAS, TEXAS (1995)[1]

We have investigated the epidemic of mental illness that has erupted in the United States during the past fifty years in a step-by-step fashion, and having reviewed the outcomes literature for each of the major disorders, there is an obvious next question to address. Why does our society believe that a "psychopharmacological revolution" has taken place during the past fifty years, when the scientific literature so clearly shows that the revolution failed to materialize? Or, to put it another way, what is the source of our remarkable societal delusion?

To answer that, we need to trace the rise of "biological psychiatry" and then look at the stories that psychiatry—once it embraced that belief system—came to tell.

Psychiatry's Season of Discontent

During the heady days of the 1950s, when it seemed that a new breakthrough drug was being discovered every year, psychiatry had reason to be optimistic about its future. It now had magic pills like the rest of medicine, and once NIMH researchers and others advanced the chemical imbalance theory of mental disorders, it seemed that these pills might indeed be antidotes to physical diseases. "American psychiatry," exclaimed former NIMH director Gerald Klerman, "accepted psychopharmacology as its domain."[2] But two decades later, those heady days were long gone, and psychiatry was mired in a deep crisis, beleaguered on so many fronts that it worried about its survival. There was a sense, said American Psychiatric Association (APA) director Melvin Sabshin in 1980, that the "profession is under severe siege and is cut off from allies."[3]

The first problem that had arisen for psychiatry was an intellectual challenge to its legitimacy, an attack launched in 1961 by Thomas Szasz, a psychiatrist at the State University of New York in Syracuse. In his book *The Myth of Mental Illness,* he argued that psychiatric disorders weren't medical in kind, but rather labels applied to people who struggled with "problems in living" or simply behaved in socially deviant ways. Psychiatrists, he said, had more in common with ministers and police than they did with physicians. Szasz's criticism rattled the field, since even mainstream publications like the *Atlantic* and *Science* found his argument to be both cogent and important, the latter concluding that his treatise was "enormously courageous and highly informative . . . bold and often brilliant."[4] As Szasz later told the *New York Times,* "In smoke-filled rooms, time and time again, I've heard the view that Szasz has killed psychiatry. I hope so."[5]

His book helped launch an "antipsychiatry" movement, and other academics in the United States and Europe—Michel Foucault, R. D. Laing, David Cooper, and Erving Goffman, just to name a few—joined the fray. All questioned the "medical model" of mental disorders and suggested that madness could be a "sane" reaction to an oppressive society. Mental hospitals might better be described as facilities for social control, rather than for healing, a viewpoint crystallized and popularized in *One Flew Over the Cuckoo's Nest,* which swept the Oscars for 1975. Nurse Ratched was the malevolent cop in that movie, which ended with Randle McMurphy (played by Jack Nicholson) being lobotomized for failing to stay in line.

The second problem that psychiatry faced was a growing competition for patients. In the 1960s and 1970s, a therapy industry blossomed in the United States. Thousands of psychologists and counselors began offering services to the "neurotic" patients that psychiatry had laid claim to ever since Freud had brought his couch to America. By 1975, the nonphysician therapists outnumbered the shrinks in the United States, and with benzodiazepines falling out of favor, the neurotic patients who had been content to pop "happy pills" in the 1960s were embracing primal scream therapy, Esalen retreats, and any number of other "alternative" therapies said to help heal the wounded soul. Partly as a result of this competition, the median earnings of a U.S. psychiatrist in the late 1970s were only $70,600, and while this was a good wage at the time, it still put psychiatry near the bottom of the medical profession. "Nonpsychiatric mental health professionals are laying claim to some, or even all, of psychiatry's task domains," wrote Tufts University psychiatrist David Adler. There was reason, he said, to worry about the "death of psychiatry."[6]

Internal divisions also ran deep. Although the field had turned toward biological psychiatry after the arrival of Thorazine, with most psychiatrists eager to speak well of the drugs, the Freudians who dominated many medical schools in the 1950s had never completely climbed on that bandwagon. While they found some use for the drugs, they still conceived of most disorders as psychological in kind. As such, during the 1970s, there was a deep philosophical split between the Freudians and those who embraced a "medical model" of psychiatric disorders. In addition, there was a third faction in the field, composed of "social psychiatrists." This group thought that psychosis and emotional distress often arose from an individual's conflict with his or her environment. If that was so, altering that environment or creating a supportive new one—as Loren Mosher had done with his Soteria Project—would be a good way to help a person heal. Like the Freudians, the social psychiatrists did not see drugs as the centerpiece of care, but rather as agents that were sometimes helpful and sometimes not. With these three approaches in conflict, the field was suffering from an "identity crisis," Sabshin said.[7]

By the end of the 1970s, the leaders of the APA regularly spoke of how their field was in a fight for "survival." In the 1950s, psychiatry had become the fastest growing specialty in medicine, but during the 1970s, the percentage of medical school graduates choosing to go into it dropped from 11 percent to less than 4 percent. This lack of interest in the field, the *New York Times* reported in an article titled "Psychiatry's Anxious Years," was "seen as a particularly painful indictment."[8]

Avoiding the Obvious

Such was psychiatry's self-assessment in the 1970s. It looked into the mirror and saw the field under attack by an "antipsychiatry" movement, threatened economically by nonphysician therapists, and split by internal disagreements. But, in fact, it was turning a blind eye to the root problem, which was that its medications were failing in the marketplace. This was what had allowed the crisis to take hold and spread.

If the first generation of psychotropics had truly worked, the public would have been pounding on psychiatrists' doors seeking prescriptions for these medicines. Szasz's argument that mental illness was a "myth" might have been seen by some as intellectually interesting, worthy of debate in academic circles, but it wouldn't have curtailed the public's appetite for drugs that made them feel and function better. Similarly, psychiatry could have brushed off the competition from psychologists and counselors as a harmless nuisance. Depressed and anxious people might have indulged in screaming therapies and mud baths, and sought out talk therapy from psychologists, but the prescription bottles would have remained in their medicine cabinets. Nor would the internal divisions have persisted. If the pills had proved to provide long-term relief, then all of psychiatry would have embraced the medical model, for the other proffered forms of care—psychoanalysis and nurturing environments—would have been perceived as too labor-intensive and unnecessary. Psychiatry fell into a crisis during the 1970s because the "miracle pill" aura around its drugs had disappeared.

From the moment that Thorazine and the neuroleptics were introduced into asylum medicine, many hospitalized patients had found them objectionable, so much so that many "tongued" the pills. This practice was so pervasive that Smith, Kline and French, in the early 1960s, developed a liquid Thorazine, which the patients could be made to swallow. Other manufacturers developed injectable forms of their neuroleptics so that hospitalized patients could be forcibly medicated. "Warning!" an ad for liquid Thorazine screamed. "Mental Patients Are Notorious DRUG EVADERS."[9] In the early 1970s, patients who had experienced such forced treatment began forming groups with names such as the "Insane Liberation Front" and the "Network Against Psychiatric Assault." At their rallies, many carried signs that read HUGS, NOT DRUGS!

One Flew Over the Cuckoo's Nest helped legitimatize that protest in the public's mind, and that movie appeared shortly after psychiatry suffered the embarrassment of news reports that the Soviet Union was using neuroleptics to torture dissidents. These drugs apparently inflicted such physical pain that quite sane people would recant their criticisms of a Communist government rather than endure repeated doses of Haldol. Dissident writings told of psychiatric drugs that turned people into "vegetables," the *New York Times* concluding that this practice could be seen as "spiritual murder."[10] Then, in 1975, when Indiana senator Birch Bayh launched an investigation of the use of neuroleptics in juvenile institutions, ex–mental patients hijacked the public hearing to testify that the drugs caused "excruciating pain" and had turned them into emotional "zombies." Antipsychotics, said one ex-patient, "are used not to heal or help, but to torture and control. It is that simple."[11]

These drugs were no longer being presented to the public as agents that made a raving madman "sit up and talk sense," as *Time* had reported in 1954, and even as this new view of antipsychotics was sinking into the public mind, the benzodiazepines fell into disrepute. The federal government classified them as schedule IV drugs, and soon Edward Kennedy was announcing that benzos had "produced a nightmare of dependence and addiction."[12] Antipsychotics and the benzodiazepines were the two classes of drugs that had launched the psychopharmacology revolution, and with both now seen by the public in a negative light, sales of psychiatric drugs plunged in the 1970s, from 223 million drugstore prescriptions in 1973 to 153 million in 1980.[13] In its article on psychiatry's "anxious years," the *New York Times* explained that a primary reason that medical school graduates were avoiding the field was because its treatments were perceived to be "low in efficacy."

This was a topic that psychiatry did not like to talk about or acknowledge. Yet, at the same time, everyone understood what gave psychiatrists a competitive advantage in the therapy marketplace. New Jersey psychiatrist Arthur Platt was at a professional meeting in the late 1970s when a keynote speaker laid it out for them: "He said, 'What is going to save us is that we're physicians,' " Platt recalls.[14] They could write prescriptions and the psychologists and social workers couldn't, and that was an economic landscape that presented the field with an obvious solution. If the image of psychotropic drugs could be rehabilitated, psychiatry would thrive.

Putting on the White Coat

The process that led to the rehabilitation of psychiatric drugs in the public's mind got under way in the 1970s. Threatened by Szasz's criticism that psychiatrists did not really function as "doctors," the APA argued that psychiatrists needed to more explicitly embrace this role. "A vigorous effort to remedicalize psychiatry should be strongly supported," said the APA's Sabshin in 1977.[15] Numerous articles appeared in the *American Journal of Psychiatry* and other journals explaining what this meant. "The medical model," wrote University of Kentucky psychiatrist Arnold Ludwig, is based on the "premise that the primary identity of the psychiatrist is as a physician."[16] Mental disorders, said Paul Blaney, from the University of Texas, were to be seen as "organic diseases."[17] The psychiatrist's focus should be on making the proper diagnosis, which arose from a cataloguing of the "symptoms and signs of illness," said Samuel Guze, from Washington University. It was only psychiatrists, he added, that had the "medical training necessary for the optimal application of the most effective treatments available today for psychiatric patients: psychoactive drugs and ECT [electroshock]."[18]

Theirs was a model of care straight out of internal medicine. The doctor in that setting took a patient's temperature, or tested blood glucose levels, or did some other diagnostic test, and then once the illness was identified, prescribed the appropriate drug. "Remedicalization" of psychiatry meant that the Freudian couch was to be trotted off to the Dumpster, and once that happened, psychiatry could expect to see its public image restored. "The medical model is most strongly linked in the popular mind to scientific truth," explained Tufts University psychiatrist David Adler.[19]

In 1974, the APA picked Robert Spitzer from Columbia University to head up the task force that would, through a revision of the APA's *Diagnostic and Statistical Manual,* prompt psychiatrists to treat patients in this way. DSM-II, which had been published in 1967, reflected Freudian notions of "neurosis," and Spitzer and others argued that such diagnostic categories were notoriously "unreliable." He was joined by four other biologically oriented psychiatrists on the task force, including Samuel Guze at Washington University. DSM-III, Spitzer promised, would serve as "a defense of the medical model as applied to psychiatric problems."[20] The manual, said APA president Jack Weinberg in 1977, would "clarify to anyone who may be in doubt that we regard psychiatry as a specialty of medicine."[21]

Three years later, Spitzer and his colleagues published their handiwork. DSM-III identified 265 disorders, all of which were said to be distinct in kind. More than one hundred psychiatrists had contributed to the five-hundred-page tome, authorship that indicated it represented the collective wisdom of American psychiatry. To make a DSM-III diagnosis, a psychiatrist would determine if a patient had the requisite number of symptoms said to be characteristic of the disease. For instance, there were nine symptoms common to "major depressive episode," and if five were present, then a diagnosis of this illness could be made. The new manual, Spitzer boasted, had been "field tested," and those trials had proven that clinicians in different facilities, when faced with the same patient, were likely to arrive at the same diagnosis, proof that diagnosis would no longer be as subjective as before. "These [reliability] results were so much better than we had expected" they would be, he said.[22]

Psychiatry now had its medical-model "bible," and the APA and others in the field rushed to extol it. DSM-III is an "amazing document . . . a brilliant tour de force," Sabshin said.[23] "The development of DSM-III," said Gerald Klerman, "represents a fateful point in the history of the American psychiatric profession . . . [and] its use represents a reaffirmation on the part of American psychiatry to its medical identity and its commitment to scientific medicine."[24] Thanks to DSM-III, wrote Columbia University psychiatrist Jerrold Maxmen, "the ascendance of scientific psychiatry became official . . . the old [psychoanalytical] psychiatry derives from theory, the new psychiatry from fact."[25]

But as critics at the time noted, it was difficult to understand why this manual should be regarded as a great *scientific* achievement. No scientific discoveries had led to this reconfiguring of psychiatric diagnoses. The biology of mental disorders remained unknown, and the authors of DSM-III even confessed that this was so. Most of the diagnoses, they said, "have not yet been fully validated by data about such important correlates as clinical course, outcome, family history, and treatment response."[26] It was also evident that the boundary lines between disease and no disease had been arbitrarily drawn. Why did it require the presence of five of nine symptoms said to be characteristic of depression for a diagnosis of the illness to be made? Why not six such symptoms? Or four? DSM-III, wrote Theodore Blau, president of the American Psychological Association, was more of "a political position paper for the American Psychiatric Association than a scientifically-based classification system."[27]

None of that mattered, however. With the publication of DSM-III, psychiatry had publicly donned a white coat. The Freudians had been vanquished, the concept of neurosis basically tossed into the trash bin, and everyone in the profession was now expected to embrace the medical model. "It is time to state forcefully that the identity crisis is over," Sabshin said.[28] Indeed, the *American Journal of Psychiatry* urged its members to "speak with a united voice, not only to secure support, but to buttress [psychiatry's] position against the numerous other mental health professionals seeking patients and prestige."[29] The medical model and DSM-III, observed University of Tennessee psychiatrist Ben Bursten in 1981, had been used to "rally the troops . . . to thwart the attackers [and] to rout the enemy within."[30]

Indeed, it wasn't only the Freudians who had been vanquished. Loren Mosher and his band of social psychiatrists also had been roundly defeated and sent packing.

When Mosher started his Soteria Project in 1971, everyone understood that it threatened the "medical model" theory of psychiatric disorders. Newly diagnosed schizophrenia patients were being treated in an ordinary home, staffed by nonprofessionals, without drugs. Their outcomes were to be compared with patients treated with drugs in a hospital setting. If the Soteria patients fared better, what would that say about psychiatry and its therapies? From the minute that Mosher proposed it, the leaders of American psychiatry had tried to make sure it would fail. Although Mosher headed up the Center for Schizophrenia Studies at the NIMH, he'd still needed to obtain funding for Soteria from the grants committee that oversaw NIMH's extramural research program, which was composed of psychiatrists from leading medical schools, and that committee slashed his initial request of $700,000 for five years to $150,000 for two years. This ensured that the project would struggle with finances from the outset, and then, in the mid-1970s, when Mosher began reporting good results for his Soteria patients, the committee struck back. The study had "serious flaws" in its design, it said. Evidence that Soteria patients had superior outcomes was "not compelling."[31] Mosher must be biased, the academic psychiatrists concluded, and they demanded that Mosher be removed as the primary investigator. "The message was clear," Mosher said, in an interview twenty-five years later. "If we were getting outcomes this good, then I must not be an honest scientist."[32] Soon after that, the grants committee shut off funding for the experiment altogether, and Mosher was pushed from his job at the NIMH, even though the committee had grudgingly concluded, in its final review of the project, that "this project has probably demonstrated that a flexible, community based, non-drug residential psychosocial program manned by non-professional staff can do as well as a more conventional community mental health program."

The NIMH never funded an experiment of this type again. Furthermore, Mosher's ouster provided everyone in the field with a clear message: Those who did not get behind the biomedical model would not have much of a future.

Psychiatry's Mad Men

Once DSM-III was published, the APA set out to market its "medical model" to the public. Although professional medical organizations have always sought to advance the economic interests of their members, this was the first time that a professional organization so thoroughly adopted the marketing practices familiar to any commercial trade association. In 1981, the APA established a "division of publications and marketing" to "deepen the medical identification of psychiatrists," and in very short order, the APA transformed itself into a very effective marketing machine.[33] "It is the task of the APA to protect the earning power of psychiatrists," said APA vice president Paul Fink in 1986.[34]

As a first step, the APA established its own press in 1981, which was expected to bring "psychiatry's best talent and current knowledge before the reading public."[35] The press was soon publishing more than thirty books a year, with Sabshin happily noting in 1983 that the books "will provide much positive public education about the profession."[36] The APA also set up committees to review the textbooks it published, intent on making sure that authors stayed on message. Indeed, in 1986, as it readied publication of *Treatment of Psychiatric Disorders,* the APA's Roger Peele—one of the organization's elected officials—worried anew about this concern. "How do we organize 32,000 members for advocacy?" he asked. "Who should be allowed to speak to the issue of the treatment of psychiatric illness? Only researchers? Only the academic elite? . . . Only members appointed by APA presidents?"[37]

Very early on, the APA realized that it would be valuable to develop a nationwide roster of "experts" that could promote the medical-model story to the media. It established a "public affairs institute" to oversee this effort, which involved training members "in techniques for dealing with radio and television." In 1985 alone, the APA ran nine "How to Survive a Television Interview" workshops.[38] Meanwhile, every district branch in the country identified "public affairs representatives" who could be called on to speak to the press. "We now have an experienced network of trained leaders who can effectively cope with all varieties of media," Sabshin said.[39]

Much like any commercial organization selling a product, the APA regularly courted the press and exulted when it received positive coverage. In December 1980, it held a daylong media conference on "new advances in psychiatry" that "was attended by representatives of some of the nation's most prestigious and widely circulated newspapers," Sabshin crowed.[40] Next, it placed "public service spots" on television to tell its story, an effort that included sponsoring a two-hour program on cable television titled *Your Mental Health*. It also developed "fact sheets" for distribution to the media that told of the prevalence of mental disorders and the effectiveness of psychiatric drugs. Harvey Rubin, chair of the APA's public affairs committee, taped a popular radio program that carried the medical-model message to listeners around the country.[41] The APA had launched an all-out media blitz—it handed out awards to journalists whose stories it liked—and every year Sabshin detailed the good publicity this effort was generating. In 1983, he noted that "with the help and urging of the Division of Public Affairs, *U.S. News and World Report* published a major cover story on depression, which included substantial quotes from prominent psychiatrists."[42] Two years later, Sabshin announced that "APA spokespersons were placed on the Phil Donahue program, *Nightline* and other network programs." That same year, it "helped develop a *Reader's Digest* book chapter on mental health."[43]

All of this paid big dividends. Newspaper and magazine headlines now regularly told of a "revolution" under way in psychiatry. Readers of the *New York Times* learned that "human depression is linked to genes" and that scientists were uncovering the "biology of fear and anxiety." Researchers, the paper reported, had discovered "a chemical key to depression."[44] Societal belief in biological psychiatry was clearly taking hold, just as the APA hoped, and in 1984, Jon Franklin of the *Baltimore Evening Sun* wrote a seven-part series titled "The Mind-Fixers" on the astonishing advances that were being made in the field.[45] He put this revolution into a historical context:

> Since the days of Sigmund Freud the practice of psychiatry has been more art than science. Surrounded by an aura of witchcraft, proceeding on impression and hunch, often ineffective, it was the bumbling and sometimes humorous stepchild of modern science. But for a decade and more, research psychiatrists have been working quietly in laboratories, dissecting the brains of mice and men and teasing out the chemical formulas that unlock the secrets of the mind. Now, in the 1980s, their work is paying off. They are rapidly identifying the interlocking molecules that produce human thought and emotion. . . . As a result, psychiatry today stands on the threshold of becoming an exact science, as precise and quantifiable as molecular genetics. Ahead lies an era of psychic engineering, and the development of specialized drugs and therapies to heal sick minds.

Franklin, who interviewed more than fifty leading psychiatrists for his series, called this new science "molecular psychiatry," which was "capable of curing the mental diseases that afflict perhaps 20 percent of the population." He was awarded the Pulitzer Prize for expository journalism for this work.

Books written by psychiatrists for the lay press at this time told a similar story. In *The Good News About Depression*, Yale University psychiatrist Mark Gold informed readers that "we who work in this new field call our science *biopsychiatry,* the new medicine of the mind. . . . It returns psychiatry to the medical model, incorporating all the latest advances in scientific research, and for the first time in history, providing a systematic method of diagnosis, treatment, cure and even prevention of mental suffering." In the past few years, Gold added, psychiatry had conducted "some of the most incredible medical research ever done. . . . We have probed the frontiers of science and human understanding wherein lie the ultimate comprehension and cure of all mental illnesses."[46]

If there was one book that cemented this belief in the public's mind, it was *The Broken Brain*. Published in 1984 and written by Nancy Andreasen, future editor of the *American Journal of Psychiatry,* it was touted as "the first comprehensive account of the biomedical revolution in the diagnosis and treatment of mental illness." In it, Andreasen concisely set forth the tenets of biological psychiatry: "The major psychiatric illnesses are diseases. They should be considered medical illnesses just as diabetes, heart disease, and cancer are. The emphasis in this model is on carefully diagnosing each specific illness from which the patient suffers, just as an internist or neurologist would."[47]

The broken brain—hers was a book with a brilliant title, one that conveyed a bottom-line message that the public could easily grasp and remember. However, what most readers failed to notice was that Andreasen, in several places in her book, confessed that researchers had not yet actually *found* that people diagnosed with psychiatric disorders have broken brains. Researchers had new tools for investigating brain function, and they hoped this knowledge would come. "Nevertheless, the *spirit* of a revolution—the sense that we are going to change things dramatically, even if the process requires a number of years—is very much present," Andreasen explained.[48]

Twenty-five years later, that breakthrough moment still lies in the future. The biological underpinnings of schizophrenia, depression, and bipolar disorder remain unknown. But the public has long since been convinced otherwise, and we can see now the marketing process that got this delusion under way. At the start of the 1980s, psychiatry was worried about its future. Sales of psychiatric drugs had notably declined in the past seven years, and few medical school graduates wanted to go into the field. In response, the APA mounted a sophisticated marketing campaign to sell its medical model to the public, and a few years later the public could only gasp in awe at the apparent advances that were being made. A revolution was under way, psychiatrists were now "mind-fixers," and as a Johns Hopkins "brain chemist," Michael Kuhar, told Jon Franklin, this "explosion of new knowledge" was going to lead to new drugs and broad changes in society that would be "fantastic!"[49]

Four-Part Harmony

Psychiatrists were not the only ones in American society who were eager to tell of a biomedical revolution in psychiatry. During the 1980s, a powerful coalition of voices came together to tell this story, and this was a group with financial clout, intellectual prestige, and moral authority. Together they enjoyed all the resources and social status necessary to convince the public of almost anything, and this storytelling coalition has stayed intact ever since.

As we saw earlier, the financial interests of pharmaceutical companies and physicians became closely aligned in 1951, when Congress gave doctors their monopolistic prescribing privileges. But in the 1980s, the APA and the industry took this relationship one step further and essentially entered into a drug marketing "partnership." The APA and psychiatrists at academic medical centers served as the front men in this arrangement, the public thereby seeing "men of science" on stage, while the pharmaceutical companies quietly provided the funds for this capitalistic enterprise.

The seed for this partnership was planted in 1974 when the APA formed a task force to assess the importance of pharmaceutical support for its future. The answer was "very," and in 1980 that led the APA to institute a policy change of transformative importance. Up to that time, pharmaceutical companies had regularly put up fancy exhibits at the APA's annual meeting and paid for social events, but they hadn't been allowed to put on "scientific" talks. However, in 1980, the APA's board of directors voted to allow pharmaceutical companies to start sponsoring scientific symposiums at its annual meeting. The drug firms paid the APA a fee for this privilege, and soon the most well-attended events at its annual meeting were the industry-funded symposiums, which provided the attendees a sumptuous meal and featured presentations by a "panel of experts." The speakers were paid handsomely to give the talks, and the drug companies made certain that their presentations went off without a hitch. "These symposia are meticulously prepared with rehearsals before the meeting, and they have excellent audio-visual content," Sabshin explained.[50]

The door to a full-fledged "partnership" had been flung open, one that would sell the medical model and the benefits of psychiatric medications to the public, and the APA now began to regularly rely on pharmaceutical money to fund many of its activities. The drug companies began "endowing" continuing education programs and psychiatric grand rounds at hospitals, and, as one psychiatrist observed, the companies were "happy to cap them with free food and booze to sweeten the love of learning."[51] When the APA launched a political action committee in 1982 to lobby Congress, this effort was funded by pharma. The industry helped pay for the APA's media-training workshops. In 1985, APA secretary Fred Gottlieb observed that the APA was now receiving "millions of dollars of drug house money" each year.[52] Two years later, an issue of the APA's newsletter, *Psychiatric News,* featured a photo of Smith, Kline and French handing a check to APA president Robert Pasnau, which led one reader to quip that the APA had become the "American Psychopharmaceutical Association."[53] The APA was prospering financially now, with its revenues jumping from $10.5 million in 1980 to $21.4 million in 1987, and it settled into a fancy new building in Washington, D.C. It openly talked about "our partners in industry."[54]

For the drug companies, the best part of this new partnership was that it enabled them to turn psychiatrists at top medical schools into "speakers," even while those doctors considered themselves "independent." The paid-for symposiums at the annual meetings greased this new relationship. The symposiums were said to be "educational" presentations, with the drug companies promising not to "control" what the experts said. Yet their presentations were *rehearsed,* and every speaker knew that if he broke from that script and started talking about the drawbacks of psychiatric medications, he would not be invited back.* There would be no industry-sponsored symposiums on "supersensitivity psychosis," or the addictive effects of benzodiazepines, or how antidepressants were no more effective than active placebo. These speakers came to be known as "thought leaders," their presence on the symposium panels elevating them to the status of "stars" in the field, and by the early 2000s, they were getting paid $2,000 to $10,000 per speech. "Some of us," confessed E. Fuller Torrey, "believe that the present system is approaching a high-class form of prostitution."[55]

These "thought leaders" also became the experts regularly quoted by the media, and they wrote the textbooks published by the APA. Psychiatry's thought leaders shaped our society's understanding of mental disorders, and once they began serving as paid speakers, the pharmaceutical companies sent money their way through multiple channels. As the *New England Journal of Medicine* observed in 2000, thought leaders "serve as consultants to companies whose products they are studying, join advisory boards and speakers' bureaus, enter into patent and royalty arrangements, agree to be the listed authors of articles ghostwritten by interested companies, promote drugs and devices at company-sponsored symposiums, and allow themselves to be plied with expensive gifts and trips to luxurious settings."[56] Nor was it just a few psychiatrists from academia that pharma courted with its dollars. The drug industry understood this was a very effective way to market their drugs, and collectively the companies began paying money to virtually every well-known figure in the field. In 2000, when the *New England Journal of Medicine* tried to find an expert to write an

---

* The academic psychiatrists also began to regularly give dinner talks to local psychiatric groups, and in 2000, University of Mississippi psychiatrist John Norton confessed in a letter to the *New England Journal of Medicine* that after he wrote about the side effects of the sponsor's drug, "my invitations to speak suddenly dropped from four to six times per month to essentially none." Prior to that experience, he said, "I deluded myself into thinking I was educating physicians, and not being swayed by the sponsors."

editorial on depression, it "found very few who did not have financial ties to drug companies that make antidepressants."

The NIMH also joined this storytelling coalition. The biological psychiatrists knew that they had successfully captured the NIMH when the Soteria Project was closed and Mosher was ousted, and during the 1980s the NIMH actively promoted the biological psychiatry story to the public, an effort that took wing under the leadership of Shervert Frazier. Prior to being picked to head the NIMH in 1984, Frazier directed the APA's Commission on Public Affairs, which had run the media-training workshops underwritten by pharmaceutical firms, and soon Frazier was announcing that the NIMH, for the first time in its forty-year history, would launch a major educational campaign called the Depression Awareness, Recognition and Treatment (DART) program. This educational effort would inform the public that depressive disorders are "common, serious and treatable," the NIMH said. Pharmaceutical companies would "contribute resources, knowledge and other forms of assistance to the project," which the NIMH promised would run for at least a decade.[57] As it helped expand the market for psychiatric medications, the NIMH even assured the public that the broken-brain story was true. "Two decades of research have shown that [psychiatric disorders] are diseases and illnesses like any other diseases and illnesses," said NIMH director Lewis Judd in 1990, even though nobody had ever been able to explain the nature of the pathology.[58]

The final group to participate in this storytelling campaign was the National Alliance for the Mentally Ill. Founded in 1979 by two Wisconsin women, Beverly Young and Harriet Shelter, it arose as a grassroots protest to Freudian theories that blamed schizophrenia on "aloof, uncaring mothers and preoccupied mothers who were unable to bond with their infants," a NAMI historian observed.[59] NAMI was eager to embrace an ideology of a different kind, and the message it sought to spread, said former NAMI president Agnes Hatfield in 1991, was that "mental illness is not a mental health problem; it is a biological illness. There is considerable clarity on the part of families that they are focusing on a physical disease."[60]

For the APA and pharma companies, the emergence of NAMI could not have come at a more opportune moment. This was a *parents'* group eager to embrace biological psychiatry, and both the APA and pharmaceutical firms pounced. In 1983, the APA "entered into an agreement with NAMI" to write a pamphlet on neuroleptic drugs, and soon the APA was encouraging its branches across the country "to foster collaborations with local chapters of the National Alliance for the Mentally Ill."[61] The APA and NAMI joined together to lobby Congress to increase funding for biomedical research, and the beneficiary of that effort, the NIMH—which saw its research budget soar 84 percent during the 1980s—thanked the parents for it. "The NIMH in a very meaningful sense is NAMI's institute," Judd told NAMI president Laurie Flynn in a 1990 letter.[62] By that time, NAMI had more than 125,000 members, most of whom were middle-class, and it was busily seeking to "educate the media, public officials, healthcare providers, educators, the business community, and the general public about the true nature of brain disorders," said one NAMI leader.[63] NAMI brought a powerful moral authority to the telling of the broken-brain story, and naturally pharmaceutical companies were eager to fund its educational programs, with eighteen firms giving NAMI $11.72 million from 1996 to 1999.[64]

In short, a powerful quartet of voices came together during the 1980s eager to inform the public that mental disorders were brain diseases. Pharmaceutical companies provided the financial muscle. The APA and psychiatrists at top medical schools conferred intellectual legitimacy upon the enterprise. The NIMH put the government's stamp of approval on the story. NAMI provided a moral authority. This was a coalition that could convince American society of almost anything, and even better for the coalition, there was one other voice on the scene that, in its own way, helped make the story bulletproof in society's eyes.

The Critics Believe in Aliens

The story of a "psychopharmacology revolution" had first been told in the 1950s and 1960s, and then, as we've seen in this chapter, it was revived in the 1980s. However, the storytellers in the 1980s were more vulnerable to criticism than the storytellers of the earlier decades simply because there was now twenty years of research that undermined their narrative. None of the drugs had proven to help people function well over the long term, and the chemical-imbalance theory of mental disorders was in the process of flaming out. As NIMH researchers had concluded in 1984, "elevations or decrements in the functioning of serotonergic systems per se are not likely to be associated with depression." Close readers of *The Broken Brain* could also see that, in fact, no great new discoveries had been made. There was a Grand Canyon–sized gap between what the broken-brain storytellers were intimating was true and what was actually known, and that same gap would appear in their stories when Prozac and the other second-generation drugs came to market. But fortunately for the proponents of biological psychiatry, criticism of the medical model and of psychiatric drugs became associated, in the public mind, with Scientology.

L. Ron Hubbard, a science-fiction writer, founded the Church of Scientology in 1952. One of the church's core tenets is that the earth is populated by souls that previously lived on other planets, an "extraterrestrial" creation myth that could have been lifted directly from a sci-fi novel. In addition, Hubbard had his own ideas about how to heal the mind. Prior to founding Scientology, he had published *Dianetics: The Modern Science of Mental Health,* which outlined the use of an "auditing" process to eliminate painful past experiences from the mind. The scientific and medical community ridiculed dianetics as quackery and dismissed Hubbard as a huckster, and he in turn developed an intense hatred for psychiatry. In 1969, Scientology and Thomas Szasz cofounded the Citizens Commission on Human Rights, and this group began waging campaigns against lobotomy, electroshock, and psychiatric drugs.

This proved to be very fortuitous for the APA and its storytelling partners as they raised the flag of biological psychiatry. Indeed, it is easy to imagine the drug companies deciding to secretly fund Scientology's protests, eager as they were to shove money to any organization that would—wittingly or unwittingly—advance their cause. For not only did Scientologists believe in extraterrestrials, they also had gained a reputation for being a secretive, litigious, and even malevolent cult. Scientology, *Time* wrote in 1991, is a "hugely profitable global racket that survives by intimidating members and critics in a Mafia-like manner."[65] Thanks to Scientology, the powers that be in psychiatry had the perfect storytelling foil, for they could now publicly dismiss criticism of the medical model and psychiatric drugs with a wave of the hand, deriding it as nonsense that arose from people who were members of a deeply unpopular cult, rather than criticism that arose from their own research. As such, the presence of Scientology in the storytelling mix served to taint all criticism of the medical model and psychiatric drugs, no matter what its source.

Those were the storytelling forces that formed in the 1980s. When Prozac arrived on the market, they were lined up perfectly for the creation—and maintenance—of a tale about psychiatry's great new leap.

The Story That Was . . . and Wasn't Told

"When it comes to dead bodies in current psychotropic
trials, there are a greater number of them in the
active treatment groups than in the placebo groups.
This is quite different from what happens in penicillin
trials or trials of drugs that really work."
—DAVID HEALY, PROFESSOR OF PSYCHIATRY AT
CARDIFF UNIVERSITY, WALES (2008)[1]

During the 1920s, owners of radios in the heartland of America regularly tuned into station KFKB, which had perhaps the most powerful signal in the country at that time, even though it emanated from tiny Milford, Kansas. "This is Dr. John R. Brinkley greeting his friends in Kansas and everywhere," they'd hear, and Dr. Brinkley did indeed have a most amazing story to tell. In 1918, he had begun transplanting goat gonads into the testicles of older men worried about their declining virility, a fifteen-minute operation, he told KFKB listeners, that had been proven to "completely restore" sexual prowess. "A man is as old as his glands," the good doctor would explain, and this rejuvenating surgery worked because the goat tissue "blends with and nourishes the human tissue, stimulating the human gland to new activity."[2]

Although Brinkley's medical credentials were of a dubious sort—he had a degree from Eclectic Medical University of Kansas City, a diploma mill—he was a masterful storyteller and something of an advertising genius. After his first few operations, he told his story to newspapers in Kansas, and soon they were publishing pictures of him cradling the first "goat-gland baby," the offspring of an older man who had undergone the operation. Older men began pouring into Milford, each paying $750 for the procedure, and Brinkley cranked up his publicity machine. He hired three press agents to write ready-to-print newspaper features, which were then distributed to "publications interested in popularizing the latest developments from the laboratories of science." Naturally, these planted articles included testimonials from satisfied customers, such as J. J. Tobias, chancellor of Chicago Law School, who—the articles said—liked to pound his chest and shout: "I'm a new man! It's one of the great things of the century!" Brinkley established his own "Scientific Press" and reported a "90% to 95% success rate" for his surgery, which, he explained, returned the body to a proper hormonal "balance." Once he began broadcasting his story on KFKB in 1923, he became so famous that three thousand letters arrived at his Milford hospital each day, and by the late 1920s, he was perhaps the wealthiest "doctor" in the United States.

Eventually, Dr. Brinkley earned a place in medical history as one of the great charlatans of all time, when the American Medical Association targeted him as a quack. But when it came to marketing his goat-gonad surgery, he employed advertising techniques and a storytelling model that have stood the test of time. He published articles that appeared scientific, courted the press, claimed a very high success rate, offered a biological rationale for why the surgery worked, and provided reporters with quotes from satisfied customers. That—as Eli Lilly and other drug manufacturers can attest—is a tried-and-true formula for turning a psychiatric drug into a commercial success.

Fibs, Lies, and a Blockbuster Drug

Today, the fraudulent nature of the story told by Eli Lilly and psychiatry about Prozac when it came to market is fairly well known, having been documented by Peter Breggin, David Healy, and Joseph Glenmullen, among others. Breggin and Healy wrote their accounts after gaining access to Eli Lilly files while serving as expert witnesses in civil lawsuits, which allowed them to see data and internal memorandums that belied what the public had been told about the drug. At the risk of going over familiar ground, we need to revisit that story briefly, for it will help us see, with considerable clarity, how our societal delusions about the merits of the "second-generation" psychiatric drugs were formed. Eli Lilly's marketing of Prozac proved to be a model that other companies followed as they brought their drugs to market, and it involved telling a false story in the scientific literature, hyping that story even more to the media, and hiding risks that could lead to disability and death for those who used the drugs.

The science of fluoxetine

Drug development begins in the laboratory, with investigation into a drug's "mechanism of action," and as we learned earlier, Eli Lilly scientists determined in the mid-1970s that fluoxetine caused serotonin to "pile up" in the synapse, which in turn triggered a series of physiological changes in the brain. Next, in animal studies, the drug was found to cause stereotyped activity in rats (repetitious sniffing, licking, etc.) and aggressive behavior in cats and dogs.[3] In 1977, Eli conducted its first small trial in humans, but "none of the eight patients who completed the four-week treatment showed distinct drug-induced improvement," Eli Lilly's Ray Fuller told his colleagues in 1978. The drug also had caused "a fairly large number of reports of adverse reactions." One patient had gone psychotic on the drug, and others had suffered from "akathisia and restlessness," Fuller said.[4]

The trials of fluoxetine had barely begun and it was clear that Eli Lilly had a big problem. Fluoxetine didn't appear to lift depression and it caused a side effect—akathisia—known to increase the risk of suicide and violence. After more reports of this kind came in, Eli Lilly amended its trial protocols. "In future studies, the use of benzodiazepines to control the agitation will be permitted," Fuller wrote on July 23, 1979.[5] The benzodiazepines would help suppress reports of akathisia, and likely boost efficacy results, as several trials of benzodiazepines for depression had shown them to be as effective as a tricyclic. Of course, as Eli Lilly's Dorothy Dobbs later confessed in court, the use of benzodiazepines was "scientifically bad," as it would "confound the results" and "interfere with the analysis of both safety and efficacy," but it enabled the company to continue development of fluoxetine.[6]

Still, even with addition of the benzodiazepines, fluoxetine failed to perform well. During the early 1980s, the company conducted a phase III trial of the drug in Germany, and in 1985, the German licensing authority, Bundesgesundheitsamt (BGA), concluded that this drug was "totally unsuitable for the treatment of depression."[7] According to the patients' "self ratings" (as opposed to the doctors' ratings), the drug produced "little response or no improvement in the clinical picture of the patients," the BGA noted.[8] At the same time, it had caused psychosis and hallucinations, and increased some patients' anxiety, agitation, and insomnia, "which as adverse effects exceed those which are considered acceptable by medical standards," the BGA wrote.[9] Most problematic of all, this drug treatment could prove fatal. "Sixteen suicide attempts were made, two of these with success," the BGA said.[10] A German Eli Lilly employee privately calculated that the incidence rate of suicidal acts for the fluoxetine patients was "5.6 times higher than under the other active medication, imipramine."[11]

With Germany having rejected its application, Eli Lilly naturally worried that it would be unable to gain FDA approval for fluoxetine.* It needed to hide the suicide data, and in a 1994 civil lawsuit, Nancy Lord, an expert in clinical trial design, explained how the company did it. First, Eli Lilly instructed investigators to record various drug-related adverse events as "symptoms of depression." As such, in the trial results submitted to the FDA, the problems were attributed to the disease rather than to fluoxetine. Second, when Eli Lilly scientists tabulated the data from case report forms, they changed individual reports of "suicidal ideation" to "depression." Third, Lilly employees went through the German data "and pulled out [suicide] cases that they didn't think were suicide."[12]

All of these shenanigans, Lord told a court in 1994, made the

---

* At the end of 1989, Eli Lilly obtained approval to market fluoxetine in Germany, but with a label that warned of the elevated risk of suicide.

entire testing process scientifically "worthless." Yet even with these statistical manipulations, Eli Lilly still struggled to present a convincing case for fluoxetine in its application to the FDA. It had conducted placebo-controlled trials at eight sites, and in four of them, the fluoxetine patients had fared no better than the placebo group, and in the others, fluoxetine was only slightly better than a placebo.[13] Meanwhile, when Peter Breggin reviewed Lilly's documents, he discovered that imipramine had proven to be more effective than fluoxetine in six of seven trials.[14] The FDA, in its March 28, 1985, review of one large trial, made the same observation: "Imipramine was clearly more effective than placebo, whereas fluoxetine was less consistently better than placebo."[15] At best, fluoxetine's efficacy was of a very marginal sort, and FDA reviewer Richard Kapit also worried about its safety. At least thirty-nine patients treated with fluoxetine had gone psychotic in the short trials, and slightly more than 1 percent had become manic or hypomanic. Other side effects included insomnia, nervousness, confusion, dizziness, memory dysfunction, tremors, and impaired motor coordination. Fluoxetine, Kapit concluded, "may negatively affect patients with depression."[16] The FDA also understood that Eli Lilly had tried to hide many of these problems, the company having engaged in "large-scale underreporting" of the harm that fluoxetine could cause, according to reviewer David Graham.[17]

While the trials may have been scientifically worthless, they nevertheless proved to be an accurate forecast of what happened after Prozac was brought to market. There were numerous anecdotal accounts of Prozac-treated patients committing horrendous crimes or killing themselves, and so many adverse-events reports flowed into the FDA's MedWatch program that Prozac quickly became America's most complained about drug. By the summer of 1997, the FDA had received thirty-nine thousand such reports about Prozac, far outstripping the number received by any other drug for that nine-year period (1988–1997). The MedWatch filings told of hundreds of suicides, and of a long list of vexing side effects, which included psychotic depression, mania, abnormal thinking, hallucinations, hostility, confusion, amnesia, convulsions, tremors, and sexual dysfunction.[18] The FDA estimates that only 1 percent of all adverse events are reported to MedWatch, which suggests that roughly 4 million Americans during that nine-year period had a bad or even fatal reaction to Prozac.[19]

The story told in the medical journals

Obviously, the record chalked up by fluoxetine in the clinical trials was not one that would support a successful launch in the marketplace. The public was not likely to embrace a medication that German's licensing authority, in its initial review, had deemed "totally unsuitable" as a treatment for depression. If Prozac was going to be successful, the psychiatrists that Eli Lilly had paid to run the trials needed to tell a very different story in the medical journals and to the public.

The first account of a U.S. trial of fluoxetine appeared in the *Journal of Clinical Psychiatry* in 1984. This novel agent, wrote James Bremner, from Northwest Psychopharmacology Research in Washington, "provides effective antidepressant activity with fewer and less troublesome side effects than imipramine. . . . None of the adverse events reported by fluoxetine patients were considered to be drug related." Fluoxetine, he added, "proved more effective than the tricyclic antidepressant."[20] Next, John Feigner, from the University of California at San Diego, reported that fluoxetine was at least equal in efficacy to imipramine (and probably superior to the tricyclic) and that "no serious side effects were observed" in his twenty-two fluoxetine patients during a five-week study.[21] A theme had been sounded—a very safe and improved antidepressant had been developed—and Eli Lilly's investigators stuck to it in the years that followed. "Fluoxetine was better tolerated than imipramine," California psychiatrist Jay Cohn reported in 1985.[22] "This drug," said Eli Lilly's Joachim Wernicke, in another article in the *Journal of Clinical Psychiatry*, "has very few serious side effects."[23] Finally, in the 1985 report on its large phase III trial, Eli Lilly announced that "fluoxetine produced greater improvement than placebo on all major efficacy parameters."[24]

While these reports did tell of a new drug that was superior to the old class of antidepressants, this still was not a narrative of a "breakthrough" medication. There was no sense of *why* this drug worked better, but as FDA approval for fluoxetine neared, a new "fact" began to appear in the scientific reports. In a 1987 article in the *British Journal of Psychiatry,* Sidney Levine wrote that "studies have shown that [serotonin] deficiency plays an important role in the psychobiology of depressive illness."[25] While this was not what had actually been found—Levine had apparently missed the 1984 NIMH report that "elevations or decrements in the functioning of serotonergic systems per se are not likely to be associated with depression"—this article set the stage for fluoxetine to be touted as a drug that fixed a chemical imbalance. Two years later, University of Louisville psychiatrists surveyed the fluoxetine literature in order to provide "prescribing guidelines for the newest antidepressant," and they wrote that "depressed patients have lower than normal concentrations of [serotonin metabolites] in their cerebrospinal fluid." A delusional belief was now spreading through the medical literature, and perhaps not surprisingly, the Kentucky psychiatrists concluded that fluoxetine, which theoretically raised serotonin levels, was "an ideal drug for the treatment of depression."[26]

This trail of reports in medical journals provided Eli Lilly with the sound bites it needed to advertise its drug to doctors. The company flooded medical journals with ads that featured good-looking people who radiated happiness, the ads touting Prozac as equal in efficacy to imipramine, and better tolerated. Science had proven that psychiatry had a new and much improved pill for depression, which appeared to correct a chemical imbalance in the brain.

The story told to the public

The story that had been told in psychiatric journals was certain to resonate with the public. However, at this point, the market for antidepressants was still moderate in size. When Prozac was approved, Wall Street analysts predicted that it could generate $135 to $400 million in annual sales for Eli Lilly. But the drug companies, the APA, and the leaders of the NIMH were keen on expanding the market for antidepressants, and the NIMH's DART "public awareness" campaign turned out to be the perfect vehicle for doing so.

After the NIMH announced its plans for DART in 1986, it had studied the public's beliefs about depression. A survey revealed that only 12 percent of American adults would take a pill to treat it. Seventy-eight percent said they "would live with it until it passed," confident they could handle it on their own. This was an attitude consistent with what the NIMH had preached only fifteen years earlier, when Dean Schuyler, head of the depressive section, had told the public that most depressive episodes "will run their course and terminate with virtually complete recovery without specific intervention." There was epidemiological wisdom in the public's belief that depression would pass, but the NIMH—once Shervert Frazier and other biological psychiatrists took the helm—was intent on delivering a different message.

The purpose of DART, the NIMH explained in 1988, was "to change public attitudes so that there is greater acceptance of depression as a disorder rather than a weakness." The public needed to understand that it regularly went "underdiagnosed and undertreated," and that it could "be a fatal disease" if left untreated. There were 31.4 million Americans who suffered from at least a mild form of depression, the NIMH said, and it was important that they get diagnosed. The public needed to be made aware that antidepressants produced recovery rates of "70% to 80% in comparison with 20% to 40% for placebo." The NIMH vowed to continue DART indefinitely in order to "inform" the public of these "facts."[27]

The NIMH officially launched DART in May 1988, five months after Prozac landed on pharmacy shelves. The NIMH enlisted "labor, religious, educational groups" and businesses to help it spread its message, and of course pharmaceutical companies and NAMI had been on board from the start. The NIMH ran advertisements in the media, and Eli Lilly helped pay for the printing and distribution of 8 million DART brochures titled "Depression: What You Need to Know." This pamphlet informed readers, among other things, of the particular merits of "serotonergic" drugs for the disease. "By making these materials on depressive illness available, accessible in physicians' offices all over the country, important information is effectively reaching the public in settings which encourage questions, discussion, treatment, or referral," said NIMH director Lewis Judd.[28]

The remaking of the American mind was under way. This selling of depression, which was being done under the guise of a "public education" campaign, turned into one of the most effective marketing efforts ever devised. Newspapers picked up on this story, sales of Prozac began to soar, and then, on December 18, 1989, the green-and-white pill officially gained celebrity status when *New York* magazine put it on its cover. BYE, BYE BLUES, the headline screamed. A NEW WONDER DRUG FOR DEPRESSION. In the article, one "anonymous" user of Prozac said that on a scale of 1 to 100, he now felt "over 100." Thanks to this new miracle pill, the magazine concluded, psychiatrists felt that their "profession has been buoyed."[29]

Other such glowing stories quickly followed. On March 26, 1990, *Newsweek*'s cover featured the green-and-white capsule floating Nirvana-like over a beautiful landscape. PROZAC: A BREAKTHROUGH DRUG FOR DEPRESSION the magazine announced. Physicians were now writing 650,000 prescriptions for the pill each month, and "nearly everyone has something nice to say about the new treatment," *Newsweek* said. Patients were loudly exclaiming, "I never felt better!"[30] Three days later, Natalie Angier of the *New York Times,* who arguably was the nation's most popular science writer, explained that antidepressants "work by restoring the balance of neurotransmitter activity in the brain, correcting an abnormal excess or inhibition of the electrochemical signals that control mood, thoughts, appetite, pain and other sensations." This new drug, Dr. Francis Mondimore told Angier, "is not like alcohol or Valium. It's like antibiotics."[31] Television shows weighed in with a similar message, and on *60 Minutes*, Lesley Stahl told the inspiring story of a woman, Maria Romero, who, after a decade of horrible depression, had been reborn on Prozac. "Somebody, something left my body and another person came in," Romero said. Stahl happily explained the biological cure that was at work: "Most doctors believe that chronic depression like Romero's is caused by a chemical imbalance in the brain. To correct it, the doctor prescribed Prozac."[32]

Scientology to the Rescue

Fairly early on, there was a moment when this wonder-drug story threatened to fall apart. The problem, of course, was that fluoxetine did in fact stir suicidal and violent thoughts in some people, and during the summer of 1990, the issue of Prozac's safety burst into the news. And it was then, at that critical moment, that Scientology proved so useful to Eli Lilly and the psychiatric establishment.

By 1990, so many people had suffered bad reactions to fluoxetine that a national Prozac Survivors Support Group had formed. Many harmed by the drug had taken their complaints to lawyers, and two lawsuits in particular grabbed the public's attention. First, on July 18, newspapers reported that a Long Island woman, Rhoda Hala, was suing Eli Lilly because, after going on Prozac, she had slashed her wrists and "other parts of her body hundreds of times."[33] Two weeks later, newspapers reported on a lawsuit related to a mass murder committed by a crazed Kentucky man. Five weeks after starting the drug, Joseph Wesbecker walked into a Louisville printing plant where he had worked and opened fire with an AK-47 assault rifle, killing eight and wounding twelve. The Citizens Commission on Human Rights quickly issued a press release urging Congress to ban this "killer drug," and that's when Eli Lilly pounced. These lawsuits, Eli Lilly loudly announced, "are being drummed up by the Scientology group, which has a history of criticizing the use of psychiatric drugs."[34]

This was the start of Eli Lilly's campaign to save its blockbuster drug. "Lilly can go down the tubes if we lose Prozac," wrote chief medical officer Leigh Thompson, in a harried 1990 memo.[35] The company quickly honed a four-point message for the media: This was an issue being raised by Scientologists; extensive clinical trials had shown that Prozac was a safe drug; the suicidal and homicidal events were "in the disease, not the drug"; and "people who could be helped are being scared away from treatment, and that's the real public menace."[36] The company ran media-training sessions for the academic psychiatrists it hired as consultants, getting them to practice their delivery of this message. "Frankly, I was unimpressed with the performance of our outside professionals," company vice-president Mitch Daniels complained to Thompson after one such practice session in April 1991. The company would "mandate" that the academic psychiatrists perform better "in their future training sessions," he said.[37]

An article that appeared in the *Wall Street Journal* on April 19, 1991, showed that Eli Lilly's training sessions had paid off. "Scientology," the paper informed its readers, was a "quasi-religious/business/paramilitary organization" that was "waging war on psychiatry." The group had attacked Prozac's safety even though "doctors unaffiliated with Lilly" had found, during the clinical trials, that there was "a lower tendency toward suicidal thinking with Prozac than with other antidepressants, or with the starch capsules given to a control group." It was, Leigh Thompson said, a "demoralizing revelation to watch twenty years of solid research by doctors and scientists shouted down in twenty-second sound bites by Scientologists and lawyers." Indeed, the *Wall Street Journal* reported, Eli Lilly, in response to concerns about Prozac's safety, had asked "suicide experts" to re-scrutinize the trial data, but they had "concluded that nothing in the clinical trials linked suicidal thinking—common in depression patients—to Prozac." It was the disease, not the drug, and that was the tragedy, explained Jerrold Rosenbaum, a Harvard psychiatrist at Massachusetts General Hospital. "The public's fear of Prozac as a result of this campaign has itself become a potentially serious public-health problem as people stay away from treatment."[38]

Rosenbaum, naturally, was one of Eli Lilly's "outside professionals." As the *Boston Globe* later reported, he "sat on a marketing advisory panel for Lilly before Prozac was launched," his relationship to Eli Lilly a "cozy" one.[39] But the *Wall Street Journal* presented him as an independent expert, one of the nation's top depression doctors, and so readers could only draw one conclusion: This was an issue conjured up by noxious Scientologists, rather than a legitimate concern. Other newspapers and magazines framed the issue in that way, with *Time,* in May of that year, publishing a scathing cover story on Scientology, calling it a "criminal organization" that attracted "psychopaths."[40]

On September 20, 1991, the FDA did convene a hearing on whether Prozac elevated the risk of suicide, but the advisory panel, which was dominated by physicians with ties to pharmaceutical companies, showed little interest in seriously investigating this question. Although more than two dozen citizens testified on the harm that the drug could cause, the panel made sure that the scientific discussion was limited to presentations that supported Eli Lilly's position that fluoxetine was perfectly safe. As the *Wall Street Journal* reported, the scientific data presented at the hearing proved that "fluoxetine doesn't lead to increased suicide or suicidal thinking, and, in fact, show that the drug helps alleviate these conditions." The entire controversy, one Lilly supporter told the *Journal,* was a "complete fiction" that had been "organized and funded by an anti-psychiatric group."[41]

At that moment, Eli Lilly and all of psychiatry had achieved a public relations victory of lasting importance. The wonder-drug aura around Prozac had been restored, and the public and the media had been conditioned to associate criticism of psychiatric drugs with Scientology. The debate over the merits of these drugs now seemed to feature the nation's top scientists and doctors on one side and religious kooks on the other, and if that were so, the public could be certain where the truth lay. Other SSRIs came to market, sales of Prozac hit the $1 billion mark in 1992, and then, in 1993, Brown University psychiatrist Peter Kramer, in his book *Listening to Prozac,* pushed the wonder-drug story up a notch. Prozac, he wrote, was making some patients "better than well." An era of "cosmetic psychopharmacology" was dawning, Kramer suggested, with psychiatry likely to have pills in the near future that could give normal people whatever personality they wanted. His book spent twenty-one weeks on the *New York Times* bestseller list, and soon *Newsweek* was warning readers that it was time for society to start grappling with the ethical questions raised by psychiatry's new powers. "The same scientific insights into the brain that led to the development of Prozac are raising the prospect of nothing less than made-to-order, off-the-shelf personalities," *Newsweek* explained in 1994. Will those who refuse to "give their brain a makeover," the magazine asked, be left behind?

Gushed neuropsychiatrist Richard Restak: "For the first time in human history, we will be in a position to design our own brains."[42]

America Fooled

As the Prozac story unfolded in the media, surely the ghost of John Brinkley was smiling somewhere. He had transfixed listeners to his radio show with tales of the wonders of transplanted goat gonads, and now here was a storytelling process that had transformed a drug "totally unsuited" for treating depression into a miracle compound, with psychiatrists publicly wringing their hands over their new godlike powers to shape the human mind. Should they worry about making people "better than well"? Would our society lose something precious if everybody were happy all the time? The widespread medicating of the American mind was now under way, and—as a very quick review will reveal—it was this same storytelling process that supported the launch of Xanax as a drug for panic disorder and the atypical antipsychotics for schizophrenia. Once those "second-generation" drugs became blockbusters, the drug companies and academic psychiatrists began touting psychiatric drugs of all kinds for use in children, this storytelling sweeping millions of American youth into the "mental illness" bin.

Xanax

Xanax (alprazolam) was approved by the FDA as an anti-anxiety agent in 1981, and then Upjohn set out to get it approved for panic disorder, which had been newly identified as a discrete condition for the first time in DSM-III (1980). As a first step, it hired former NIMH director Gerald Klerman to co-chair its "steering committee" for the testing process, and it paid Daniel Freedman, editor of the *Archives of General Psychiatry,* to be an assistant to its "division of medical affairs."[43] This was just part of the company's efforts to co-opt academic psychiatry: "The most senior psychiatrists in the world were flooded with offers of consultancies" from

Upjohn, said Isaac Marks, an expert in anxiety disorders at the Institute of Psychiatry in London.[44]

Klerman and Upjohn designed Upjohn's Cross National Collaborative Panic Study in a manner that could be expected to produce a poor placebo response. Patients who had been on benzodiazepines were allowed into the study, which meant that many in the placebo group would in fact be going through the horrors of benzodiazepine withdrawal, and thus could be expected to be extremely anxious during the first weeks of the trial. Nearly one-fourth of the placebo patients had traces of benzodiazepines in their blood when the treatment period began.[45]

Benzodiazepines are known to work quickly, and that proved true in this study. At the end of four weeks, 82 percent of the alprazolam patients were "moderately improved" or "better," versus 43 percent of the placebo group. However, during the next four weeks, the placebo patients continued to improve, while the alprazolam patients did not, and by the end of the eighth week, there "was no significant difference between the groups" on most of the rating scales, at least among the patients who remained in the study. The alprazolam group also experienced a variety of troubling side effects: sedation, fatigue, slurred speech, amnesia, and poor coordination. One of every twenty-six alprazolam patients suffered a "serious" reaction to the drug, such as mania or aggressive behavior.[46]

At the end of eight weeks, the patients were tapered from their medication for four weeks and then followed while medication-free for another two weeks. The results were predictable. Thirty-nine percent of those withdrawn from alprazolam "deteriorated significantly," their panic and anxiety skyrocketing to such an extent they had to start taking the medication again. Thirty-five percent of the alprazolam patients suffered "rebound" panic and anxiety symptoms more severe than when the study began, and an equal percentage suffered a host of debilitating new symptoms, including confusion, heightened sensory perceptions, depression, a feeling that insects were crawling over them, muscle cramps, blurred vision, diarrhea, decreased appetite, and weight loss.[47]

In sum, at the end of fourteen weeks, the drug-exposed patients were worse off than the placebo group: They were more phobic,

The Xanax Study

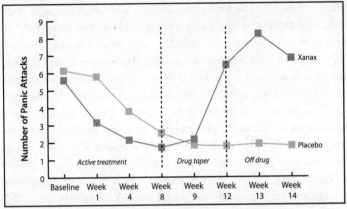

In Upjohn's study of Xanax, patients were treated with the drug or placebo for eight weeks. Then this treatment was slowly withdrawn (weeks 9 through 12), and during the last two weeks patients didn't receive any treatment. The Xanax patients fared better during the first four weeks, which is the result that the Upjohn investigators focused on in their journal articles. However, once the Xanax patients began withdrawing from the the the drug, they suffered many more panic attacks than the placebo patients, and at the end of the study were much more symptomatic. Source: Ballenger, C. "Alprazolam in panic disorder and agoraphobia." *Archives of General Psychiatry* 45 (1988): 413–22. Pecknold, C. "Alprazolam in panic disorder and agoraphobia." *Archives of General Psychiatry* 45 (1988): 429–36.

more anxious, more panic stricken, and doing worse on a "global scale" that assessed overall well-being. Forty-four percent had been unable to get off the drug, on their way to a lifetime of addiction. In every way, the results painted a powerful portrait of the benzo trap: This was a drug that worked for a short time, then its efficacy over a placebo petered out, and yet when patients tried to go off the drug, they became quite sick and many couldn't kick the habit. The first few weeks of relief came at a very high long-term cost, with those stuck on the drug—as previous benzodiazepine studies had shown—likely to end up physically, emotionally, and cognitively impaired.

The Upjohn investigators published three articles in the *Archives of General Psychiatry* in May 1988, and anyone who carefully reviewed the data could see the harm caused by alprazolam. But in order for Xanax to be successfully marketed, Upjohn needed its investigators to draw a different sort of conclusion, and so they did, particularly in the abstracts of the three articles. First, they focused their attention on the four-week results (rather than the eight-week outcomes at the end of the treatment period), announcing that "alprazolam was found to be effective and well-tolerated."[48] Next, they noted that 84 percent of the alprazolam patients had finished the eight-week study, which was evidence that "patient acceptance of alprazolam was high." Although their alprazolam patients regularly exhibited such problems as "slurred speech, amnesia" and other signs of "impaired mentation," they still concluded that the drug had "few side effects and is well tolerated."[49] Finally, while they acknowledged that some alprazolam patients fared poorly when the drug was withdrawn, they reasoned that it had been used for *too short* a period and the withdrawal done too abruptly. "We recommend that patients with panic disorder be treated for a longer period, at least six months," they said.[50]

In London, Isaac Marks and several of his colleagues at the Institute of Psychiatry subsequently pointed out how transparently ridiculous this all was. In a letter to the *Archives of General Psychiatry*, they observed that since the alprazolam patients "were in a worse state than patients receiving placebo" at the end of the study, the finding by the Upjohn investigators that the drug was effective and well tolerated could only be seen as "biased and arguable."[51] The entire affair, Marks subsequently wrote, "is a classic demonstration of the hazards of research funded by industry."[52]

Yet the fact that the alprazolam patients came to such a bad end, with many on a path to a lifelong addiction, did not deter Upjohn, Klerman, the APA, and the NIMH from touting Xanax's benefits to the American public. The same marketing machinery that had made Prozac a bestseller was rolled out again. Upjohn sponsored a symposium at the APA's 1988 meeting where the "expert panel" highlighted the four-week results. Robert Pasnau, who had been head of the APA in 1987, sent a glossy booklet on the *Consequences of Anxiety* to APA members, an "educational" effort paid for by Upjohn. Both Shervert Frazier and Gerald Klerman penned a "Dear Doctor" letter that Upjohn included in the promotional literature it sent to doctors about Xanax as a treatment for panic disorder. Upjohn also gave $1.5 million to the APA so that it could mount a

DART-like campaign to "educate" psychiatrists, health-care workers, and the public about panic disorder, which was said to be "under-recognized and undertreated."[53] Finally, the NIMH chipped in too, identifying panic disorder as a priority concern and sponsoring a conference in 1991 on it, with its panel of experts designating "high potency benzodiazepines"—this would be Xanax—as one of the two "treatments of choice."[54]

The FDA approved Xanax as a treatment for panic disorder in November 1990, and many newspapers and magazines ran the usual features. IN A PANIC? HELP IS ON THE WAY, a *St. Louis Post-Dispatch* headline announced. Treatment, the paper said, helped 70 to 90 percent of those with the debilitating condition, which af-flicted "4 million adults in this country."[55] The Associated Press ex-plained that "a biochemical malfunctioning in the brain is believed to be one of the causes of panic attacks. Xanax can block the at-tacks by interacting with several different systems in the brain."[56] In the *Chicago Sun-Times*, Dr. John Zajecka at Rush Medical College in Chicago announced that "Xanax is the fastest acting and least toxic" of medications for the disorder.[57] Once again, a very effec-tive, safe drug had arrived on the market, and in 1992, Xanax be-came the fifth most frequently prescribed medication in the United States.[58]

Not so atypical

Even as Xanax was on the way to market as a treatment for panic disorder, Janssen was conducting tests of risperidone, a new drug for schizophrenia. By this time, the methods that pharmaceutical firms were employing to create new "blockbuster" psychotropics were becoming quite well practiced, with nearly everyone employ-ing the Prozac model of drug development, and so Janssen, like Eli Lilly and Upjohn, designed trials that were biased in favor of its drug. In particular, Janssen compared multiple doses of risperidone to a high dose of haloperidol (Haldol), as it could then be relatively certain that one of the risperidone doses would have a good safety profile in comparison to the old "standard" neuroleptic. As FDA reviewers noted, these studies were "incapable" of providing any meaningful comparison of the two drugs.[59] In the FDA's letter of approval to Janssen, Robert Temple, director of the Office of Drug Evaluation, made this clear:

> We would consider any advertisement or promotion labeling for RISPERDAL false, misleading, or lacking fair balance under section 502 (a) and 502 (n) of the ACT if there is presentation of data that conveys the impression that risperidone is superior to haloperidol or any other marketed antipsychotic drug product with regard to safety or effectiveness.[60]

However, while the FDA could prohibit Janssen from placing advertisements touting its drug as superior to haloperidol, it did not have authority over what the academic psychiatrists hired by Janssen could say. This was the commercial beauty of the "partnership" that had emerged between psychiatry and the pharmaceutical industry during the 1980s—the academic doctors could make claims, both in their medical journals and to the public, that the FDA considered false in kind. In this case, they published more than twenty articles in psychiatric journals touting risperidone as equal or superior to haloperidol in reducing positive symptoms of schizophrenia (psychosis) and superior to haloperidol in improving negative symptoms (lack of emotion). The academic doctors reported that risperidone reduced hospital stays, improved the patient's ability to function socially, and reduced hostility. "Risperidone has important advantages compared with haloperidol," they wrote in the *Journal of Clinical Psychiatry*. "When administered in an effective dose range, risperidone produced greater improvements on all five dimensions of schizophrenia."[61]

Once again, this was a scientific story of a new and improved treatment, and in their interviews with the media, Janssen's investigators told of a wonder drug. This new agent, the *Washington Post* reported, "represents a glimmer of hope for a disease that until recently had been considered hopeless." Risperidone, it explained, did not "cause sedation, blurred vision, impaired memory or muscle stiffness, side effects commonly associated with an earlier generation of antipsychotic drugs."[62] The *New York Times,* quoting

Richard Meibach, Janssen's clinical research director, reported that "no major side effects" had appeared in the two-thousand-plus patients treated with risperidone in the clinical trials.* The drug was thought to "relieve schizophrenia symptoms by blocking excessive flows of serotonin or dopamine, or both," the paper said.[63]

The atypical revolution was on. Risperdal apparently restored sanity by balancing *multiple* neurotransmitters in the brain, and it seemed to cause *no* side effects of any note. In 1996, Eli Lilly brought Zyprexa (olanzapine) to market, and the public story of the wonders of atypicals got ramped up another notch.

As had become customary, Eli Lilly employed trials that were "biased by design" against haloperidol, the FDA concluded. As a result, its large phase III trial, which wasn't placebo controlled, provided "little useful efficacy data." As for olanzapine's safety profile, twenty patients treated with the drug during the trials died, 22 percent suffered a "serious" adverse event (higher than in the haloperidol patients), and two-thirds failed to complete the studies. Olanzapine, the data suggested, made patients sleepy and fat, and caused such problems as Parkinsonian symptoms, akathisia, dystonia, hypotension, constipation, tachycardia, diabetes, seizures, leaking breasts, impotence, liver abnormalities, and white blood cell disorders. Furthermore, warned the FDA's Paul Leber, since olanzapine blocked receptors for many types of neurotransmitters, "no one should be surprised if, upon marketing, events of all kinds and severity not previously identified are reported in association with olanzapine's use."[64]

That was the story told by the trial data. The story that Eli Lilly wanted to appear in the medical journals and newspapers was that Zyprexa was better than Janssen's Risperdal, and so that's the story that its hired guns told. Psychiatrists from academic medical schools announced that olanzapine worked in a more "comprehensive" manner than either risperidone or haloperidol. It was a well-tolerated

---

* In fact, eighty-four patients treated with risperidone had suffered a "serious adverse event," which the FDA defined as a life-threatening event or one that required hospitalization.

agent that led to global improvement—it reduced positive symptoms, caused fewer motor side effects than other antipsychotics, and improved negative symptoms and cognitive function.[65] This second atypical was better than the first, and the *Wall Street Journal* ran with that angle. Zyprexa, it announced, "has substantial advantages" over other current therapies. "The real world," explained John Zajecka, from Rush Medical College, "is finding that Zyprexa has fewer extrapyramidal side effects than Risperdal."[66] Zyprexa is "a potential breakthrough of tremendous magnitude," Stanford University psychiatrist Alan Schatzberg told the *New York Times*.[67]

The only question now seemed to be whether Zyprexa was truly better than Risperdal, and after AstraZeneca brought a third atypical to market, Seroquel, the media settled on the notion that collectively the new atypicals were a dramatic improvement over the older drugs. They were, *Parade* told its readers, "far safer and more effective in treating negative symptoms, such as difficulty in reasoning and speaking in an organized way."[68] The newer drugs, the *Chicago Tribune* announced, "are safer and more effective than older ones. They help people go to work."[69] Wrote the *Los Angeles Times,* "It used to be that schizophrenics were given no hope of improving. But now, thanks to new drugs and commitment, they're moving back into society like never before."[70] NAMI chimed in, too, publishing a book titled *Breakthroughs in Antipsychotic Medications,* which helpfully explained that these new drugs "do a better job of balancing all of the brain chemicals, including dopamine and serotonin."[71] On and on it went, and finally NAMI's executive director, Laurie Flynn, told the press that the promised land had at last been reached: "These new drugs truly are a breakthrough. They mean we should finally be able to keep people out of the hospital, and it means that the long-term disability of schizophrenia can come to an end."[72]

Lancet Asks a Question

That was the sequence of storytelling that led to the explosive rise in the use of psychiatric drugs in the United States. First, American psychiatrists touted Prozac as a wonder drug, next they hailed Xanax as a safe and effective therapy for panic disorder, and finally they informed the public that atypical antipsychotics were "breakthrough" medications for schizophrenia. In this way, they rejuvenated the market for psychiatric medications, even though the clinical studies of the new drugs had not told of any therapeutic advance.

At least in scientific circles, the "wonder drug" glow around the second-generation psychotropics has long since disappeared. As we learned earlier, the SSRIs were reported in 2008 to provide a meaningful clinical benefit only to severely depressed patients. Xanax is now understood to be much more addictive than Valium, with various investigators determining that two-thirds of people who take it for any length of time have trouble getting off it.[73] As for the top-selling atypicals, the hyping of these drugs is now viewed as one of the more embarrassing episodes in psychiatry's history, as one government-funded study after another failed to find that they were any better than the first-generation antipsychotics. In 2005, the NIMH's "CATIE Trial" determined that there were "no significant differences" between the atypicals and their predecessors, and even more troubling, in this study neither the new drugs nor the old ones could really be said to work. Seventy-four percent of the 1,432 patients were unable to stay on the medications, mostly because of their "inefficacy or intolerable side effects."[74] A study by the U.S. Department of Veterans Affairs came to a similar conclusion about the relative merits of atypicals and the older drugs, and then, in 2007, British psychiatrists reported that schizophrenia patients, if anything, had a better "quality of life" on the old drugs than on the new ones.[75] All of this led two prominent psychiatrists to write in the *Lancet* that the story of the atypicals as breakthrough medications could now be "regarded as invention only," a tale concocted "by the drug industry for marketing purposes and only now being exposed." Yet, they wondered, "how is it that for nearly two decades we have, as some have put it, 'been beguiled' into thinking they were superior?"[76]

History, as readers of this book can attest, reveals the answer to that question. The seed for the atypicals story was planted in the early 1980s, when the APA embraced "biological psychiatry" as a story that could be successfully marketed to the public. This was also a story that the field, as a whole, desperately wanted to believe in, and soon Nancy Andreasen and others were telling of a revolution that was under way, with mental illnesses finally giving up their biological secrets, even though nobody could precisely explain what those secrets were. That story gained steam, prepping the public to believe that therapeutic advances were on the way, and as pharmaceutical companies brought new medications to market, they hired the top psychiatrists in the country to tell of how these new wondrous drugs "balanced" brain chemistry. And it was that co-opting of academic medicine that gave the story its credibility. This was a story told by *Harvard Medical School* psychiatrist Jerrold Rosenbaum, by former *NIMH director* Gerald Klerman, and by *Stanford University* psychiatrist Alan Schatzberg.

Of course we, as a society, believed it.

Silencing Dissent

As we have seen, American psychiatry has told the public a false story over the past thirty years. The field promoted the idea that its drugs fix chemical imbalances in the brain when they do no such thing, and it grossly exaggerated the merits of the second-generation psychotropics. In order to keep that tale of scientific progress afloat (and to protect its own belief in that tale), it has needed to squelch talk about the harm that the drugs can cause.

Psychiatry's policing of its own ranks began in earnest in the late 1970s, when Loren Mosher was ousted from the NIMH for having run his Soteria experiment. The next prominent psychiatrist to end up on psychiatry's hit list was Peter Breggin. Although he is known today for his "antipsychiatry" writings, he, too, had once been on the fast track at the NIMH. After finishing his residency at a Harvard Medical School hospital, Breggin went to the NIMH in 1966 to work on developing community mental health centers. "I was still the young hotshot guy," he recalled, in an interview. "I thought

I would be the youngest professor of psychiatry in the history of Harvard Medical School. That was the trajectory I was on."[77] However, he saw that the future belonged to biological psychiatry, as opposed to the social psychiatry that interested him, and he left the NIMH to go into private practice. Soon he began writing about the hazards of electroshock and psychiatric drugs, which, he argued, "worked" by disabling the brain. After a number of heated battles with the APA's leaders, Breggin appeared in 1987 on Oprah Winfrey's television show, where he spoke about tardive dyskinesia and how that dysfunction was evidence that neuroleptics damaged the brain. His comments so infuriated the APA that it sent a transcript of the show to NAMI, which in turn filed a complaint with the Maryland State Commission on Medical Discipline, asking that it take away Breggin's medical license on the grounds that his statements had caused schizophrenia patients to stop taking their medications (and thus caused harm). Although the commission decided not to take any action, it did conduct an inquiry (rather than summarily dismissing NAMI's complaint), and the message to everyone in the field was, once again, quite clear.

"I think the interesting thing is that Loren [Mosher] and I took on scientifically the two sides of the issue," Breggin said. "Loren took on the issue that there is a better treatment than drugs for schizophrenia. I took on the treatments—the drugs, electroshock, and psychosurgery. And what this showed is that it didn't matter which end you wanted to take, they were willing to destroy your career. That is the lesson."

The career setback that Irish psychiatrist David Healy experienced was, in some ways, reminiscent of Mosher's fall from grace. During the 1990s, he earned a reputation as one of the field's leading historians, his writings focusing on the psychopharmacology era. He had served as secretary of the British Association for Psychopharmacology, and in early 2000, he accepted an offer from the University of Toronto's Centre for Addiction and Mental Health to head up its mood and anxiety program. Up until that moment, he was very much part of the psychiatric establishment, just as Mosher had been. However, for several years he had been interested in the question of whether SSRIs could stir suicide, and he had recently completed a "healthy volunteers" study. Two of the twenty volunteers had become suicidal after they were exposed to an SSRI, which clearly showed that the drug could cause such thoughts. Not long after he accepted the Toronto job, he presented his results at a meeting of the British Association for Psychopharmacology. There, one of the most prominent figures in American psychiatry warned him to knock it off. "He told me that my career would be destroyed if I kept on showing results like the ones I'd just shown, that I had no right to bring out hazards of the pills like these," Healy said.[78]

In November of 2000, only a few months before he was scheduled to start his new job at the University of Toronto, Healy gave a talk on the history of psychopharmacology at a colloquium organized by the school. In his presentation, Healy spoke about problems that had arisen with neuroleptics since their introduction in the 1950s, briefly reviewed the data showing that Prozac and other SSRIs elevated the risk of suicide, and then observed in passing that outcomes for affective disorders are worse today than they were a century ago. This, he observed, shouldn't be happening if "our drugs really worked."[79]

Although the audience subsequently rated his talk as the colloquium's best for content, by the time Healy arrived back in Wales, the University of Toronto had rescinded the job offer. "While you are held in high regard as a scholar of the history of modern psychiatry, we do not feel your approach is compatible with the goals for development of the academic and clinical resources that we have," wrote the Centre's head psychiatrist, David Goldbloom, in an e-mail.[80] Once more, others in the field could draw only one lesson. "The message is that it is a bad idea to speak out, and that the idea that treatments might not work or might not be best managed by being entrusted to doctors is beyond the pale," Healy said in an interview.[81]

Numerous others can attest to the fact that it is a "bad idea" to speak out. Nadine Lambert, a psychologist at the University of California at Berkeley, conducted a long-term study of children treated with Ritalin and found that, as young adults, they had elevated rates of cocaine abuse and cigarette smoking. After she reported her results at a 1998 NIH conference, the National Institute on Drug

Abuse stopped funding her work. In 2000, when Joseph Glenmullen, a clinical instructor in psychiatry at Harvard Medical School, authored *Prozac Backlash,* which detailed the many problems associated with the use of SSRIs, Eli Lilly mounted a campaign to discredit him. A public-relations firm gathered critical comments from several prominent psychiatrists, who derided Glenmullen as a "nobody" in the field, and then it mailed these "reviews" to various newspapers. "It's a dishonest book, it's manipulative, it's mischievous," said Harvard Medical School psychiatrist Jerrold Rosenbaum, even though he was a colleague of Glenmullen's. The press release naturally did not mention that Rosenbaum was an Eli Lilly consultant.[82] Next up on the chopping block: Gretchen LeFever, a psychologist at East Virginia Medical School. After she published research showing that an overly high number of children in Virginia schools were being diagnosed with ADHD, an anonymous "whistle-blower" charged her with scientific misconduct. Her federal research funds were cut off and her computers were seized, and while she was subsequently cleared of any misconduct, her career had still been derailed.

Said Healy: "The thought-control aspect of things in psychiatry today is like old-style Eastern European social control."

Hiding the Evidence

The third aspect to the storytelling process that has led to our societal delusion about the merits of psychiatric drugs is easy to document. Imagine what our beliefs would be today if, over the past twenty years, we had opened our newspapers and read about the following findings, which represent but a sampling of the outcome studies we reviewed earlier in the book:

> 1990: In a large, national depression study, the eighteen-month stay-well rate was highest for those treated with psychotherapy (30 percent) and lowest for those treated with an antidepressant (19 percent). (NIMH)

1992: Schizophrenia outcomes are much better in poor countries like India and Nigeria, where only 16 percent of patients are regularly maintained on antipsychotics, than in the United States and other rich countries, where continual drug usage is the standard of care. (World Health Organization)

1995: In a six-year study of 547 depressed patients, those who were treated for the disorder were nearly seven times more likely to become incapacitated than those who weren't, and three times more likely to suffer a "cessation" of their "principal social role." (NIMH)

1998: Antipsychotic drugs cause morphological changes in the brain that are associated with a worsening of schizophrenia symptoms. (University of Pennsylvania)

1998: In a World Health Organization study of the merits of screening for depression, those diagnosed and treated with psychiatric medications fared worse—in terms of their depressive symptoms and their general health—over a one-year period than those who weren't exposed to the drugs. (WHO)

1999: When long-term benzodiazepine users withdraw from the drugs, they become "more alert, more relaxed, and less anxious." (University of Pennsylvania)

2000: Epidemiological studies show that long-term outcomes for bipolar patients today are dramatically worse than they were in the pre-drug era, with this deterioration in modern outcomes likely due to the harmful effects of antidepressants and antipsychotics. (Eli Lilly; Harvard Medical School)

2001: In a study of 1,281 Canadians who went on short-term disability for depression, 19 percent of those who took an antidepressant ended up on long-term disability, versus 9 percent of those who didn't take the medication. (Canadian investigators)

2001: In the pre-drug era, bipolar patients did not suffer cognitive decline over the long term, but today they end up almost as cognitively impaired as schizophrenia patients. (Sheppard Pratt Health System in Baltimore)

2004: Long-term benzodiazepine users suffer cognitive deficits "moderate to large" in magnitude. (Australian scientists)

2005: Angel dust, amphetamines, and other drugs that induce psychosis all increase D_2 HIGH receptors in the brain; antipsychotics cause this same change in the brain. (University of Toronto)

2005: In a five-year study of 9,508 depressed patients, those who took an antidepressant were, on average, symptomatic nineteen weeks a year, versus eleven weeks for those who didn't take any medication. (University of Calgary)

2007: In a fifteen-year study, 40 percent of schizophrenia patients off antipsychotics recovered, versus 5 percent of the medicated patients. (University of Illinois)

2007: Long-term users of benzodiazepines end up "markedly ill to extremely ill" and regularly suffer from symptoms of depression and anxiety. (French scientists)

2007: In a large study of children diagnosed with ADHD, by the end of the third year "medication use was a significant marker not of beneficial outcome, but of deterioration." The medicated children were also more likely to engage in delinquent behavior; they ended up slightly shorter, too. (NIMH)

2008: In a national study of bipolar patients, the major predictor of a poor outcome was exposure to an antidepressant. Those who took an antidepressant were nearly four times as likely to become rapid cyclers, which is associated with poor long-term outcome. (NIMH)

A check of newspaper archives reveals that the psychiatric establishment has thoroughly succeeded in keeping this information from the public. I searched for accounts of these studies in the *New York Times* archives and in the LexisNexis database, which covers most

U.S. newspapers, and I couldn't find a *single* instance where the results were accurately reported.*

Newspapers, of course, would have been happy to publish these study results. However, medical news is typically generated in this way: The scientific journals, the NIH, medical schools, and pharmaceutical companies issue press releases touting certain findings as important, and reporters then sift through the releases to identify the ones they deem worthy of writing about. If no press releases are issued, or there is no other effort by the medical community to publicize the findings, then no stories appear. We can even document this blackout process at work in the NIMH's handling of Martin Harrow's outcomes study. In 2007, the year he published his results in the *Journal of Nervous and Mental Disease,* the NIMH issued eighty-nine press releases, many on inconsequential matters. But it did not issue one on Harrow's findings, even though his was arguably the best study of the long-term outcomes of schizophrenia patients that had *ever* been done in the United States.[83] It's fair to say that if the results had been the reverse, the NIMH would have sounded the press-release gong and newspapers across the country would have touted the findings.

Although reports about most of the studies listed above simply never appeared in newspapers, there were a couple of instances when psychiatrists were forced to say something to reporters about one of the studies, and each time they spun the results. For example, when the NIMH announced the three-year results from its MTA study of ADHD treatments, it did not inform the public that stimulant usage during the third year was a "marker of deterioration." Instead, it put out a press release with this headline: IMPROVEMENT

---

* There were newspaper reviews of my book *Mad in America* that mentioned the WHO study of better schizophrenia outcomes in poor countries where patients were not regularly maintained on the drugs, and since then, this information has become somewhat known. In addition, I mentioned Martin Harrow's fifteen-year schizophrenia study in a talk I gave at Holy Cross College in February 2009, and that led to a February 8, 2009, article in the *Worcester Telegram and Gazette* (Mass.) that discussed Harrow's work. That was the first time that news of his study had appeared in any American newspaper.

FOLLOWING ADHD TREATMENT SUSTAINED FOR MOST CHILDREN. That headline told of drugs that had been *beneficial,* and while the text of the release did state that "continuing medication was no longer associated with better outcomes by the third year," it also included a canned quote from lead author Peter Jensen stating that there was still plenty of reason to keep children on Ritalin. "Our results suggest that medication can make a long-term difference for some children if it's continued with optimal intensity, and not started or added too late in a child's clinical course."[84]

If we want to get another look at this spinning process, we can turn to a 1998 *New York Times* article that briefly told of the WHO study on schizophrenia outcomes in rich and poor countries. After interviewing psychiatrists about the study, the *Times* reporter wrote that "schizophrenics generally responded better to treatment in less developed countries than in more technologically developed countries."[85] *Responded better to treatment*—readers could only assume that schizophrenia patients in India and Nigeria responded better to antipsychotics than patients in the United States and other rich countries did. They had no way to know that "treatment" for 84 percent of the schizophrenia patients in the poor countries consisted of being off the drugs.

In July 2009, I also searched the NIMH and NAMI websites for some mention of the studies listed above, and I found zilch. For instance, the NIMH website did not discuss the remarkable decline in bipolar outcomes in modern times, even though Carlos Zarate, who coauthored the 2000 article that documented this decline, was head of the NIMH's mood and anxiety disorders research unit in 2009. Similarly, NAMI's website didn't provide any information about Harrow's study, even though it provides reason for parents of schizophrenic children to be *optimistic.* Forty percent of those off medications recovered over the long term! But that finding directly contradicted the message that NAMI has promoted to the public for decades, and NAMI's website is sticking to that message. Antipsychotics, it informs the public, "correct an imbalance in the chemicals that enable brain cells to communicate with each other."[86]

Finally, the entire outcomes history documented in this book is missing from the 2008 edition of the APA's *Textbook of Psychiatry,* which means that medical students training to be psychiatrists are kept in the dark about this history.[87] The book does not discuss "supersensitivity psychosis." It does not mention that antidepressants may be depressogenic agents over the long term. It does not report that bipolar outcomes are much worse today than they were forty years ago. There is no discussion of rising disability rates. There is no talk about the cognitive impairment that is seen in longtime users of psychotropic drugs. The textbook authors are clearly familiar with many of the sixteen studies listed above, but, if they do mention them, they don't discuss the relevant facts about medication usage. The long-running study by Harrow, the textbook states, reveals that there are some schizophrenia patients who "are able to function without the benefit of continuous antipsychotic treatment." The authors of that sentence didn't mention the stunning difference in recovery rates for the unmedicated and medicated groups; instead they crafted a sentence that told of the *benefit of continuous antipsychotic treatment*. In a similar vein, while the textbook briefly discusses the WHO study on the better outcomes of schizophrenia patients in poor countries like India and Nigeria, it does not mention that patients in those countries weren't regularly maintained on antipsychotics. In a section on benzodiazepines, the authors acknowledge that there are concerns about their addictive properties, but then state that long-term outcomes for those who stay on benzodiazepines are generally good, as most patients "maintain their therapeutic gains."

There is a story that psychiatry doesn't dare tell, which shows that our societal delusion about the benefits of psychiatric drugs isn't entirely an innocent one. In order to sell our society on the soundness of this form of care, psychiatry has had to grossly exaggerate the value of its new drugs, silence critics, and keep the story of poor long-term outcomes hidden. That is a willful, conscious process, and the very fact that psychiatry has had to employ such storytelling methods reveals a great deal about the merits of this paradigm of care, much more than a single study ever could.

Tallying Up the Profits

*"Receiving $750 checks for chatting with some
doctors during a lunch break was such easy money
that it left me giddy."*
—PSYCHIATRIST DANIEL CARLAT (2007)[1]

The walk from Jenna's group home in Montpelier, Vermont, to the town's Main Street is only two blocks long, and yet, on the late spring morning I visited, it took us twenty minutes to travel that distance, for Jenna had to stop every few steps and catch her balance, with her aide, Chris, constantly putting his hand up behind her in case she fell.* Jenna had first taken an antidepressant twelve years earlier, when she was fifteen years old, and now she was on a daily cocktail of eight drugs, including one for drug-induced Parkinsonian symptoms. As we sat outside a café, Jenna told me her story, although at times—because of her problems with motor control—it was difficult to understand her. Her tremors are so severe that when she dunked her pastry, the coffee spilled and she had trouble bringing the pastry to her lips.

"I'm sooooooo messed up," she says.

I had gone to the interview thinking that Jenna had been diagnosed with tardive dyskinesia, an antipsychotic side effect that can disable people. But it wasn't clear whether her motor impairments

---

* Although Jenna said that I could use her last name, her mother and stepfather, who have legal guardianship, requested that I use her first name only.

were due to that particular type of drug-induced dysfunction or to a more idiosyncratic drug-related process, and by the time the interview was over, Jenna had raised a new issue for me to think about. She told of how psychiatrists and other mental health workers had always resisted seeing any of her physical or emotional difficulties as drug-caused, but instead had regularly blamed everything on her illness, and, from her point of view, that was a thinking process dictated by monetary interests. If you wanted to understand the care she'd received, you had to understand that she was valuable to the pharmaceutical companies as a "consumer" of their medications. "Nobody," Chris explains, "has addressed the fact that the drugs may be causing her problems."

The first time that Jenna had been exposed to a psychiatric drug was when she was in the second grade, and that episode suggested that she would not be a good responder to psychotropics. Up until that time Jenna had been a healthy child, a star on a local swim team; only then she developed seizures, and when she was put on an anticonvulsive agent, she developed severe motor problems, her mother said, in a phone interview. But eventually the seizures went away and once Jenna stopped taking the anticonvulsant, her motor problems disappeared. Jenna took up horseback riding, excelling in show-jumping competition. "She was back to being totally normal," her mother recalled.

When Jenna entered ninth grade, her mother and stepfather decided to send her to an elite boarding school in Massachusetts, as they didn't trust the public schools in Tennessee, and it was then that her behavioral and emotional problems began. She was kicked out of that first school and sent to a second one for troubled teens, where she "got into all that Gothic stuff" and began "acting out" sexually, her mother said. Then, on a dare one night, Jenna stole a package of condoms from a drugstore and "freaked out" when she was arrested. Now she was sent to a third boarding school and prescribed Paxil.

"The minute she takes that drug, she starts shaking," her mother said. "I tell the doctor, 'Oh my gosh, it is from the medicine.' The doctor says, 'Oh no, it's not the medicine.' I said, 'Yes it is.' We went from one doctor to another, doing test after test, but they couldn't find anything and so they kept her on the medications, which made everything worse. They just wouldn't listen to me."

In addition to the tremors, Jenna became suicidal while taking Paxil, and soon her life transformed into a psychiatric nightmare. She began cutting herself regularly, and at one point, she used an electric saw to take off the middle finger on her left hand. The Paxil gave way to cocktails of Klonopin, Depakote, Zyprexa, and other medications, and during a nearly four-year stay in a psych hospital, she ended up on a cocktail of fifteen or so drugs, so doped up she didn't even know where she was. "I don't know the exact date," Jenna says, summing up this history, "but slowly my speech and my walking and my balance and the shaking got really bad at that hospital. And they just kept on adding drugs. That's how f-f-f-fucked up they are."

Today, Jenna's psychiatric problems remain severe. On the day we met, her wrist was bandaged, as she had recently tried to cut herself, and thus the medications haven't been much help in that regard, either. But, she says, "I don't see anything different happening. I have brought up the issue of taking me off the meds billions of times."

Before we left our sidewalk table, Chris provided me with the details of Jenna's daily cocktail: two antidepressants, an antipsychotic, a benzodiazepine, a Parkinson's medication, and three others for physical problems likely related to the psychiatric drugs. Later, I calculated that even if generics were prescribed whenever possible, she was consuming $800 of medication monthly, or roughly $10,000 annually. She had been on psychiatric medications for twelve years, which meant that her Rx bill for psychiatric medications might already have surpassed $100,000, and given that she will likely remain on the drugs for the rest of her life, this bill could eventually end up well north of $200,000.

"They are making a lot of money on me," Jenna says. "But these drugs have ruined my life. They make me all f-f-f-fucked up."

A Business Triumph

Jenna's perspective on her care was not an unusual one. Many of the people on SSI and SSDI that I interviewed spoke about how they felt they were caught in the tangles of a business enterprise. "There is a reason we are called *consumers*" was a comment I heard several times. They are right of course that the pharmaceutical companies want to build a market for their products, and when we view the psychopharmacology "revolution" through this prism, as a business enterprise first and a medical enterprise second, we can easily see why psychiatry and the pharmaceutical companies tell the stories they do, and why the studies detailing poor long-term outcomes have been kept from the public. That information would derail a business enterprise that brings profits to so many.

As we saw earlier, during the late 1970s psychiatry was worried about its survival. The public viewed its therapies as "low in efficacy," and sales of psychiatric drugs were in decline. Then, in what might be called a "rebranding" effort, psychiatry published DSM-III and began telling the public that mental disorders were "real" diseases, just like diabetes and cancer, and that their drugs were chemical antidotes to those diseases, just like "insulin for diabetes." That story, while it may have been false in kind, created a powerful conceptual framework for selling psychiatric medications of all types. Everyone could understand the chemical-imbalance metaphor, and once the public came to understand that notion, it became relatively simple for pharmaceutical companies and their story-telling allies to build markets for psychiatric drugs of various types. They ran "educational" campaigns to make the public more "aware" of the various disorders the drugs were approved to treat, and, at the same time, they expanded the diagnostic boundaries of mental disorders.

After Prozac was introduced, NIMH's DART campaign informed the public that depression regularly went "undiagnosed and untreated." Upjohn partnered with the APA to tell the public that "panic disorder" was a common affliction. In 1990, the NIMH launched its "Decade of the Brain," telling the public that 20 percent of Americans suffered from mental disorders (and thus might be in need of psychiatric medications). Soon psychiatric groups and others were promoting "screening programs," which from a business perspective are best described as customer-recruitment efforts. NAMI, for its part, understood that its "educational" efforts served a commercial end, writing in a 2000 document filed with the government that "providers, health plans, and pharmaceutical companies want to grow their markets and to increase their share of the market. . . . NAMI will cooperate with these entities to grow the market by making persons aware of the issues involving severe brain disorders."[2]

The APA is in charge of defining diagnostic categories in our society, and DSM-IV, an 886-page tome published in 1994, listed 297 disorders, 32 more than DSM-III. New and expanded diagnoses invite more people into the psychiatric drugstore, and one of the best examples of this type of market-building occurred in 1998, when GlaxoSmithKline got the FDA to approve Paxil for "social anxiety disorder." In the past, this might have been perceived as a character trait (shyness), but GlaxoSmithKline hired a PR firm, Cohn & Wolfe, to promote awareness of this newly recognized "disease," and soon newspapers and television shows were telling of how SAD afflicted 13 percent of the American population, making it "the third most common psychiatric disorder in the United States, after depression and alcoholism." Those afflicted with this illness, the public learned, were in some ways biologically "allergic to people."[3]

Diagnostic changes lay behind the bipolar boom, too. In DSM-III (1980), bipolar illness was identified for the first time (the old manic-depressive cohort was splintered into different groups), and then psychiatry steadily loosened the diagnostic boundaries for this illness, such that today the field talks about bipolar I, bipolar II, and a "bipolarity intermediate between bipolar disorder and normality." This once rare disease is now said to afflict 1 to 2 percent of the adult population, and if the "intermediate" bipolar folk are counted, 6 percent. As this diagnostic expansion happened, pharmaceutical companies and their allies mounted their usual "educational" campaigns. Abbott Laboratories and NAMI teamed up to promote a "Bipolar Awareness Day"; in 2002, Eli Lilly joined with the Depression and Bipolar Support Alliance to launch a new online destination, bipolarawareness.com. Today many websites offer visitors a quick question-and-answer test to see if they have this illness.

Naturally, pharmaceutical companies want to sell their drugs to people of all ages, and they built the pediatric market for psychotropics step by step. First, in the 1980s, the prescribing of stimulants to "hyperactive" children took off. Next, in the early 1990s, psychiatrists began regularly prescribing SSRIs to teenagers. But that meant prepubertal children weren't being prescribed these new wonder drugs, and in 1997, the *Wall Street Journal* reported that the manufacturers of SSRIs were "taking aim at a controversial new market: children." The drug firms were "preparing their medications in easy-to-swallow forms that will be more palatable to even the youngest tykes," the newspaper said, with Eli Lilly formulating a "minty liquid" Prozac for the tots to down.[4] The *New York Times,* in its coverage of this initiative, explained quite clearly what was driving it: "The adult market for [SSRIs] has become saturated. . . . The companies are looking for expanded markets."[5] Psychiatry quickly provided a medical cover for this marketing effort, with the American Academy of Child and Adolescent Psychiatry announcing that 5 percent of all children in the United States were clinically depressed. "Many of these young patients now are inadequately treated, experts say, often leading to long-term emotional and behavioral problems, drug abuse, or even suicide," the *Wall Street Journal* reported.[6]

The creation of the "juvenile bipolar" market was a bit more complicated. Prior to the 1990s, psychiatry thought that bipolar illness simply didn't occur in prepubertal children, or was extremely rare. But children and teenagers prescribed stimulants and antidepressants often suffered manic episodes, and thus pediatricians and psychiatrists began to see more youth with "bipolar" symptoms. At the same time, once Janssen and Eli Lilly brought their atypical antipsychotics to market, they were looking for a way to sell those drugs to children, and during the mid-1990s, Joseph Biederman at Massachusetts General Hospital in Boston provided the diagnostic framework that made that possible. In 2009, while being deposed in a legal case, he explained his handiwork.

All psychiatric diagnoses, he said, "are subjective in children and in adults." As such, he and his colleagues decided that children who in the past had been seen as having pronounced behavioral problems should instead be diagnosed with juvenile bipolar illness. "The conditions that we see in front of us are reconceptualized," Biederman testified. "These children have been called in the past conduct disorder, oppositional-defiant disorder. It's not that these children did not exist, they were just under different names."[7] Biederman and his colleagues decided that "severe irritability" or "affective storms" would be the telltale signs of juvenile bipolar disorder, and with this new diagnostic criteria in hand, they announced in 1996 that many children diagnosed with ADHD were in fact "bipolar" or else "comorbid" for both illnesses.[8] The illness was a "much more common condition than was previously thought," often appearing when children were only four or five years old, Biederman said.*[9] Soon parents in the United States were reading newspaper articles about this newly recognized illness and buying *The Bipolar Child*, a book published by Random House in 2000. Child psychiatrists, meanwhile, began treating it with atypical antipsychotics.

That was the marketing machinery that lured more and more Americans into the psychiatric drugstore. As new drugs were brought to market, disease "awareness" campaigns were conducted and diagnostic categories were expanded. Now, once a business gets a customer into its store, it wants to keep that customer and get that customer to buy multiple products, and that's when the psychiatric "drug trap" kicks in.

The "broken brain" story helps with customer retention, of course, for if a person suffers a "chemical imbalance," then it makes sense that he or she will have to take the medication to correct it indefinitely, like "insulin for diabetes." But more important, the drugs *create* chemical imbalances in the brain, and this helps turn a first-time customer into a long-term user, and often into a buyer of multiple drugs. The patient's brain adapts to the first drug, and that

* During Biederman's February 26, 2009, deposition, an attorney asked him about his rank at Harvard Medical School. "Full professor," he replied. "What's above that?" the attorney asked. "God," Biederman replied.

makes it difficult to go off the medication. The store's exit door is hard to squeeze through, so to speak. At the same time, since psychiatric drugs perturb normal function, they regularly cause physical and psychiatric problems, and this greases the path to polypharmacy. The hyperactive child is put on a stimulant that rouses him during the day; at night he needs a sleeping pill to go to sleep. An atypical causes people to feel depressed and lethargic; psychiatrists may prescribe an antidepressant to treat that problem. Conversely, an antidepressant may stir a bout of mania; in that case an atypical antipsychotic may be prescribed to tamp down the mania. The first drug triggers a need for a second, and so on.

Eli Lilly even capitalized on this fact when it brought Zyprexa to market. As it well knew, Prozac and other SSRIs could trigger manic episodes, and so it instructed its sales representatives to tell psychiatrists that Zyprexa "is a great mood stabilizer, especially for patients whose symptoms were aggravated by an SSRI."[10] In essence, Eli Lilly was telling doctors to prescribe its second drug to fix the psychiatric problems caused by its first one. We can also see this cascading effect operating at a societal level. The SSRIs came to market and suddenly bipolar patients were cropping up everywhere, and then this new group of patients provided a market for the atypicals.*

All of this has produced a growth industry of impressive dimensions. In 1985, outpatient sales of antidepressants and antipsychotics in the United States amounted to $503 million.[11] Twenty-three years later, U.S. sales of antidepressants and antipsychotics reached $24.2 billion, nearly a fiftyfold increase. Antipsychotics—a class of drugs previously seen as extremely problematic in kind, useful only in severely ill patients—were the top revenue-producing class of drugs in 2008, ahead even of the cholesterol-lowering agents.[12] Total sales of all psychotropic drugs in 2008 topped $40 billion. Today—and this

---

* In a similar vein, pharmaceutical companies have pounced on the fact that many of the drugs initially prescribed for a target symptom don't work very well. "Two out of three people treated for depression still have symptoms," a Bristol-Myers Squibb commercial informed television viewers in 2009. The solution? Add an atypical antipsychotic, Abilify, to the mix.

shows how crowded the drugstore has become—one in every eight Americans takes a psychiatric drug on a regular basis.[13]

The Money Tree

Naturally, this flourishing business enterprise generates great personal wealth for executives at pharmaceutical companies, and money also flows in fairly copious amounts to the academic psychiatrists who tout their drugs. Indeed, the profits from this enterprise trickle down to nearly all of those who tell the "psychiatric drugs are good" story to our society. To get a sense of the amounts involved, we can look at the money that the different players in this enterprise receive.

We can start with Eli Lilly, as it serves as a good example of the profits that go to a drug company's shareholders and its executives.

Eli Lilly

In 1987, Eli Lilly's pharmaceutical division generated $2.3 billion in revenues. The company did not have a central nervous system drug of any importance, as its three bestselling drugs were an oral antibiotic, a cardiovascular drug, and an insulin product. Eli Lilly began selling Prozac in 1988, and four years later it became the company's first billion-dollar drug. In 1996, Eli Lilly brought Zyprexa to market, and it became a billion-dollar drug in 1998. By 2000, these two drugs accounted for nearly half of the company's revenues of $10.8 billion.

Prozac soon after lost its patent protection, and thus the wealth-generating effects of the two drugs can best be assessed across a thirteen-year period, from 1987 to 2000. During this time, Eli Lilly's value on Wall Street rose from $10 billion to $90 billion. An investor who bought $10,000 of Eli Lilly stock in 1987 would have seen that investment grow to $96,850 in 2000, and along the way the investor would have received an additional $9,720 in dividends. At the same time, Eli Lilly's executives and employees, in addition to their salaries and bonuses, netted around *$3.1 billion* from the stock options they exercised.[14]

Academic psychiatrists

The pharmaceutical companies would not have been able to build a $40 billion market for psychiatric drugs without the help of psychiatrists at academic medical centers. The public looks to doctors for information about illnesses and how best to treat them, and so it was the academic psychiatrists—paid by drug companies to serve as consultants, on advisory boards, and as speakers—who in essence acted as the salesmen for this enterprise. The pharmaceutical companies, in their internal memos, accurately call these psychiatrists "key opinion leaders," or KOLs for short.

Thanks to a 2008 investigation by Iowa senator Charles Grassley, the public got a glimpse of the amount of money that the pharmaceutical companies pay their KOLs. The academic psychiatrists regularly receive federal NIH grants, and as such, they are required to inform their institutions how much they receive from pharmaceutical companies, with the medical schools expected to manage the "conflict of interest" whenever this amount exceeds $10,000 annually. Grassley investigated the records of twenty or so academic psychiatrists, and he found that not only were many making much more than $10,000 a year, they were also hiding this fact from their schools.

Here are a few examples of the money paid to KOLs in psychiatry.

- From 2000 to 2007, Charles Nemeroff, chair of the psychiatry department at Emory Medical School, earned at least $2.8 million as a speaker and consultant for drug firms, with GlaxoSmithKline alone paying him $960,000 to promote Paxil and Wellbutrin. He is a coauthor of the APA's *Textbook of Psychopharmacology,* which is the bestselling textbook in the field. He also wrote a trade book about psychiatric medications, *The Peace of Mind Prescription,* for the general public. He has served on the editorial boards of more than sixty medical journals and for a time was editor in chief of

Neuropsychopharmacology. In December of 2008, he resigned as chair of Emory's psychiatry department, as he had failed to inform Emory of his drug-company paychecks.[15]

- Zachary Stowe, also a professor of psychiatry at Emory, received $250,000 from GlaxoSmithKline in 2007 and 2008, partly to promote the use of Paxil by breast-feeding women. Emory "reprimanded" him for failing to properly disclose these payments to the school.[16]

- Another member of GlaxoSmithKline's speaker bureau was Frederick Goodwin, a former director of the NIMH. The company paid him $1.2 million from 2000 to 2008, mostly to promote the use of mood stabilizers for bipolar illness (GlaxoSmithKline sells Lamictal, which is a mood stabilizer). Goodwin is the coauthor of *Manic-Depressive Illness,* the authoritative textbook on this disorder, and he also was the longtime host of a popular radio show, *The Infinite Mind,* which was carried on NPR stations nationwide. His show regularly featured discussions of psychiatric medications, with Goodwin, in a program broadcast on September 20, 2005, warning that if children with bipolar disorder were not treated, they could suffer brain damage. Goodwin has been a speaker or consultant for a number of other pharmaceutical companies; the $1.2 million was what he received from GlaxoSmithKline alone. In an interview with the *New York Times,* Goodwin explained that he was only "doing what every other expert in the field does."[17]

- From 2000 to 2005, Karen Wagner, director of child and adolescent psychiatry at the University of Texas, collected more than $160,000 from GlaxoSmithKline. She promoted the use of Paxil in children, and did so in part by coauthoring an article that falsely reported the results of a pediatric trial of the drug.

  In a confidential document written in October 1998, GlaxoSmithKline concluded that in the study, Paxil "failed to demonstrate a statistically significant difference from placebo on the primary efficacy measures."[18] In addition, five of the ninety-three adolescents treated with Paxil in the study suffered "extreme lability," versus one in the placebo group, which meant that the drug markedly elevated the suicide risk. The study had shown Paxil to be neither safe nor effective in adolescents. However, in a 2001 article published in the *Journal of the American Academy of Child & Adolescent Psychiatry*, Wagner and twenty-one other leading child psychiatrists stated that the study proved that Paxil is "generally well tolerated and effective for major depression in adolescents."[19] They did not discuss the sharply elevated suicide risk, writing instead that only one child treated with Paxil had suffered a serious adverse event, with that child developing a "headache." New York State attorney general Eliot Spitzer sued GlaxoSmithKline for fraudulently marketing Paxil to adolescents, a case which was settled out of court.

All told, Wagner has been a consultant or advisor to at least seventeen pharmaceutical companies. The $160,000 was the amount she received from GlaxoSmithKline alone; she told her school that she had received $600.[20]

• From 1999 to 2006, Jeffrey Bostic, a psychiatrist at Massachusetts General Hospital in Boston, collected more than $750,000 from Forest Laboratories to promote the prescribing of Celexa and Lexapro to children and adolescents. He gave more than 350 talks in twenty-eight states during this period, leading one Forest sales rep to boast: "Dr. Bostic is the man when it comes to child psych!"[21] In March of 2009, the federal government charged Forest with illegally marketing these drugs to this patient population, alleging that it had paid "kickbacks, including lavish meals and cash payments disguised as grants and consulting fees, to induce doctors to prescribe the drugs." Dr. Bostic, the federal government said, served as the company's "star spokesman" in this scheme. The federal government noted that the company had also failed to disclose the results of a study of these drugs in children that had produced "negative" results.

• From 2003 to 2007, Melissa DelBello, an associate professor of psychiatry at the University of Cincinnati, received at least $418,000 from AstraZeneca. She promoted the prescribing of atypical antipsychotics, including AstraZeneca's Seroquel, to juvenile bipolar patients. DelBello worked for at least seven other pharmaceutical companies. "Trust me, I don't take much" from drug firms, she told the New York Times prior to Grassley's report.[22]

- Joseph Biederman may have been the KOL who did the most to help the pharmaceutical industry build a market for its products. To a large extent, juvenile bipolar illness was his creation, and children and adolescents so diagnosed are often treated with drug cocktails. Pharmaceutical companies paid him $1.6 million for his various services from 2000 to 2007, with much of this money coming from Janssen, the division of Johnson & Johnson that sells Risperdal.[23]

Biederman also got the company to pay $2 million from 2002 to 2005 to create the Johnson & Johnson Center for Pediatric Psychopathology at Massachusetts General Hospital.[24] In a 2002 report on the center, he candidly set forth its aims. The center, he explained, was a "strategic collaboration" that would "move forward the commercial goals of J&J." He and his colleagues would develop screening tests for juvenile bipolar illness, and then teach CME (continuing medical education) courses to train pediatricians and psychiatrists to use them. Their research, Biederman wrote, would "alert physicians to the existence of a large group of children who might benefit from treatment with Risperdal." In addition, the center would promote the understanding that "pediatric mania evolves into what some have called mixed or atypical mania in adulthood, [which] will provide further support for the chronic use of Risperdal from childhood through adulthood."* In the past, Biederman noted, he had successfully led the medical profession to conceive of ADHD

---

* Biederman here is describing the course of children who are diagnosed with bipolar illness and then medicated; those children do tend to become chronically ill in the way he describes. But there is no medical literature showing that there is a disease that takes this course in unmedicated children.

as a "chronic" illness, and now he would do the same for bipolar disorder.[25]

Biederman has been the Pied Piper of pediatric bipolar illness in our society, and in this document we can see the future that he was laying out for the children given this diagnosis. They were being groomed to be lifelong consumers of psychiatric medications. The child diagnosed with bipolar disorder would be put on an antipsychotic, and that child could then be expected to become chronically ill, and that would require a lifetime of "aggressive treatments such as Risperdal." Perhaps there is a file tucked away in a drug company cabinet that estimates the expected lifetime consumption of psychiatric medications by a child diagnosed with bipolar illness; all we can say, in this book, is that every child so diagnosed is, from a business standpoint, a new Jenna.

The next tier down

The KOLs are the "stars" of the field, as they are the ones who "influence" their peers at a national and international level, but the pharmaceutical companies also pay physicians to promote their drugs on a more local basis, with these speakers giving talks at dinners or to other physicians in their offices. Pay typically starts at $750 per event and rises from there. Two states, Minnesota and Vermont, have passed "sunshine" laws that disclose these payments, and their reports provide insight into the flow of money to these doctors.

In 2006, pharmaceutical firms gave $2.1 million to Minnesota psychiatrists, up from $1.4 million in 2005. From 2002 to 2006, the recipients of drug-company money included seven past presidents of the Minnesota Psychiatric Society and seventeen faculty psychiatrists at the University of Minnesota. John Simon, who was a member of the state's Medicaid formulary committee, which guides the state's spending on drugs, was the top-paid psychiatrist, earning $570,000 for his services to drug companies. All told, 187 of 571 psychiatrists in Minnesota received pharmaceutical money for some reason or other during this period, a percentage that was "much higher" than for any other specialty. Their collective take was $7.4 million.[26]

Vermont's reports tell much the same story. Of all the medical specialties, psychiatry received the most money from the drug companies.

The community psychiatrist

The pharmaceutical companies also provide freebies to community psychiatrists. They invite them to free dinners where the KOLs and the local experts give their talks, and their sales representatives regularly come to their offices bearing small gifts. "Gave Dr. Child a cupcake sized peanut butter cup," wrote an Eli Lilly sales representative, in a 2002 report to her boss. "He was kind of tickled." Or as she said after another sales call: "Doc and staff loved the goodie box I brought in, filled with useful items for their new clinic."[27] These are very small bribes, but even a small gift helps build a social bond. A California group surveyed the drug firms and found that they do set a limit on the freebies that are offered to a psychiatrist each year; GlaxoSmithKline's was $2,500 per physician, while Eli Lilly's was $3,000. There are many companies that sell psychiatric drugs, and thus any psychiatrist who welcomes sales reps can enjoy a regular supply of goodies.

NAMI and all the rest

Eli Lilly now posts on the Web a list of the "educational" and "philanthropy" grants it makes, and this provides a peek at the money going to patient advocacy groups and various educational organizations. In the first quarter of 2009 alone, Eli Lilly gave $551,000 to NAMI and its local chapters, $465,000 to the National Mental Health Association, $130,000 to CHADD (an ADHD patient-advocacy group), and $69,250 to the American Foundation for Suicide Prevention. The company gave more than $1 million to various educational organizations, including $279,533 to the Antidote Education Company, which runs a "continuing medical education" course. Those are the amounts from one pharmaceutical company for three months; any full accounting of the flow of money to patient advocacy groups and educational organizations would require adding up the grants from all of the makers of psychiatric drugs.[28]

We All Pay the Tab

According to a 2009 report by the federal Agency for Healthcare Research and Quality, spending on mental health services is now rising at a faster rate than for any other medical category.[29] In 2008, the United States spent about $170 billion on mental health services, which is twice the amount it spent in 2001, and this spending is projected to increase to $280 billion in 2015. The public, primarily through its Medicaid and Medicare programs, picks up close to 60 percent of the nation's spending on mental health services.[30]

Such is the story of the psychiatric drug business. The industry has excelled at expanding the market for its drugs, and this generates a great deal of wealth for many. However, this enterprise has depended on the telling of a false story to the American public, and the hiding of results that reveal the poor long-term outcomes with this paradigm of care. It also is exacting a horrible toll on our society. The number of people disabled by mental illness during the past twenty years has soared, and now this epidemic has spread to our children. Indeed, millions of children and adolescents are being groomed to be lifelong users of these drugs.

From a societal and moral point of view, that is a bottom-line that cries out for change.

part five

Solutions

I 6

Blueprints for Reform

"I think it is time for another hunger strike."
—VINCE BOEHM, 2009

On July 28, 2003, six "psychiatric survivors" associated with MindFreedom International, a patients' rights organization, announced a "fast for freedom." David Oaks, Vince Boehm, and four others sent a letter to the American Psychiatric Association, NAMI, and the U.S. Office of the Surgeon General stating that they would begin a hunger strike unless one of the organizations provided "scientifically valid evidence" that the various stories they told to the public about mental disorders were true. Among other things, the MindFreedom group asked for evidence proving that major mental illness are "biologically-based brain diseases," and for evidence that "any psychiatric drug can correct a chemical imbalance" in the brain. The MindFreedom Six had put together a scientific panel to review the organizations' replies, an advisory group that included Loren Mosher, and they demanded that if the APA and the others couldn't provide such scientific evidence, "you publicly admit to media, government officials, and the general public that you are unable to do so."[1]

Here's how the APA responded: "The answers to your questions are widely available in the scientific literature, and have been for years," wrote medical director James Scully. He suggested that they read the U.S. Surgeon General's 1999 *Mental Health* report, or an

APA textbook coedited by Nancy Andreasen. "This is a 'user-friendly' textbook for persons just being introduced to the field of psychiatry," he explained.[2]

Only the uneducated, it seemed, asked such dumb questions. But Scully had failed to list any citations, and so the six "psychiatric survivors" began their hunger strike, and when their scientific advisors reviewed the texts that Scully had referred them to, they found no citations there, either. Instead, the texts all grudgingly acknowledged the same bottom line. "The precise causes [etiology] of mental disorders are not known," U.S. surgeon general Satcher confessed in his 1999 report. MindFreedom's scientific panel, in its August 22 reply to Scully, observed that the strikers had asked "clear questions about the science of psychiatry," and yet the APA had brushed them off. "By not giving specific answers to the specific questions posed by the hunger strikers, you appear to be affirming the very reason for the hunger strike."[3]

The APA never answered that letter. Instead, after the Mind-Freedom group broke their fast (several started to have health problems), it issued a press release, stating that the APA, NAMI, and the rest of the psychiatric community "will not be distracted by those who would deny that serious mental disorders are real medical conditions that can be diagnosed accurately and treated effectively."[4] But it was clear to all observers who had won this battle. The strikers had called the APA's bluff, and the APA had come up empty. It hadn't come up with a single citation that supported the "brain disease" story it told to the public. The MindFreedom Six, along with their scientific panel, then issued a clarion call for help:

> We urge members of the public, journalists, advocates, and officials reading this exchange to ask for straightforward answers to our questions from the APA. We also ask Congress to investigate the mass deception that the "diagnosis and treatment of mental disorders," as promoted by bodies such as the APA and its powerful allies, represents in America today.[5]

The strike, noted MindFreedom executive director David Oaks, stirred articles in the *Washington Post* and the *Los Angeles Times*.

"The purpose of the strike was to educate the public. It was about empowering the public and getting them to talk about these issues, which affect everyone. It was about challenging the corporate bullying of the [public] mind."[6]

Lessons from a Hunger Strike

When I first thought about writing a "solutions" chapter, I figured that I would simply report on programs, both in the United States and abroad, that involve using psychiatric medications in a selective, cautious manner (or not at all), and are producing good results. But then I thought of the hunger strike, and I realized that the MindFreedom group had precisely identified the bigger issue at hand.

The real question regarding psychiatric medications is this: When and how should they be used? The drugs may alleviate symptoms over the short term, and there are some people who may stabilize well over the long term on them, and so clearly there is a place for the drugs in psychiatry's toolbox. However, a "best" use paradigm of care would require psychiatry, NAMI, and the rest of the psychiatric establishment to think about the medications in a scientifically honest way and to speak honestly about them to the public. Psychiatry would have to acknowledge that the biological causes of mental disorders remain unknown. It would have to admit that the drugs, rather than fix chemical imbalances in the brain, perturb the normal functioning of neurotransmitter pathways. It would have to stop hiding the results of long-term studies that reveal that the medications are worsening long-term outcomes. If psychiatry did that, it could figure out how to use the medications judiciously and wisely, and everyone in our society would understand the need for alternative therapies that don't rely on the medications or at least minimize their use.

In his 1992 book *How to Become a Schizophrenic*, John Modrow—who had been so diagnosed—wrote the following: "How then are we to help 'schizophrenics'? The answer is simple:

Stop the lies!"[7] In essence, that's what the MindFreedom Six were demanding, and as their advisory panel observed, this is a perfectly rational request. And that, I think, sums up the challenge that we, as a society, now face. How do we break up the psychiatry-and-drug-company partnership that, as we have seen, regularly does lie to us? How can we insist that our society's mental health system be driven by honest science rather than by a partnership that is constantly seeking to expand the market for psychiatric drugs?

There is no easy answer to that question. But clearly our society needs to have a conversation about it, and so I thought that the rest of this "solutions" chapter should be devoted to interviews and investigations of alternative programs that could help make that conversation a fruitful one.

An Artful Form of Care

David Healy is a professor of psychiatry at Cardiff University and tends to psychiatric patients at the District General Hospital in North Wales, where he has been since 1990. His office is located a few feet from a closed ward, and naturally, he regularly prescribes psychiatric medications. Indeed, although he has come to be perceived by many in psychiatry as a "maverick," he recoils at that word. In the 1980s, he notes, he researched serotonin reuptake in depressed patients. He participated as a clinical investigator in a trial of Paxil. He has authored more than a dozen books and published more than 120 articles, with much of his writing focusing on the history of psychiatry and the psychopharmacology era. His CV speaks of a psychiatrist and historian who, until he began writing about problems with the SSRIs, was embraced by the psychiatric establishment. "I don't think I've changed much at all," he said. "I think the mainstream has left me."[8]

His thoughts on how psychiatric drugs should be used (and what they really do) have been deeply influenced both by his writings on the history of psychiatry and by a study he has conducted that compares outcomes of the mentally ill in North Wales a century ago with outcomes in the region today. The population hasn't changed in this period, with around 240,000 in the area, and whereas all the seriously mentally ill were treated at the North Wales Asylum in Denbigh a century ago, today all psychiatric patients needing to be hospitalized are treated at the District General Hospital in Bangor. By poring over records of the two institutions, Healy and his assistants have been able to determine the number of people who were treated back then and the number treated today, as well as the frequency of their hospitalizations.

The common belief, Healy notes, is that the old asylums were bulging with lunatics. Yet from 1894 to 1896, there were only forty-five people per year admitted to the North Wales Asylum (for mental problems). Furthermore, as long as the patients didn't succumb to tuberculosis or some other infectious disease, they regularly got better over the course of three months to a year and went home. Fifty percent were discharged as "recovered" and another 30 percent as "relieved." In addition, the overwhelming majority of patients admitted for a first episode of illness were discharged and never again rehospitalized, and that was true even for psychotic patients. This latter group averaged only 1.23 hospitalizations in a ten-year period (that number includes the initial hospitalization).

Today, the assumption is that patients fare much better than they used to thanks to psychiatric medications. However, in 1996, there were 522 people admitted to the psychiatric ward at the District General Hospital in Bangor—nearly twelve times the number admitted to the Denbigh asylum a century earlier. Seventy-six percent of the 522 patients had been there before, part of a large group of patients in North Wales that cycle regularly through the hospital. Although the patients spent a shorter time in the hospital than they did in 1896, only 36 percent were discharged as recovered. Finally, the patients admitted for a first episode of psychosis in the 1990s averaged 3.96 hospitalizations over the course of ten years—more than three times the number a century earlier. Patients today are clearly more chronically ill than they were a century ago, with modern treatments apparently having set up a "revolving door."[9]

"We have been surprised by how poor the five-year outcomes are today," Healy said. "Each time we look at the current data, at the first batch of five-year outcomes [for a particular diagnostic group], we think, 'God, that can't be the case.' "

Their study sends a fairly clear message about how and when psychiatric medications should be used. "A bunch of people used to recover," Healy explained, but if you immediately put all patients on medications, you run the risk of "giving them a chronic problem they wouldn't have had in the old days." Healy now tries to "watch and wait" before giving psychiatric drugs to first-episode patients, as he wants to see if this type of natural recovery can take hold. "I try to use the drugs cautiously in reasonably low doses, and I tell the patient, 'If the drug isn't doing what we want it to do, we are going to halt it,' " he said. If psychiatrists listened to their patients about how the drugs were affecting them, he concluded, "we would have only a few patients on them long-term."

There it is: a simple prescription for using the medications judiciously. Once a physician realizes that many people who experience a bout of psychosis or a deep depression can recover naturally, and that long-term use of psychotropics is associated with increased chronicity, then it becomes apparent that the drugs need to be used in a selective, limited manner. Healy has seen this approach work with his patients, many of whom initially insist that they need the drugs. "I say to them, 'We can do more harm than good,' " he said. "They don't realize just how much harm we can do."

Healing the "In-Between"

For a long time, western Lapland in Finland had one of the highest rates of schizophrenia in Europe. There are about 70,000 people who live there, and during the 1970s and early 1980s, twenty-five or so new cases of schizophrenia appeared each year—an incidence rate double and even triple the norm for other parts of Finland and the rest of Europe. Furthermore, those patients regularly became chronically ill. But today the long-term outcomes of psychotic patients in western Lapland are the best in the Western world, and this region now sees very few new cases of schizophrenia.

This is a medical success that has been decades in the making, and it began in 1969 when Yrjö Alanen, a Finnish psychiatrist who had psychoanalytic training, arrived at the psychiatric hospital in Turku, a port city in southwest Finland. At that time, few psychiatrists in the country thought that psychotherapy could help schizophrenics. However, Alanen believed that the hallucinations and paranoid utterances of schizophrenic patients, when carefully parsed, told meaningful stories. Hospital psychiatrists, nurses, and staff needed to *listen* to the patients. "It's almost impossible for anyone meeting with these patients' families to not understand that they have difficulties in life," Alanen explained in an interview at the psychiatric hospital in Turku. They are "not ready" to be adults, and "we can help with this development."[10]

Over the next fifteen years, Alanen and a handful of other Turku psychiatrists, most notably Jukka Aaltonen and Viljo Räkköläinen, created what they called the "need-adapted" treatment of psychotic patients. Since psychotic patients are a very heterogeneous group, they decided that treatment needed to be "case specific." Some first-episode patients would need to be hospitalized, and others would not. Some would benefit from low doses of psychiatric medications (either benzos or neuroleptics), and others would not. Most important, the Turku psychiatrists settled on group family therapy—of a particularly collaborative type—as the core treatment. Psychiatrists, psychologists, nurses, and others trained in family therapy all served on two- and three-member "psychosis teams," which would meet regularly with the patient and his or her family. Decisions about the patient's treatment were made jointly at those meetings.

In those sessions, the therapists did not worry about getting the patient's psychotic symptoms to abate. Instead, they focused the conversation on the patient's past successes and achievements, with the thought that this would help strengthen his or her "grip on life." The hope, said Räkköläinen, "is that they haven't lost the idea that they can be like others." The patient might also receive individual psychotherapy to help this process along, and eventually the patient would be encouraged to construct a new "self-narrative" for going forward, the patient imagining a future where he or she was integrated into society, rather than isolated from it. "With the biological conception of psychosis, you can't see the past achievements" or the future possibilities, Aaltonen said.

During the 1970s and 1980s, the outcomes for psychotic patients in the Turku system steadily improved. Many chronic patients were discharged from the hospital, and a study of first-episode schizophrenic-type patients treated from 1983 to 1984 found that 61 percent were asymptomatic at the end of five years and only 18 percent were on disability. This was a very good result, and from 1981 to 1987, Alanen coordinated the Finnish National Schizophrenia Project, which determined that the need-adapted model of care developed in Turku could be successfully introduced into other cities. Two decades after Alanen and the others had initiated their Turku project, Finland had decided that psychotherapy could indeed help psychotic patients.

However, the question of the best use of antipsychotics remained, and in 1992, Finland mounted a study of first-episode patients to answer it. All six sites in the study provided the newly diagnosed patients with need-adapted treatment, but in three of the centers, the patients were not put on antipsychotics during the first three weeks (benzos could be used), with drug therapy initiated only if the patient hadn't improved during this period. At the end of two years, 43 percent of the patients from the three "experimental" sites had never been exposed to neuroleptics, and overall outcomes at the experimental sites were "somewhat better" than they were at the centers where nearly all of the patients had been exposed to the drugs. Furthermore, among the patients at the three experimental sites, those who had never been exposed to neuroleptics had the best outcomes.[11]

"I would advise case-specific use [of the drugs]," Räkköläinen said. "Try without antipsychotics. You can treat them better without medication. They become more interactive. They become themselves." Added Aaltonen: "If you can postpone medication, that's important."

It might seem that Finnish psychiatry, given the outcomes of the study, would have then embraced—on a national level—this "no immediate use of neuroleptics" model of care. Instead, Alanen and the other creators of need-adapted treatment retired, and during the 1990s, Finland's treatment of psychosis became much more "biologically" oriented. Even in Turku, first-episode patients are regularly treated with antipsychotics today, and Finnish guidelines now call for the patients to be kept on the drugs for at least five years after a first episode. "I am a bit disappointed," Alanen confessed at the end of our interview.

Fortunately, one of the three "experimental" sites in the 1992–1993 study did take the results to heart. And that site was Tornio, in western Lapland.

On my way north to Tornio, I stopped to interview Jaakko Seikkula, a professor of psychotherapy at the University of Jyväskylä. In addition to working at Keropudas Hospital in Tornio for nearly twenty years, he has been the lead author on several studies documenting the extraordinary outcomes of psychotic patients in western Lapland.

The transformation of care at Keropudas Hospital, from a system in which patients were regularly hospitalized and medicated to one in which patients are infrequently hospitalized and only occasionally medicated, began in 1984, when Räkköläinen visited and spoke about need-adapted treatment. The Keropudas staff, Seikkula recalled, immediately sensed that holding "open meetings," where every participant freely shared his or her thoughts, would provide psychotic patients with a very different experience from conventional psychotherapy. "The language we use when the patient is sitting with us is so different from the language we use when we [therapists] are by ourselves and discussing the patient," he said. "We do not use the same words, and we have to listen more to the patient's ideas about what is going on, and listen more to the family."

Eventually, Seikkula and others in Tornio developed what they called open-dialogue therapy, which was a subtle variation of

Turku's need-adapted model. As was the case in Turku, patient outcomes in western Lapland improved during the 1980s, and then Tornio was selected to be one of the three experimental sites in Finland's 1992–93 first-episode study. Tornio enrolled thirty-four patients, and at the end of two years, twenty-five had never been exposed to neuroleptics. Nearly all of the never-medicated patients in the national study (twenty-five of twenty-nine) had actually come from this one site, and thus it was only here that hospital staff observed the longer-term course of unmedicated psychosis. And they found that while recovery from psychosis often proceeds at a fairly slow pace, it regularly happens. The patients, Seikkula said, "went back to their work, to their studies, to their families."[12]

Encouraged by the results, Keropudas Hospital immediately started a new study, charting the long-term outcomes of all first-episode psychotic patients in western Lapland from 1992 through 1997. At the end of five years, 79 percent of the patients were asymptomatic and 80 percent were working, in school, or looking for work. Only 20 percent were on government disability. Two-thirds

Five-Year Outcomes for First-Episode Psychotic Patients in Finnish Western Lapland Treated with Open-Dialogue Therapy

Patients (N=75)	
Schizophrenia (N=30)	
Other psychotic disorders (N=45)	
Antipsychotic use	
Never exposed to antipsychotics	67%
Occasional use during five years	33%
Ongoing use at end of five years	20%
Psychotic symptoms	
Never relapsed during five years	67%
Asymptomatic at five-year follow-up	79%
Functional outcomes at five years	
Working or in school	73%
Unemployed	7%
On disability	20%

Source: Seikkula, J. "Five-year experience of first-episode nonaffective psychosis in open-dialogue approach." *Psychotherapy Research* 16 (2006): 214–28.

of the patients had never been exposed to antipsychotic medication, and only 20 percent took the drugs regularly.[13] Western Lapland had discovered a successful formula for helping psychotic patients recover, with its policy of no immediate use of neuroleptics in first-episode patients critical to that success, as it provided an "escape valve" for those who could recover naturally.

"I am confident of this idea," Seikkula said. "There are patients who may be living in a quite peculiar way, and they may have psychotic ideas, but they still can hang on to an active life. But if they are medicated, because of the sedative action of the drugs, they lose this 'grip on life,' and that is so important. They become passive, and they no longer take care of themselves."

Today, the psychiatric facilities in western Lapland consist of the fifty-five-bed Keropudas Hospital, which is located on the outskirts of Tornio, and five mental-health outpatient clinics. There are around one hundred mental-health professionals in the district (psychiatrists, psychologists, nurses, and social workers), and most have completed a nine-hundred-hour, three-year course in family therapy. Many of the staff—including psychiatrist Birgitta Alakare and psychologists Tapio Salo and Kauko Haarakangas—have been there for decades, and today open-dialogue therapy is a well-polished form of care.

Their conception of psychosis is quite distinct in kind, as it doesn't really fit into either the biological or psychological category. Instead, they believe that psychosis arises from severely frayed social relationships. "Psychosis does not live in the head. It lives in the in-between of family members, and the in-between of people," Salo explained. "It is in the relationship, and the one who is psychotic makes the bad condition visible. He or she 'wears the symptoms' and has the burden to carry them."[14]

With most of the staff in the district trained in family therapy, the system is able to respond quickly to a psychotic crisis. Whoever is first contacted—by a parent, a patient seeking help, or perhaps a school administrator—is responsible for organizing a meeting within twenty-four hours, with the family and patient deciding where the meeting should be held. The patient's home is the preferred place. There must be at least two staff members present at the meeting, and preferably three, and this becomes a "team" that ideally will stay together during the patient's treatment. Everyone goes to that first meeting aware that they "know nothing," said nurse Mia Kurtti. Their job is to promote an "open dialogue" in which everybody's thoughts can become known, with the family members (and friends) viewed as coworkers. "We are specialists in saying that we are not specialists," Birgitta Alakare said.

The therapists consider themselves guests in the patient's home, and if an agitated patient runs off to his or her room, they simply ask the patient to leave the door open, so that he or she can listen to the conversation. "They hear voices, we meet them, and we try to reassure them," Salo said. "They are psychotic, but they are not violent at all." Indeed, most patients want to tell their story, and when they speak of hallucinations and paranoid thoughts, the therapists simply listen and reflect upon what they've heard. "I think [psychotic symptoms] are very interesting," Kurtti said. "What's the difference between voices and thoughts? We are having a conversation."

No mention is made of antipsychotics in the first few meetings. If the patient begins sleeping better and bathing regularly, and in other ways begins to reestablish societal connections, the therapists know that the patient's "grip on life" is strengthening, and that medication will not be needed. Now and then, Alakare may prescribe a benzodiazepine to help a person sleep or to dampen the patient's anxiety, and eventually she may prescribe a neuroleptic at a low dose. "Usually I suggest that the patient use it for some months," Alakare said. "But when the problems go away, after six months or a year, or maybe even after three years, we try to stop the medication."

From the outset, the therapists strive to give both the patient and family a sense of hope. "The message that we give is that we can manage this crisis. We have experience that people can get better, and we have trust in this kind of possibility," Alakare said. They have found that it can take a long time—two, three, or even five years—for a patient to recover. Although a patient's psychotic symptoms may abate fairly quickly, they are focused on the patient's "grip on life" and repairing his or her relationship to society, and that is a much bigger task. The team continues to meet with the patient and family, and as this process unfolds, teachers and prospective employers are asked to attend too. "It's about restoring social connections," Salo said. "The 'in-between' starts working again, with family and with friends."

Over the past seventeen years, open-dialogue therapy has transformed "the picture of the psychotic population" in western Lapland. Since the 1992–93 study, not a single first-episode psychotic patient has ended up chronically hospitalized. Spending on psychiatric services in the region dropped 33 percent from the 1980s to the 1990s, and today the district's per-capita spending on mental-health services is the lowest among all health districts in Finland. Recovery rates have stayed high: From 2002 to 2006, Tornio participated in a multinational study by Nordic countries of first-episode psychosis, and at the end of two years, 84 percent of the patients had returned to work or school, and only 20 percent were taking antipsychotics. Most remarkable of all, schizophrenia is now disappearing from the region. Families in western Lapland have become so comfortable with this gentle form of care that they call the hospital (or one of the outpatient clinics) at the first sign of psychosis in a loved one, with the result being that today first-episode patients typically have had psychotic symptoms for less than a month and, with treatment initiated at this early stage, very few go on to develop schizophrenia (the diagnosis is made after a patient has been psychotic for longer than six months). Only two or three new cases of schizophrenia appear each year in western Lapland, a 90 percent drop since the early 1980s.[15]

Tornio's success has drawn the attention of mental-health-care providers in other European countries, and during the past twenty years, two or three other groups in Europe have reported that the combination of psychosocial care and limited use of neuroleptics has produced good outcomes.[16] "This really happened," Seikkula said. "It's not just a theory."

. . .

On my way back to Helsinki, I kept puzzling over this one thought: Why are the group meetings in Tornio so therapeutic? Given the outcomes literature for neuroleptics, I could understand why selective use of the drugs had proven to be so helpful. But why did open-dialogue therapy help psychotic patients heal?

During my two days in Tornio, I sat in on three group sessions, and although I don't speak Finnish, it was nevertheless possible to gain a sense of the meetings' emotional tenor and to observe how the conversation flowed. Everyone sat in a circle, in a very relaxed and calm manner, and before anyone spoke, there often was a split-second moment of silence, as if whoever was going to speak next was gathering his or her thoughts. Now and then someone laughed, and I couldn't identify a time when anyone was interrupted, and yet no individual seemed to go on speaking too long, either. The conversation seemed graced by gentility and humility, and both family members and patients listened with rapt attention whenever the therapists turned and spoke to each other. "We like to know what they really think, rather than just have them give us advice," said the parents in one of the meetings.

But that was the sum of it. It was all a bit mystifying, and even the staff at Keropudas Hospital hadn't really been able to explain why these conversations were so therapeutic. "The severe symptoms begin to pass," Salo said with a shrug. "We don't know how it happens, but [open-dialogue therapy] must be doing something, because it works."

A Natural Antidepressant

In the early 1800s, Americans regularly turned to a book written by Scottish physician William Buchan for medical advice. In *Domestic Medicine*, Buchan prescribed this pithy remedy for melancholy:

> The patient ought to take as much exercise in the open air as he can bear . . . A plan of this kind, with a strict attention to

diet, is a much more rational method of cure, than confining the patient within doors, and plying him with medicines.[17]

Two centuries later, British medical authorities rediscovered the wisdom of Buchan's advice. In 2004, the National Institute for Health and Clinical Excellence, which acts as an advisory panel to the country's National Health Service, decided that "antidepressants are not recommended for the initial treatment of mild depression, because the risk-benefit ratio is poor." Instead, physicians should try non-drug alternatives and advise "patients of all ages with mild depression of the benefits of following a structured and supervised exercise programme."[18]

Today, general practitioners in the UK may write a *prescription* for exercise. "The evidence base for exercise as a treatment for depression is quite good," said Andrew McCulloch, executive director of the Mental Health Foundation, a London-based charity that has been promoting this alternative. "It also reduces anxiety. It's good for self-esteem, control of obesity, et cetera. It has a broad-spectrum effect."[19]

In terms of its short-term efficacy as an antidepressant, studies have shown that exercise produces a "substantial improvement" within six weeks, that its effect size is "large," and that 70 percent of all depressed patients respond to an exercise program. "These success rates are quite remarkable," German investigators wrote in 2008.[20] In addition, over time, exercise produces a multitude of "side benefits." It enhances cardiovascular function, increases muscle strength, lowers blood pressure, and improves cognitive function. People sleep better, they function better sexually, and they also tend to become more socially engaged.

A 2000 study by James Blumenthal at Duke University also revealed that it is unwise to combine exercise with drug therapy. He randomized 156 older depressed patients into three groups—exercise, Zoloft, and Zoloft plus exercise—and at the end of sixteen weeks, those treated with exercise alone were doing as well as those in the other two groups.[21] Blumenthal then tracked the patients for another six months, with the patients free to choose whatever

The Long-Term Benefit of Exercise for Depression

Treatment During First Four Months	Percentage of Patients in Remission at End of Four Months	Percentage of Remitted Patients Who Relapsed in Six-Month Follow-up	Percentage of Patients Depressed at End of Ten Months
Zoloft alone	69%	38%	52%
Zoloft plus exercise therapy	66%	31%	55%
Exercise therapy alone	60%	8%	30%

In this study by Duke researchers, older patients with depression were treated for 16 weeks in one of three ways, and then followed for another six months. Patients treated with exercise alone had the lowest rates of relapse during the following six months, and as a group, they were much less likely to be suffering from depressive symptoms at the end of ten months. Source: Babyak, M. "Exercise treatment for major depression." *Psychosomatic Medicine* 62 (2000): 633–38. 100–11.

treatment they wanted during this period, and at the end the patients treated initially with exercise alone were doing the best. Only 8 percent of those who had been well at the end of sixteen weeks had relapsed during the follow-up, and by the end of ten months 70 percent of the exercise-only group were asymptomatic. In the two Zoloft-exposed groups, more than 30 percent of the patients who had been well at the end of sixteen weeks relapsed, and fewer than 50 percent were asymptomatic by the study's end. The "Zoloft plus exercise" group had fared no better than the "Zoloft alone" patients, which suggested that exposure to Zoloft *negated* the benefits of exercise. "This was an unexpected finding, because it was assumed that combining exercise with medication would have, if anything, an additive effect," Blumenthal wrote.[22]

In 2003, when Britain's Mental Health Foundation launched its exercise-for-depression campaign, it took advantage of the fact that general practitioners in Britain were already "prescribing" exercise to patients with diabetes, hypertension, osteoporosis, and other physical conditions. The delivery of this medical care requires physicians to collaborate with local YMCAs, gyms, and recreational facilities, with these collaborations known as "exercise-referral schemes," and thus the foundation simply needed to get the GPs to start prescribing exercise to their depressed patients too.

Today, more than 20 percent of the GPs in the UK prescribe exercise to depressed patients with some frequency, which is four times the percentage who did in 2004.

A "prescription" for exercise typically provides the patient with twenty-four weeks of treatment. An exercise professional assesses the patient's fitness and develops an appropriate "activity plan," with the patient then given discounted or free access to the collaborating YMCA or gym. Patients work out on exercise machines, swim, and take various exercise classes. In addition, many exercise-referral schemes provide access to "green gyms." The outdoor programs may involve group walks, outdoor stretching classes, and volunteer environmental work (managing local woodlands, improving footpaths, creating community gardens, etc.). Throughout the six months of treatment, the exercise professional monitors the patient's health and progress.

As might be expected, patients have found "exercise-on-prescription" treatment to be quite helpful. They told the Mental Health Foundation that exercise allowed them to "take control of their recovery" and to stop thinking of themselves as "victims" of a disease. Their confidence and self-esteem increased; they felt calmer and more energetic. Treatment was now focused on their "health," rather than on their "illness."

"The fathers of medicine wouldn't be surprised about what we are doing," McCulloch said. "They would say, 'Hasn't science gone any further? Diet and exercise? This is what is new?' If they could travel in a time machine, they would think we were mad, because people have been saying these things for thousands of years."

These Kids Are Awesome

The children who end up living at Seneca Center in San Leandro, California, have come to the last stop for severely disturbed youth in the northern part of the state. The children, five to thirteen years old, have usually cycled through several foster homes and have had multiple hospitalizations, and their behavior has been so difficult that there are no foster homes or hospitals left that want to see them again. In bureaucratic terms, they are "level-14" kids, which is the designation given to the most troubled kids in California, but since these children have flunked out of other level-14 facilities, they are better described as "level-14-plus-plus" youth. Counties pay Seneca Center $15,000 a month to shelter a child and, not surprisingly, when the children arrive at the center, most are on heavy-duty drug cocktails. "They are so drugged up that they are asleep most of the day," said Kim Wayne, director of the residence program.[23]

And then their lives begin to change dramatically.

I visited one of Seneca Center's two residences for younger children in the summer of 2009, and when I entered, here is what I saw: a young African American girl wearing headphones singing along to a Jordin Sparks song; a second slightly older African American girl sitting at the kitchen table, leafing through photos of their recent group trip to Disneyland; and two African American boys at the table goofing around with each other and racing to see who could drink a glass of water the fastest. A Caucasian girl sat on the couch, and the sixth resident of the house, I later learned, was off at a swimming lesson. Within a short while, the girl with the headphones was singing a cappella (and quite well), and the girl huddled over the photo album had started calling me Bob Marley, apparently because I knew who Jordin Sparks was. Now and then, one of the children erupted into laughter.

"The kids are so grateful to be off the drugs," said therapist Kari Sundstrom. "Their personalities come back. They are people again."

The two Seneca Center homes may be the last residential facilities in the United States where severely troubled children under county or state control are treated without psychiatric drugs. Indeed, in most child-psychiatry circles, this would be considered unethical. "I've been told, 'If your child had a disease, would you deny your child medication that helped him get better?'" said Seneca Center founder and CEO Ken Berrick. And even within the agency, which has a staff of around seven hundred and provides a variety of services to two thousand troubled children and youth in northern California, the residence program is an anomaly.

When the center opened in 1985, Berrick and others sought to hire consulting psychiatrists who would use psychiatric medications in a "conservative" fashion and never for purposes of "behavioral control." Some used the drugs more than others, and then there was Tony Stanton, whom the agency hired in 1987 to oversee the children's residential program. In the 1960s, he had trained at Langley Porter Hospital in San Francisco, which at the time emphasized the "importance of environment" to a child's mental health. Stanton's own "attachment theory" convinced him of the importance of emotional relationships to a child's well-being. Then, in the late 1970s, while he was in charge of a psychiatric ward for children at a county hospital, he assigned a "mentor" to every child. The children weren't medicated, and he saw a number of them become attached to their mentors and "blossom."

"That experience allowed me to see this therapeutic principle in action," Stanton said. "You just can't organize yourself without a connection to another human being, and you can't make that connection if you embalm yourself with drugs."

When a child enters Seneca Center's residential program, Stanton does not ask "what's wrong" with the child, but rather "what happened to them." He gets the department of social services, schools, and other agencies to send him all of the records they have on the child, and then he spends eight to ten hours constructing a "life chart." As might be expected, the charts regularly tell of children who have been sexually abused, physically abused, and horribly neglected. But Stanton also tracks their medication history and how their behavior may have changed after they were put on a particular drug, and given that the children who arrive at Seneca Center are seriously disturbed, these medical histories regularly tell of psychiatric care that has worsened their behavior. "I'll have people say, 'We want to try the child on Risperdal now,' and I'll say, 'Let's take a look at the chart and see what happened before. I don't think it will be helpful,' " Stanton said.

The children regularly arrive at the center on drug cocktails, and thus it can take a month or two to withdraw the medications. Often the children, having been repeatedly told that they need the drugs, are nervous about this process—"One kid told me 'What do you mean you are taking me off my meds? I'll destroy your program,' "

Stanton said—and often they do become more aggressive for a time. Staff may have to use "physical restraints" more frequently (they have been trained to hold the kids in "safe" ways). However, these behavioral problems usually begin to abate and by the end of the withdrawal process, the child has "come alive."

"It's wonderful," Kim Wayne said. "Most times when the kids come in, they can't keep their heads up, they are lethargic, they are just a blank and there is minimal engagement. You just can't get through to them. But when they come off their meds, you can engage them and you get to see who they are. You get a sense of their personality, their sense of humor, and what kinds of things they like to do. You may have to use physical restraints for a time, but to me, it's worth it."

Once they are off meds, the children begin to think of themselves in a new way. They see that they can control their own behavior, and this gives them a sense of "agency," Stanton said. The Seneca Center uses behavior-modification techniques to promote this self-control, with the children constantly having to abide by a well-defined set of rules. They have to ask permission to go to the bathroom and enter bedrooms, and if they don't comply with the rules, they may be sent to a "time-out" or lose a privilege. But the staff tries to focus on reinforcing positive behaviors, offering words of praise and rewarding the kids in various ways. The children are required to keep their rooms clean and perform a daily chore, and at times they will help prepare the evening meal.

"The question of feeling in charge of yourself and being responsible for yourself is the central issue in their lives," Stanton said. "They may only partially get there while they are with us, but when we are really successful, we see them develop this sense of 'Oh, I can do this; I want to be in control of myself and my own life.' They see themselves as having that power."

Even more important, once the children are off the medications they are better able to form emotional bonds with the staff, and the staff with them. They have known rejection all their lives, and they need to form relationships that nurture a belief that they are worthy of being loved, and when that happens, their "internal narrative" can switch from "I'm a bad kid" to "I'm a good kid."

"They come in thinking, 'I'm crazy, you are going to hate me, you are going to get rid of me, I'm going to be the worst kid you have ever seen,'" said therapist Julie Kim. "But then they become willing to form [emotional] attachments, and that's such an amazing thing. You can see the power of a relationship to change a kid, and even the kids who seem the toughest when they come in here, who don't make any progress at first, eventually do."

Although Kim and others can tell anecdotal stories of children discharged from the residence program who have returned to ordinary schools and done well, the center has not done a long-term follow-up of the children that have gone through their residence program. The only statistical information the center has to show that its residence program works is this: 225 children lived at its residences from 1995 to 2006, and nearly all were discharged to lower-level group homes or to a foster home or to their biological families. Their time at Seneca Center at least turned their lives in a new direction. And yet, it is difficult to be optimistic that their lives continue down that path. Their emotional and behavioral problems do not completely go away, and so many of the discharged children—and perhaps most—are remedicated. They return to a world where that is the norm. Their time at Seneca Center may primarily provide them with a temporary oasis from a society prone to asking "what's wrong with them," and thus, if we want to assess whether the no-medication policy of the center's residence program is providing the children with a "benefit," instead of looking to the future, perhaps we should focus on the present and look at what it is like for the children to have this opportunity to "come alive" for a time and fully feel the world.

I spent two days at the center, and there were three children in particular I had a chance to interact with. One was a twelve-year-old boy I'll call Steve. When he'd arrived at Seneca Center a year earlier, he'd been so filled with suicidal and self-destructive habits that doctors thought he had suffered brain damage from all of his head-banging episodes. Since then he'd become very attached to Stacy, one of the male staff at his house, and during our interview, he flopped down into a chair, grinned, and immediately took over the conversation. "I hate taking medicine. It is real boring being on drugs," he said, and then he began telling us about migratory turtles, a raccoon that had been poking around their house, a trip to McDonald's with Stacy, and what people needed to do to prepare for an earthquake. All of that was prelude to a story about a comic book he wanted to write, titled *The Adventures of Sam Dune and Rock*, which featured numerous "good and evil" characters, including one who needed to take drugs to keep from going mad. Steve held center stage for at least an hour, and afterward he happily informed Stacy that the interview had been "cold, real cold," which of course meant that he had enjoyed himself immensely.

I'll call the two African American girls I met in the Los Reyes house Layla (the a cappella singer) and Takeesha. Their "life charts" both told of nightmarish pasts, and that was particularly true for Takeesha. When she'd arrived at the Seneca Center in 2006, at age seven, she was described as delusional, guarded, suspicious, uncooperative, and very sedated. After we spent thirty minutes or so at the kitchen table, talking about *American Idol* and the trip they had taken to Disneyland, Takeesha asked if we could go outside and play catch with a football. We did that for a while, and then Takeesha got permission to ride her bike in the street, but only if she promised to go only a few houses away in either direction, and suddenly she came to a screeching halt in the driveway. "I'm going to Burger King. What do you want?" she announced. Seconds later she proudly returned holding an imaginary bag filled with a Whopper, French fries, and a Coke, which I paid for with an equally imaginary five-dollar bill, asking if she would please make change. When it came time to say good-bye, Layla asked for a hug, and then Takeesha—having scurried into her bedroom to find something—held out what appeared to be a package of gum, except for the fact that the piece sticking out was clearly metallic in kind.

"It's just gum!" she squealed when I felt the slight buzz.

The next day I sat in on their class. I spoke briefly with the teacher and several of the aides, and they all said the same thing. "These kids are awesome! We could drug the kids into submission, but for what purpose? I love this place!" I was there with Tony Stanton, and after a while it became evident that our presence was causing a dilemma for both Layla and Takeesha. They were supposed to be paying attention to the teacher, and they knew that if they didn't, they would be sent to time-out (there was a steady march of children to the time-out corner), and yet both were clearly intent on making contact with us. We were sitting by the sink, and at last both girls decided they just *had* to wash their hands. As Layla went back to her seat, she couldn't resist giving us a high-five, even though this was a breach of class protocol. Meanwhile, as Takeesha passed by my chair, she whispered, "Bob Marley, what are you doing here?"

At that moment, I couldn't imagine any outcome data of a more powerful sort.

On the Drawing Board

Psychiatry and the rest of medicine regularly proclaim that treatments should be "evidence-based." The solutions we've reviewed in this chapter all meet that standard. David Healy's belief that the psychiatric medications should be used in a cautious manner, the open-dialogue program in Tornio, and the prescribing of exercise as a first-line therapy for mild-to-moderate depression are all rooted in good science. The same can be said of Tony Stanton's medication-withdrawal policy. Earlier in the book, we saw that children put on stimulants, antidepressants, and antipsychotics often worsen over the long term, and that those who end up on drug cocktails can be said to be suffering from an iatrogenic illness. The medications can be viewed as pathological agents, and thus when Tony Stanton takes the Seneca Center children off the drugs, he is—in essence—providing treatment for a "disease." The proof that the treatment works can be found in the staff's observation that the children "come alive."

Given this perspective, it would be helpful if we could identify a mainstream medication-withdrawal program in adults, one that arises from research into this process. How quickly should the drugs be withdrawn? After the drugs are withdrawn, how long does it take for the brain to "renormalize?" Or does it? Do neuronal feedback mechanisms reset? Do presynaptic neurons begin releasing normal amounts of the neurotransmitter? Do receptor densities return to normal? Psychiatry has been using psychotropic medications for more than fifty years, yet all of these questions basically remain unanswered. Indeed, people who want to stop taking the drugs have been mostly left to fend for themselves, sharing information on the Internet and through their various peer networks.

However, in the fall of 2009, a major provider of mental-health services in eastern and central Massachusetts, Advocates, drew up a plan for a medication-withdrawal study. Advocates provides services to several thousand people with psychiatric difficulties, and in 2008, when it asked its clients for "new ideas," many put this at the top of their wish list, said Keith Scott, director of recovery and peer support services. "A number said, 'Geez, it would be great if there would be a place where I could try to stop taking my medication without being threatened with losing my housing or my services and the relationships that are important to me.' That seemed extremely reasonable to me."[24]

The medical director of Advocates, Chris Gordon, who is an assistant clinical professor of psychiatry at Harvard Medical School, said that he hoped to obtain funding from either the state Department of Mental Health or a federal agency. Advocates plans to provide both medical and social support to patients in the "drug reduction/elimination" study, and Gordon said that if patients begin to struggle during the withdrawal process, he'd like to see if they can be helped through that crisis without restarting the medications. He'd like to follow the patients in the program for five years, so Advocates can get a sense of their long-term outcomes.

This initiative, Gordon said, is being driven in part by the fact that the mentally ill are now dying twenty-five years earlier than their peers, and that it is clear that the atypical antipsychotics, which regularly cause metabolic dysfunction, are contributing to that early death problem. "We see it all the time. We could name a terrible list of people we know personally and care about who died way too young," he said.[25]

The Alaska Project

If I had to identify one person in the United States who was doing the most to "change the system," I would pick Alaska attorney Jim Gottstein. A 1978 graduate of Harvard Law School, Gottstein was hospitalized twice in the 1980s because of bouts of mania, and that personal experience has inspired a lifelong career of fighting to improve the plight of the mentally ill in our society.

During the 1980s and 1990s, Gottstein joined other attorneys in an epic lawsuit by the Alaska Mental Health Association against the state. In 1956, Congress allowed Alaska's territorial administrators to set aside one million acres of prime federal land as an asset that would fund mental-health programs, but in 1978 the state legislature redesignated the acreage as "general grant lands," leaving the mentally ill out in the cold. The state basically "stole" the land, Gottstein said, and eventually he and other attorneys negotiated a $1.1 billion settlement.[26] The state gave $200 million and nearly a million acres of land to a newly created Mental Health Trust Authority, with the trust allowed to spend this money as it sees fit, without the legislature's approval.

In 2002, Gottstein founded a non-profit organization, PsychRights, and the first thing that it did was mount a "public information" campaign. PsychRights brought various people to Anchorage to speak to judges, lawyers, psychiatrists, and the general public about the outcomes literature for antipsychotics.* Gottstein believed that this would provide a foundation for a lawsuit challenging the state's right to medicate patients forcibly, and for lobbying the Mental Health Trust Authority to fund a Soteria-like home, where psychotic patients who didn't want to take neuroleptics could get help.

"The public opinion is that the meds work, and that if people weren't crazy, they would know that the drugs are good for them," Gottstein said. "But if we can get judges and lawyers to understand

---

* In the interest of full disclosure, I was one of the speakers at several of those events.

that it's not necessarily good for the person and potentially very harmful, they would tend to honor a person's legal right to refuse treatment. In the same vein, if the public knew that there are other non-drug approaches like Soteria that work better, they would support alternatives, right?"

State case laws governing the forced treatment of psychiatric patients date back to the late 1970s. Although state supreme courts typically ruled that patients have a right to refuse treatment (in non-emergency situations), they nevertheless noted that antipsychotics were understood to be "a medically sound treatment of mental disease," and thus hospitals could apply to a court to sanction forced treatment. At such hearings, hospitals regularly argue that no competent person would refuse "medically sound treatment," and thus courts consistently order patients to be medicated.[27] But in 2003, Gottstein initiated a forced-drugging lawsuit on behalf of a woman named Faith Myers, and he put the medication on trial, arguing that the state could not show that it was in her best medical interest to take an antipsychotic. He got Loren Mosher and a second psychiatrist who knows the outcomes literature well, Grace Jackson, to serve as his expert witnesses, and he also filed copies of the many research studies that tell of how neuroleptics can worsen long-term outcomes.

Having become versed in the scientific literature, the Alaska Supreme Court gave PsychRights a stunning legal victory in 2006. "Psychotropic medication can have profound and lasting negative effects on a patient's mind and body," the court wrote. These drugs "are known to cause a number of potentially devastating side effects." As such, it ruled in *Myers v. Alaska Psychiatric Institute* that a psychiatric patient could be forcibly medicated only if a court "expressly finds by clear and convincing evidence that the proposed treatment is in the patient's best interest and that no less intrusive alternative is available."[28] In Alaska case law, antipsychotics are no longer viewed as treatment that will necessarily help psychotic people.

In 2004, Gottstein launched an effort to get the Mental Health Trust Authority to fund a Soteria home in Anchorage, which would offer psychotic patients the type of care that Loren Mosher's Soteria

Project did in the 1970s. Once again, he relied on the persuasive powers of the scientific literature to carry his argument, and in the summer of 2009, a seven-bedroom Soteria home opened a few miles south of downtown. The director of the project, Susan Musante, formerly led a psychiatric rehabilitation program at the University of New Mexico Mental Health Center; the consulting psychiatrist, Aron Wolf, is a well-respected figure in Alaskan psychiatry.

"We want to work with younger people who have been on psychiatric medications for only a short time, and by getting them off the meds and helping them get better, we hope to keep them from going down the path of chronic illness," Musante said. "Our expectation is that people will recover. We expect them to go to work or to school, to return to age-appropriate behavior. We are here to help them to dream again and to pursue those dreams. We are not set up to funnel them onto SSI or SSDI."[29]

Gottstein now has his sights set on a legal challenge national in scope. He has been filing lawsuits that challenge the medicating of foster children and poor children in Alaska (the poor are covered by Medicaid), and ultimately he hopes to take one of these cases to the U.S. Supreme Court. He sees this as a 14th Amendment issue, with the children being deprived of their liberty without due process of law. At the heart of any such case would be a scientific question: Are the foster children being treated with medications that help, or are they being treated with tranquilizing drugs that cause long-term harm?

"I analogize it to *Brown v. Board of Education*," Gottstein said. "Before that decision, there was widespread acceptance in the United States that segregation is OK. The Supreme Court had previously said that segregation was OK. But then in *Brown v. Board of Education*, the court said it wasn't OK, and that really changed public opinion. Today you can't get anyone to say segregation is OK. And that's how I visualize this whole effort."

We the People

As a society, we put our trust in the medical profession to develop the best possible clinical care for diseases and ailments of all types. We expect that the profession will be honest with us as it goes about this task. And yet, as we look for ways to stem the epidemic of disabling mental illness that has erupted in this country, we cannot trust psychiatry, as a profession, to fulfill that responsibility.

For the past twenty-five years, the psychiatric establishment has told us a false story. It told us that schizophrenia, depression, and bipolar illness are known to be brain diseases, even though—as the MindFreedom hunger strike revealed—it can't direct us to any scientific studies that document this claim. It told us that psychiatric medications fix chemical imbalances in the brain, even though decades of research failed to find this to be so. It told us that Prozac and the other second-generation psychotropics were much better and safer than the first-generation drugs, even though the clinical studies had shown no such thing. Most important of all, the psychiatric establishment failed to tell us that the drugs worsen long-term outcomes.

If psychiatry had been honest with us, the epidemic could have been curbed long ago. The long-term outcomes would have been publicized and discussed, and that would have set off societal alarms. Instead, psychiatry told stories that protected the image of its drugs, and that storytelling has led to harm done on a grand and terrible scale. Four million American adults under sixty-five years old are on SSI or SSDI today because they are disabled by mental illness. One in every fifteen young adults (eighteen to twenty-six years old) is "functionally impaired" by mental illness. Some 250 children and adolescents are added to the SSI rolls daily because of mental illness. The numbers are staggering, and still the epidemic-making machinery rolls on, with two-year-olds in our country now being "treated" for bipolar illness.

As I noted earlier in this chapter, I believe the MindFreedom Six showed what must be done if we are going to halt this epidemic. We need to become informed about the long-term outcomes literature reviewed in this book, and then we need to ask the NIMH, NAMI, the APA, and all those who prescribe the medications to address the many questions raised by that literature. In other words, we need to have an honest scientific discussion. We need to talk about what is truly known about the biology of mental disorders, about what the drugs actually do, and about how the drugs increase the risk that people will become chronically ill. If we could have that discussion, then change surely would follow. Our society would embrace and promote alternative forms of non-drug care. Physicians would prescribe the medications in a much more limited, cautious manner. We would stop putting foster children on heavy-duty cocktails and pretending that it was medical care. In short, our societal delusion about a "psychopharmacology" revolution could at last fade away, and good science could illuminate the path to a much better future.

Epilogue

"Few dare to announce unwelcome truth."
—EDWIN PERCY WHIPPLE (1866)[1]

This book tells a history of science that leads readers to a socially awkward place. Our society believes that psychiatric medications have led to a "revolutionary" advance in the treatment of mental disorders, and yet these pages tell of a drug-induced epidemic of disabling mental illness. Society sees the beautiful woman, and this book directs the reader's gaze to the old woman. It's never easy to hold a belief that is out of sync with what the rest of society believes, and in this instance, it's particularly difficult because the story of progress is told by figures of scientific authority—the APA, the NIMH, and psychiatrists at prestigious universities such as Harvard Medical School. Disagree with the common wisdom on this topic, and it seems that you must be a card-carrying member of the flat-Earth society.

But for those readers still wondering about the history told here, I offer one last story. You can read it and decide for yourself whether you are now, metaphorically speaking, in the flat-Earth camp.

After I interviewed Jaakko Seikkula at the University of Jyväskylä, he asked me to give a short talk on the history of antipsychotics to a few of his colleagues. Now, Seikkula and others at Keropudas Hospital in Tornio did not decide to use antipsychotics in a selective manner because they thought that the drugs *worsened* psychotic symptoms over the long term. Instead, they observed that many people did better when off them. Thus, when I spoke to Seikkula's colleagues at the University of Jyväskylä, this notion that antipsychotics can make people chronically ill was something they hadn't thought much about before, and at the end of my talk, one of the members of our circle asked if this could be true of antidepressants, too. He and others had been researching the long-term outcomes of depressed patients in Finland, and charting too whether they had used the drugs, and they had been startled by their results.

So, dear readers, ask yourself this: What do you think they found? And are you surprised?

Afterword: Research Update

Since *Anatomy* was published, a number of studies have appeared in medical journals relevant to the question of how psychiatric drugs affect long-term outcomes. A review of that literature provides an opportunity to update the evidence for the argument made in this book. In addition, as *Anatomy* was translated into other languages, I gathered data on the number of disability pensions in those countries due to mental illness. The disability numbers also add to the "evidence base" for rethinking psychiatric care.

Disability Pensions

Many critics of *Anatomy* argued that the rise in the number of people in the United States on the SSI or SSDI disability roles due to mental illness could be explained by social factors: welfare reform that reduced aid to the poor, difficult economic times, the lack of national health insurance, etc. People in the United States were turning to the disability system in order to obtain financial support and access to health care. While that may be partly true, a dramatic rise in disability due to mental illness has occurred in country after country that has adopted the widespread use of psychiatric drugs, including those that offer extensive social support to their citizens.*

For instance, in Australia, there were 57,008 adults on government disability due to mental illness in 1990. That number rose to 241,335 in 2011, a fourfold increase.[1] The data from New Zealand tells the same story. In 1998, there were 21,972 adults, ages 18 to 64, on disability due to psychiatric conditions. Thirteen years later, that number had more than doubled, to 50,979.[2]

Societies are also reporting that their annual number of new disability awards due to mental illness keeps going up. In Iceland, with its stable population, the number of new cases of disability due to a psychiatric problem increased from 84 per 100,000 adults in 1992 to 217 per 100,000 adults in 2007.[3] In Denmark there were 3,550 new disability awards due to psychiatric disorders in 1999; eleven years later, this number had jumped to 8,812.[4] The same is true in Sweden. In 1999, about 25 percent of all new disability claims were due to psychiatric disorders; by 2011, this percentage had risen to nearly 60 percent.[5] Finally, in Germany, the number of adults going on government disability because of a psychiatric disorder rose from 39,037 in 2000 to 70,946 in 2010.[6]

The Death of the Chemical Imbalance Story

While it may still be possible to read on websites that mental disorders are due to chemical imbalances, academic psychiatrists in the United States have stopped telling that story to the media. The official burial date for the chemical-imbalance story could be said to have occurred on July 11, 2011, when Ronald Pies, editor-in-chief emeritus of the *Psychiatric Times,* published an article titled "Psychiatry's New Brain-Mind and the Legend of the 'Chemical Imbalance.'" Pies wrote that American psychiatry, in fact, had never promoted this idea.

---

* This was true of disability numbers for all six foreign countries that I reviewed.

I am not one who easily loses his temper, but I confess to experiencing markedly increased limbic activity whenever I hear someone proclaim, "Psychiatrists think all mental disorders are due to a chemical imbalance!" In the past 30 years, I don't believe I have ever heard a knowledgeable, well-trained psychiatrist make such a preposterous claim, except perhaps to mock it. On the other hand, the "chemical imbalance" trope has been tossed around a great deal by opponents of psychiatry, who mendaciously attribute the phrase to psychiatrists themselves. And, yes—the "chemical imbalance" image has been vigorously promoted by some pharmaceutical companies, often to the detriment of our patients' understanding. In truth, the "chemical imbalance" notion was always a kind of urban legend—never a theory seriously propounded by well-informed psychiatrists.[7]

"Preposterous, an urban legend" . . . those are words that tell of a profession eager to wash its hands of the entire affair.

At the same time, a handful of researchers in the past few years have been writing about how the drugs, rather than fix a chemical imbalance, induce compensatory adaptations the "opposite of what is originally intended." In 2014, Peter Gøtzsche, a cofounder of the Cochrane Collaboration, which is an international network of researchers known for its rigorous reviews of the risks and benefits of medical treatments, wrote about this in a blog post titled "Psychiatry Gone Astray":

The theories that patients with depression lack serotonin and that patients with schizophrenia have too much dopamine have long been refuted. The truth is just the opposite. There is no chemical imbalance to begin with, but when treating mental illness with drugs, we create a chemical imbalance.[8]

That is a concise summary of the information presented in chapter five of this book, "The Hunt for Chemical Imbalances."

A Heretical Idea Goes Mainstream

In 2010, the idea that antipsychotics impaired long-term recovery for people diagnosed with schizophrenia and other psychotic disorders was considered heresy. Antipsychotics were seen as an essential treatment, so much so that our society was led to understand that if patients didn't want to take these medications, it was because they lacked "insight" into their disease (and thus, in many instances, they should be forcibly ordered to take these drugs).

Today, the evidence that drugs impair long-term recovery rates is becoming so convincing that even mainstream psychiatric journals have run editorials urging that the use of these drugs should be rethought.

Brain Volumes

Although Nancy Andreasen conceded in a 2008 interview with the *New York Times* that antipsychotics caused the "prefrontal cortex to slowly atrophy," she had not—at that time—presented that conclusion in a research paper. In 2011, she dropped her bombshell finding into the scientific literature. In an article published in the *Archives of General Psychiatry,* she reported that long-term use of the old standard antipsychotics, the new atypicals, and clozapine were all "associated with smaller brain tissue volumes." She found that this brain shrinkage was dose related; the more drug a person was given, the greater the association "with smaller grey matter volumes." A loss in white matter volume was also "most evident among patients who received more antipsychotic treatment." Illness severity and substance abuse had "minimal or no effects" on brain volumes, she concluded.[9]

Together, Andreasen's various reports revealed an iatrogenic process at work. Antipsychotics block dopamine activity in the brain and this leads to brain shrinkage, which in turn is associated with a worsening of negative symptoms and cognitive impairment. Several other researchers subsequently scoured the literature for studies examining antipsychotic use and brain volumes, and their work adds to the evidence that the drugs have this iatrogenic effect.

In 2012, a European group reported that in a review of forty-three brain-imaging studies of patients being treated for a first episode of psychosis, the loss of gray matter volume was "significantly more severe in medicated patients."[10] The researchers noted that the drugs reduce "frontal cerebral blood flow" and that this "could be a mechanism underlying smaller brain tissue volumes." Next, in 2013, Chinese investigators found an "acute reduction" in white matter in the frontal lobe following six weeks of antipsychotic treatment for first-episode schizophrenia.[11] Finally, in 2014, German investigators conducted an exhaustive review of the literature, and they concluded that "there is evidence for grey and white matter volume changes of the frontal brain, which cannot be explained by the severity of the disease alone but are also very likely a manifestation of long-term effects of antipsychotics." The German scientists advised that the use of antipsychotics should be rethought:

> Considering the contribution of antipsychotics to the changes in brain structure, which seem to depend on cumulative dosage and can exert adverse effects on neurocognition, negative and positive symptoms and psychosocial functioning, the guidelines for antipsychotic long-term drug treatment should be reconsidered. . . . Treatment approaches which can help to minimize antipsychotic medication or even administer them only selectively are of increasing importance.[12]

Although this is understood to be a long-term effect, the shrinkage—as seen in the Chinese study—begins to occur rather quickly, during the first year of drug use.

Harrow Updates His Findings

When Martin Harrow published his 2007 report on the fifteen-year outcomes of schizophrenia patients, he did not attribute the better outcomes of the unmedicated patients to their avoidance of antipsychotics. Instead, he reported that it was those patients with a good prognosis at entry into the study that were more likely to go off the drugs, and this explained why the unmedicated group had better long-term outcomes.

Although I wrote about his explanation, stating that it was those with a better internal sense of self who were more likely to go off the medications, I always thought it was belied by his own data. In every patient subset—good prognosis schizophrenia, bad prognosis schizophrenia, and milder psychotic disorders—those who got off did better, and most telling of all, the schizophrenia patients off antipsychotics did better than those with milder psychotic disorders who stayed on the drugs. In a series of papers written since 2010, Harrow noted that was true, and he also reported new data that further fleshed out the marked differences in outcomes for the medicated and unmedicated patients. He also directly raised the question of whether the drugs were, in fact, to blame for the difference in outcomes.

In 2012, Harrow reported on the patients' twenty-year outcomes.[13] This time he grouped those with a diagnosis of schizoaffective disorder and a diagnosis of schizophrenia into a single "schizophrenia spectrum" category. Starting at the 4.5-year follow-up, the patients off antipsychotics were less psychotic, less anxious, and had lower relapse rates. They also had better cognitive functioning and were much more likely to enjoy "sustained periods of recovery." This dramatic difference in global outcomes continued at each of the remaining follow-up assessments in the twenty-year study.

In this paper, Harrow also compared functional outcomes for those patients who were off antipsychotics by the end of the second year and never took the medications again with those of patients who were on antipsychotics at the end of the second year and continued to take them throughout the study. The first group could be said to be consistently noncompliant, going against what was said to be best for schizophrenia patients, while the second group complied with the doctors' orders. The differences between the two groups were stunning: 87 percent of the off-antipsychotic group had *two or more* sustained periods of recovery, whereas only 17 percent of the medication-compliant patients had even *one* sustained period of recovery. To be in recovery in this study, the patient had to be working more than 50 percent of the time, and few of the medicated patients worked long enough to meet that standard. At the conclusion of that paper, Harrow asked the obvious question, "Is very long-term treatment with antipsychotic medications undesirable?"

Next, in a 2013 paper that appeared the *Schizophrenia Bulletin*, Harrow sought to answer his own question.[14] He first revisited his 2007 article. Although it was true that patients in the good prognosis category were more likely to go off medication than those with a bad prognosis, he noted—once again—that within each of these patient subsets, it was the off-med group that did better. He also noted that whereas in relapse studies, it was the drug-withdrawn patients that had the higher relapse rates, the opposite was true in his study. Once patients got stable off medication, they had extremely low relapse rates, much lower than the medicated patients. In an effort to explain this seeming paradox, Harrow turned to the research showing that antipsychotics increased the density of D_2 receptors. This could be the reason that people relapsed so frequently when coming off the drugs, he wrote. The high-relapse rate, which was the evidence that psychiatry relied upon to justify long-term use, was at least in part a drug-withdrawal effect, as opposed to the return of the "disease." At the same time, the fact that so many of the medicated patients in his study remained psychotic was consistent with the idea that the increase in D_2 receptors made a person more biologically vulnerable to psychosis, and this, over the long term, could lead to tardive psychosis. "How unique among medical treatments is it that the apparent efficacy of antipsychotics could diminish over time or become ineffective or harmful?" Harrow concluded. "There are many examples for other medications of similar long-term effects, with this often occurring as the body readjusts, biologically, to the medications."

With each successive publication, Harrow was going a step further in questioning the merits of antipsychotics. Finally, in a 2014 paper, he honed in on the question of whether the drugs reduced psychotic symptoms over the long term. This is the benefit the drugs are supposed to provide, and if the drugs don't do that, then there is nothing left on the benefit side of the ledger for these drugs. Harrow reported that 72 percent of the patients who were "always on antipsychotics" throughout the twenty years were persistently psychotic (e.g., psychotic at four or more of the follow-up assessments). Forty-six percent of those who were "sometimes" on antipsychotics fell into this category, and only 7 percent of those who never used antipsychotics after year two did.[15]

This was data that powerfully supported the hypothesis that antipsychotic drugs induce biological changes that make people more psychotic over the long term. The drugs, over the long term, appear to worsen the very symptom they are supposed to treat.

Other Clinical Studies

As convincing as Harrow's data may seem, his was a naturalistic study, rather than a randomized one, and defenders of conventional beliefs about antipsychotics regularly pointed to that fact. In a naturalistic study, a researcher simply collects outcomes data for all of the patients, and those who choose to go off medication may be different in some ways—such as the baseline severity of their symptoms—than those who choose to stay on the medication. Harrow had initially explained his fifteen-year results in that way. It was only when he reported the twenty-year data that he backed away from that explanation. But to the defenders of conventional wisdom, studies that randomized patients to different treatments are the gold standard in research, and until the field had such a study, Harrow's work could be dismissed.

In 2013, Dutch researcher Lex Wunderink filled in that gap. In his randomized study, psychotic patients who had stabilized on an antipsychotic were then either maintained on the drug or withdrawn from it (or tapered to a very low dose). At the end of two years, the drug-withdrawn/low-dose group had a higher relapse rate (43 percent versus 21 percent), but by the end of seven years, it had a slightly lower relapse rate (62 percent versus 69 percent). More important, at the end of seven years, the withdrawn/low-dose group had a much higher recovery rate (40 percent versus 18 percent). This higher recovery rate was due to the fact that those in the withdrawn/low-dose group had much better functional outcomes.[16]

Wunderink drew two conclusions from his studies. The first was that antipsychotics "might compromise important mental functions, such as alertness, curiosity, drive, and activity levels, and aspects of executive functional capacity to some extent." The second was that psychiatric researchers, by focusing on drug-withdrawal studies as a measure of long-term efficacy, had missed the bigger picture:

> The results of this study lead to the following conclusions: schizophrenia treatment strategy trials should include recovery or functional remission rates as their primary outcome and should also include long-term follow-up for more than 2 years, even up to 7 years or longer. In the present study, short-term drawbacks, such as higher relapse rates, were leveled out in the long term, and benefits that were not evident in short-term evaluation, such as functional gains, only appeared in long-term monitoring.

In 2013, Australian researchers also published a very revealing finding. In their study, patients who had stabilized on antipsychotics following a first episode of schizophrenia were randomized either to treatment as usual or to a program designed to improve medication compliance. Their hypothesis was that increased compliance would produce better outcomes. However, while the program did achieve its goal of getting patients to stay on their antipsychotic medication, the increased compliance was associated with "decreases in psychosocial functioning and increases in negative symptoms."[17] Once again, increased antipsychotic use was associated with a worse functional outcome.

A Need to Rethink Antipsychotics
All of this literature ultimately comes together to tell a convincing story. Antipsychotics induce changes in the brain that increase a person's biological vulnerability to psychosis, and the drugs also decrease brain volumes, with this shrinkage associated with an increase in negative symptoms and functional impairment and a

worsening of cognitive function. And given those facts, then it is to be expected that Harrow, Wunderink, and the Australian researchers would report the results they did. Although research may show that some schizophrenia patients need the medications, the literature nevertheless tells of drugs that worsen long-term outcomes in the aggregate. At some point, the collection of evidence becomes overwhelming.

In 2012, the *British Journal of Psychiatry*, in an editorial by Peter Tyrer titled "The End of the Psychopharmacological Revolution," acknowledged that the time had come for the field to rethink its use of antipsychotics.

> It is time to reappraise the assumption that antipsychotics must always be the first line of treatment for people with psychosis. This is not a wild cry from the distant outback, but a considered opinion by influential researchers. . . . [There is] an increasing body of evidence that the adverse effects of [antipsychotic] treatment are, to put it simply, not worth the candle.[18]

The following year, after Wunderink published his findings, *JAMA Psychiatry,* in an editorial by Patrick McGorry titled "Less Is More," similarly wrote that the field needed to change its ways.

> In moving to a more personalized or stratified medicine, we first need to identify the very small number of patients who may be able to recover from first episode psychosis with intensive psychosocial interventions alone. For everyone else, we need to determine which medication, for how long, in what minimal dose, and what range of intensive psychosocial interventions will be needed to help them get well, stay well, and lead fulfilling and productive lives. These factors have rarely been the goal in the real world of clinical psychiatry—something we must finally address now that we are armed with stronger evidence to counter poor practice.[19]

If that last editorial is carefully parsed, McGorry is recommending the selective-use protocol employed in Open Dialogue therapy to such great success. *JAMA Psychiatry* is embracing a drug-use model put forth as a solution in *Anatomy* three years earlier.

They Call It Tardive Dysphoria

When I reported on the STAR*D study for this book, I struggled to find a report that clearly told of the percentage of depressed patients who were still doing well at the end of one year. Based on information in several published articles, I calculated that fewer than 20 percent of the patients who entered the study remitted and then stayed well and in the trial throughout the one-year follow-up. This study, funded by the NIMH, is touted as the largest antidepressant trial ever conducted in "real-world" patients, and thus the bottom-line result—the one-year stay-well rate—is of considerable significance. It turns out the actual stay-well rate was much lower than what I had calculated. Psychologist Ed Pigott pored over the published data with a careful eye and was finally able to make sense of a hard-to-understand graphic published in one of the STAR*D reports. Only 108 of the 4,041 depressed patients who entered the study remitted, and then stayed well and in the trial for one year.[20] That is a documented stay-well rate of 3%. When Pigott published his findings, one of the STAR*D investigators, Mauricio Fava, acknowledged that the 3 percent figure was correct. This outcome, *Medscape Medical News* noted, pointed "to a lack of long-term efficacy for antidepressants."[21]

In fact, this finding supported the notion that SSRIs are depressogenic agents over the long term, and thus increase the chronicity of the disorder. Other recent studies support this conclusion. To wit:

- MN Community Measurement is a nonprofit organization that gathers data on health outcomes in Minnesota. In 2010, it determined that only 1,131 of 23,887 patients (4.5 percent) treated for major depression or dysthymia in 2009 were in remission at the end of twelve months. The remaining 95 percent

were still symptomatic, evidence that they were now chronically depressed.[22]

- Researchers in the Netherlands followed 172 patients for two
years after their depression had initially gone into remission
and found that during this follow-up the relapse rate was 60
percent for those who continuously took an antidepressant,
64 percent for those who intermittently took one, and 26 percent for those who didn't take an antidepressant at all. The
higher relapse rate for the patients who took antidepressants,
the investigators concluded, was consistent with the idea that
"continued antidepressant treatment may oppose the initial
acute effects of [the] antidepressant . . . [and] neurobiological
mechanism(s) may be involved in increasing vulnerability" to
relapse.[23]

- Paul Andrews, an assistant professor at McMaster University
in Canada, determined that patients who remitted on an antidepressant in a clinical trial and then stopped taking the drug
were much more likely to relapse in the next three months
than patients who remitted on placebo during a clinical trial
(and stayed off medication). In a meta-analysis of forty-six
studies, he found that the relapse rate for the drug-treated
group was 45 percent compared to 25 percent for the placebo
patients. In the discussion of his results, Andrews noted that
in response to an SSRI, the brain diminishes its own serotonergic activity, and thus develops an "oppositional tolerance"
to the drug. When the antidepressant is withdrawn, the "oppositional forces" that have arisen in response to the drug operate "unopposed," and this may increase the risk of relapse,
he wrote.[24]

- In a somewhat similar vein, French researchers, in a study of
more than 35,000 first-episode patients, found that the
longer patients were treated with an antidepressant before
withdrawing from it, the higher the rate of relapse. Those
who were exposed to an antidepressant for longer than six

months had more than twice the risk of relapse compared to those exposed for less than one month.[25]

With such findings appearing in the medical literature, Giovanna Fava revisited this issue of the long-term effects of antidepressants in 2011. Researchers were reporting that initial exposure to an antidepressant increased the risk of relapse upon drug withdrawal, and they were speculating that this was due to "oppositional tolerance"—the brain's attempt to compensate for the presence of the drug.* Fava summed up the research in this way: "When we prolong treatment over 6–9 months, we may recruit processes that oppose the initial acute effects of antidepressant drugs." These drug-induced changes "may propel the illness to a malignant and treatment-unresponsive course."[26]

All of these researchers, as they wrote about oppositional tolerance, were seeking to provide a biological explanation for the poor long-term outcomes seen in depressed patients treated with SSRIs. In 2011, American psychiatrist Rif El-Mallakh tackled this topic in a paper titled "Tardive Dysphoria: The Role of Long-Term Antidepressant Use in Inducing Chronic Depression." In the early 1990s, before the widespread use of SSRIs, only about 10 percent to 15 percent of patients with major depression ended up "treatment-resistant," he noted. Fifteen years later, researchers were reporting that nearly 40 percent of drug-treated patients were now ending up in this chronically depressed state.[27] Even when patients initially have a good response to an SSRI, El-Mallakh observed, they may end up with chronic depression. Up to 80 percent of patients maintained on antidepressants suffer a recurrence of symptoms, and once that "initial treatment response is lost," continued efforts to treat the relapsed patient with an antidepressant frequently results in "poor response and the rise of treatment-resistant depression." El-Mallakh also noted that people treated with antidepressants for other reasons—anxiety, and so forth—often became depressed, evidence that

---

* This is the compensatory process described by Stephen Hyman in 1996 (pages 83–84), and also described by Giovanna Fava in his writings on antidepressants (pages 159–160).

antidepressants could induce depression over the long term. Having reviewed the relevant literature, he proposed this hypothesis:

> A chronic and treatment-resistant depressive state is proposed to occur in individuals who are exposed to potent antagonists of serotonin reuptake pumps (SSRIs) for prolonged time periods. Due to the delay in the onset of this chronic depressive state, it is labeled tardive dysphoria. Tardive dysphoria manifests as a chronic dysphoric state that is initially transiently relieved by—but ultimately becomes unresponsive to—antidepressant medication. Serotonergic antidepressants may be of particular importance in the development of tardive dysphoria.

There was one other haunting possibility raised by both Fava and El-Mallakh. Both worried that after a person has been on an SSRI for a longer period of time, the brain may not be able to return to normal functioning even after the drug is withdrawn. At least in some people, the drug-induced changes might be permanent. El-Mallakh, as he concluded his paper, wrote what might be considered a black box warning for all psychiatric drugs: "Continued drug treatment may induce processes that are the opposite of what the medication originally produced." This may "cause a worsening of the illness, continue for a period of time after discontinuation of the medication, and may not be reversible."

Stimulants: No Long-Term Benefit

The NIMH's MTA study of ADHD treatments is still seen as the best long-term study of stimulants that has ever been done. That study found that stimulants did not provide any benefit, on any domain, over the long term, and, if anything, it showed worse outcomes for the medicated patients at the end of three years and six years. More recent studies of Australian children and Quebec youth have produced the same result.

In 2009, the Western Australian Department of Health, in a study of the ten-year outcomes of children with ADHD, reported that by the end of the study, the medicated youth had slightly worse ADHD symptoms, elevated blood pressure, and were ten times more likely to be identified by teachers as performing poorly in school than the unmedicated youth. The researchers concluded that treating ADHD with stimulants does not translate into long-term benefits to the child's social and emotional outcomes, school-based performance, or symptom improvement.[28]

The Canadian Institutes of Health Research funded the Quebec study, which relied on data from the National Longitudinal Survey of Canadian Youth. In 1994, Canadian researchers surveyed more than 16,000 children, ages 0 to 11, and then followed their progress through childhood, with follow-up assessments done every two years, through 2008. This data set provided information on whether the children had symptoms of ADHD, and the investigators in this study assessed whether prescribing stimulants to such youth translated into better long-term outcomes. Here is what the researchers found:

> The increase in medication use is associated with increases in unhappiness and a deterioration in relationship with parents. These emotional and social effects are concentrated among girls, who also experience increases in anxiety and depression. We also see some evidence of deterioration in contemporaneous educational outcomes including grade repetition and mathematics scores. When we turn to an examination of long-term outcomes, we find that increases in medication use are associated with increases in the probability that boys dropped out of school and with marginal increases in the probability that girls have ever been diagnosed with a mental or emotional disorder.[29]

The prescribing of stimulants to ADHD youth began to take off in the 1980s, and today, thirty years later, studies have failed to show that this treatment helps children grow up and thrive. In a 2012 op-ed published in the *New York Times*, Alan Sroufe, a professor of psychology at the University of Minnesota's Institute of Child Development, told of this bottom-line finding: "To date, no study has found any long-term benefit of attention-deficit medication on academic performance, peer relationships, or behavior problems, the very things we want to improve. . . . The drugs can also have serious side effects, including stunting growth."[30]

Finally, in 2014, Spanish investigators published an "exhaustive review" of the "scientific evidence regarding the short and long term effectiveness" of stimulants for ADHD. "The result," they concluded, "is disappointing and should lead to a modification of the CPGs [clinical practice guidelines] to the use of drugs as tools of last resort, in a small number of cases and limited and short periods of time."[31]

Anatomy Four Years Later

This book, when published in 2010, set forth a provocative argument. While psychiatric medications may be effective over the short term, and while some people may fare well on them over longer periods of time, on the whole they worsen the long-term outcomes of major mental disorders. They increase the likelihood that a person will become chronically ill, and ill with new and more severe symptoms.

In science, the past should help predict the future. If research over a fifty-year period told of medications that worsened long-term outcomes, then studies published since 2010 should corroborate that essential finding. That has been the case here. The updated research deepens what might be called the "case against psychiatric drugs." And given that this is so, it would seem that psychiatry and our society now have more reason than ever to fundamentally rethink the use of these medications and our current drug-based paradigm of care.

To read many of the source documents listed here, go to madinamerica.com or robertwhitaker.org

Chapter 1: A Modern Plague

1. J. Bronowski, *The Ascent of Man* (New York: Little, Brown & Co., 1973), 153.
2. IMS Health, "2007 top therapeutic classes by U.S. sales."
3. U.S. Department of Health and Human Services, *Mental Health: A Report of the Surgeon General* (1999), 3, 68, 78.
4. E. Shorter, *A History of Psychiatry* (New York: John Wiley & Sons, 1997), 255.
5. R. Friedman, "On the Horizon, Personalized Depression Drugs," *New York Times,* June 19, 2007.
6. *Boston Globe* editorial, "When Kids Need Meds," June 22, 2007.
7. Address by Carolyn Robinowitz, APA Annual Conference, Washington, D.C., May 4, 2008.
8. C. Silverman, *The Epidemiology of Depression* (Baltimore: Johns Hopkins Press, 1968), 139.
9. Social Security Administration, annual statistical reports on the SSDI and SSI programs, 1987–2008. To calculate a total disability number for 1987 and 2007, I added the number of recipients under age sixty-five receiving an SSI payment that year and the number receiving an SSDI payment due to mental illness, and then I adjusted the total to reflect the fact that one in every six SSDI recipients also receives an SSI payment. Thus, mathematically speaking: SSI recipients + (.833 × SSDI recipients) = total number of disabled mentally ill.
10. Silverman, *The Epidemiology of Depression,* 139.
11. The annual Social Security Administration reports don't provide data on the specific

diagnoses of SSI and SSDI recipients disabled by mental illness. However, various researchers have reported that affective disorders now make up 37 percent (or more) of the disabled mentally ill. See, for instance, J. Cook, "Results of a multi-site clinical trials study of employment models for mental health consumers," available at: psych.uic.edu/EIDP/eidp-3-20-03.pdf.

12. U.S. Government Accountability Office, "Young adults with serious mental illness" (June 2008).

13. Social Security Administration, annual statistical reports on the SSI program, 1996–2008; and *Social Security Bulletin, Annual Statistical Supplement,* 1988–1992.

Chapter 2: Anecdotal Thoughts

1. Adlai Stevenson, speech at University of Wisconsin, October 8, 1952. As cited by L. Frank, *Quotationary* (New York: Random House, 2001), 430.

Chapter 3: The Roots of an Epidemic

1. J. Young, *The Medical Messiahs* (Princeton, NJ: Princeton University Press, 1967), 281.

2. Chemical Heritage Foundation, "Paul Ehrlich, Pharmaceutical Achiever," accessed at chemheritage.org.

3. P. de Kruif, *Dr. Ehrlich's Magic Bullet* (New York: Pocket Books, 1940), 387.

4. L. Sutherland, *Magic Bullets* (Boston: Little, Brown and Company, 1956), 127.

5. L. Garrett, *The Coming Plague* (New York: Penguin, 1995), 49.

6. T. Mahoney, *The Merchants of Life* (New York: Harper & Brothers, 1959), 14.

7. "Mind Is Mapped in Cure of Insane," *New York Times,* May 15, 1937.

8. "Surgery Used on the Soul-Sick," *New York Times,* June 7, 1937.

9. A. Deutsch, *The Shame of the States* (New York: Harcourt Brace, 1948), 41.

10. E. Torrey, *The Invisible Plague* (New Brunswick, NJ: Rutgers University Press, 2001), 295.

11. G. Grob, *The Mad Among Us* (Cambridge, MA: Harvard University Press, 1994), 189.

12. "Need for Public Education on Psychiatry Is Stressed," *New York Times,* November 16, 1947.

Chapter 4: Psychiatry's Magic Bullets

1. E. Valenstein, *Blaming the Brain* (New York: The Free Press, 1998), 38.

2. J. Swazey, *Chlorpromazine in Psychiatry* (Cambridge, MA: MIT Press, 1974), 78.

3. Ibid, 79.

4. Ibid, 105.

5. Ibid, 134–35.

6. F. Ayd Jr., *Discoveries in Biological Psychiatry* (Philadelphia: Lippincott, 1970), 160.

7. Symposium proceedings, *Chlorpromazine and Mental Health* (Philadelphia: Lea and Fabiger, 1955), 132.

8. Ayd, *Discoveries in Biological Psychiatry,* 121.

9. M. Smith, *Small Comfort* (New York: Praeger, 1985), 23.

10. Ibid, 26.

11. Ibid, 72.

12. "TB and Hope," *Time*, March 3, 1952.

13. Valenstein, *Blaming the Brain*, 38.

14. "TB Drug Is Tried in Mental Cases," *New York Times*, April 7, 1957.

15. M. Mintz, *The Therapeutic Nightmare* (Boston: Houghton Mifflin, 1965), 166.

16. Ibid, 488.

17. Ibid, 481.

18. Ibid, 59, 62.

19. T. Mahoney, *The Merchants of Life* (New York: Harper & Brothers, 1959), 4, 16.

20. Mintz, *The Therapeutic Nightmare*, 83.

21. Swazey, *Chlorpromazine in Psychiatry*, 190.

22. "Wonder Drug of 1954?" *Time*, June 14, 1954.

23. "Pills for the Mind," *Time*, March 7, 1955.

24. "Wonder Drugs: New Cures for Mental Ills?" *U.S. News and World Report*, June 17, 1955.

25. "Pills for the Mind," *Time*, March 7, 1955.

26. "Don't-Give-a-Damn Pills," *Time*, February 27, 1956.

27. Smith, *Small Comfort*, 67–69.

28. "To Nirvana with Miltown," *Time*, July 7, 1958.

29. "Wonder Drug of 1954?" *Time*, June 14, 1954.

30. "TB Drug Is Tried in Mental Cases," *New York Times*, April 7, 1957.

31. Smith, *Small Comfort*, 70.

32. "Science Notes: Mental Drug Shows Promise," *New York Times*, April 7, 1957.

33. "Drugs and Depression," *New York Times*, September 6, 1959.

34. H. Himwich, "Psychopharmacologic drugs," *Science* 127 (1958): 59–72.

35. Smith, *Small Comfort*, 110.

36. Ibid, 104.

37. The NIMH Psychopharmacology Service Center Collaborative Study Group, "Phenothiazine treatment in acute schizophrenia," *Archives of General Psychiatry* 10 (1964): 246–61.

38. Valenstein, *Blaming the Brain*, 70–79. Also see David Healy, *The Creation of Psychopharmacology* (Cambridge, MA: Harvard University Press, 2002), 106, 205–206.

39. J. Schildkraut, "The catecholamine hypothesis of affective disorders," *American Journal of Psychiatry* 122 (1965): 509–22.

40. Valenstein, *Blaming the Brain*, 82.

41. A. Baumeister, "Historical development of the dopamine hypothesis of schizophrenia," *Journal of the History of the Neurosciences* 11 (2002): 265–77.

42. Swazey, *Chlorpromazine in Psychiatry*, 4.

43. Ibid, 8.

44. Ayd, *Discoveries in Biological Psychiatry*, 215–16.

45. Ibid, 127.

46. Ibid, 195.

Chapter 5: The Hunt for Chemical Imbalances

1. T. H. Huxley, *Critiques and Addresses* (London: Macmillan & Co., 1873), 229.

2. E. Azmitia, "Awakening the sleeping giant," *Journal of Clinical Psychiatry* 52 (1991), suppl. 12: 4–16.

3. M. Bowers, "Cerebrospinal fluid 5-hydroxyindoleacetic acid and homovanillic acid in psychiatric patients," *International Journal of Neuropharmacology* 8 (1969): 255–62.

4. R. Papeschi, "Homovanillic and 5-hydroxyindoleacetic acid in cerebrospinal fluid of depressed patients," *Archives of General Psychiatry* 25 (1971): 354–58.

5. M. Bowers, "Lumbar CSF 5-hydroxyindoleacetic acid and homovanillic acid in affective syndromes," *Journal of Nervous and Mental Disease* 158 (1974): 325–30.

6. D. L. Davies, "Reserpine in the treatment of anxious and depressed patients," *Lancet* 2 (1955): 117–20.

7. J. Mendels, "Brain biogenic amine depletion and mood," *Archives of General Psychiatry* 30 (1974): 447–51.

8. M. Asberg, "Serotonin depression: A biochemical subgroup within the affective disorders?" *Science* 191 (1976): 478–80; M. Asberg, "5-HIAA in the cerebrospinal fluid," *Archives of General Psychiatry* 33 (1976): 1193–97.

9. H. Nagayama, "Postsynaptic action by four antidepressive drugs in an animal model of depression," *Pharmacology Biochemistry and Behavior* 15 (1981): 125–30. Also see H. Nagayama, "Action of chronically administered antidepressants on the serotonergic postsynapse in a model of depression," *Pharmacology Biochemistry and Behavior* 25 (1986): 805–11.

10. J. Maas, "Pretreatment neurotransmitter metabolite levels and response to tricyclic antidepressant drugs," *American Journal of Psychiatry* 141 (1984): 1159–71.

11. J. Lacasse, "Serotonin and depression: a disconnect between the advertisements and the scientific literature," *PLoS Medicine* 2 (2005): 1211–16.

12. C. Ross, *Pseudoscience in Biological Psychiatry* (New York: John Wiley & Sons, 1995), 111.

13. Lacasse, "Serotonin and depression."

14. D. Healy, "Ads for SSRI antidepressants are misleading," *PLoS Medicine* news release, November 2005.

15. I. Creese, "Dopamine receptor binding predicts clinical and pharmacological potencies of antischizophrenic drugs," *Science* 192 (1976): 481–83; P. Seeman, "Antipsychotic drug doses and neuroleptic/dopamine receptors," *Nature* 261 (1976): 177–79.

16. "Schizophrenia: Vast effort focuses on four areas," *New York Times*, November 13, 1979.

17. M. Bowers, "Central dopamine turnover in schizophrenic syndromes," *Archives of General Psychiatry* 31 (1974): 50–54.

18. R. Post, "Cerebrospinal fluid amine metabolites in acute schizophrenia," *Archives of General Psychiatry* 32 (1975): 1063–68.

19. J. Haracz, "The dopamine hypothesis: an overview of studies with schizophrenic patients," *Schizophrenia Bulletin* 8 (1982): 438–58.

20. T. Lee, "Binding of ^{3}H-neuroleptics and ^{3}H-apomorphine in schizophrenic brains," *Nature* 374 (1978): 897–900.

21. D. Burt, "Antischizophrenic drugs: chronic treatment elevates dopamine receptor binding in brain," *Science* 196 (1977): 326–27.

22. M. Porceddu, "[^{3}H]SCH 23390 binding sites increase after chronic blockade of d-1 dopamine receptors," *European Journal of Pharmacology* 118 (1985): 367–70.

23. A. MacKay, "Increased brain dopamine and dopamine receptors in schizophrenia," *Archives of General Psychiatry* 39 (1982): 991–97.

24. J. Kornhuber, "^{3}H-spiperone binding sites in post-mortem brains from schizophrenic patients," *Journal of Neural Transmission* 75 (1989): 1–10.

25. J. Martinot, "Striatal D_2 dopaminergic receptors assessed with positron emission tomography and bromospiperone in untreated schizophrenic patients," *American Journal of Psychiatry* 147 (1990): 44–50; L. Farde, "D_2 dopamine receptors in neuroleptic-naïve schizophrenic patients," *Archives of General Psychiatry* 47 (1990): 213–19; J. Hietala, "Striatal D_2 dopamine receptor characteristics in neuroleptic-naïve schizophrenic patients studied with positron emission tomography," *Archives of General Psychiatry* 51 (1994): 116–23.

26. P. Deniker, "The neuroleptics: a historical survey," *Acta Psychiatrica Scandinavica* 82, suppl. 358 (1990): 83–87. Also: "From chlorpromazine to tardive dyskinesia," *Psychiatric Journal of the University of Ottawa* 14 (1989): 253–59.

27. J. Kane, "Towards more effective antipsychotic treatment," *British Journal of Psychiatry* 165, suppl. 25 (1994): 22–31.

28. E. Nestler and S. Hyman, *Molecular Neuropharmacology* (New York: McGraw Hill, 2002), 392.

29. J. Mendels, "Brain biogenic amine depletion and mood," *Archives of General Psychiatry* 30 (1974): 447–51.

30. P. Deniker, "The neuroleptics: a historical survey," *Acta Psychiatrica Scandinavica* 82, suppl. 358 (1990): 83–87. Also: "From chlorpromazine to tardive dyskinesia," *Psychiatric Journal of the University of Ottawa* 14 (1989): 253–59.

31. D. Healy, *The Creation of Psychopharmacology* (Cambridge, MA: Harvard University Press, 2002), 217.

32. E. Valenstein, *Blaming the Brain* (New York: The Free Press, 1998), 96.

33. U.S. Department of Health and Human Services, *Mental Health: A Report of the Surgeon General* (1999), 3, 68, 78.

34. J. Glenmullen, *Prozac Backlash* (New York: Simon & Schuster, 2000), 196.

35. Lacasse, "Serotonin and depression."

36. R. Fuller, "Effect of an uptake inhibitor on serotonin metabolism in rat brain," *Life Sciences* 15 (1974): 1161–71.

37. D. Wong, "Subsensitivity of serotonin receptors after long-term treatment of rats with fluoxetine," *Research Communications in Chemical Pathology and Pharmacology* 32 (1981): 41–51.

38. J. Wamsley, "Receptor alterations associated with serotonergic agents," *Journal of Clinical Psychiatry* 48, suppl. (1987): 19–25.

39. A. Schatzberg, *Textbook of Psychopharmacology* (Washington, DC: American Psychiatric Press, 1995), 8.

40. C. Montigny, "Modification of serotonergic neuron properties by long-term treatment with serotonin reuptake blockers," *Journal of Clinical Psychiatry* 51, suppl. B (1990): 4–8.

41. D. Wong, "Subsensitivity of serotonin receptors after long-term treatment of rats with fluoxetine," *Research Communications in Chemical Pathology and Pharmacology* 32 (1981): 41–51.

42. C. Montigny, "Modification of serotonergic neuron properties by long-term treatment with serotonin reuptake blockers," *Journal of Clinical Psychiatry* 51, suppl. B (1990): 4–8.

43. R. Fuller, "Inhibition of serotonin reuptake," *Federation Proceedings* 36 (1977): 2154–58.

44. B. Jacobs, "Serotonin and behavior," *Journal of Clinical Psychiatry* 52, suppl. (1991): 151–62.

45. Schatzberg, *Textbook of Psychopharmacology,* 619.

46. S. Hyman, "Initiation and adaptation: A paradigm for understanding psychotropic drug action," *American Journal of Psychiatry* 153 (1996): 151–61.

Chapter 6: A Paradox Revealed

1. E. Stip, "Happy birthday neuroleptics!" *European Psychiatry* 17 (2002): 115–19.

2. M. Boyle, "Is schizophrenia what it was?" *Journal of the History of Behavioral Science* 26 (1990): 323–33; M. Boyle, *Schizophrenia: A Scientific Delusion?* (New York: Routledge, 1990).

3. P. Popenoe, "In the melting pot," *Journal of Heredity* 14 (1923): 223.

4. J. Cole, editor, *Psychopharmacology* (Washington, DC: National Academy of Sciences, 1959), 142.

5. Ibid, 386–87.

6. N. Lehrman, "Follow-up of brief and prolonged psychiatric hospitalization," *Comprehensive Psychiatry* 2 (1961): 227–40.

7. R. Warner, *Recovery from Schizophrenia* (Boston: Routledge & Kegan Paul, 1985), 74.

8. L. Epstein, "An approach to the effect of ataraxic drugs on hospital release rates," *American Journal of Psychiatry* 119 (1962): 246–61.

9. C. Silverman, *The Epidemiology of Depression* (Baltimore: Johns Hopkins Press, 1968), 139.

10. J. Swazey, *Chlorpromazine in Psychiatry* (Cambridge, MA: MIT Press, 1974), 247.

11. Cole, *Psychopharmacology,* 144, 285.

12. Ibid, 285.

13. Ibid, 347.

14. R. Baldessarini, *Chemotherapy in Psychiatry* (Cambridge, MA: Harvard University Press, 1977), 29.

15. A. Schatzberg, editor, *Textbook of Psychopharmacology* (Washington, DC: American Psychiatric Press, 1995), 624.

16. P. Gilbert, "Neuroleptic withdrawal in schizophrenic patients," *Archives of General Psychiatry* 52 (1995): 173–88.

17. J. Geddes, "Prevention of relapse," *New England Journal of Medicine* 346 (2002): 56–58.

18. L. Dixon, "Conventional antipsychotic medications for schizophrenia." *Schizophrenia Bulletin* 21 (1995): 567–77.

19. Stip, "Happy birthday, neuroleptics!"

20. N. Schooler, "One year after discharge," *American Journal of Psychiatry* 123 (1967): 986–95.

21. R. Prien, "Discontinuation of chemotherapy for chronic schizophrenics," *Hospital and Community Psychiatry* 22 (1971): 20–23.

22. G. Gardos and J. Cole, "Maintenance antipsychotic therapy: is the cure worse than the disease?" *American Journal of Psychiatry* 133 (1977): 32–36.

23. G. Gardos and J. Cole, "Withdrawal syndromes associated with antipsychotic drugs," *American Journal of Psychiatry* 135 (1978): 1321–24. Also see Gardos and Cole, "Maintenance antipsychotic therapy."

24. J. Bockoven, "Comparison of two five-year follow-up studies," *American Journal of Psychiatry* 132 (1975): 796–801.

25. W. Carpenter, "The treatment of acute schizophrenia without drugs," *American Journal of Psychiatry* 134 (1977): 14–20.

26. M. Rappaport, "Are there schizophrenics for whom drugs may be unnecessary or contraindicated?" *International Pharmacopsychiatry* 13 (1978): 100–11.

27. S. Mathews, "A non-neuroleptic treatment for schizophrenia," *Schizophrenia Bulletin* 5 (1979): 322–32.

28. J. Bola, "Treatment of acute psychosis without neuroleptics," *Journal of Nervous and Mental Disease* 191 (2003): 219–29.

29. Carpenter, "The treatment of acute schizophrenia."

30. G. Paul, "Maintenance psychotropic drugs in the presence of active treatment programs," *Archives of General Psychiatry* 27 (1972): 106–14.

31. T. Van Putten, "The board and care home: does it deserve a bad press?" *Hospital and Community Psychiatry* 30 (1979): 461–64.

32. Gardos and Cole, "Maintenance antipsychotic therapy."

33. P. Deniker, "Are the antipsychotic drugs to be withdrawn?" in C. Shagass, editor, *Biological Psychiatry* (New York: Elsevier, 1986), 1–9.

34. G. Chouinard, "Neuroleptic-induced supersensitivity psychosis," *American Journal of Psychiatry* 135 (1978): 1409–10.

35. G. Chouinard, "Neuroleptic-induced supersensitivity psychosis: Clinical and pharmacologic characteristics," *American Journal of Psychiatry* 137 (1980): 16–20.

36. G. Chouinard, "Neuroleptic-induced supersensitivity psychosis, the 'Hump Course,' and tardive dyskinesia," *Journal of Clinical Psychopharmacology* 2 (1982): 143–44.

37. G. Chouinard, "Severe cases of neuroleptic-induced supersensitivity psychosis," *Schizophrenia Research* 5 (1991): 21–33.

38. P. Muller, "Dopaminergic supersensitivity after neuroleptics," *Psychopharmacology* 60 (1978): 1–11.

39. L. Martensson, "Should neuroleptic drugs be banned?" *Proceedings of the World Federation of Mental Health Conference in Copenhagen,* 1984, accessed via www.larsmartensson.com, 10/30/08.

40. P. Breggin, *Brain Disabling Treatments in Psychiatry* (New York: Springer Publishing Company, 1997), 60.

41. S. Snyder, *Drugs and the Brain* (New York: Scientific American Library, 1986), 88.

42. C. Harding, "The Vermont longitudinal study of persons with severe mental illness," *American Journal of Psychiatry* 144 (1987): 727–34; C. Harding, "The Vermont longitudinal study of persons with severe mental illness, II," *American Journal of Psychiatry* 144 (1987): 727–35.

43. P. McGuire, "New hope for people with schizophrenia," *APA Monitor* 31 (February 2000).

44. C. Harding, "Empirical correction of seven myths about schizophrenia with implications for treatment," *Acta Psychiatrica Scandinavica* 384, suppl. (1994): 14–16.

45. A. Jablensky, "Schizophrenia: manifestations, incidence and course in different cultures," *Psychological Medicine* 20, monograph (1992): 1–95.

46. Ibid. See tables on page 60 for medication usage by individual centers; see table on page 64 for medication usage by developing and developed countries.

47. K. Hopper, "Revisiting the developed versus developing country distinction in course and outcome in schizophrenia," *Schizophrenia Bulletin* 26 (2000): 835–46.

48. J. Wade, "Tardive dyskinesia and cognitive impairment," *Biological Psychiatry* 22 (1987): 393–95.

49. M. Myslobodsky, "Central determinants of attention and mood disorder in tardive dyskinesia," *Brain and Cognition* 23 (1993): 56–70.

50. H. Wisniewski, "Neurofibrillary pathology in brains of elderly schizophrenics treated with neuroleptics," *Alzheimer Disease and Associated Disorders* 8 (1994): 211–27.

51. M. Chakos, "Increase in caudate nuclei volumes of first-episode schizophrenic patients taking antipsychotic drugs," *American Journal of Psychiatry* 151 (1994): 1430–36; A. Madsen, "Neuroleptics in progressive structural brain abnormalities in psychiatric illness," *Lancet* 352 (1998): 784–85; R. Gur, "A follow-up of magnetic resonance imaging study of schizophrenia," *Archives of General Psychiatry* 55 (1998): 145–52.

52. R. Gur, "Subcortical MRI volumes in neuroleptic-naïve and treated patients with schizophrenia," *American Journal of Psychiatry* 155 (1998): 1711–17.

53. P. Seeman, "Dopamine supersensitivity correlates with D$_2$ HIGH states, implying many paths to psychosis," *Proceedings of the National Academy of Science* 102 (2005): 3513–18.

54. B. Ho, "Progressive structural brain abnormalities and their relationship to clinical outcome," *Archives of General Psychiatry* 60 (2003): 585–94.

55. N. Andreasen, "Longitudinal changes in neurocognition during the first decade of schizophrenia illness," *International Congress on Schizophrenia Research* (2005): 348.

56. C. Dreifus, "Using imaging to look at changes in the brain," *New York Times,* September 16, 2008.

57. T. McGlashan, "Rationale and parameters for medication-free research in psychosis," *Schizophrenia Bulletin* 32 (2006): 300–302.

58. M. Harrow, "Factors involved in outcome and recovery in schizophrenia patients not on antipsychotic medications," *Journal of Nervous and Mental Disease* 195 (2007): 406–14.

59. National Institute of Mental Health, "The Numbers Count," accessed at www.nimh.nih.gov on 3/7/2008.

Chapter 7: The Benzo Trap

1. S. Garfield, "Valium's 40th Birthday," *Observer,* February 2, 2003.

2. E. Shorter, *A History of Psychiatry* (New York: John Wiley & Sons, 1997), 161, 181.

3. A. Tone, *The Age of Anxiety* (New York: Basic Books, 2009), 15.

4. American Psychiatry Association, *Diagnostic and Statistical Manual of Mental Disorders* (1952), 31.

5. C. Silverman, *The Epidemiology of Depression* (Baltimore: Johns Hopkins Press, 1968), 139.

6. L. Hollister, "Drugs for emotional disorders," *Journal of the American Medical Association* 234 (1975): 942–47.

7. F. Ayd Jr., *Discoveries in Biological Psychiatry* (Philadelphia: Lippincott, 1970), 127.

8. D. Greenblatt, "Meprobamate: a study of irrational drug use," *American Journal of Psychiatry* 127 (1971): 33–39.

9. C. Essig, "Addiction to nonbarbiturate sedative and tranquillizing drugs," *Clinical Pharmacology & Therapeutics* 5 (1964): 334–43.

10. "Letdown for Miltown," *Time,* April 30, 1965.

11. Tone, *The Age of Anxiety,* 171.

12. M. Smith, *Small Comfort* (New York: Praeger, 1985), 78.

13. Tone, *The Age of Anxiety,* 172.

14. G. Cant, "Valiumania," *New York Times,* February 1, 1976.

15. R. Hughes, *The Tranquilizing of America* (New York: Harcourt Brace Jovanovich, 1979), 8.

16. Tone, *The Age of Anxiety,* 176.

17. Committee on the Review of Medicines, "Systematic review of the benzodiazepines," *British Medical Journal* 280 (1980): 910–12.

18. Editorial, "Benzodiazepines on trial," *British Medical Journal* 288 (1984): 1101–12.

19. Smith, *Small Comfort,* 32.

20. S. Stahl, "Don't ask, don't tell, but benzodiazepines are still the leading treatments for anxiety disorder," *Journal of Clinical Psychiatry* 63 (2002): 756–67.

21. IMS Health, "Top therapeutic classes by U.S. dispensed prescriptions," 2006 and 2007 reports.

22. K. Solomon, "Pitfalls and prospects in clinical research on antianxiety drugs," *Journal of Clinical Psychiatry* 39 (1978): 823–31.

23. A. Shapiro, "Diazepam: how much better than placebo?" *Journal of Psychiatric Research* 17 (1983): 51–73.

24. C. Gudex, "Adverse effects of benzodiazepines," *Social Science & Medicine* 33 (1991): 587–96.

25. J. Martin, "Benzodiazepines in generalized anxiety disorder," *Journal of Psychopharmacology* 21 (2007): 774–82.

26. Malcolm Lader interview, January 12, 2009.

27. B. Maletzky, "Addiction to diazepam," *International Journal of Addictions* 11 (1976): 95–115.

28. A. Kales, "Rebound insomnia," *Science* 201 (1978): 1039–40.

29. H. Petursson, "Withdrawal from long-term benzodiazepine treatment," *British Medical Journal* 283 (1981): 643–35.

30. H. Ashton, "Benzodiazepine withdrawal," *British Medical Journal* 288 (1984): 1135–40.

31. H. Ashton, "Protracted withdrawal syndromes from benzodiazepines," *Journal of Substance Abuse Treatment* 9 (1991): 19–28.

32. P. Cowen, "Abstinence symptoms after withdrawal of tranquillising drugs," *Lancet* 2, 8294 (1982): 360–62.

33. H. Ashton, "Benzodiazepine withdrawal," *British Medical Journal* 288 (1984): 1135–40.

34. H. Ashton, *Benzodiazepines: How They Work and How to Withdraw* (Newcastle upon Tyne: University of Newcastle, 2000), 42.

35. H. Ashton, "Protracted withdrawal syndromes from benzodiazepines," *Journal of Substance Abuse Treatment* 9 (1991): 19–28.

36. K. Rickels, "Long-term benzodiazepine users 3 years after participation in a discontinuation program," *American Journal of Psychiatry* 148 (1991): 757–61.

37. K. Rickels, "Psychomotor performance of long-term benzodiazepine users before, during, and after benzodiazepine discontinuation," *Journal of Clinical Psychopharmacology* 19 (1999): 107–13.

38. S. Patten, "Self-reported depressive symptoms following treatment with corticosteroids and sedative-hypnotics," *International Journal of Psychiatry in Medicine* 26 (1995): 15–24.

39. Ashton, *Benzodiazepines*, 8.

40. A. Pelissolo, "Anxiety and depressive disorders in 4,425 long term benzodiazepine users in general practice," *Encephale* 33 (2007): 32–38.

41. Hughes, *The Tranquilizing of America*, 17.

42. S. Golombok, "Cognitive impairment in long-term benzodiazepine users," *Psychological Medicine* 18 (1988): 365–74.

43. M. Barker, "Cognitive effects of long-term benzodiazepine use," *CNS Drugs* 18 (2004): 37–48.

44. WHO Review Group, "Use and abuse of benzodiazepines," *Bulletin of the World Health Organization* 61 (1983): 551–62.

45. Maletzky, "Addiction to diazepam."

46. R. Caplan, "Social effects of diazepam use," *Social Science & Medicine* 21 (1985): 887–98.

47. H. Ashton, "Tranquillisers," *British Journal of Addiction* 84 (1989): 541–46.

48. Ashton, *Benzodiazepines*, 12.

49. Stevan Gressitt interview, January 9, 2009.

50. U.S. Department of Health & Human Services, SAMHSA, *Mental Health, United States* (2002).

51. Government Accountability Office, *Young Adults with Serious Mental Illness,* June 2008.

52. R. Vasile, "Results of a naturalistic longitudinal study of benzodiazepine and SSRI use in the treatment of generalized anxiety disorder and social phobia," *Depression and Anxiety* 22 (2005): 59–67.

53. Malcolm Lader interview, January 12, 2009.

Chapter 8: An Episodic Illness Turns Chronic

1. C. Dewa, "Depression in the workplace," A Report to the Ontario Roundtable on Appropriate Prescribing, November 2001.

2. A. Solomon, *The Noonday Demon* (New York: Simon & Schuster, 2001), 289.

3. C. Goshen, editor, *Documentary History of Psychiatry* (New York: Philosophical Library, 1967), 118–20.

4. Solomon, *The Noonday Demon*, 286.

5. E. Wolpert, editor, *Manic-Depressive Illness* (New York: International Universities Press, 1977), 34.

6. C. Silverman, *The Epidemiology of Depression* (Baltimore: Johns Hopkins Press, 1968), 44, 139. The first-admission and residence data in Silverman's book is for all manic-depressive patients; the unipolar patients comprised about 75 percent of that total.

7. Ibid, 79, 142.

8. F. Ayd, *Recognizing the Depressed Patient* (New York: Grune & Stratton, 1961), 13.

9. A. Zis, "Major affective disorder as a recurrent illness," *Archives of General Psychiatry* 36 (1979): 835–39.

10. G. Winokur, *Manic Depressive Illness* (St. Louis: The C.V. Mosby Company, 1969), 19–20.

11. T. Rennie, "Prognosis in manic-depressive psychoses," *American Journal of Psychiatry* 98 (1941): 801–14. See table on page 811.

12. G. Lundquist, "Prognosis and course in manic-depressive psychoses," *Acta Psychiatrica Scandinavica*, suppl. 35 (1945): 7–93.

13. D. Schuyler, *The Depressive Spectrum* (New York: Jason Aronson, 1974), 49.

14. J. Cole, "Therapeutic efficacy of antidepressant drugs," *Journal of the American Medical Association* 190 (1964): 448–55.

15. N. Kline, "The practical management of depression," *Journal of the American Medical Association* 190 (1964): 122–30.

16. Winokur, *Manic Depressive Illness*, 19.

17. Schuyler, *The Depressive Spectrum*, 47.

18. Medical Research Council, "Clinical trial of the treatment of depressive illness," *British Medical Journal* 1 (1965): 881–86.

19. A. Smith, "Studies on the effectiveness of antidepressant drugs," *Psychopharmacology Bulletin* 5 (1969): 1–53.

20. A. Raskin, "Differential response to chlorpromazine, imipramine, and placebo," *Archives of General Psychiatry* 23 (1970): 164–73.

21. R. Thomson, "Side effects and placebo amplification," *British Journal of Psychiatry* 140 (1982): 64–68.

22. I. Elkin, "NIMH treatment of depression collaborative research program," *Archives of General Psychiatry* 47 (1990): 682–88.

23. A. Khan, "Symptom reduction and suicide risk in patients treated with placebo in antidepressant clinical trials," *Archives of General Psychiatry* 57 (2000): 311–17.

24. E. Turner, "Selective publication of antidepressant trials and its influence on apparent efficacy," *New England Journal of Medicine* 358 (2008): 252–60.

25. I. Kirsch, "Initial severity and antidepressant benefits," *PLoS Medicine* 5 (2008): 260–68.

26. G. Parker, "Antidepressants on trial," *British Journal of Psychiatry* 194 (2009): 1–3.

27. C. Barbui, "Effectiveness of paroxetine in the treatment of acute major depression in adults," *Canadian Medical Association Journal* 178 (2008): 296–305.

28. J. Ioannidis, "Effectiveness of antidepressants," *Philosophy, Ethics, and Humanities in Medicine* 3 (2008): 14.

29. Hypericum Trial Study Group, "Effect of Hypericum perforatum in major depressive disorder," *Journal of the American Medical Association* 287 (2002): 1807–14.

30. J.D. Van Scheyen, "Recurrent vital depressions," *Psychiatria, Neurologia, Neurochirurgia* 76 (1973): 93–112.

31. Ibid.

32. R. Mindham, "An evaluation of continuation therapy with tricyclic antidepressants in depressive illness," *Psychological Medicine* 3 (1973): 5–17.

33. M. Stein, "Maintenance therapy with amitriptyline," *American Journal of Psychiatry* 137 (1980): 370–71.

34. R. Prien, "Drug therapy in the prevention of recurrences in unipolar and bipolar affective disorders," *Archives of General Psychiatry* 41 (1984): 1096–1104. See table 6 and figure 2.

35. M. Shea, "Course of depressive symptoms over follow-up," *Archives of General Psychiatry* 49 (1992): 782–87.

36. A. Viguera, "Discontinuing antidepressant treatment in major depression," *Harvard Review of Psychiatry* 5 (1998): 293–305.

37. P. Haddad, "Antidepressant discontinuation reactions," *British Medical Journal* 316 (1998): 1105–6.

38. G. Fava, "Do antidepressant and antianxiety drugs increase chronicity in affective disorders?" *Psychotherapy and Psychosomatics* 61 (1994): 125–31.

39. G. Fava, "Can long-term treatment with antidepressant drugs worsen the course of depression?" *Journal of Clinical Psychiatry* 64 (2003): 123–33.

40. Ibid.

41. G. Fava, "Holding on: depression, sensitization by antidepressant drugs, and the prodigal experts," *Psychotherapy and Psychosomatics* 64 (1995): 57–61; G. Fava, "Potential sensitizing effects of antidepressant drugs on depression," *CNS Drugs* 12 (1999): 247–56.

42. R. Baldessarini, "Risks and implications of interrupting maintenance psychotropic drug therapy," *Psychotherapy and Psychosomatics* 63 (1995): 137–41.

43. R. El-Mallakh, "Can long-term antidepressant use be depressogenic?" *Journal of Clinical Psychiatry* 60 (1999): 263.

44. "Editorial sparks debate on effects of psychoactive drugs," *Psychiatric News,* May 20, 1994.

45. Consensus Development Panel, "Mood disorders," *American Journal of Psychiatry* 142 (1985): 469–76.

46. R. Hales, editor, *Textbook of Psychiatry* (Washington, DC: American Psychiatric Press, 1999), 525.

47. J. Geddes, "Relapse prevention with antidepressant drug treatment in depressive disorders," *Lancet* 361 (2003): 653–61.

48. L. Judd, "Does incomplete recovery from first lifetime major depressive episode herald a chronic course of illness?" *American Journal of Psychiatry* 157 (2000): 1501–4.

49. R. Tranter, "Prevalence and outcome of partial remission in depression," *Journal of Psychiatry and Neuroscience* 27 (2002): 241–47.

50. Hales, *Textbook of Psychiatry,* 547.

51. J. Rush, "One-year clinical outcomes of depressed public sector outpatients," *Biological Psychiatry* 56 (2004): 46–53.

52. Ibid.

53. D. Warden, "The star*d project results," *Current Psychiatry Reports* 9 (2007): 449–59.

54. NIMH, *Depression* (2007): 3. (NIH Publication 07–3561.)

55. D. Deshauer, "Selective serotonin reuptake inhibitors for unipolar depression," *Canadian Medical Association Journal* 178 (2008): 1293–1301.

56. C. Ronalds, "Outcome of anxiety and depressive disorders in primary care," *British Journal of Psychiatry* 171 (1997): 427–33.

57. E. Weel-Baumgarten, "Treatment of depression related to recurrence," *Journal of Clinical Pharmacy and Therapeutics* 25 (2000): 61–66.

58. S. Patten, "The impact of antidepressant treatment on population health," *Population Health Metrics* 2 (2004): 9.

59. D. Goldberg, "The effect of detection and treatment on the outcome of major depression in primary care," *British Journal of General Practice* 48 (1998): 1840–44.

60. Dewa, "Depression in the workplace."

61. W. Coryell, "Characteristics and significance of untreated major depressive disorder," *American Journal of Psychiatry* 152 (1995): 1124–29.

62. J. Moncrieff, "Trends in sickness benefits in Great Britain and the contribution of mental disorders," *Journal of Public Health Medicine* 22 (2000): 59–67.

63. T. Helgason, "Antidepressants and public health in Iceland," *British Journal of Psychiatry* 184 (2004): 157–62.

64. R. Rosenheck, "The growth of psychopharmacology in the 1990s," *International Journal of Law and Psychiatry* 28 (2005): 467–83.

65. M. Posternak, "The naturalistic course of unipolar major depression in the absence of somatic therapy," *Journal of Nervous and Mental Disease* 194 (2006): 324–29.

66. Ibid. Also see M. Posternak, "Untreated short-term course of major depression," *Journal of Affective Disorders* 66 (2001): 139–46.

67. J. Cole, editor, *Psychopharmacology* (Washington, DC: National Academy of Sciences, 1959), 347.

68. NIMH, "The numbers count," accessed at www.nimh.nih.gov on 3/7/2008; W. Eaton, "The burden of mental disorders," *Epidemiologic Reviews* 30 (2008): 1–14.

69. M. Fava, "A cross-sectional study of the prevalence of cognitive and physical symptoms during long-term antidepressant treatment," *Journal of Clinical Psychiatry* 67 (2006): 1754–59.

70. M. Kalia, "Comparative study of fluoxetine, sibutramine, sertraline and defenfluramine on the morphology of serotonergic nerve terminals using serotonin immunohistochemistry," *Brain Research* 858 (2000): 92–105. Also see press release by Thomas Jefferson University Hospital, "Jefferson scientists show several serotonin-boosting drugs cause changes in some brain cells," 2/29/2000.

Chapter 9: The Bipolar Boom

1. D. Healy, *Mania* (Baltimore: Johns Hopkins University Press, 2008), 16, 41, 43.

2. I calculated these estimates by applying the 25 percent figure to the 1955 data on patients in state and county mental hospitals with a diagnosis of manic-depressive illness.

3. C. Silverman, *The Epidemiology of Depression* (Baltimore: Johns Hopkins University Press, 1968), 139.

4. G. Winokur, *Manic Depressive Illness* (St. Louis: The C.V. Mosby Company, 1969), 19.

5. F. Wertham, "A group of benign chronic psychoses," *American Journal of Psychiatry* 9 (1929): 17–78.

6. G. Lundquist, "Prognosis and course in manic-depressive psychoses," *Acta Psychiatrica Scandinavica,* suppl. 35 (1945): 7–93.

7. M. Tsuang, "Long-term outcome of major psychoses," *Archives of General Psychiatry* 36 (1979): 1295–1301.

8. Winokur, *Manic Depressive Illness,* 21.

9. NIMH, *The Numbers Count: Mental Disorders in America,* accessed at www.nimh.nih.gov on 3/7/2008.

10. C. Baethge, "Substance abuse in first-episode bipolar I disorder," *American Journal of Psychiatry* 162 (2005): 1008–10; E. Frank, "Association between illicit drug and

alcohol use and first manic episode," *Pharmacology Biochemistry and Behavior* 86 (2007): 395–400.

11. S. Strakowski, "The effects of antecedent substance abuse on the development of first-episode psychotic mania," *Journal of Psychiatric Research* 30 (1996): 59–68.

12. J. Goldberg, "Overdiagnosis of bipolar disorder among substance use disorder inpatients with mood instability," *Journal of Clinical Psychiatry* 69 (2008): 1751–57.

13. M. Van Laar, "Does cannabis use predict the first incidence of mood and anxiety disorders in the adult population?" *Addiction* 102 (2007): 1251–60.

14. G. Crane, "The psychiatric side effects of iproniazid," *American Journal of Psychiatry* 112 (1956): 494–501.

15. J. Angst, "Switch from depression to mania," *Psychopathology* 18 (1985): 140–54.

16. American Psychiatric Association, *Practice Guidelines for Major Depressive Disorder in Adults* (Washington, DC: APA, 1993), 22.

17. A. Martin, "Age effects on antidepressant-induced manic conversion," *Archives of Pediatrics & Adolescent Medicine* 158 (2004): 773–80.

18. J. Goldberg, "Risk for bipolar illness in patients initially hospitalized for unipolar depression," *American Journal of Psychiatry* 158 (2001): 1265–70.

19. R. El-Mallakh, "Use of antidepressants to treat depression in bipolar disorder," *Psychiatric Services* 53 (2002): 58–84.

20. Interview with Fred Goodwin, "Advances in the diagnosis and treatment of bipolar disorder," *Primary Psychiatry*, accessed via Internet on 3/6/09 at primarypsychiatry.com.

21. G. Fava, "Can long-term treatment with antidepressant drugs worsen the course of depression?" *Journal of Clinical Psychiatry* 64 (2003): 123–33.

22. L. Judd, "The prevalence and disability of bipolar spectrum disorders in the US population," *Journal of Affective Disorders* 73 (2003): 123–31.

23. J. Angst, "Toward a re-definition of subthreshold bipolarity," *Journal of Affective Disorders* 73 (2003): 133–46.

24. Ibid; Judd, "The prevalence and disability."

25. R. Fieve, *Moodswing* (New York: William Morrow and Company, 1975), 13.

26. For a history of lithium, see Healy, *Mania,* and J. Moncrieff, *The Myth of the Chemical Cure* (New York: Palgrave MacMillan, 2008).

27. S. Tyrer, "Lithium in the treatment of mania," *Journal of Affective Disorders* 8 (1985): 251–57.

28. J. Baker, "Outcomes of lithium discontinuation," *Lithium* 5 (1994): 187–92.

29. R. Baldessarini, "Discontinuing lithium maintenance treatment in bipolar disorders," *Bipolar Disorders* 1 (1999): 17–24.

30. G. Faedda, "Outcome after rapid v. gradual discontinuation of lithium treatment in bipolar disorders," *Archives of General Psychiatry* 50 (1993): 448–55.

31. J. Himmelhoch, "On the failure to recognize lithium failure," *Psychiatric Annals* 24 (1994): 241–50.

32. J. Moncrieff, *The Myth of the Chemical Cure* (London: Palgrave Macmillan, 2008), 199.

33. G. Goodwin, "Recurrence of mania after lithium withdrawal," *British Journal of Psychiatry* 164 (1994): 149–52.

34. H. Markar, "Efficacy of lithium prophylaxis in clinical practice," *British Journal of Psychiatry* 155 (1989): 496–500; J. Moncrieff, "Lithium revisited," *British Journal of Psychiatry* 167 (1995): 569–74.

35. J. Goldberg, "Lithium treatment of bipolar affective disorders under naturalistic follow-up conditions," *Psychopharmacology Bulletin* 32 (1996): 47–54.

36. M. Gitlin, "Relapse and impairment in bipolar disorder," *American Journal of Psychiatry* 152 (1995): 1635–40.

37. J. Moncrieff, "Lithium: evidence reconsidered," *British Journal of Psychiatry* 171 (1997): 113–19.

38. F. Goodwin, *Manic-Depressive Illness* (New York: Oxford University Press, 1990), 647.

39. A. Zis, "Major affective disorder as a recurrent illness," *Archives of General Psychiatry* 36 (1979): 835–39.

40. A. Koukopoulos, "Rapid cyclers, temperament, and antidepressants," *Comprehensive Psychiatry* 24 (1983): 249–58.

41. N. Ghaemi, "Diagnosing bipolar disorder and the effect of antidepressants," *Journal of Clinical Psychiatry* 61 (2000): 804–809.

42. N. Ghaemi, "Antidepressants in bipolar disorder," *Bipolar Disorders* 5 (2003): 421–33.

43. R. El-Mallakh, "Use of antidepressants to treat depression in bipolar disorder," *Psychiatric Services* 53 (2002): 580–84.

44. A. Koukopoulos, "Duration and stability of the rapid-cycling course," *Journal of Affective Disorders* 72 (2003): 75–85.

45. R. El-Mallakh, "Antidepressant-associated chronic irritable dysphoria in bipolar disorder," *Journal of Affective Disorders* 84 (2005): 267–72.

46. N. Ghaemi, "Treatment of rapid-cycling bipolar disorder," *American Journal of Psychiatry* 165 (2008): 300–301.

47. C. Schneck, "The prospective course of rapid-cycling bipolar disorder," *American Journal of Psychiatry* 165 (2008): 370–77.

48. L. Judd, "The long-term natural history of the weekly symptomatic status of bipolar I disorder," *Archives of General Psychiatry* 59 (2002): 530–37.

49. L. Judd, "A prospective investigation of the natural history of the long-term weekly symptomatic status of bipolar II disorder," *Archives of General Psychiatry* 60 (2003): 261–69.

50. R. Joffe, "A prospective, longitudinal study of percentage of time spent ill in patients with bipolar I or bipolar II disorders," *Bipolar Disorders* 6 (2004): 62–66.

51. R. Post, "Morbidity in 258 bipolar outpatients followed for 1 year with daily prospective ratings on the NIMH life chart method," *Journal of Clinical Psychiatry* 64 (2003): 680–90.

52. L. Judd, "Residual symptom recovery from major affective episodes in bipolar disorders and rapid episode relapse/recurrence," *Archives of General Psychiatry* 65 (2008): 386–94.

53. C. Zarate, "Functional impairment and cognition in bipolar disorder," *Psychiatric Quarterly* 71 (2000): 309–29.

54. Gitlin, "Relapse and impairment."

55. P. Keck, "12-month outcome of patients with bipolar disorder following hospitalization for a manic or a mixed episode," *American Journal of Psychiatry* 155 (1998): 646–52.

56. D. Kupfer, "Demographic and clinical characteristics of individuals in a bipolar disorder case registry," *Journal of Clinical Psychiatry* 63 (2002): 120–25.

57. N. Huxley, "Disability and its treatment in bipolar disorder patients," *Bipolar Disorders* 9 (2007): 183–96.

58. T. Goldberg, "Contrasts between patients with affective disorders and patients with schizophrenia on a neuropsychological test battery," *American Journal of Psychiatry* 150 (1993): 1355–62.

59. J. Zihl, "Cognitive deficits in schizophrenia and affective disorders," *Acta Psychiatrica Scandinavica* 97 (1998): 351–57.

60. F. Dickerson, "Outpatients with schizophrenia and bipolar I disorder," *Psychiatry Research* 102 (2001): 21–27.

61. G. Malhi, "Neuropsychological deficits and functional impairment in bipolar depression, hypomania and euthymia," *Bipolar Disorders* 9 (2007): 114–25.

62. V. Balanza-Martinez, "Persistent cognitive dysfunctions in bipolar I disorder and schizophrenic patients," *Psychotherapy and Psychosomatics* 74 (2005): 113–19; A Martinez-Aran, "Functional outcome in bipolar disorder," *Bipolar Disorders* 9 (2007): 103–13.

63. M. Pope, "Determinants of social functioning in bipolar disorder," *Bipolar Disorders* 9 (2007): 38–44.

64. C. Zarate, "Antipsychotic drug side effect issues in bipolar manic patients," *Journal of Clinical Psychiatry* 61, suppl. 8 (2000): 52–61.

65. C. Zarate, "Functional impairment and cognition in bipolar disorder," *Psychiatric Quarterly* 71 (2000): 309–29.

66. D. Kupfer, "The increasing medical burden in bipolar disorder," *Journal of the American Medical Association* 293 (2005): 2528–30.

67. L. Citrome, "Toward convergence in the medication treatment of bipolar disorder and schizophrenia," *Harvard Review of Psychiatry* 13 (2005): 28–42.

68. Huxley, "Disability and its treatment."

69. M. Harrow, "Factors involved in outcome and recovery in schizophrenia patients not on antipsychotic medications," *Journal of Nervous and Mental Disorders* 195 (2007): 406–14.

70. W. Eaton, "The burden of mental disorders," *Epidemiology Review* 30 (2008): 1–14.

Chapter 10: An Epidemic Explained

1. Interview with Amy Upham, June 14, 2009.

2. M. Morgan, "Prospective analysis of premature mortality in schizophrenia in relation to health service engagement," *Psychiatry Research* 117 (2003): 127–35;

C. Colton, "Congruencies in increased mortality rates, years of potential life lost, and causes of death among public mental health clients in eight states," *Preventing Chronic Disease* 3 (April 2006).

3. S. Saha, "A systematic review of mortality in schizophrenia," *Archives of General Psychiatry* 64 (2007): 1123–31; L. Appleby, "Sudden unexplained death in psychiatric in-patients," *British Journal of Psychiatry* 176 (2000): 405–406; M. Joukamaa, "Schizophrenia, neuroleptic medication, and mortality," *British Journal of Psychiatry* 188 (2006): 122–27.

Chapter 11: The Epidemic Spreads to Children

1. B. Carey, "What's wrong with a child? Psychiatrists often disagree," *New York Times,* November 11, 2006.

2. R. Kessler, "Mood disorders in children and adolescents," *Biological Psychiatry* 49 (2001): 1002–14.

3. J. O'Neal, *Child and Adolescent Psychopharmacology Made Simple* (Oakland, CA: New Harbinger Publications, 2006), 6.

4. R. Mayes, *Medicating Children* (Cambridge, MA: Harvard University Press, 2009), 46.

5. G. Jackson, "Postmodern psychiatry," unpublished paper, September 2, 2002.

6. Mayes, *Medicating Children,* 54.

7. Ibid, 61.

8. R. Mayes, "ADHD and the rise in stimulant use among children," *Harvard Review of Psychiatry* 16 (2008): 151–66.

9. G. Golden, "Role of attention deficit hyperactivity disorder in learning disabilities," *Seminars in Neurology* 11 (1991): 35–41.

10. NIH Consensus Development Conference statement, "Diagnosis and treatment of attention deficit hyperactivity disorder," November 16–18, 1998.

11. P. Breggin, *Talking Back to Ritalin* (Cambridge, MA: Perseus Publishing, 2001), 180.

12. S. Hyman, "Initiation and adaptation: a paradigm for understanding psychotropic drug action," *American Journal of Psychiatry* 153 (1996): 151–61.

13. Breggin, *Talking Back to Ritalin,* 83.

14. H. Rie, "Effects of methylphenidate on underachieving children," *Journal of Consulting and Clinical Psychology* 44 (1976): 250–60.

15. C. Cunningham, "The effects of methylphenidate on the mother-child interactions of hyperactive identical twins," *Developmental Medicine & Child Neurology* 20 (1978): 634–42.

16. N. Fiedler, "The effects of stimulant drugs on curiosity behaviors of hyperactive boys," *Journal of Abnormal Child Psychology* 11 (1983): 193–206.

17. T. Davy, "Stimulant medication and short attention span," *Journal of Developmental & Behavioral Pediatrics* 10 (1989): 313–18.

18. D. Granger, "Perceptions of methylphenidate effects on hyperactive children's peer interactions," *Journal of Abnormal Child Psychology* 21 (1993): 535–49.

19. J. Swanson, "Effects of stimulant medication on learning in children with ADHD," *Journal of Learning Disabilities* 24 (1991): 219–30.

20. Breggin, *Talking Back to Ritalin*, 92.

21. J. Richters, "NIMH Collaborative Multisite Multimodal Treatment Study of Children with ADHD," *Journal of the American Academy of Child & Adolescent Psychiatry* 34 (1995): 987–1000.

22. T. Spencer, "Pharmacotherapy of attention-deficit hyperactivity disorder across the life cycle," *Journal of the American Academy of Child & Adolescent Psychiatry* 35 (1996): 409–32.

23. E. Sleator, "How do hyperactive children feel about taking stimulants and will they tell the doctor?" *Clinical Pediatrics* 21 (1982): 474–79.

24. D. Jacobvitz, "Treatment of attentional and hyperactivity problems in children with sympathomimetic drugs," *Journal of the American Academy of Child & Adolescent Psychiatry* 29 (1990): 677–88.

25. A. Sroufe, "Treating problem children with stimulant drugs," *New England Journal of Medicine* 289 (1973): 407–13.

26. Ibid.

27. Rie, "Effects of methylphenidate."

28. R. Barkley, "Do stimulant drugs improve the academic performance of hyperkinetic children?" *Clinical Pediatrics* 8 (1978): 137–46.

29. Swanson, "Effects of stimulant medication."

30. C. Whalen, "Stimulant pharmacotherapy for attention-deficit hyperactivity disorders," in S. Fishberg and R. Greenberg, eds., *From Placebo to Panacea* (New York: John Wiley & Sons, 1997), 329.

31. R. Schachar, "Attention-deficit hyperactivity disorder," *Canadian Journal of Psychiatry* 47 (2002): 337–48.

32. Whalen, "Stimulant pharmacotherapy," 327.

33. P. Breggin, "Psychostimulants in the treatment of children diagnosed with ADHD," *International Journal of Risk & Safety in Medicine* 12 (1993): 3–35.

34. Ibid.

35. Richters, "NIMH Collaborative Multisite."

36. P. Jensen, "3-year follow-up of the NIMH MTA study," *Journal of the American Academy of Child & Adolescent Psychiatry* 46 (2007): 989–1002. See chart on page 997 for medication use.

37. The MTA Cooperative Group, "A 14-month randomized clinical trial of treatment strategies for attention-deficit/hyperactivity disorder," *Archives of General Psychiatry* 56 (1999): 1073–86.

38. Jensen, "3-year follow-up."

39. B. Molina, "Delinquent behavior and emerging substance use in the MTA at 36 months," *Journal of the American Academy of Child & Adolescent Psychiatry* 46 (2007): 1028–39.

40. B. Molina, "MTA at 8 years," *Journal of the American Academy of Child & Adolescent Psychiatry* 48 (2009): 484–500.

41. C. Miranda, "ADHD drugs could stunt growth," *Daily Telegraph* (UK), November 12, 2007.

42. Breggin, *Talking Back to Ritalin;* K. Bolla, "The neuropsychiatry of chronic cocaine abuse," *Journal of Neuropsychiatry and Clinical Neurosciences* 10 (1998): 280–89.

43. S. Castner, "Long-lasting psychotomimetic consequences of repeated low-dose amphetamine exposure in rhesus monkeys," *Neuropsychopharmacology* 20 (1999): 10–28.

44. W. Carlezon, "Enduring behavioral effects of early exposure to methylphenidate in rats," *Biological Psychiatry* 54 (2003): 1330–37.

45. C. Bolanos, "Methylphenidate treatment during pre- and periadolescence alters behavioral responses to emotional stimuli at adulthood," *Biological Psychiatry* 54 (2003): 1317–29.

46. J. Zito, "Rising prevalence of antidepressants among US youths," *Pediatrics* 109 (2002): 721–27.

47. R. Fisher, *From Placebo to Panacea* (New York: John Wiley & Sons, 1997), 309.

48. T. Delate, "Trends in the use of antidepressants in a national sample of commercially insured pediatric patients, 1998 to 2002," *Psychiatric Services* 55 (2004): 387–91.

49. Editorial, "Depressing research," *Lancet* 363 (2004): 1335.

50. T. Laughren, Memorandum, "Background comments for Feb. 2, 2004 meeting of psychopharmacological drugs advisory committee," January 5, 2004. Accessed at fda.gov.

51. J. Leo, "The SSRI trials in children," *Ethical Human Psychology and Psychiatry* 8 (2006): 29–41.

52. C. Whittington, "Selective serotonin reuptake inhibitors in childhood depression," *Lancet* 363 (2004): 1341–45.

53. Editorial, "Depressing research," *Lancet* 363 (2004): 1335.

54. J. Jureidini, "Efficacy and safety of antidepressants for children and adolescents," *British Medical Journal* 328 (2004): 879–83.

55. T. Wilens, "A systematic chart review of the nature of psychiatric adverse events in children and adolescents treated with selective serotonin reuptake inhibitors," *Journal of Child and Adolescent Psychopharmacology* 13 (2003): 143–52.

56. T. Gualtieri, "Antidepressant side effects in children and adolescents," *Journal of Child and Adolescent Psychopharmacology* 16 (2006): 147–57.

57. P. Breggin, *Brain-Disabling Treatments in Psychiatry* (New York: Springer Publishing Company, 2008), 153.

58. D. Papolos, *The Bipolar Child* (New York: Broadway Books, 2000), xiv.

59. C. Moreno, "National trends in the outpatient diagnosis and treatment of bipolar disorder in youth," *Archives of General Psychiatry* 64 (2007): 1032–39.

60. J. Kluger, "Young and Bipolar," *Time,* August 19, 2002.

61. L. Lurie, "Psychoses in children," *Journal of Pediatrics* 36 (1950): 801–9.

62. Ibid.

63. B. Hall, "Our present knowledge about manic-depressive states in childhood," *Nervous Child* 9 (1952): 319–25.

64. J. Anthony, "Manic-depressive psychosis in childhood," *Journal of Child Psychology and Psychiatry* 1 (1960): 53–72.

65. W. Weinberg, "Mania in childhood," *American Journal of Diseases of Childhood* 130 (1976): 380–85.

66. R. DeLong, "Lithium carbonate treatment of select behavior disorders in children suggesting manic-depressive illness," *Journal of Pediatrics* 93 (1978): 689–94.

67. M. Strober, "Bipolar illness in adolescents with major depression," *Archives of General Psychiatry* 39 (1982): 549–55.

68. P. Lewinsohn, "Bipolar disorders in a community sample of older adolescents," *Journal of the American Academy of Child & Adolescent Psychiatry* 34 (1995): 454–63.

69. G. Carlson, "Manic symptoms in psychiatrically hospitalized children—what do they mean?" *Journal of Affective Disorders* 51 (1998): 123–35.

70. J. Kluger, "Young and Bipolar."

71. D. Janowsky, "Proceedings: effect of intravenous d-amphetamine, l-amphetamine and methylphenidate in schizophrenics," *Psychopharmacology Bulletin* 19 (1974): 15–24.

72. E. Cherland, "Psychotic side effects of psychostimulants," *Canadian Journal of Psychiatry* 44 (1999): 811–13.

73. K. Gelperin, "Psychiatric adverse events associated with drug treatment of ADHD," FDA, Center for Drug Evaluation and Research, March 3, 2006.

74. D. Papolos, "Bipolar disorder, co-occuring conditions, and the need for extreme caution before initiating drug treatment," *Bipolar Child Newsletter* 1 (November 1999).

75. M. DelBello, "Prior stimulant treatment in adolescents with bipolar disorder," *Bipolar Disorders* 3 (2001): 53–57.

76. J. Biederman, "Attention-deficit hyperactivity disorder and juvenile mania," *Journal of the American Academy of Child & Adolescent Psychiatry* 35 (1996): 997–1008.

77. J. Jain, "Fluoxetine in children and adolescents with mood disorders," *Journal of Child & Adolescent Psychopharmacology* 2 (1992): 259–65.

78. G. Emslie, "A double-blind, randomized, placebo-controlled trial of fluoxetine in children and adolescents with depression," *Archives of General Psychiatry* 54 (1997): 1031–37.

79. P. Breggin, *The Anti-Depressant Fact Book* (Cambridge, MA: Perseus Publishing, 2001), 116.

80. A. Martin, "Age effects on antidepressant-induced manic conversion," *Archives of Pediatrics & Adolescent Medicine* 158 (2004): 773–80.

81. G. Faedda, "Pediatric onset bipolar disorder," *Harvard Review of Psychiatry* 3 (1995): 171–95.

82. B. Geller, "Bipolar disorder at prospective follow-up of adults who had prepubertal major depressive disorder," *American Journal of Psychiatry* 158 (2001): 125–27.

83. D. Cicero, "Antidepressant exposure in bipolar children," *Psychiatry* 66 (2003): 317–22.

84. D. Papolos, "Antidepressant-induced adverse effects in juvenile-onset bipolar

disorder," paper presented at the Fifth International Conference on Bipolar Disorder, June 12–14, 2003, Pittsburgh, PA.

85. G. Faedda, "Pediatric bipolar disorder," *Bipolar Disorders* 6 (2004): 305–13.

86. M. Hellander, "Children with bipolar disorder," *Journal of the American Academy of Child & Adolescent Psychiatry* 38 (1999): 495.

87. H. Marano, "Crisis on the campus," *Psychology Today,* May 2, 2002.

88. C. Reichart, "Earlier onset of bipolar disorder in children by antidepressants or stimulants," *Journal of Affective Disorders* 78 (2004): 81–84. Also see abstracts presented at the Fourth International Conference on Bipolar Disorder in Pittsburgh, June 2001.

89. B. Geller, "Child and adolescent bipolar disorder," *Journal of the American Academy of Child & Adolescent Psychiatry* 36 (1997): 1168–76.

90. Papolos, "Antidepressant-induced adverse effects."

91. G. Faedda, "Treatment-emergent mania in pediatric bipolar disorder," *Journal of Affective Disorders* (82): 149–58.

92. R. Perlis, "Long-term implications of early onset in bipolar disorder," *Biological Psychiatry* 55 (2004): 875–81.

93. B. Birmaher, "Course and outcome of bipolar spectrum disorder in children and adolescents," *Development and Psychopathology* 18 (2006): 1023–35.

94. M. DelBello, "Twelve-month outcome of adolescents with bipolar disorder following first hospitalization for a manic or mixed episode," *American Journal of Psychiatry* 164 (2007): 582–90.

95. T. Goldstein, "Psychosocial functioning among bipolar youth," *Journal of Affective Disorders* 114 (2009): 174–83.

96. B. Geller, "Two-year prospective follow-up of children with a prepubertal and early adolescent bipolar disorder phenotype," *American Journal of Psychiatry* 159 (2002): 927–33.

97. "Hayes says new treatments for pediatric bipolar disorder not ready for prime time" (December 3, 2008 press release), accessed at hayesinc.com, August 2, 2009.

98. Social Security Administration, annual statistical reports on the SSI program, 1996–2008; *Social Security Bulletin, Annual Statistical Supplement,* 1988–1992.

99. Pediatric Academic Societies, "Pediatric psychiatry admissions on the rise," May 16, 2000, press release.

100. D. Satcher, *Report of Surgeon General's Conference on Children's Mental Health* (U.S. Dept. of Health and Human Services, 2001).

101. B. Whitford, "Depression, eating disorders and other mental illnesses are on the rise," *Newsweek,* August 27, 2008.

102. U.S. Government Accountability Office, "Young adults with serious mental illness" (June 2008).

Chapter 12: Suffer the Children

1. J. Zito, "Psychotropic medication patterns among youth in foster care," *Pediatrics* 121 (2008): 157–63.

Chapter 13: The Rise of an Ideology

1. C. Ross, *Pseudoscience in Psychiatry* (New York: John Wiley & Sons, 1995).

2. G. Klerman, "A debate on DSM-III," *American Journal of Psychiatry* 141 (1984): 539–42.

3. M. Sabshin, "Report of the medical director," *American Journal of Psychiatry* 137 (1980): 1308.

4. See blurbs for second edition of *The Myth of Mental Illness*, published by Harper & Row in 1974.

5. B. Nelson, "Psychiatry's anxious years," *New York Times*, November 2, 1982.

6. D. Adler, "The medical model and psychiatry's tasks," *Hospital and Community Psychiatry* 32 (1981): 387–92.

7. Sabshin, "Report of the medical director."

8. Nelson, "Psychiatry's anxious years."

9. Copy from a Smith Kline and French advertisement that ran monthly in *Mental Hospitals* in 1962.

10. L. Thorne, "Inside Russia's psychiatric jails," *New York Times Magazine*, June 12, 1977.

11. U.S. Senate, Committee on the Judiciary, Subcommittee to Investigate Juvenile Delinquency, *Drugs in Institutions*, 94th Cong., 1st sess., 1975.

12. A. Tone, *The Age of Anxiety* (New York: Basic Books, 2009), 176.

13. M. Smith, *Small Comfort* (New York: Praeger, 1985), 32.

14. Interview with Arthur Platt, June 8, 2009.

15. M. Sabshin, "On remedicalization and holism in psychiatry," *Psychosomatics* 18 (1977): 7–8.

16. A. Ludwig, "The medical basis of psychiatry," *American Journal of Psychiatry* 134 (1977): 1087–92.

17. P. Blaney, "Implications of the medical model and its alternatives," *American Journal of Psychiatry* 132 (1975): 911–14.

18. S. Guze, "Nature of psychiatric illness," *Comprehensive Psychiatry* 19 (1978): 295–307.

19. Adler, "The medical model."

20. M. Wilson, "DSM-III and the transformation of American psychiatry," *American Journal of Psychiatry* 150 (1993): 399–410.

21. S. Kirk, *The Selling of DSM* (New York: Aldine de Gruyter, 1992), 114.

22. Ibid, 134.

23. M. Sabshin, "Turning points in twentieth-century American psychiatry," *American Journal of Psychiatry* (1990): 1267–74.

24. Klerman, "A debate on DSM-III."

25. J. Maxmen, *The New Psychiatrists* (New York: New American Library, 1985), 35, 31.

26. H. Kutchins, *Making Us Crazy* (New York: The Free Press, 1997), 248.

27. Kirk, *The Selling of DSM*, 115.

28. M. Sabshin, "Report of the medical director" (1980), 1308.

29. L. Havens, "Twentieth-century psychiatry," *American Journal of Psychiatry* 138 (1981): 1279–87.

30. B. Bursten, "Rallying 'round the medical model," *Hospital and Community Psychiatry* 32 (1981): 371.

31. Sources for this political battle include reviews by NIMH's "Clinical Programs Projects Research Review Committee" on April 27, 1970; April 1–2, 1973; April 1974; April 21, 1975; June 27, 1977; December 1, 1977; February 17–18, 1978; and June 26–27, 1978.

32. Interview with Loren Mosher, December 1, 2000.

33. M. Sabshin, "Report of the medical director," *American Journal of Psychiatry* 138 (1981): 1418–21.

34. P. Breggin, *Toxic Psychiatry* (New York: St. Martin's Press, 1991), 360.

35. Sabshin, "Report of the medical director" (1981).

36. M. Sabshin, "Report of the medical director," *American Journal of Psychiatry* 140 (1983): 1398–1403.

37. R. Peele, "Report of the speaker-elect," *American Journal of Psychiatry* 143 (1986): 1348–50.

38. M. Sabshin, "Report of the medical director," *American Journal of Psychiatry* 143 (1986): 1342–46.

39. M. Sabshin, "Report of the medical director," *American Journal of Psychiatry* 145 (1988): 1338–42.

40. Sabshin, "Report of the medical director" (1981).

41. M. Sabshin, *Changing American Psychiatry* (Washington, DC: American Psychiatric Publishing, Inc., 2008), 78.

42. Sabshin, "Report of the medical director" (1983).

43. Sabshin, "Report of the medical director" (1986).

44. *New York Times,* November 26, 1981; September 7, 1982; July 29, 1984.

45. J. Franklin, "The Mind-Fixers," *Baltimore Evening Sun,* July 1984.

46. M. Gold, *The Good News About Depression* (New York: Villard Books, 1987), xi–xiii.

47. N. Andreasen, *The Broken Brain* (New York: Harper & Row, 1984), 29–30.

48. Ibid, 138.

49. Franklin, "The Mind-Fixers."

50. Sabshin, *Changing American Psychiatry,* 194.

51. M. Dumont, "In bed together at the market," *American Journal of Orthopsychiatry* 60 (1990): 484–85.

52. F. Gottlieb, "Report of the speaker," *American Journal of Psychiatry* 142 (1985): 1246–49.

53. Breggin, *Toxic Psychiatry,* 46, 357.

54. P. Breggin, *Medication Madness* (New York: St. Martin's Press, 2008), 150.

55. S. Boseley, "Scandal of scientists who take money for papers ghostwritten by drug companies," *Guardian,* February 7, 2002.

56. M. Angel, "Is academic medicine for sale?" *New England Journal of Medicine* 342 (2000): 1516–18.

57. D. Regier, "The NIMH depression awareness, recognition, and treatment program," *American Journal of Psychiatry* 145 (1988): 1351–57.

58. Breggin, *Toxic Psychiatry,* 14.

59. E. Foulks, "Advocating for persons who are mentally ill," *Administration and Policy in Mental Health and Mental Health Services Research* 27 (2000): 353–67.

60. A. Hatfield, "The National Alliance for the Mentally Ill," *Community Mental Health Journal* 27 (1991): 95–103.

61. E. Benedek, "Report of the secretary," *American Journal of Psychiatry* 144 (1987): 1381–88.

62. Breggin, *Toxic Psychiatry,* 363.

63. Foulks, "Advocating for persons."

64. K. Silverstein, "Prozac.org," *Mother Jones,* November/December 1999.

65. R. Behar, "The thriving cult of greed and power," *Time,* May 6, 1991.

Chapter 14: The Story That Was . . . and Wasn't Told

1. D. Healy, *Mania* (Baltimore: Johns Hopkins University Press, 2008), 132.

2. G. Carson, *The Roguish World of Doctor Brinkley* (New York: Rinehart & Co., 1960).

3. P. Breggin, *Brain-Disabling Treatments in Psychiatry* (New York: Springer Publishing Co., 2008), 390.

4. "Fluoxetine project team meeting," July 31, 1978, accessed at healyprozac.com.

5. "Fluoxetine project team meeting," July 23, 1979, accessed at healyprozac.com.

6. J. Cornwell, *The Power to Harm* (New York: Viking, 1996), 147–48.

7. D. Healy, *Let Them Eat Prozac* (New York: New York University Press, 2004), 39.

8. Ibid, 128.

9. Ibid, 249.

10. BGA letter to Eli Lilly, May 25, 1984, *Forsyth v. Eli Lilly* trial documents, exhibit 42. See baumhedlundlaw.com/media/timeline.

11. *Forsyth v. Eli Lilly* trial documents, exhibit 58.

12. Cornwell, *The Power to Harm,* 198.

13. Healy, *Let Them Eat Prozac,* 35.

14. P. Breggin, *Talking Back to Prozac* (New York: St. Martin's Press, 1994), 41.

15. Ibid, 46.

16. Ibid, 90. Also see P. Breggin, *Brain-Disabling Treatments in Psychiatry,* 79, 86, 91.

17. D. Graham, "Sponsor's ADR submission on fluoxetine dated July 17, 1990," FDA document, September 1990.

18. T. Moore, "Hard to Swallow," *Washingtonian,* December 1997.

19. D. Kessler, "Introducing MEDWatch," *Journal of the American Medical Association* 269 (1993): 2765–68.

20. J. Bremner, "Fluoxetine in depressed patients," *Journal of Clinical Psychiatry* 45 (1984): 414–19.

21. J. Feigner, "A comparative trial of fluoxetine and amitriptyline in patients with major depressive disorder," *Journal of Clinical Psychiatry* 46 (1985): 369–72.

22. J. Cohn, "A comparison of fluoxetine, imipramine, and placebo in patients with major depressive disorder," *Journal of Clinical Psychiatry* 46 (1985): 26–31.

23. J. Wernicke, "The side effect profile and safety of fluoxetine," *Journal of Clinical Psychiatry* 46 (1985): 59–67.

24. P. Stark, "A review of multicenter controlled studies of fluoxetine vs. imipramine and placebo in outpatients with major depressive disorder," *Journal of Clinical Psychiatry* 46 (1985): 53–58.

25. S. Levine, "A comparative trial of a new antidepressant, fluoxetine," *British Journal of Psychiatry* 150 (1987): 653–55.

26. R. Pary, "Fluoxetine: prescribing guidelines for the newest antidepressant," *Southern Medical Journal* 82 (1989): 1005–9.

27. D. Regier, "The NIMH depression awareness, recognition and treatment program," *American Journal of Psychiatry* 145 (1988): 1351–57.

28. Healy, *Let Them Eat Prozac,* 9.

29. F. Schumer, "Bye-Bye, Blues," *New York,* December 18, 1989.

30. G. Cowley, "Prozac: A Breakthrough Drug for Depression," *Newsweek,* March 26, 1990.

31. N. Angier, "New antidepressant is acclaimed but not perfect," *New York Times,* March 29, 1990.

32. B. Duncan, "Exposing the mythmakers," *Psychotherapy Networker,* March/April 2000.

33. M. Waldholz, "Prozac said to spur idea of suicide," *Wall Street Journal,* July 18, 1990.

34. Ibid. Also see S. Shellenbarger, "Eli Lilly stock plunges $4.375 on news of another lawsuit over Prozac drug," *Wall Street Journal,* July 27, 1990.

35. Memo from Leigh Thompson to Allan Weinstein, February 7, 1990, accessed at healyprozac.com

36. Memo from Mitch Daniels to Leigh Thompson, "Upcoming TV appearance," April 15, 1991, accessed at healyprozac.com.

37. Ibid.

38. T. Burton, "Medical flap: Anti-depression drug of Eli Lilly loses sales after attack by sect," *Wall Street Journal,* April 19, 1991.

39. L. Garnett, "Prozac revisited," *Boston Globe,* May 7, 2000.

40. R. Behar, "The Thriving Cult of Greed and Power," *Time,* May 6, 1991.

41. T. Burton, "Panel finds no credible evidence to tie Prozac to suicides and violent behavior," *Wall Street Journal,* September 23, 1991.

42. S. Begley, "Beyond Prozac," *Newsweek,* February 7, 1994.

43. P. Breggin, *Toxic Psychiatry* (New York: St. Martin's Press, 1991), 348–50. In this book, Breggin detailed the bad science involved in the Xanax trials, the co-opting of academic psychiatry, and the involvement of the APA in marketing the drug.

44. "High Anxiety," *Consumer Reports,* January 1993.

45. C. Ballenger, "Alprazolam in panic disorder and agoraphobia," *Archives of General Psychiatry* 45 (1988): 413–22.

46. R. Noyes, "Alprazolam in panic disorder and agoraphobia," *Archives of General Psychiatry* 45 (1988): 423–28.

47. J. Pecknold, "Alprazolam in panic disorder and agoraphobia," *Archives of General Psychiatry* 45 (1988): 429–36.

48. Ballenger, "Alprazolam in panic disorder."

49. Noyes, "Alprazolam in panic disorder."

50. Pecknold, "Alprazolam in panic disorder."

51. I. Marks, "The 'efficacy' of alprazolam in panic disorder and agoraphobia," *Archives of General Psychiatry* 46 (1989): 668–72.

52. I. Marks, "Reply to comment on the London/Toronto study," *British Journal of Psychiatry* 162 (1993): 790–94.

53. Breggin, *Toxic Psychiatry*, 344–53.

54. F. Pollner, "Don't overlook panic disorder," *Medical World News*, October 1, 1991.

55. J. Randal, "In a panic?" *St. Louis Post-Dispatch*, October 7, 1990.

56. H. Brown, "Panic attacks keeps thousands from malls, off roads," Associated Press, November 19, 1990.

57. R. Davis, "When panic is disabling," *Chicago Sun-Times*, June 29, 1992.

58. "High Anxiety," *Consumer Reports*.

59. FDA reviews of risperidone data included the following written commentaries: reviews by Andrew Mosholder, May 11, 1993, and November 7, 1993; David Hoberman, April 20, 1993; and Thomas Laughren, December 20, 1993.

60. Approval letter from Robert Temple to Janssen Research Foundation, December 29, 1993.

61. S. Marder, "The effects of risperidone on the five dimensions of schizophrenia derived by factor analysis," *Journal of Clinical Psychiatry* 58 (1997): 538–46.

62. "New hope for schizophrenia," *Washington Post*, February 16, 1993.

63. "Seeking safer treatments for schizophrenia," *New York Times*, January 15, 1992.

64. FDA reviews of olanzapine data included the following written commentaries: reviews by Thomas Laughren on September 27, 1996; by Paul Andreason on July 29 and September 26, 1996; and by Paul Leber on August 18 and August 30, 1996.

65. C. Beasley, "Efficacy of olanzapine," *Journal of Clinical Psychiatry* 58, suppl. 10 (1997): 7–12.

66. "Psychosis drug from Eli Lilly racks up gains," *Wall Street Journal*, April 14, 1998.

67. "A new drug for schizophrenia wins approval from the FDA," *New York Times*, October 2, 1996.

68. "Schizophrenia, close-up of the troubled brain," *Parade*, November 21, 1999.

69. "Mental illness aid," *Chicago Tribune*, June 4, 1999.

70. "Lives recovered," *Los Angeles Times*, January 30, 1996.

71. P. Weiden, *Breakthroughs in Antipsychotic Medications* (New York: W.W. Norton, 1999), 26

72. *Wall Street Journal*, "Psychosis drug from Eli Lilly."

73. "High Anxiety," *Consumer Reports*.

74. J. Lieberman, "Effectiveness of antipsychotic drugs in patients with schizophrenia," *New England Journal of Medicine* (2005): 1209–33.

75. L. Davies, "Cost-effectiveness of first- v. second-generation antipsychotic drugs." *British Journal of Psychiatry* 191 (2007): 14–22.

76. P. Tyrer, "The spurious advance of antipsychotic drug therapy," *Lancet* 373 (2009): 4–5.

77. Interview with Peter Breggin, October 10, 2008.

78. Healy interview on CBS News and *Current Affairs*, June 12, 2001.

79. D. Healy, "Psychopharmacology and the government of the self," talk given November 30, 2000, at the University of Toronto.

80. E-mail from David Goldbloom to David Healy, December 7, 2000.

81. Interview with Healy by e-mail, July 4, 2009.

82. Memo from Larry Carpman to Steve Kurkjian, April 11, 2000.

83. "Science News from 2007," NIMH website, accessed on July 2, 2009.

84. NIMH press release, July 20, 2007.

85. J. Sharkey, "Delusions; paranoia is universal," *New York Times,* August 2, 1998.

86. Search of NAMI website on July 7, 2009.

87. R. Hales, *The American Psychiatric Publishing Textbook of Psychiatry* (Arlington, VA: American Psychiatric Publishing, 2008).

Chapter 15: Tallying Up the Profits

1. D. Carlat, "Dr. Drug Rep," *New York Times,* November 25, 2007.

2. NAMI IRS 990 Form, 2000.

3. B. Koerner, "First you market the disease, then you push the pills to treat it," *Guardian,* July 30, 2002.

4. E. Tanouye, "Antidepressant makers study kids' market," *Wall Street Journal,* April 4, 1997.

5. B. Strauch, "Use of antidepression medicine for young patients has soared," *New York Times,* August 10, 1997.

6. Tanouye, "Antidepressant makers."

7. Deposition of Joseph Biederman in legal case of *Avila v. Johnson & Johnson Co.,* February 26, 2009, pages 139, 231, 232, 237.

8. J. Biederman, "Attention-deficit hyperactivity disorder and juvenile mania," *Journal of the American Academy of Child & Adolescent Psychiatry* 35 (1996): 997–1008.

9. Deposition of Joseph Biederman, p. 158.

10. Margaret Williams, report on a sales call, May 17, 2002.

11. J. J. Zorc, "Expenditures for psychotropic medications in the United States in 1985," *American Journal of Psychiatry* 148 (1991): 644–47

12. "Top therapeutic classes by U.S. sales, 2008," IMS Health.

13. S. Giled, "Better but not best," *Health Affairs* 28 (2009): 637–48.

14. These calculations are based on Eli Lilly's annual 10-K reports filed with the SEC from 1987 to 2000. Capitalization figures for 1987 and 2000 are based on prices in the fourth quarter of each year.

15. J. Pereira, "Emory professor steps down," *Wall Street Journal,* December 23, 2008.

16. C. Schneider, "Emory psychiatrist reprimanded over outside work," *Atlanta Journal-Constitution,* June 11, 2009.

17. G. Harris, "Radio host has drug company ties," *New York Times,* November 22, 2008.

18. GlaxoSmithKline internal memo, "Seroxat/Paxil adolescent depression. Position piece on the phase III studies," October 1998.

19. M. Keller, "Efficacy of paroxetine in the treatment of adolescent major depression," *Journal of the American Academy of Child & Adolescent Psychiatry* 40 (2001): 762–72.

20. E. Ramshaw, "Senator questions doctors' ties to drug companies," *Dallas Morning News,* September 24, 2008.

21. L. Kowalczyk, "US cites Boston psychiatrist in case vs. drug firm," *Boston Globe,* March 6, 2009.

22. G. Harris, "Lawmaker calls for registry of drug firms paying doctors," *New York Times,* August 4, 2007.

23. G. Harris, "Researchers fail to reveal full drug pay," *New York Times,* June 8, 2008.

24. *Avila v. Johnson & Johnson,* deposition of Joseph Biederman, February 26, 2009, 119.

25. J. Biederman, *Annual Report 2002: The Johnson & Johnson Center for Pediatric Psychopathology at the Massachusetts General Hospital.*

26. J. Olson, "Drug makers step up giving to Minnesota psychiatrists," *Pioneer Press,* August 27, 2007.

27. Margaret Williams, reports on sales calls, April 20, 2001, and April 8, 2002.

28. Eli Lilly grant registry, 2009, 1st quarter.

29. E. Mundell, "U.S. spending on mental health care soaring," *HealthDay,* August 6, 2009.

30. T. Mark, "Mental health treatment expenditure trends, 1986–2003," *Psychiatric Services* 58 (2007): 1041–48. Seven percent of national health expenditures in 2008 went to mental health services; by 2015, this figure is expected to rise to 8 percent. Data on national health expenditures in 2008, and projected expenditures in 2015, are from the U.S. Department of Health and Human Services.

Chapter 16: Blueprints for Reform

1. MindFreedom, "Original statement by the fast for freedom in mental health," July 28, 2003.

2. Letter from James Scully to David Oaks, August 12, 2003.

3. Letter from MindFreedom scientific panel to James Scully, August 22, 2003.

4. APA statement on "diagnosis and treatment of mental disorders," September 26, 2003.

5. Letter from MindFreedom scientific panel to James Scully, December 15, 2003.

6. Interview with David Oaks, October 4, 2009.

7. J. Modrow, *How to Become a Schizophrenic* (Seattle: Apollyon Press, 1992), ix.

8. Interview with David Healy in Bangor, Wales, September 4, 2009.

9. D. Healy, "Psychiatric bed utilization," *Psychological Medicine* 31 (2001): 779–90;

D. Healy, "Service utilization in 1896 and 1996," *History of Psychiatry* 16 (2005): 37–41. Also, Healy, unpublished data on readmission rates for first-episode psychosis, 1875–1924, and 1994–2003.

10. Interviews with Yrjö Alanen, Jukka Aaltonen, and Viljo Räkköläinen in Turku, Finland, September 7, 2009.

11. V. Lehtinen, "Two-year outcome in first-episode psychosis treated according to an integrated model," *European Psychiatry* 15 (2000): 312–20.

12. Interview with Jaakko Seikkula in Jyväskylä, Finland, September 9, 2009.

13. J. Seikkula, "Five year experience of first-episode nonaffective psychosis in open-dialogue approach," *Psychotherapy Research* 16 (2006): 214–28. Also see: J. Seikkula, "A two-year follow-up on open dialogue treatment in first episode psychosis," *Society of Clinical Psychology* 10 (2000): 20–29; J. Seikkula, "Open dialogue, good and poor outcome," *Journal of Constructivist Psychology* 14 (2002): 267–86; J. Seikkula, "Open dialogue approach: treatment principles and preliminary results of a two-year follow-up on first episode schizophrenia," *Ethical Human Sciences Services* 5 (2003): 163–82.

14. Interviews with staff at Keropudas Hospital in Tornio, Finland, September 10 and 11, 2009.

15. Outcomes for 2002–2006 study and for spending in western Lapland on psychiatric services from interviews with Jaakko Seikkula and Birgitta Alakare. See also the published papers by Seikkula, op. cit.

16. J. Cullberg, "Integrating intensive psychosocial therapy and low dose medical treatment in a total material of first episode psychotic patients compared to treatment as usual," *Medical Archives* 53 (1999): 167–70.

17. W. Buchan, *Domestic Medicine* (Boston: Otis, Broaders, and Co., 1846), 307.

18. National Institute for Health and Clinical Excellence, "Depression," December 2004.

19. Interview with Andrew McCulloch in London, September 3, 2009.

20. F. Dimeo, "Benefits from aerobic exercise in patients with major depression," *British Journal of Sports Medicine* 35 (2001): 114–17; K. Knubben, "A randomized, controlled study on the effects of a short-term endurance training programme in patients with major depression," *British Journal of Sports Medicine* 41 (2007): 29–33; A. Ströhle, "Physical activity, exercise, depression and anxiety disorders," *Journal of Neural Transmission* 116 (2009): 777–84.

21. J. Blumenthal, "Effects of exercise training on older patients with major depression," *Archives of Internal Medicine* 159 (1999): 2349–56.

22. Ibid.

23. Interviews with Tony Stanton and staff at Seneca Center in San Leandro, California, July 13 and 14, 2009.

24. Interviews with Keith Scott and Chris Gordon, Framingham, Massachusetts, October 1, 2009.

25. Ibid.

26. Interview with Jim Gottstein in Anchorage, Alaska, May 10, 2009.

27. M. Ford, "The psychiatrist's double bind," *American Journal of Psychiatry* 137 (1980): 332–39.

28. *Myers v. Alaska Psychiatric Institute*, Alaska Supreme Court No. S-11021.

29. Interview with Susan Musante in Anchorage, Alaska, May 10, 2009.

Epilogue

1. E. Whipple, *Character and Characteristic Men* (Boston: Ticknor & Fields, 1866), 1.

Afterword: Research Update (2010–2014)

1. Australian government, "Characteristics of Disability Support Pension Recipients" (June 2011).

2. New Zealand Ministry of Social Development, "National Benefits Factsheets" (2004–2011).

3. S. Thorlacus, "Increased incidence of disability due to mental and behavioural disorders in Iceland, 1990–2007," *Journal of Mental Health* 19 (2010): 176–83.

4. Danish government, The Appeals Board, Statistics on Early Retirement.

5. OECD Mental Health at Work: Sweden (2013).

6. Letter from the federal government to the minority members of Jutta Krellman, Sabine Zimmermann, Dr. Martina Bunge, and other Members of the Group of the Left, printed paper 17/9478, "Psychological stress in the workplace."

7. R. Pies, "Psychiatry's new brain-mind and the legend of the 'chemical imbalance,'" *Psychiatric Times,* July 11, 2011.

8. P. Gøtzsche, blog post, "Psychiatry Gone Astray," January 21, 2014, accessed at http://davidhealy.org/psychiatry-gone-astray/ on 6/17/2014.

9. B. Ho, "Long-term antipsychotic treatment and brain volumes," *Archives of General Psychiatry* 68 (2011): 128–37.

10. J. Radua, "Multimodal meta-analysis of structural and functional changes in first episode psychosis and the effects of antipsychotic medications," *Neuroscience and Biobehavioral Review* 36 (2012): 2325–33.

11. Q. Wang, "White-matter microstructure in previously drug naïve patients with schizophrenia after 6 weeks of treatment," *Psychological Medicine* 43 (2013): 2301–9.

12. V. Aderhold. "Heinzfrontale Hirnvolumenminderung durch Antipsycotika?" *Der Nervenarzt.* May 2014

13. M. Harrow. "Do all schizophrenia patients need antipsychotic treatment continuously throughout their lifetime? A 20-year longitudinal study," *Psychological Medicine* 42 (2012): 2145–55.

14. M. Harrow, "Does long-term treatment of schizophrenia with antipsychotic medications facilitate recovery?" *Schizophrenia Bulletin* 39 (2013): 962–5.

15. M. Harrow, "Does treatment of schizophrenia with antipsychotic medications eliminate or reduce psychosis?" *Psychological Medicine* (2014): DOI:10.1017/S0033291714000610.

16. L. Wunderink, "Recovery in remitted first-episode psychosis at 7 years of follow-up of an early dose reduction/discontinuation of maintenance treatment strategy," *JAMA Psychiatry,* 70 (2013): 913–20.

17. J. Gleeson, "A randomized controlled trial of relapse prevention therapy for first-episode psychosis patients," *Schizophrenia Bulletin* 39 (2013): 436–48.

18. P. Tyrer, "The end of the psychopharmacological revolution," *British Journal of Psychiatry* 201 (2012): 168.

19. P. McGorry, "Antipsychotic medication during the critical period following remission from first-episode psychosis: less is more," *JAMA Psychiatry,* published online July 3, 2013.

20. E. Pigott, "Efficacy and effectiveness of antidepressants," *Psychotherapy and Psychosomatics* 79 (2010): 267–79.

21. D. Brauser, "Broad review of FDA trials suggests antidepressants only marginally better than placebo," *Medscape Medical News*, August 24, 2010.

22. MN Community Measurement, "2010 Health Care Quality Report."

23. C. Bockting, "Continuation and maintenance use of antidepressants in recurrent depression," *Psychotherapy and Psychosomatics* 77 (2008): 17–26.

24. P. Andrews, "Primum non nocere: an evolutionary analysis of whether antidepressants do more harm than good," *Frontiers in Psychology* 3 (2012): 1–18.

25. H. Verdoux, "Impact of duration of antidepressant treatment on the risk of occurrence of a new sequence of antidepressant treatment," *Pharmopsychiatry* 44 (2011): 96–101.

26. G. Fava, "The mechanisms of tolerance in antidepressant action," *Progress in Neuro-Psychopharmacology & Biological Psychiatry* 35 (2011): 1593–1602.

27. R. El-Mallakh, "Tardive dysphoria: the role of long-term antidepressant use in inducing chronic depression," *Medical Hypotheses* 76 (2011): 769–73.

28. Western Australian Department of Health, "Raine ADHD study: long-term outcomes associated with stimulant medication in the treatment of ADHD children," 2009, accessed at www.health.wa.gov.au/publications/documents/MICADHD_Raine_ADHD_study_report_022010.pdf.

29. J. Currie, "Do stimulant medications improve educational and behavioral outcomes for children with ADHD?," NBER working paper 19105, June 2013.

30. A. Sroufe, "Ritalin Gone Wrong," *New York Times,* January 28, 2012.

31. M. Valverde, "Outreach and limitations of the pharmacological treatment of Attention Deficit Disorder with Hyperactivity (ADHD) in children and adolescents and Clinical Practice Guidelines." *Revista de la Asociación Española de Neuropsiquiatría* 34 (2014): 37–74.

ACKNOWLEDGMENTS

As I began reporting this book, I reached out to leaders of various "consumer" groups for help in locating "patients" to interview. I wanted to find people with different diagnoses and of various ages, and before long I had a list of more than 100 people willing to tell me their stories. I am deeply grateful to all those who helped me find patients to interview, and to all of those who spoke to me about their lives. In addition to those named in the book, I want to thank the following people: Camille Santoro, Jim Rye, Sara Sternberg, Monica Cassani, Brenda Davis, Lauren Tenney, Cheryl Stevens, Ellen Liversidge, Howard Trachtman, Jennifer Kinzie, Kathryn Cascio, Shauna Reynolds, Maggie McClure, Renee LaPlume, Chaya Grossberg, Lyle Murphy, Oryx Cohen, Will Hall, Evelyn Kaufman, Dianne Dragon, Melissa Parker, Amanda Green, Nicki Glasser, Stan Cavers, Cindy Votto, Eva Dech, Dennis Whetsel, Diana Petrakos, Bert Coffman, Janice Sorensen, Joe Carson, Rich Winkel, Pat Risser, Susan Hoffman, Les Cook, Amy Philo, Benjamin Bassett, Antti Seppala, Chris LaBrusciano, Kermit Cole, David Oaks, Darby Penney, and Michael Gilbert.

At every turn, the people I interviewed were extraordinarily gracious with their time. In Syracuse, Gwen Oates, Sean Oates,

Jason Smith, and Kelley Smith welcomed me into their homes. In California, Tony Stanton organized two days of interviews with administrators, staff, and children at the Seneca Center. Throughout this project, David Healy answered my inquiries, and when I interviewed him in North Wales, he and his wife, Helen, proved to be gracious hosts. The architects of Open Dialogue therapy in Finland collectively spent a week with me. I'm deeply indebted to Yrjö Alanen, Jaakko Seikkula, and Birgitta Alakare for making my trip there possible, and to Tapio Salo and his family for a wonderful evening of conversation in Tornio.

As I worked on this book, I regularly drew sustenance from friends and family. Thanks to Jang-Ho Cha, I was able to attend a brain-cutting seminar at Massachusetts General Hospital. Matt Miller, an associate professor at the Harvard School of Public Health, proved to be an invaluable sounding board for thinking about how medical therapies are evaluated and assessed. Cynthia Frawley, my next-door office "neighbor," drew the many charts that grace the book. And thanks to Joe Layden, Winnie Yu, and Chris Ringwald for our regular conversations about the ups and downs of the writer's life.

This is my fourth book, and I am now more convinced than ever that writing a book—from the moment of first conception to the day of publication—is best described as a collective enterprise. My agent, Theresa Park, helped me shape the proposal and provided me with invaluable guidance as I worked on the project. My editor, Sean Desmond, pushed me to broaden the book's scope and its narrative arc, and when it came time to edit the manuscript, he improved it in innumerable ways. Every writer should be so lucky to have an agent as supportive as Theresa Park and an editor as talented as Sean Desmond. I am also indebted to Rick Willett for his skillful copyediting; to Laura Duffy for her eye-catching cover; to SongHee Kim for her wonderful layout; to Stephanie Chan for her diligent management of the project; and to the many others at Crown who contributed their talents to this book. And finally, I am deeply grateful to Tina Constable for believing that the history told in *Anatomy of an Epidemic* is one that deserves to be known.

INDEX

Page numbers of illustrations appear in italics.

Aaltonen, Jukka, 337
Abbott Laboratories, 317
Abilify (aripiprazole), 144–45, 212, 320n
acetylcholine, 61
Adderall (amphetamine), 252
Advocates, Inc., 214, 354
Age of Anxiety, The (Tone), 132
akathisia, 232, 249, 285, 301
Alakare, Birgitta, 341
Alanen, Yrjö, 337, 338, 339
Alaska Mental Health Assn., 355–57
Ambien (zolpidem), 23
American Foundation for Suicide
   Prevention, 327
American Medical Association, 39; drug
   company alliances, 54–57
American Psychiatric Association (APA),
   161–64, 168–69, 264; annual meeting,
   4–5, 11, 115–18, 172–77; diagnostic
   categories and market growth, 161–62,
   168, 317; drug company alliances,
   172–73, 273, 276–89, 278n, 298–99;
   lithium approval and, 183; lobbying of
   Congress, 277, 280; marketing of
   antidepressants, 289–91; medical
   (biological) model, 269–76, 304;
   practice guide to depression, 180–81;
   silencing of dissent, 304–7; *Textbook of
   Neuropsychiatry*, 221; *Textbook of
   Psychiatry*, 161, 225–26, 311–12;

Textbook of Psychopharmacology, 82,
   322; *Treatment of Psychiatric
   Disorders*, 272–73; wooing of media,
   273–74
amitriptyline, 73, 74n
amphetamines, 64, 219, 228–29, 236. *See
   also* Benzedrine; Ritalin
Andreasen, Nancy, 113–14, 275, 304, 332
Angier, Natalie, 291
anti-anxiety agents, 4, 51–53, 60, 65,
   126–47; bipolar illness and, 142, 144,
   148; disability numbers and, 146–47;
   long-term effects, 136–38; side effects,
   29, 140, 296–97; withdrawal from,
   133–36, 134. *See also* benzodiazepine;
   specific brand names
antibiotics, 41–42, 45, 51, 56, 57
antidepressants, 4, 60, 61, 62, 70, 73,
   79–82, 148–71; bipolar disorder and,
   175–77, 180, 181, 186–96, 193, 195;
   case studies, 24–26, 148–50, 171,
   196–204, 211–12; as cause of mental
   illness, 26, 28, 30, 81–82, 157–60,
   169–71, 197, 234; children given,
   160–61, 229–32; disability numbers
   and, 167–68, 168; hiding the evidence,
   308–9, 312; marketing of, 74, 289–91 ;
   nondrug outcomes vs. , 153–57,
   164–69, 164n, 166, 166n, 167, 169,
   185–96, 193, 195, 362; paradigm for
   psychotropic drugs, 83–84; relapse risk
   and, 158, 162, 169, 186; sales and use,
   3, 320; side effects, 175–76, 191,

211–12; tricyclics, 153–55, 157, 158, 186, 198, 199, 229, 234, 240, 249, 285, 288 withdrawal psychosis, 250. *See also* SSRIs; *specific brand names*
antipsychotics. *See* neuroleptics
Antipsychotics and Mood Stabilizers (Stahl), 192
anxiety, 28, 51–53, 126–47; case studies, 139–45; disability and, 5, 140, 146–47, 209; drug-based treatment, 129–39; hiding the evidence, 307–12; iatrogenic effects of drugs, 209; social anxiety disorder (SAD), 317; treatment before Miltown, 127–29. *See also* benzodiazepines; panic disorder
Asberg, Marie, 72–73
Ashton, Heather, 134–35, 137, 138
AstraZeneca, 174, 302, 324–25
Ativan (lorazepam), 18, 140–41, 212
attention deficit/hyperactivity disorder (ADHD), 10, 216–29, 325–26; ADHD to Bipolar Pathway, *238*, 238; bipolar disorder and, 319; case studies, 251–53, 258–60; drug therapy, 31–34, 220, 236–38; etiology unknown, 220–21; hiding the evidence, 309; low dopamine theory, 77–78, 221; silencing of dissent, 307. *See also* Ritalin
Ayd, Frank, Jr., 64, 151–52

Badillo, George, 20–24, 120, 121
Baldessarini, Ross, 96–97, 158, 160, 184, 188, 191, 193–94
Banks, Brandon, 200–202
Barrow, Jonathan, 255–56
Bayer, 41
Bayh, Birch, 267
Beard, George, 127
benzedrine, 219
benzodiazepine, 28, 29, 126–47, 202, 267–68; addiction, 129–30, 140–41; brain damage, 137–38; case studies, 139–45; disability and, 131, 138; fall from favor, 129–31, 265, 267–68; hiding the evidence, 308–9, 312; long-term effects, 136–38, 159; short-term efficacy, 131, 132–33; side effects, 213; withdrawal, 129–30, 133–36, *134*. *See also* Klonopin; Miltown
Berger, Frank, 51–52, 65, 128–29
Berrick, Ken, 348–49
Biederman, Joseph, 173, 232, 238, 242, 318–19, 319n, 325–26, 325n
Bipolar Child, The (Papolos), 233, 319
bipolar disorder, 14, 17, 172–204; academics paid by drug companies, 323; anti-anxiety agents and, 142, 144,

148; antidepressants and, 175–77, 180, 181, 186; case studies, 16–20, 24–30, 196–204, 247–60; DBSA and, 13; diagnostic boundaries and, 242, 317–18; disability and, 5, 7, 15, 25, 178, 179, 188, 194, 193, 196, 210; drug-based treatment and worsening of, 177, 184–87; drug cocktails, 190, 191, 192, 200–202; drug side effects, 13, 26, 181, 189–91, 191n; as epidemic, 179–80, 235; etiology unknown, 275; Harrow long-term study, 194–96, *195*; hiding the evidence, 307–12; juvenile bipolar disorder, 10, 32, 33, 173, 217, 232–46, *255*, 318–19, 325, 325n, 353, 358; lithium and, 175, 182–86, 189–90, 198, 200; long-term outcomes, drug vs. non-drug, 177–79, 185–96, *193*, *195*; marketing of, 317–18; number of cases, 179, 182, 193, 195–96, 210; Patty Duke and, 174; rapid cycling, 175, 186–87, 199, 237, 239, 243; "ultra, ultra rapid cycling," 243
Blaming the Brain (Valenstein), 61, 78
Blau, Theodore, 270
Bleuler, Eugen, 90
Bockoven, J. Sanborne, 100, 118
Bola, John, 102–3
Bostic, Jeffrey, 324
Bowers, Malcolm, 71, 75
Boyer, Francis, 58–61
Bradley, Charles, 219, 222, 223–24, 233
brain, 61–64, 67–68, 68, 69–70, 69, 77, 80–81, 106–7; benzodiazepines and GABA inhibition, 135–36, 139; chemical imbalance theory and, 10, 17, 33, 61–64, 70–85; damage from psychotropic drugs, 104, 106–7, 111–12, 113–14, 137–38, 159–60, 170, 189–90, 192; D1 and D2 receptors, 75–76, 82, 105, 106, 107, 113, 309; Ritalin and, 221–22
Breggin, Peter, 230, 284, 287, 304–5
Briggs, Monica, 24–26, 197
Brinkley, John R., 283–84, 295
Bristol-Myers Squibb, 172, 320n
Brodie, Bernard, 61–62
Broken Brain, The (Andreasen), 275
Bronowski, Jacob, 3
Buchan, William, 344–45
Burke, Tomie, 240
Burns, Geraldine, 139–41, 142

Carlat, Daniel, 313
Carlson, Gabrielle, 234–35
Carpenter, William, 100–101, 103–4, 118, 119, 209

Carter Products, 59
catecholamines, 62, 63
Celexa (citalopram), 324
Cha, Jang-Ho, 67
chemical imbalance theory, 10, 17, 33,
   61–85, 74n, 264; disproved, 77–79,
   358; marketing of drug therapy and,
   291, 319–20; societal belief in, 78
Child and Adolescent
   Psychopharmacology Made Simple
   (O'Neal), 218
children and adolescents: academics paid
   by drug companies and, 323–26, 325n;
   ADHD in, 10, 31–34, 218–29; ADHD
   to Bipolar Pathway, 238; alternative
   treatment, 347–53; apathy syndrome,
   232; case studies, 31–34, 247–60,
   313–15; delinquency, crime, and mental
   illness, 227, 257; depression in, 10,
   217, 229–32, 318; diagnosis of mental
   disorders, 10–11, 216–18; drug
   cocktails and, 32, 33, 173, 244–45,
   249, 254, 258, 313–15, 320, 349–50,
   353, 359; as drug company market,
   318–19; drug therapy, 31–34, 160–61,
   218, 220, 231–32, 238–42, 318; drug
   therapy, long-term outcomes, 34, 35,
   222–29, 243–45; drug therapy, side
   effects, 32, 222–29, 231–32, 244n,
   247–60; epidemic of mental illness in,
   8–9, 239–46, 241, 246; foster children,
   medicating of, 253–57, 347, 348, 357,
   359; GAO figures on, 246; juvenile
   bipolar disorder, 10, 32, 33, 173, 217,
   232–45, 255, 318–19, 325, 325n, 353,
   358; lawsuits brought on behalf of,
   357; number receiving SSI for mental
   illness, 3, 8, 241, 245–46, 246, 358;
   rarity of pediatric mania, prior to drug
   therapies, 233–34
Children and Adults with Attention Deficit
   Hyperactivity Disorder (CHADD), 220,
   221, 327
Chouinard, Guy, 105–7, 108, 119, 176–77
Ciba-Geigy, 219, 220
Citizens Commission of Human Rights,
   281
Clayborn, Sam, 254–56
Clemens, James, 79–82
clonidine, 253
Clozaril (clozapine), 250
Cochrane Collaboration, 96n
Cogentin (benztropine), 18
Cole, Jonathan, 95, 99, 104–5, 118,
   152–53
Concerta (methylphenidate), 32, 252,
   259
Costello, E. Jane, 216

Crane, George, 180
Creation of Psychopharmacology, The
   (Healy), 78

DelBello, Melissa, 237, 244, 324–25
de Montigny, Claude, 81
Deniker, Pierre, 49–50, 77, 78, 105
Depakote (divalproex), 33, 200, 203, 249,
   255, 315
depression, 68, 68–69, 70 , 81–82,
   148–71; case studies, 24–26, 148–50,
   171, 211–12, 214–15; in children, 10,
   217, 229–32, 318; disability and
   unemployment, 5, 7, 15, 149, 166,
   167–68, 168, 209–10 ; drug therapy,
   13, 53–54, 162–64; drug therapy and
   worsening, 157–64, 170; drug therapy
   vs. nondrug outcomes, 153–57,
   164–69, 164n, 166, 166n, 167, 362;
   etiology unknown, 275; exercise
   therapy, 344–47, 346; hiding the
   evidence, 307–12; low-serotonin
   hypothesis, 71–75, 74n, 77, 289;
   marketing of, 291; number of cases
   163–64, 210, 290; revision of
   diagnosis, 161–64; Saint-John's-wort
   and, 156–57; as self-limiting in nature,
   152–53; "selling of," 291; selling of
   Prozac for, 289–95
Depression and Bipolar Support Alliance
   (DBSA), 12–15, 25, 26, 29, 181, 198;
   drug company alliances, 317–18
desipramine, 24, 197
Deutsch, Albert, 44, 91
Dewa, Carolyn, 148, 165–67, 166n, 167
dextroamphetamine, 252
Diagnostic and Statistical Manual of
   Mental Disorders (DSM), 5, 10, 128,
   177, 219; II (DSM-II), 269; III
   (DSM-III), 218, 220, 269–70, 271,
   295; III-Revised (DSM-III Rev), 220;
   IV (DSM-IV), 317
Dobbs, Dorothy, 285–86
Domestic Medicine (Buchan), 344–45
dopamine, 61, 62, 63–64, 68, 69, 69, 70,
   71; ADHD and low dopamine theory,
   77–78, 221; D2 receptors blocked by
   antipsychotics, 75–76, 82, 114;
   schizophrenia and, 63–64, 69, 70,
   75–77, 78; supersensitivity psychosis,
   105–7
drug cocktails, 18: for bipolar disorder, 28,
   177, 190, 192, 196–97, 200–202;
   children given, 32, 33, 173, 244–45,
   249, 254, 258, 313–15, 320, 349–50,
   359; iatrogenic illness and, 192,
   353–54; side effects, 211–15
Drugs and the Brain (Snyder), 108–9

Duke, Patty, 174
Durham-Humphrey Amendment, 56, 57

Effexor, 155, 171, 213
Ehrlich, Paul, 39–41
electroconvulsive therapy (ECT), 44, 103n,
    157, 171, 180–81, 197, 281
Eli Lilly, 42, 47, 172, 187, 320; drug
    revenues, 321–22; drug trials, skewing
    of, 230–31, 285–86, 288–89; fraud
    and, 284–85; grants and payments to
    influence opinion, 293, 294, , 317–18
    327–28; lawsuits against, 292; Prozac
    and, 74, 79–81, 154–56, 239, 284–91,
    286n, 292–95, 318, 320; Zyprexa and,
    208, 301, 320
encephalitis lethargica, 50, 90–91, 219
Epidemiology of Depression, The
    (Silverman), 151
Essential Psychopharmacology, 74
Evarts, Edward, 95

Faedda, Gianni, 240, 242, 243
Fava, Giovanni, 159–60, 161, 165, 181
Fieve, Ronald, 182
Fink, Paul, 272
Flugman, Hal, 141–43
fluoxetine. *See* Prozac
Flynn, Laurie, 280, 302
Food and Drug Administration (FDA),
    55–56, 94; MedWatch Prozac
    complaints, 287–88; MedWatch report
    on Ritalin risk, 236–37; Paxil approved
    for "social anxiety disorder," 317;
    prescription-only requirement for
    drugs, 55–56, 56n; Prozac hearing,
    294; Risperdal trials and, 300
Ford, Betty, 131
Forest Laboratories, 324
Franklin, Jon, 274, 276
Frazer, Alan, 71, 72, 78
Frazier, Jean, 173
Frazier, Shervert, 290, 298
Freedman, Daniel, 295
Freud, Sigmund, 127, 128, 265

GABA, 135–36, 139
Gately, Theresa, 253–54
Geodon (Ziprasidone), 173, 176, 203, 213
Ghaemi, Nassir, 172, 175, 177, 187
GlaxoSmithKline: academics paid, 322–23;
    fraud and, 324; freebies to
    psychiatrists, 327; Paxil and, 317, 322,
    323–24
Glenmullen, Joseph, 78, 284, 307
Gold, Mark, 274–75
Good News About Depression, The
    (Gold), 274–75

Goodwin, Frederick, 175–76, 181–82,
    186, 323
Gordon, Chris, 354
Gottstein, Jim, 355–57
Grassley, Charles, 322
Gressitt, Stevan, 138

Haarakangas, Kauko, 341
Hagler, Dennis, 14
Hala, Rhoda, 292
Halcion (triazolam), 18
Haldol (haloperidol), 17, 18, 21, 200, 267,
    299–300
Harding, Courtenay, 109–10, 118, 119,
    193n
Harrow, Martin, 115–18, *116*, *117*, 119,
    174–75, 185, 193n, 194–96, *195*, 209,
    227, 310, 310n, 311, 312
Hayes, Inc., 244
Healy, David, 74–75, 78, 230, 283, 284,
    305–6, 307, 353
Hellander, Martha, 240
History of Psychiatry, A (Shorter), 4
Hoffman-La Roche, 52, 60, 126, 129,
    138
Houtsmuller, Elisabeth, 244
How to Become a Schizophrenic
    (Modrow), 333–34
Hubbard, L. Ron, 281
Hyman, Steve, 77, 83–84, 85, 222

imipramine, 60, 62, 65, 70–71, 74n, 153,
    249, 287. *See also* tricyclics
Infinite Mind, The (radio show), 323
iproniazid, 53–54, 60, 62, 70–71, 84–85,
    180

Jackson, Grace, 356
Jamison, Kay, 28
Janssen company, 299–302, 325
Jenner, Alec, 126
Jensen, Peter, 226, 311
Jones, Barry, 105–7, 108, 119, 176–77
Judd, Lewis, 162, 182, 187, 279, 280, 291

Kefauver, Estes, 56
Kendler, Kenneth, 78–79
Kennedy, Edward, 131, 267–68
Keropudas Hospital, Tornio, Finland,
    339–44, *340*, 361–62
Kessler, Ronald, 217
Kim, Julie, 351
Klein, Rachel, 213–14
Klerman, Gerald, 264, 270, 295–96, 298,
    304
Kline, Nathan, 47, 53, 65, 153
Klonopin (clonazepam), 29, 141–46, 212,
    315

Kraepelin, Emil, 90, 151, 152, 169, 175, 178, 186, 193n, 194, 198
Kramer, Peter, 294
Kuhar, Michael, 276
Kuhn, Roland, 65
Kurtti, Mia, 342

Lader, Malcolm, 133–34, 135, 137–38, 147
Lamictal (lamotrigine), 145, 323
Lappen, Steve, 13, 14, 198–99
Laughren, Thomas, 230
LeFever, Gretchen, 307
Leonhard, Karl, 178
Levin, Cathy, 16–20, 120–21
Lexapro (escitalopram), 145, 324
Librium (chlordiazepoxide), 52, 60, 129, 145
life expectancy, 176, 211, 214–15, 354
Listening to Prozac (Kramer), 294
lithium, 25–26, 17, 33, 145, 175, 182–86, 189, 190, 197, 198, 200, 205, 212
lobotomy, 44, 45, 49, 84, 281
Lord, Nancy, 286–87
Luvox (fluvoxamine), 239, 249

Mad in America (Whitaker), 16, 310n
"magic bullet" medicine, 39–42, 47, 49, 51, 54–61, 65, 78, 84–85, 206–7, 263–64
Magic Bullets (Sutherland), 41
Maine Benzo Study Group, 138
Manic-Depressive Illness (Goodwin), 175, 323
Manic Depressive Illness (Winokur), 178
MAOIs (monoamine oxidase inhibitors), 153, 171
March of Medicine (TV show), 57, 58
Marks, Isaac, 295, 298
Marsilid (iproniazid), 53, 84
McCulloch, Andrew, 345, 347
McGlashan, Thomas, 100–101, 103–4, 114
McWade, Mathew, 256
Mendels, Joseph, 71, 72, 78
Mental Health (Satcher), 4, 9, 78
mental illness, 353; biological psychiatry and, 304; chemical imbalance theory, 10, 17, 33, 61–64, 67–85; in children, 5, 10, 216–46, 241, 246; deinstitutionalization of patients, 93, 206; drugs and revolutionizing of treatment, 4–5, 9; economics of, after passage of Medicare and Medicaid, 93, 206; epidemic, past 50 years, 5–9, 7, 39–46, 169–71; epidemic, social factors, 208–10; epidemic as iatrogenic, 9, 11, 30, 195, 195–96, 205–15, 239–46, 241, 353; etiology unknown, 78–79, 220, 332, 358; history of

treatment, 12, 42–46; hospitalized mentally ill, 6, 6, 44, 91, 100, 205; milieu therapy, 103n; as self-limiting, 100; social policy and, 91–92, 206; spending on mental health services, 328. See also children and adolescents; specific disorders
mental illness, reform of treatment, 331–59; Alaska Project, 355–57; alternative treatment, 43, 332, 335–36; "best" use paradigm, 332, 334–35, 353; children and, 347–53; David Healy and, 334–36, 353; as evidence-based, 353; exercise therapy, 344–47, 346; Lapland, open-dialogue therapy, 339–44, 340; Lapland need-adapted treatment, 336–39; medication withdrawal programs, 353–54; MindFreedom International hunger strike, 331–33; truth in research and marketing, 332–33
mephenesin, 51, 52
meprobamate. See Miltown
Merck, 41, 55, 60
Miltown (meprobamate), 52, 59, 65, 84, 126, 128–29, 146
MindFreedom International, 331–34, 358
Modrow, John, 333
Moniz, Egas, 49
Moodswing (Fieve), 182
Mosher, Loren, 102–3, 107, 118, 119, 209, 265, 271, 279, 304, 305, 356
M-Power, 18, 148, 214
Musante, Susan, 357
Myers, Faith, 356
Myers v. Alaska Psychiatric Institute, 356
Myth of Mental Illness, The (Szasz), 264

Nash, John, 204
National Alliance on Mental Illness (NAMI), 174, 302; drug company alliances, 279–80, 317, 327; hiding the evidence, 311; silencing dissent, 305
National Institute of Mental Health (NIMH), 46, 153; bias for drug therapy, 64, 272, 279; bipolar child, description of, 237; bipolar disorder, rates, 179; bipolar disorder vs. schizophrenia and cognitive function study, 189–90; CATIE Trial, 303; Center for Schizophrenia Studies, 271–72; chemical imbalance theory, 61–63; chronicity of depression and drug treatment, 158; Collaborative Program on the Psychobiology of Depression, 162, 168; depressed patients and probably outcome, 163–64; Depression Awareness,

Recognition and Treatment (DART) program, 279, 289–91, 316; depression study, "naturalistic" outcomes, 167, *168*; dopamine hypothesis, 75, 77; drug company alliances, 289–91, 295, 298, 299, 316–17, 323; Harrow long-term study of schizophrenia, 115–18, *116*, *117*, 174–75, 193n, 194–96, *195*, 209, 227, 310, 311, 312; hiding the evidence, 307–12; Hyman paper, 83–84; imipramine trial, 154; low-serotonin theory of depression, 73–75, 74n; marketing of antidepressants and, 289–91; neuroleptics testing, 94–98, 96n, 118; Psychopharmacology Service Center, *95*, *96*; Ritalin studies, 224, 226–27; silencing of dissent, 304–7; Soteria Project and, 271–72, 279, 304; STAR*D trial, 163; STEP-BD study, 243–44; studies of schizophrenia, 100–102, *101*; study of first-episode psychotic patients, 1946-1950, 92; Thorazine trial, 60–61

National Mental Health Act, 45–46
National Mental Health Association, 327
National Science Foundation, 42
Nemeroff, Charles, 322–23
neuroleptics, 4, 14, 50, 61, 64, 89–125, 107, 183; American spending on, yearly, 3; atypical antipsychotics, 13, 14, 15, 16, 18, 19, 120, 244, 295, 299–302, 318, 319, 325; Bayh investigation, 267; blocking of D2 receptors, 75–76, 82, 113, 114; brain damage and, 104, 106–7, 111–14, 115, 192; case for, *95*, 96–99, 96n, 108; case studies, 20–24, 121–25, 213–14; hiding the evidence, 308–9; how they alter the course of schizophrenia, 98–104, *101*; long-term outcomes, 29, 89, 98–120, *101*, *116*, *117*, 159, 356, 361–62; as magic bullet medicine, 61; MRI studies, 112; NIMH trials, 94–99, 96n, 118; paradigm for understanding, 83–84; as psychosis-inducing, 64, 82, 99–102, 107, 108–14, 120, 250; review of the evidence, 118–20; sales and use of, 320–21; side effects, 13, 19, 20, 22, 29, 99, 104–5, 107, 108, 111–14, 122, 191, 191n, 211; societal belief in, 154–55; supersensitivity psychosis, 105–7, 109; unpopularity with patients, 267; used in children, 244, 318, 319. *See also* Thorazine; Zyprexa
Neurontin (gabapentin), 145, 200
norepinephrine, 61, 62, 68
Norton, John, 278n

Oates, Gwendolyn and Sean, 31–32, 257, 258–60
O'Neal, John, 218
One Flew Over the Cuckoo's Nest (film), 264–65, 267
Orr, Louis M., 39
Oxford Textbook of Clinical Psychopharmacology and Drug Therapy, 223

panic disorder, 295
Papolos, Demitri, 233, 237, 239–40, 242, 243
Parents of Bipolar Children, 240
Pasnau, Robert, 298
Paxil, 149, 155, 314, 315, 317, 322, 323, 334; used in children, 323–24
Peele, Roger, 272–73
peer recovery movement, 24, 26, 148, 214
Pelham, William, 227
Pfizer, 41, 57, 172, 176
phenelzine, 153
phenothiazines, 48–51
Platt, Arthur, 268
Post, Robert, 75, 175, 176, 187
promethazine, 48–49
Prozac (fluoxetine), 4, 5, 7, 74, 79–82, 80n, 171, 240, 284–91, 286n; children dosed, 32, 229, 239, 318; drug trials, 154–56, 230–31, 285–88; Eli Lilly campaign to save, 292–95; fraud and, 284–85; lawsuits against, 292; marketing of, 282, 294; as model for drug development, 299, 303; sales figures, 289, 321; side effects, 230, 285–88, 292, 320; silencing of dissent, 307; story told in medical journals, 288–89; story told to the public, 289–91, 358
Prozac Backlash (Glenmullen), 78, 307
Prozac Survivors Group, 292
Pseudoscience in Biological Psychiatry (Ross), 74
psychiatry, 4, 11, 20, 127–28, 266: academics paid by drug companies, 276–80, 278n, 288–89, 322–27; "alternative" therapies, 265; antipsychiatry movement, 264–66, 304; biological psychiatry, 63, 263–82, 304; categories of disorders, 128; charlatans and, 283–84, 295; children, diagnosis of mental disorders, 10–11, 216–18; critics, discrediting, 280–82, 292–95, 304–7; depression, pre-drug therapy, 151–53; diagnostic boundaries expanded, 209, 242; drug-based treatment paradigm, 4–5, 59–60, 177, 265, 266–76, 270; drug company

alliances, 94–95, 276–89, 293–302, 304, 322–27; false story told by, 358–59; financial incentives for drug therapy, 313–28; hiding the evidence, 307–12; history of treatment, 3, 4, 42–46; "key opinion leaders" (KOLs), 322–26; "magic bullet" medicine and, 263–64, 267; marketing of drug therapy, 283–312; median earnings, 1970s, 265; psychopharmacology revolution, 4, 47–66, 78, 265, 361; rebranding of, 316–21; social psychiatrists, 265

psychopharmacology, 4, 39, 205–15; biological psychiatry and, 263–82; development of drug treatment paradigm, 47–66; drug sales in 1967, 64; drug sales to children promoted, 218; expectations for drug therapy, 64–65; financial incentives, 313–28; long-term safety of agents, 65, 211–15; "magic bullet" medicine and, 58–61, 78, 84–85, 185; medical-related disability and, 196; paradigm for understanding psychotropic drugs, 83–84, 207; Prozac marketing, 288–95; psychiatrists profiting from drugs, 57, 295–302; thought experiment, 207–8; Xanax marketing, 295–99, *297*; "young lady/old hag" analogy, 205, *206*, 361

psychotherapy, 103n

PsychRights, *355*, 356

Putnam, Robert, 208

Räkköläinen, Viljo, 337, 338, 339

Rappaport, Maurice, *101*, 101–2, 107, 118, 119, 209

Recognizing the Depressed Patient (Ayd), 151–52

reserpine, 61–62, 72

Rhône-Poulenc, 48, 49, 51

Risperdal (risperidone), 18, 32, 33, 113, 200, 213, *255*, 259, 325; biased drug trials, 299–300; marketing of, 299–302; side effects, 18–19, 113, 120–21, 301n

Ritalin (methylphenidate), 77, 219, 220, 221–29, 221n, 252; case studies, 31–34, 251–53, 255–56; as cause of juvenile bipolar disorder, 234–38, *241*, 242; hiding the evidence, 309, 311; risks/side effects, 219, 224–29, 236–38, 252; silencing dissent, 306–7

Robinowitz, Carolyn, 5, 11, 172

Rosenbaum, Jerrold, 293, 304, 307

Ross, Colin, 74

Rubin, Harvey, 273

Sabshin, Melvin, 264, *265*, 268, 270, 271, 272, 273, 277

Saint-John's-wort, 156–57

Salo, Tapio, 341, 342

Sances, Melissa, 148–50, 171

Satcher, David, 4, 9, 78, 245

Schildkraut, Joseph, 62–63, 68, 70, 71–72, 78

schizophrenia 63– 64, 90–91, 109, 112–13, 151, 193, 193n; atypical antipsychotics and, 295, 299–305; case studies, 20–24, 120, 121–25; cognitive impairment in, 189–91; discharge rate, 93, 100, 103n; dopamine hypothesis, 63–64, 69, 70, 71, 75–77, 78, 236; drug treatment as psychosis-inducing, 107, 108–14, 192; disability and employment, 93, 99, 100, 109–10, 111, 115, 120; etiology unknown, 275; Harrow long-term study, 115–18, *116*, *117*, 174–75, 193n, 194–96, *195*, 209, 227, 310, 310n, 311, 312 ; hiding the evidence, 307–12; how antipsychotics alter the course of, 98–104, *101*; Lapland non-drug treatment, 336–44; long-term outcomes drug treatment vs. non-drug, 89, 90, 92–94, 98–120, *101*, 103n, *116*, *117*, 209, 312, 335–36; Mosher's theory of cause, 102; MRI studies, 112, 113–14, 119; natural history of disorder, 90–94, 92n; neuroleptic risk-benefit profile, 104–5; NIMH drug trials, 94–99, 96n, 118; relapse studies, 97–98, 97n, 99, 104; "revolving door syndrome," 99, 103; Risperdal, marketing of, 299–302; short-term drug success, 95, 96n, 97–98, 99; silencing of dissent, 304–7; Soteria Project, 102–3, *265*, 271–72, 279, 304, *355*–57; supersensitivity psychosis, 105–7, 109, 176–77; tardive dyskinesia and, 111–12; Thorazine and, 92, 93

Schuyler, Dean, 153, 290

Scientology, 280–82, 292–95

Scott, Keith, 354

Seeman, Philip, 75, 107, 112–13

Seikkula, Jaakko, 339–41, *340*, 343, 361–62

Seneca Center, 347–53

Seroquel (quetiapine), 23, 145, 200, 302

serotonin, 61, 62, *68*, 68–69, 71; depression and, 68–69, 70, 71–75, 74n, 289; "reuptake" inhibitors, 62, 73, 74, 79–82, 80n

Serzone (nefazodone), 155

Sexton, Scott, 214–15

Shader, Richard, 129

Shame of the States, The (Deutsch), 44
Shorter, Edward, 4
Silver, Ann, 120
Silverman, Charlotte, 151
Simon, John, 326
Smith, Jason and Kelley, 33–34, 257–58
Smith Kline and French, 57, 58, 59–60, 267
Snyder, Solomon, 75, 108–9
Solomon, Harry, 100
Soteria House, 102–3, 265, 271–72, 279, 304, 355–57
Spitzer, Robert, 269–70
Squib, 41
SSRIs (selective serotonin reuptake inhibitors), 74, 79–82, 155–57, 170, 181, 303; as cause of chemical imbalance, 81–82, 170; children given, 160–61, 229–32, 238–42, 318; disability and, 167–68, *168*; lawsuits against, 230; sales and use, 160–61, 294; side effects, 170, 231–32, 305–6; silencing of dissent, 305–6; suicide risk, 230, 285, 286, 287, 292, 305–6, 315. *See also* Prozac
Stahl, Stephen, 131–32, 192
Stanton, Tony, 349, 350, 352, 353
Stevens, Andrew, 251–53
stimulants, 177, 180, 219; ADHD to Bipolar Pathway, 238, *238. See also* Ritalin
Stip, Emmanuel, 89, 98, 118
Stotland, Nada Logan, 172
Stowe, Zachery, 323
Strober, Michael, 234–35
Suavitil (benactyzine), 60
suicide risk, 25, 230, 243, 285, 286, 287, 292, 305–6, 315
supersensitivity psychosis, 105–7, 109, 160, 176–77
Supplemental Security Income (SSI) or Social Security Disability Insurance (SSDI), 6, 18, 206; anxiety disorders, 7, 140, 146–47, 209; bipolar illness, 142, 196, 199, 256; cost of, 10; depression, 149, 209–10; "entitlement trap," 208–9; number receiving for mental illness, 3, 7–8, 210, *241*, 245–46, *246*, *358*
Sutherland, Louis, 41
Szasz, Thomas, 264, 266, 268, 281

tardive dyskinesia, 19, 104, 105, 107, 108–9, 111–12, 304, 313
Tegretol (carbamazepine), 18

Thorazine (chlorpromazine), 4, 39, 58, 82, 84, 92–94, 105–7, 183, 200, 206, 267; development of treatment, 49–51; "magic bullet" medicine and, 58–59, 206–7; NIMH trials, 60–61, 96–98, 96n; rise in disabled mentally ill, 120; side effects, 50, 63, 104–5, 107; supersensitivity psychosis, 105–7
Tohen, Mauricio, 187, 189
Tone, Andrea, 132
Touched by Fire (Jamison), 28
tricyclics. *See* antidepressants

Upham, Amy, 204, 211–12
Upjohn, 131; APA partnership, 316; marketing of Xanax, 295–99, *297*; paid psychiatrists, 295–96, 298

Valenstein, Elliot, 61, 78
Valium (diazepam), 126, 130–33, *134*, 145, 147, 149, 303
Van Rossum, Jacques, 64, 70, 75
Vierling-Claassen, Dorea, 27–30, 196–97
Viguera, Adele, 97n

Wagner, Karen, 323–24
Wallace Laboratories, 52, 59
Wayne, Kim, 350
weight gain and drug therapy, 13, 29, 122, 140, 191, 203, 207, 214, 244, 249, 250, 301
Weinberg, Jack, 269
Weinstein, Haskell, 57
Wellbutrin (bupropion), 145, 322
Whipple, Edwin Percy, 361
Winokur, George, 153, 178–79, 183, 188
World Health Organization (WHO): depression study, 165, *166*; schizophrenia studies, 110–11, 118, 119, 308, 310n, 312; Paxil trials, 156

Xanax (alprazolam), 131, 213, 296–97, *297*, 298, 303; marketing of, 295–99, *297*, 303

Zajecka, John, 299, 302
Zarate, Carlos, 187, 189, 311
Zoloft (sertraline), 149, 156–57, 171, 249, 345–46, *346*
Zubin, Joseph, 96, 98, 169
Zyprexa (olanzapine), 27, 29, 113, 200, 214–15, 249, 301, 315, 320, 321; marketing, 301–2; thought experiment, 207–8; weight gain, 13, 29, 214–15, 249, 250, 301